Pauperism and Poor Laws

ROBERT PASHLEY

CAMBRIDGE
UNIVERSITY PRESS

CAMBRIDGE UNIVERSITY PRESS

Cambridge, New York, Melbourne, Madrid, Cape Town,
Singapore, São Paolo, Delhi, Tokyo, Mexico City

Published in the United States of America by Cambridge University Press, New York

www.cambridge.org
Information on this title: www.cambridge.org/9781108037006

This edition first published 1852
This digitally printed version 2011

ISBN 978-1-108-03700-6 Paperback

CAMBRIDGE LIBRARY COLLECTION

Books of enduring scholarly value

History

The books reissued in this series include accounts of historical events and movements by eye-witnesses and contemporaries, as well as landmark studies that assembled significant source materials or developed new historiographical methods. The series includes work in social, political and military history on a wide range of periods and regions, giving modern scholars ready access to influential publications of the past.

Pauperism and Poor Laws

Robert Pashley (1805–59), lawyer, economist, traveller, and fellow of Trinity College, Cambridge, is famous for his travel memoirs as well as his legal achievements. First published in 1852, his history of pauperism and the poor laws in England analyses the history of poverty and the various attempts at reform, including legislation in the reign of Elizabeth I, the statute of Charles II for the Removal of the Poor, and the pauper legislation of 1834. In the final chapters, Pashley asserts the necessity for a total repeal of the existing legislation, including the Poor Law Amendment Act of 1834, arguing that the provisions for raising and administering relief to paupers should be consolidated into one statute and suggesting a national levy on property to aid poor relief. Pashley's work was influential, although reform of the system did not begin until the creation of the Local Government Board in 1871.

Cambridge University Press has long been a pioneer in the reissuing of out-of-print titles from its own backlist, producing digital reprints of books that are still sought after by scholars and students but could not be reprinted economically using traditional technology. The Cambridge Library Collection extends this activity to a wider range of books which are still of importance to researchers and professionals, either for the source material they contain, or as landmarks in the history of their academic discipline.

Drawing from the world-renowned collections in the Cambridge University Library, and guided by the advice of experts in each subject area, Cambridge University Press is using state-of-the-art scanning machines in its own Printing House to capture the content of each book selected for inclusion. The files are processed to give a consistently clear, crisp image, and the books finished to the high quality standard for which the Press is recognised around the world. The latest print-on-demand technology ensures that the books will remain available indefinitely, and that orders for single or multiple copies can quickly be supplied.

The Cambridge Library Collection will bring back to life books of enduring scholarly value (including out-of-copyright works originally issued by other publishers) across a wide range of disciplines in the humanities and social sciences and in science and technology.

PAUPERISM

AND

POOR LAWS.

London:
Spottiswoodes and Shaw,
New-street-Square.

PAUPERISM

AND

POOR LAWS

BY ROBERT PASHLEY

ONE OF HER MAJESTY'S COUNSEL

LATE FELLOW OF TRINITY COLLEGE CAMBRIDGE

AUTHOR OF *TRAVELS IN CRETE*

LONDON

LONGMAN BROWN GREEN AND LONGMANS

1852

PREFACE.

Some years before I was called to the Bar, my attention was especially drawn to the operation of the Poor Laws on the well-being of our labouring population; and, during nearly the whole of my professional practice, I have had ample opportunities of seeing the actual working, and of forming an opinion on the character and tendency, of those laws. It therefore seems to me, that the setting forth of my views, thus formed on the Pauperism and Poor Laws of England, may tend to promote the progress of truth, and so prove useful to the public in a matter of great social importance.

It was my hope and intention to go to press, with some such book as the present, in 1851; and, in March and April of that year, I wrote several of the chapters now printed. But ill health suspended my labours. I was obliged to pass the whole summer, in perfect idleness, in the south of Germany, and only returned to England in time to resume my professional labours in Michaelmas Term. The Christmas Vacation enabled me to complete the work.

For the Index appended to the volume, I am indebted to Mr. George Tayler, of the Common Law Bar.

R. P.

Temple,
9th February, 1852.

CORRECTIONS AND ADDITIONS.

Page 5. *line* 1. for "5,789,533," read "5,789,583."
9. „ 17. for "126,569," read "126,582."
11. „ 3. for "58,331," read "58,731."
35. „ 2. for "715,680," read "741,722."
61. „ 11. for "4*s*. 6*d*." read "9*s*."
81. „ 1. for "1,102,359," read "1,102,349."
116. „ 2. of note *, for "second," read "third."
124. „ 3. of note †, for "*adulterior*," read "*adulterio*."
139. „ 5. of note ‡, for "Smynæ," read "Smyrnæ."
144. „ 1. of note †, the Canon referred to is Canon V. Concilii Matisconensis ii. A.D. 585, and is found in *Labbe*, tom. ix. pp. 951, 952. ed. Florent. 1763.
ib. „ 1. of note ‡, for "decimam," read "suam decimam."
157. „ 31. of note, for "were," read "was."
201. „ 1. of note *, for "was," read "was, as it was said."
204. „ 1. for "14 Eliz. c. 3." read "14 Eliz. c. 5."
237. „ 14. for "1692," read "1691."
251. „ 7. for "towards," read "during."
4. „ 17. the † after the word "souls" has fallen out: at *page* 114. *line* 26. the letter "y" has fallen out of the word "universality," and at *page* 227. *line* 7. "f" has fallen out of the word "of."

CONTENTS.

PAUPERISM

AND

THE POOR LAWS.

CHAPTER I.

THE NUMBER AND COST OF PAUPERS IN ENGLAND.

> Non secus ac si qua penitus vi terra dehiscens,
> Infernas reserat sedes, et regna recludat
> Pallida, dis invisa. VIRGIL.

THE pauperism of England, notwithstanding the present general prosperity, still extends to vast numbers of the people, and the sum annually disbursed, under the administration of the poor law, in maintenance and relief alone, amounts to upwards of five millions sterling. It has become, therefore, most important to inquire, whether the law of settlement and removal of the poor does not exercise an injurious influence on the physical and moral condition of the working classes, especially of labourers in agriculture; and whether the repeal of that law will not alleviate the pecuniary burden of rate-payers, and tend also to diminish the sufferings, and to elevate the character, of the whole body of our labouring population.

Before entering on the consideration of defects in the poor law, which have produced or aggravated many of the existing evils of our pauperism, I will endeavour to ascertain the number of paupers at present distributed over the whole country, and the cost of their support.

Pauperism in England may be said to be relieved from three entirely distinct sources.

The first of these consists in the various parochial and other charities, founded mainly by the piety and benevolence of former ages, and dispensing an annual income of upwards of 1,200,000*l*.

Respecting these Charities, ample information is found in the voluminous Reports of the Commissioners of Inquiry into Public Charities; and the Summary of those Reports, presented to parliament by command of Her Majesty, and printed in 1842, shows that their income is derived from 442,915 acres of land, from between five and six millions of money in the public funds, and from other property. Its exact annual amount appears, by the Summary, to be 1,209,395*l.* 12*s.* 8*d.*: a sum of about 200,000*l.* a year is appropriated to schools and other educational objects.

The character of the innumerable foundations which yield this large annual revenue of 1,209,395*l.*, becomes sufficiently apparent on the inspection of any page of the Digest of Reports of the Commissioners, arranged according to counties. By far the greater part of the whole amount is simply in the nature of direct relief to the poor. The separate enumeration of charities giving such relief, fills 336 folio pages.

That the large amount of money thus distributed would, if it formed part of the ordinary fund for the relief of the poor, be of far greater service to the community, including the industrious poor themselves, can hardly be doubted.

Commissioners of Inquiry into the Administration of the Poor Laws, whose Report preceded the passing of the Poor Law Amendment Act of 1834, state their conviction that these charities, distributed as they are among the same classes who are also receivers of the poor rate, are often wasted and often mischievous. "In some cases they have a quality of evil peculiar to themselves. The majority of them are distributed among the poor inhabitants of particular parishes and towns. The places intended to be favoured with large charities attract, therefore, an undue proportion of the poorer classes, who, in the hope of trifling benefits to be obtained without labour, often linger in spots most unfavourable to the exercise of their industry. Poverty is thus not only collected, but created in the very neighbourhood whence the benevolent founders have manifestly expected to make it disappear."*

It is very remarkable that three centuries before the date of this Report, the legislature had not only expressed a view similar to that now taken by these commissioners, in respect of such foundations, but, in the very first statute which provides for the raising of a common fund for relief of the poor, had wholly merged all the proceeds of such foundations in the fund to be distributed under the statute. The 27 Henry VIII. c. 25., passed in 1536, only a few years before the final dissolution of the abbeys, "for the avoiding of all such inconveniences as oftentimes have and daily do chance among the people by common and open doles, and that the most commonly unto such doles many persons do resort which have no need of the same," enacts, "that no manner of person shall make any common dole, or give any ready money in alms, otherwise than to the common boxes and common gatherings for the putting in due execution of the good intents and purposes contained in the act, upon pain to forfeit ten times the value;" and the same statute further directs, that all persons bound to give any money, food, or other sustentation to poor people, should give the same to the said common boxes, "towards the common alms and relief of the poor people." †

The next source of relief, for our existing pauperism, is found in the various hospitals, infirmaries, and other charitable

* Report, 20th February, 1834, p. 361.

† An Ordinance of the King of France, of 9th July, 1547, which will be again referred to in Chapter IV. of this book, makes a precisely similar provision, and for exactly the same reason. Poor boxes, *troncs et boëtes des pauvres*, are to be placed in all churches and parishes; and all abbeys, priories, chapters and colleges, *qui d'ancienne fondation furent tenus faire aumosnes publiques, d'autant que la dite aumosne* était occasion d'attraire les valides, et les detournerait d'œuvrer et travailler; *furent tenus bailler et fournir en deniers* à la paroisse, *à laquelle les dits abbayes etc. étaient assis, la valeur de la dite aumosne publique.*"

institutions established throughout the country, and mainly supported by voluntary contributions. The amount thus raised is very large, and is difficult to ascertain with any near approach to the truth. It cannot be far short of 2,000,000*l.* yearly, and may greatly exceed that sum.

It appears, therefore, that, beyond the whole amount of what is given by individual Christian charity, the sum of money expended on the indigent poor of England, by what may be termed the organisation of public charity, wholly independent of the relief bestowed under the poor law, amounts to from 3,000,000*l.* to 4,000,000*l.* yearly.*

Lastly comes the relief of paupers under the poor law; and here we have a vast expenditure, respecting which official statistics give us accurate information.

During the three years 1748, 1749, and 1750, the average annual sum so expended was 689,971*l.*, and the then population of the country was 6,455,672 souls. During the three years 1848, 1849, and 1850, the corresponding average annual sum has been 5,789,583*l.*, the average population of those three years having been 17,488,821.

England, therefore, has almost trebled her population in a single century; and during the same period has increased her

* Eden, *State of the Poor*, i. 465., with a poor-rate for England and Wales of only 2,167,749*l.*, and a population of only 8,000,000, estimated the whole yearly amount "disbursed in the various objects of permanent or occasional charity," at upwards of six millions; adding to his estimate, that "it is probably much below the truth." I do not think that 4,000,000*l.*, nearly double the then amount of the poor-rate, can have been distributed to the poor of England by voluntary charity in 1783, 1784, or 1785. Baron De Gérando, speaking of 1835 and 1836, when the poor-rate was from 6,000,000*l.* to 7,000,000*l.*, says, with a nearer approach to the truth, "On estime que les bienfaits répandus, soit par des associations philantropiques, soit par la charité individuelle, ajoutent encore au moins 3 ou 4 millions sterling aux secours distribués en Angleterre et dans le pays de Galles."—*De la Bienfaisance Publique*, tom. iv. p. 147. Colquhoun also, *Treatise on Indigence*, London, 1806, is probably within the truth when, pp. 60, 61, he puts down relief from poor rate 4,267,965*l.*, from charitable bequests 400,000*l.*, and from public and private charity 3,332,035*l.*; making a total of 8,000,000*l.* for 1803.

† The average pauperism of the years 1748, 1749, and 1750, was ascertained under an order of the House of Commons, made on 20th March, 1750.

absolute official pauperism in the proportion of 5,789,533 to 689,971, that is, of more than eight to one.

It is to be observed that, in 1750, the outlay, in relief of the poor, was little more than 2*s.* per head on the whole population: it is now nearly three times as great. And in several years, between 1840 and 1850, it has exceeded 6*s.* per head on the population, on the average of the whole country, while, in many extensive districts, even now in 1851, it amounts to 10*s.* per head on the population.

Great as has been the increase, during the last century, in the value of the property rateable to the relief of the poor, such value has not increased uniformly throughout the country, nor has it increased at an equal rate with the localised pauperism preying on it. But the existing distribution of the pauperism of England, as found in the metropolis and in the agricultural and manufacturing districts respectively, will call for separate consideration. At present it will suffice to ascertain the aggregate cost and numbers of this official pauperism, leaving for subsequent pages the distribution of its burden.

The poor law reform of 1834 put an end to numerous inveterate abuses in the mere administration of relief to the poor, and thereby effected a considerable diminution in the yearly cost of pauperism. That effect was fully produced in the year ended at Lady-day, 1837, in which the sum expended in the relief of the poor was only 4,044,741*l.*

From 1837 there has been a considerable increase of expenditure in relief of the poor, as recorded in the annual official reports of the Poor Law Commissioners: its maximum of 6,180,764*l.* was attained in 1848.

The great prosperity of nearly all classes, in England, since the repeal of the corn laws, has been accompanied by a considerable diminution, since 1848, in the total *money* cost of pauperism: the sum expended in relief, for the year ended in March, 1851, has probably been less, by one million sterling, than was expended in the year ended in March, 1848. Nevertheless, even in 1851, the year's expenditure in actual relief of the poor is still 5,000,000*l.* sterling, under these most favourable circumstances, and with wheat at 40*s.* the quarter.

During the last ten years the mean population of England and Wales has been 16,918,458: the mean expenditure for the relief of the poor, during the same period, will be seen by the following statement:

Year.	Sum expended in Relief of the Poor for the Year ended 25th March.	Cost of Wheat per Quarter.	Number of Quarters of Wheat for which the Money could have been exchanged.
	£	*s.* *d.*	
1841	4,760,929	65 3	1,459,288
1842	4,911,498	64 0	1,534,843
1843	5,208,027	54 4	1,917,065
1844	4,976,093	51 5	1,935,595
1845	5,039,703	49 2	2,050,048
1846	4,954,204	53 3	1,860,733
1847	5,298,787	59 0	1,796,199
1848	6,180,764	64 6	1,916,515
1849	5,792,963	49 1	2,360,460
1850	5,395,022	42 7	2,533,865
Total	52,517,990	- -	19,364,611
Average	5,251,799	54 2	1,936,461

The amount of money *levied* for the poor-rate, (including as it does county rate, police rate, and other matters, besides the mere relief of the poor,) is always a much larger sum than that expended in relief. Thus the amount so *levied*, for the year which ended at Lady-day, 1850, was 7,270,493*l.*; while the sum *expended* in relief, for the same year, was 5,395,022*l.**

* Since an account of sums so "*levied* for poor-rate" includes many large items wholly unconnected with the relief of the poor, we need not wonder that a return (in the Parliamentary Paper 690, House of Commons, 1851) of the rate "*levied for the relief of the poor*" in several metropolitan parishes, should present St. George's Hanover Square at an apparent rating of 1*s.* 8*d.* in the pound on its rental, although, in truth, the yearly relief of the poor in that parish does not require a rate of more than 6*d.* or 7*d.* in the pound.

It is obvious that such an undiscriminating return wholly fails to give any idea of the inequality in the incidence of the poor-rate, so far as the real burden of pauperism is concerned. It even tends to mislead, when headed "Poor Relief," as if its amount were applied to relieving the poor. Every parish included in the return in question is under 10 Geo. IV. c. 44. (An Act for Improving

It is to be observed, that the sum expended in relief of the poor for the year ended Lady-day, 1850, notwithstanding the general prosperity of all classes, excepting the agricultural, throughout the country, exceeds by 143,223*l.* the average amount of that relief for each of the last ten years; and that, if the quantity of wheat, for which the 5,395,022*l.* expended in 1850 could have been then exchanged, be looked at, the last year of the series has been the most costly of them all.

Important as it is to know the amount of money expended yearly in relieving the poor, it is not less important to determine the number of indigent persons among whom the vast yearly sum is divided. I will now endeavour to show what proportion of the whole population of England is thus under the sad necessity of obtaining yearly the means of subsistence, in part at least, from the poor-rate.

The questions to be determined will be:

1. What number of persons are admitted yearly into workhouses and there relieved?

2. What number of persons are relieved yearly as out-door poor?

It is greatly to be regretted that these important questions do not admit of any direct answer, by a mere reference to the voluminous Blue Books, folio and octavo, published at the instance of the Poor Law Commissioners, or the Poor Law Board. Ample materials, however, exist, at Somerset House, or Gwydyr House, for answering them; and, even while those materials are still a sealed book to the public, we may approximate closely to the truth of the required answer to each of the questions.

Ever since 1848, the clerks to boards of guardians have returned half-yearly, to the Poor Law Board, a "Statistical Statement," for the half-year, of the cost and numbers of the poor persons relieved in their respective unions; and, so far

the Police in and near the Metropolis), and sec. 20. of that statute directs parish overseers to levy the whole of the police rate "as part of the rate for the relief of the poor." Similarly the county rate is payable "out of the money to be collected for the relief of the poor."

as the money amount of such relief is concerned, the Poor Law Board have published the result of those returns. The number of poor persons, so relieved in each *half-year*, has, however, not been published by the Poor Law Board; the only published returns of the number receiving relief having been confined to those receiving it on two days, the 1st January and the 1st July, in each year.

The published returns, therefore, at the most, only supply the average number of mouths that are constantly yawning for relief; but no more exhibit the number of persons relieved in a year, than the number of hundreds of persons in Coldbath Fields Prison, or in St. Thomas's Hospital, on any given day, would represent the thousands received into, and discharged from, those establishments in a year. However, referring to what has been made public by the Poor Law Board, we obtain the following figures.

The Third Annual Report of the Poor Law Board gives the total number of persons receiving relief in 595 unions in England and Wales, on the 1st January, 1850, as 881,206.

But these 595 unions contained a population of only 13,724,508 inhabitants out of a whole population of England and Wales (in 1841) of 15,911,737, and the whole population now, in 1851, has become 17,922,768. It therefore follows that, in round numbers, we must add one-sixth to the poor law returns for its 595 unions, in order to obtain the true number of poor persons relieved throughout England and Wales on the day in question. Adding, therefore, 146,867 to the 881,206 persons then relieved in unions, we obtain 1,028,073 as the number of paupers relieved on the 1st January, 1850.

An examination of many other official returns shows that it may be safely taken that, on the average of the last ten years, the number of poor persons *constantly* receiving relief, or, in poor law phraseology, *chargeable*, has been not much, if at all, less than 1,000,000. The number of poor persons relieved on the 1st January in each of the years 1847, 1848, and 1849, was greater than the number so relieved on the 1st January, 1850.

With this datum of 1,000,000 paupers as the average number of persons maintained, under the poor law, at the expense of their neighbours, we must try to ascertain the number of different persons relieved during any part of the year. There is certainly no necessary or invariable proportion between the number of paupers relieved on a given day, and those who are compelled for a longer or a shorter period of the year to become and remain chargeable to the poor-rate.

The statistics of the Poor Law Administration of Ireland, for 1849 and 1850, strikingly show, how uncertain a criterion of the extent of pauperism, is afforded by the mere number of poor persons receiving relief on any given day.

The total number relieved in workhouses, in Ireland, during the year ended on 29th September, 1849, was 932,284; and the number so relieved, during the following year, was 805,702: a decrease of no less than 126,569. Yet, in the latter year, when the whole number of paupers relieved in workhouses was so greatly reduced, the number of such paupers in workhouses, during each week of the year, was larger than in each corresponding week of the year 1849. The very obvious explanation, given by the Poor Law Commissioners for Ireland, in their Fourth Annual Report is, that "in 1850 there was far less fluctuation by way of admission into, and discharge from, the workhouse than in former years, and that, cousequently, the average duration of residence in the workhouse was greater than it had been previously."

In the year ended 25th September, 1850, the highest number of inmates of workhouses in Ireland, at any one time, was in the week ended 22nd June, when it was 264,048. The lowest number was in the week ended 28th September, when it was 155,173. In round numbers there were, on the average, about 200,000 inmates of workhouses, in Ireland, during the year 1850; in other words, even in 1850, the number of persons relieved, at some period or other of the year, was nearly four times as great as the mean number of those who were receiving relief on any given day.

Having found it utterly impossible, on the published Annual Reports of the Poor Law Board, to determine the number of paupers relieved in *a year* in England, I have been obliged to make applications to clerks of boards of guardians for returns of facts and figures, which, though mostly contained in the "Statistical Statement" furnished half-yearly to the Poor Law Board by the same clerks, have not, as yet, been made public. In many of my applications, I have failed to obtain returns; and such failures make me feel the more obliged to those clerks of boards of guardians whose kindness has furnished me with returns, which others would not take the trouble of making. The unions, respecting which I have been favoured with full and accurate information, include a population of upwards of 2,000,000. I have also other returns, in answer to a limited inquiry as to the corresponding numbers, in the metropolitan district, of in-door and out-door poor on the same day; and these latter returns include an additional population of nearly 1,000,000. Upon the whole, therefore, I possess a sufficient sample of the pauperism of all England.

These returns seem to show, clearly enough, that the number of out-door paupers relieved, in a year, throughout England and Wales, is fully three times as great as the average number so relieved on each day. The account of each *half-year's* pauperism, even as it has been returned, for several years past, from each union, to Somerset House, shows plainly enough how great is the change, in the course of each half-year, in the persons chargeable, and how much larger is the mighty host of English pauperism, than the mere number of rations served out to it *daily* would indicate.

The number of persons who become chargeable during the summer half-year, is much less than that of the winter half-year. From the returns in my possession, I select the summer half-year of prosperous 1850, in order to contrast the average daily number of persons relieved as out-door poor, with the number so relieved even during that summer half-year.

My returns are, on this point, upwards of thirty in number; they include a population of 1,773,376; and, as will be seen by reference to the subjoined table*, the average number of persons receiving *out-door* relief on each *day* of the year is 58,331, and the whole corresponding number of persons receiving *out-door* relief in the summer *half-year* (25th March to 25th September), is no less than 121,562.

It would appear clear, therefore, that the number of persons relieved, for a longer or shorter term, during even the summer *half-year*, is more than twice as great as the average number of paupers chargeable on each day of the year. The number of paupers, on the relief lists, is still greater in the winter half-year than in the summer half; but a proportion of those who are relieved in the winter half-year, have been relieved, and have ceased to be chargeable, in the summer half-year. The relief lists of the several relieving officers extend over each half-year only, so that any one, who had gone off the list in one half-year, and been entered again in the next, would appear *twice*, once in each list. Making sufficient allowance for this double entry †, I find, on a careful comparison of all the returns before me, ample ground for the inference that, during each of the last ten years, the annual pauperism of England has numbered in its ranks about three times as many paupers, as, on the average, have been relieved or chargeable on each day of each year. The single million relieved on each day of the year, represents, therefore,

* See Appendix.

† Many of the returns which I have obtained, give the exact deduction to be made on account of the double entries in the lists of the second half-year. The clerks of unions, in their half-yearly return of the official "Statistical Statement" to the Poor Law Board, merely show the absolute number of different persons relieved in *each half-year;* and although no single person is twice entered in *one* half-year, yet any one who both receives relief, and ceases to be chargeable, in the first half-year, and then becomes again chargeable in the second half-year would be entered again on the new relief list of that second half-year, so that the simple addition together of the numbers appearing by the lists to have been relieved in the two half-years, would contain a certain number of persons counted twice over: my returns have corrected this. The master of each workhouse is able to apply the correction for the in-door poor, and the relieving officer, if intelligent, and willing to take trouble about the matter, can do it for the out-door. The number of such double entries varies considerably in different localities.

three millions of paupers relieved during some part of the year.

In-door relief is given to about 300,000 of the year's paupers; and the corresponding number of the out-door poor is nearly 2,700,000.

Throughout the whole of England and Wales, the average number of persons receiving out-door relief, on each day, for several years past, has been upwards of seven times as great as the number of those on the same day receiving in-door relief. For instance, in 1850, on the 1st January, (a season when the proportion of in-door paupers is above the average,) there were, in the 595 unions of England and Wales, only 109,307 persons receiving in-door relief, while there were as many as 769,687 receiving out-door relief; and on the 1st July, in the same year, the former class amounted to 86,352 only, and the latter to 708,571.

But, throughout the great and populous region of the metropolis, the out-door poor is hardly three times as numerous as the in-door. It follows, therefore, that in some parts of the country, the number of persons receiving out-door relief must be very much more than seven times as great as the number of those relieved in workhouses.

The districts in which, mainly, this large proportion of out-door relief is bestowed, in which the "workhouse test" has been most sparingly applied, and has, in truth, long ceased to be applied at all, will probably be sufficiently indicated by a subjoined table.* It exhibits the average number of the in-door and out-door recipients of relief, in several manufacturing towns, on each day of the year ended 25th March, 1851.

The average number of persons so relieved appears to have been:

In-door - - -	2,124
Out-door - - -	26,131

so that, for every one in-door pauper, there are, on the average, more than twelve out-door.

* See Appendix.

Such is the result of the endeavour so severely made, by the administrators of the Poor Law Amendment Act, for some time after its passing in 1834, to make the workhouse the only place of relief for the poor!

Assuming that, on the average of the ten years, 1841-1850, the number of paupers always receiving relief has been 1,000,000, and the corresponding number relieved during the course of each year nearly 3,000,000, (from one in six to one in five on the whole population,) it remains to consider the character of the different classes of poor persons who constitute this great army of pauperism.

The whole number of *adult* paupers receiving relief *daily* in England and Wales, during the last few years, has been from 600,000 to 650,000, and the remaining 350,000 to 400,000 daily recipients of relief have been children under sixteen years of age. Of the 600,000 or 650,000 adult paupers, it is important to ascertain what proportion, on the average, have been *able-bodied*. The number of able-bodied adult paupers,—poor persons both willing and physically able to work, but unable to obtain employment so as to earn their daily bread,—is most variable, differing greatly, not only in different years, but in different parts of the same year.

Able-bodied adults are the class of paupers who have given rise to the worst, if not to the greater part, of our past pauper legislation, and the class on whose condition and numbers a great change may possibly be produced by future legislation. The proportion of able-bodied adult paupers to the total number of paupers relieved on two given days in 1850, was as follows:

	Total Number of Paupers relieved in 595 Unions.	Total Number of able-bodied Adults relieved In-door and Out-door.
1st January, 1850 -	881,206*	170,502†
1st July, 1850 -	796,318	138,578

* Third Annual Report of the Poor Law Board, 1850, p. 125.
† Ibid. p. 137.

It is not necessary to correct this table, so as to make it represent the pauperism of all England instead of that of 595 unions only, for the *proportion* of able-bodied adults to the total number relieved, would remain unaltered.

The number of able-bodied adult persons relieved on the 1st January, appears, therefore, to be more than one-fifth of the whole number then receiving relief; and their number on the 1st July, is little more than one-sixth of the whole number then receiving relief. This state of things might be expected. The able-bodied can more easily find work, especially in the agricultural districts, in July than in January, and they are not likely to remain so long on the relief list as the other pensioners on public support. Hence, a quarter's or half-year's relief list will contain a still larger proportion of able-bodied adult paupers out of the whole number relieved, than is found in their respective numbers on a given day.

Prior to, and in 1848, the Poor Law Commissioners endeavoured to compare the general pauperism, not of a single day or of a whole year, but of a single *quarter* of a year, with the able-bodied pauperism of the same period. The omission to exclude vagrants from the returns then obtained and used by the Poor Law Commissioners, renders the figures a mere approximation, where much greater accuracy might easily have been obtained. Their table is as follows *:

Quarter ended Lady-day.	Number of Paupers relieved in the Quarter.	Total Number of *able-bodied* Paupers relieved in the Quarter.
1842	1,427,187	411,890
1843	1,539,490	466,585
1844	1,477,561	431,484
1845	1,470,970	420,096
1846	1,332,089	382,417
1847	1,721,350	562,355
1848	1,876,541	666,338

Vagrants having been included in these returns, and the same pauper having been entered as a vagrant in different

* See Report of Commissioners for administering the Laws for the Relief of the Poor in England and Wales, 1848, p. 60.

unions in the course of the same quarter, the number of able-bodied—the class to which vagrants mainly belong—is exaggerated beyond its true amount.

Although the returns in question are certainly inaccurate, in the respect just mentioned, they do not appear by any means to deserve the censure with which they have been recently visited, in an official report, by the Poor Law Board.* It is there said, "As regards the number of paupers relieved, it has been the practice heretofore to take the number relieved during the quarter ended at Lady-day in each year, as representing the aggregate number of paupers; and thus a quarter, ordinarily the heaviest in point of destitution, became the standard for estimating the extent of pauperism. Moreover, as there is frequently an interruption in the relief, the same paupers with their families were by this course entered more than once during the quarter, and were on each occasion counted as distinct persons. Such an estimate must obviously have greatly exceeded the number actually in receipt of relief. In like manner the number of vagrants relieved was made to appear much greater than it really was, as every individual of that class was returned by each of the several unions in which he had been relieved during the quarter."

It would seem that this criticism is, in some respects, wholly unfounded. First: "An interruption in the relief" would not, as is here supposed, cause paupers to be entered twice on a relief list of the same quarter. In the former relief list, which was for each quarter, and not, like the present relief list, for a whole half-year†, one single entry of the pauper's name was made on his first receiving relief; each subsequent occasion of relief, during the quarter, whether his chargeability had been interrupted or not, would be set down, by the relieving officer, in a column appropriated to the week in which the relief was given, and opposite to the original and single entry of the man's name. Clearly, therefore, no such cause of inaccuracy arises as is

* Constituted under the statute 10 & 11 Vict. c. 109., which came into operation on the 17th December, 1847.

† See *antè*, p. 11., and note, ib.

here suggested. In the next place, the quarter's return, if ever used as "a standard for estimating the extent of pauperism," was used in such a manner, that no one could, by the selection of the winter quarter, rather than that of spring, summer, or autumn, be led into any error whatever.

The use mainly made of the Return, by the Poor Law Commissioners themselves, seems to have been in comparing the pauperism of different years. Now and then they ventured to estimate the absolute number of paupers relieved in a whole year: for instance, on the 1st May, 1845, after stating the number of paupers relieved in the March quarter, they subjoin: "From this statement it appears that the total number of persons relieved in the three months ending Lady-day, 1844, amounted to nearly a million and a half, and were about $9\frac{1}{5}$ per cent. of the entire population, according to the census of 1841. Of the million and half of persons thus relieved, a large proportion were permanent paupers: but the number of new cases in the other three quarters may be safely estimated at half a million; so that the number of persons relieved in England and Wales in the course of the parochial year, 1844, may be taken at about two millions, or nearly one-eighth part of the actual population. In other words, about 1 person in 8, through the entire population, received relief from the poor's-rate at some time during the year."*

Manifestly, the Poor Law Commissioners do not use the single quarter as an absolute standard; but merely act on the supposition, that the relief of destitution, during a single quarter, cannot embrace all the paupers of the entire year; and they certainly make a very moderate allowance, which, when made, must have seemed to be a vague estimate or guess, and which now appears to be below the truth, in respect of the additional paupers relieved in the remaining nine months of the year. After all, as a means of approximating towards the great desideratum, the number of poor people relieved in a year, these much abused returns are

* Eleventh Annual Report of the Poor Law Commissioners, p. 3.

of more use, even now, than the perfectly accurate record of a single day's pauperism, as recently published by the Poor Law Board, though of much less use, for such a purpose, than the unpublished returns, of the persons relieved in a whole half-year, would be.

The inferences drawn by the Poor Law Board, in the same Report, from comparison of the two classes of returns, seem to be equally unfounded. "The mode formerly adopted for ascertaining the number of persons in receipt of relief, although affording a means of comparing the pauperism of one year with that of another, has led to erroneous conclusions, in regard to the extent of pauperism. The returns set forth in our last report, were obtained under the former mode, and show that 1,626,201 * persons, out of a population of 14,453,000, were relieved during the quarter ended at Lady-day, 1848. From this it has been supposed, that 1 in every 9 of the population was a pauper. The returns of which the foregoing table is a summary, show, however, that the number actually in receipt of relief on the 1st July, 1848, was 893,743, out of a population of 14,501,000, or less than 1 pauper in every 16 of the population." †

If I understand aright this passage, it is intended to show that the two modes are each a measure of *the same thing*, and that one of them ascertains it accurately, which the other does not. How the facts, first, that the number of persons relieved on a given day, were 1 in 16 on the population, and secondly, that those relieved, in the course of that or any other quarter of the year, were as many as 1 in 9 on the population, can be supposed to be necessarily inconsistent, I am at a loss to discover.

The extreme importance of judging correctly of the proportion which able-bodied adult pauperism bears to the general pauperism of the country, has prevented me from resting satisfied with the data given by the above-mentioned returns, and has led me to bestow a special attention on the

* The number of poor persons relieved in the 592 *unions* which existed in 1848: see the First Annual Report of the Poor Law Board, 1848, p. 3.

† Second Annual Report of the Poor Law Board, p. 10.

question. Since the able-bodied adults are likely to be chargeable for very much shorter periods than other classes of the indigent poor, it is manifest that mere returns, such as have been published by the Poor Law Board, of the proportion of the able-bodied adults to the whole number of poor on a single day, give no more aid, probably give even less, than did the former returns of the Poor Law Commissioners, towards determining the proportion between the able-bodied adults and the whole number of paupers of any given year.

An accurate comparison between able-bodied adult paupers and the corresponding number of paupers of all classes receiving relief on given days, and during an entire half-year, is furnished by a subjoined table*, founded on returns obtained, in this instance, from a population of 850,895. The following are some of the results of my table.

Number of adult able-bodied Males receiving Out-door Relief on 1st July, 1850.	Total Number receiving Out-door Relief on 1st July, 1850.	Number of adult able-bodied Males receiving Relief during some part of the Half-year	Total Number receiving Relief during some part of the Half-year.
1461	28,740	6120	60,596

In other words, it appears that the able-bodied adult males are only about 1 in 20 on the whole number of poor relieved on a given day, and are 1 in 10 on the whole number relieved in the summer half-year. The winter half-year would exhibit a still greater disproportion.

It appears also that the number of different able-bodied *men* relieved even in one half-year, is four times as great as the number of that class receiving relief on a given day, although the total number of all classes of out-door poor relieved in the half-year is little more than double the number relieved on any given day. The average duration of the chargeability of able-bodied *men*, is manifestly only one-half of the general average duration of chargeability.

It may safely be concluded that the able-bodied men who receive parish relief, do not, on the average, remain

* See Appendix.

chargeable longer than two months: in other words, that there are relieved, of this particular class of paupers, in the course of the year, six times as many as are, on the average, receiving relief on each day of the year.

The mean number of able-bodied adult males relieved on the 1st January and the 1st July, 1849, was as follows:

In-door - - - - -	7,925
Out-door - - - -	47,715
Total - -	55,640

During the year, the whole number of the men thus relieved would therefore be $55{,}640 \times 6 = 333{,}840$; and each of these men is *able-bodied*, able to serve his country either in peace or war; he only wants employment to become, or remain, a useful member of society.* This band of brothers, upwards of 300,000, "nourris par la patrie" in their state of destitution, constitute an army greater, in its numerical force at least, than that of the 228,889 men, recently raised in countries inhabited by 17,902,295 subjects of a great military monarchy, the Austrian Empire.†

If pauperism were not ashamed of showing itself, and wore a badge, as it once did, we should meet pauper pensioners at every turn in England, just as, in Austria in 1851, soldiers are met at every place of public resort; and the men in uniform seem almost to equal, in number, those in plain clothes.

Women form by far the largest part of the whole number of adult paupers. The observation has been made long ago by Villermé and others, and applies to the pauperism of France and Belgium, as well as to our own. The table referred to in the last page, exemplifies this law of pauperism. The

* Who does not remember the words of the poet?

Gratum est, quod patriæ civem populoque dedisti,
Si facis, ut patriæ sit idoneus, utilis agris,
Utilis et bellorum et pacis rebus agendis:
Plurimum enim intererit, quibus artibus, et quibus hunc tu
Moribus instituas.

† See Appendix. The figures in the text are from "Tafeln zur Statistik der Oesterreichischen Monarchie, für die Jahre 1845 und 1846." Vienna, 1850.

published returns of the Poor Law Board show that it always obtains. On the 1st January, 1850, a period of the year when the proportion of female to that of male adults, receiving relief, is lower than it is in the summer or autumn, the numbers relieved in the parishes *in union* in England and Wales were as follows: —

Adult Males	- - - - -	178,068
Adult Females	- - - - -	350,446
Children under Sixteen	- - - -	350,480
	Total - -	878,994

A view of the number of the indigent poor receiving the out-door relief of *secours à domicile*, administered by the Bureaux de Bienfaisance in Paris, shows the same excess of women over men in the persons receiving relief.* The proportion of children relieved is, however, much smaller than ours, as might be expected in a country where population is progressing at a much slower rate than with us.

It is to be observed that, among the Parisian children, the girls are only a little more numerous than the boys; but, among the adults, there are, in the twelfth arrondissement, 4643 women, and only 2759 men: in other words, there are about 7 women to 4 men; nearly the same enormous disproportion as exists between the sexes in the pauperism of England.

Widows form a numerous class of the chargeable poor. The proportion which they bear to the total number of poor receiving relief on given days, will be seen by a subjoined table.†

It appears that the number of widows is full 6·80 per cent. of the whole number of poor persons receiving out-door relief. But the ordinary proportion of widows and widowers, taken together, to the whole population, is 7 per cent. only.‡ The

* See, in the Appendix to this chapter, the table given by M. Buret, *De la Misère des Classes laborieuses en Angleterre et en France*, tom. i. p. 267.

† See Appendix.

‡ This proportion seems to be invariable; but the proportion between the

proportion of widows found in the ranks of pauperism is, therefore, one among many indications of the excessive mortality, which is generally prevalent throughout the poorer classes of our community.

Awfully great as is the number of these 350,000 children under 16, found in the daily list of English pauperism, it by no means represents the whole number of children under 16, who, in the course of any given year, are relieved, for a longer or a shorter period, out of the poor rate. The whole number of children so relieved cannot, I fear, be less than 1,000,000.

Such of these children as are numbered among the outdoor poor need no special consideration, for they are wholly under the care of parents, or natural guardians; and the administration of the Poor Law deals with them merely as members of the family to which they belong. But in respect of such children, when relieved in workhouses, the position of the givers of relief is very different. The average daily number of children under 16, who, for some years past, have been inmates of workhouses, has varied mainly from 40,000 to 50,000. About one-half of them are "orphans, or children relieved without their parents."*

It may be supposed that this number of children in workhouses will be liable to a much less fluctuation than the number of adult paupers there. We are now enabled, by means of a valuable report, made by Mr. Doyle to the Poor Law Board, and published since most of these pages were written, to ascertain pretty closely the proportion between

widows and widowers who constitute the 7 per cent, varies greatly in different countries: in France there are more than two widows to one widower; in England more than four: Moreau de Jonnès, *Eléments de Statistique*, p. 264.

* The number of this class on 1st July, 1849, was 22,485; on 1st January, 1850, 23,596. I do not understand why Mr. Doyle concludes (in his report of 31st December, 1850), that of the whole number of children, who are at any one time in workhouses, not more than about 15 per cent. should be considered from orphanage, and from being deserted, "as being permanently chargeable, and, therefore, wholly under the control of the guardians." It appears to me, that their number is fully 50 per cent. of the whole number of children receiving, on any given day, in-door relief. This class of orphan and deserted children is, of course, that which will mainly supply the inmates of district schools.

the number of children under 16, in workhouses on a given day, and the whole number of such children admitted into the same workhouses during an entire year. Mr. Doyle's report comprehends unions in the counties of Chester and Salop, and in Wales. The number of children in workhouses in those unions on the 1st December, 1849, and the number admitted into the same workhouses during the next year, were as follows:

Number of Children in the Workhouses on 1st Dec. 1849.			Number admitted from 1st Dec. 1849 to 1st Dec. 1850.			Total relieved in the Workhouses during the Year.		
Boys.	Girls.	Total.	Boys.	Girls.	Total.	Boys.	Girls.	Total.
1,003	779	1,782	1,782	1,629	3,411	2,785	2,408	5,193

The day's total, 1782, indicates a year's total of 5193, so that the number of pauper children on a given day is one third of that of the year. The number of children, therefore, who, in the course of every year, are inmates of our workhouses, will be not less than 120,000 to 150,000, since the average daily number there appears to be from 40,000 to 50,000.

Among the many things in the administration of the Poor Law which urgently require reform, the condition of these helpless children of indigence, especially such of them as have only the State for a parent, holds a foremost place. If they are to be clothed, and fed, and lodged at the expense of rate-payers, surely it concerns the interest of such rate-payers, as well as that of the poor outcasts themselves, that each of them should be removed from the contamination of the workhouse, and be so dealt with, as to have a reasonable chance of becoming an honest and industrious man or woman.*

Every one agrees that the poor-rate is to maintain these pauper children: it must, therefore, be worth while, even

* Even the heathen poet could exclaim,

Nil dictu fœdum visuque hæc limina tangat
Intra quæ puer est!

on pecuniary grounds, to relieve them from the pernicious influences of common workhouses, and to bestow on them such opportunities of an industrial, moral, and religious training, as may make them worthy members of a civilised Christian community. There can be no difficulty about even religious training in the case of pauper orphans. No class of the destitute seems so urgently to need some amelioration in its condition. For the pauper child, the workhouse is, in many cases, a prison; and its administration may easily be so conducted as to exercise an influence more powerful for evil to the child, than the ordinary contamination of a prison is to the adult. The neglect of these unhappy children, in workhouses, "has long been visited in bitter retribution on the country. 'A very large proportion of the inmates of all the London prisons,' writes Mr. Hickson, who made an extensive inquiry and report on the subject, 'have passed, as a preparatory step, some portion of their lives in workhouses. In Tothill Fields Prison I examined twenty-five boys, whom I found at the treadmill, thirteen of whom were workhouse boys. In the Coldbath Fields Prison, the House of Correction at Brixton, Clerkenwell New Prison, the Penitentiary, and other prisons, I examined a considerable number who had passed through workhouses. In the Euryalus convict ship, 25 boys out of 150 had lived in workhouses.'"

The above is the language of Mr. Tufnell, in a valuable Appendix to a Report on the Training of Pauper Children, and on District Schools, published ten years ago by the Poor Law Commissioners. In that Report (p. ix.), the commissioners, after speaking of their own recommendation of district schools to the House of Commons, subjoin, that their own subsequent experience abundantly proved, that such an arrangement was *necessary* to the success of their efforts to place, in a career of virtuous and successful industry, orphans and other children deprived of their natural protectors. In similar terms speak the different assistant commissioners, whose views, with most satisfactory and apparently conclusive reasons for them, are appended to the Report. "If the class of workhouse children is to be effectually saved from future pauperism and vice," says Sir Edmund Head (p. 379.), "*district schools, and nothing else,* must be looked upon as the means."

A common popular argument, against the establishment of efficient district schools, for poor children in workhouses, is sufficiently refuted by Mr. Tufnell, in one of the papers appended to the last-mentioned report. He says: "It would be said that we should be giving the pauper children a better education than that obtained by the independent labourer's child. While I allow and lament this truth, I wholly deny its force. Because the schooling of children out of the workhouse is neglected, is this a valid reason and excuse for wholly neglecting those who are within it? According to this argument, not a single ray of moral or religious knowledge should be allowed to illumine the mind of a pauper child; he should be brought up a perfect brute, since it is certain that this is the lot of innumerable independent children." Again: "The extreme ignorance of most children when they first enter the workhouse, together with the great ease with which, in a well-conducted school, they appear to be taught and reformed, affords a pleasing presage of the good that might result to society, were all those, whose condition seems cast irrevocably among the most degraded, thus furnished, as they easily might be, with that internal safeguard against future misconduct which a sound education affords. On entering the workhouse it frequently happens that children, even those who are fourteen or fifteen years old, do not know a letter, have never heard the Lord's Prayer, nor even of a God; but their docility is usually unbounded. From the perfect control that the circumstance of their boarding in the house gives the master, and their consequent freedom from all corrupt external influences, and those petty interruptions to constant attendance that so frequently thin the ranks of a village school, the instruction is imbibed with a rapidity that far surpasses the progress in day schools. It is also worthy of remark, that those children who most distinguish themselves for ability and good conduct are, very generally, those who are orphans or entirely deserted. The cause is obvious.—Those who consider this question on the low ground of economy, should calculate the incidental expenses that arise, owing to the present defective system, as every boy who stays in the house a year beyond the time at which, under improved management, he would be able to get work, costs his parish at least 8*l.* The cost should also be taken into account, of relieving those in after life, who, in consequence of their early inefficient training, have not the energy or the talent to preserve independence, and are hence constant recipients of relief, and pass their latter days as pensioners on the parish purse. To this should also be added the expense of those whom this bad education may lead into courses of crime, and who prey upon society, to the average amount, according to the constabulary report, of not less than 25*s.* weekly."

When it was once understood that, by a small extra outlay in educating these children of workhouses, much could be done towards the prevention of future pauperism and crime, parliament was induced to adopt the views so strongly recommended to their consideration; and, in the year 1844, by the statute 7 & 8 Vict. c. 101. s. 40., the Poor Law Commissioners are authorised, "as and when they may see fit," to combine unions and parishes "into school districts, for the management of any class or classes of infant poor, not above the age of *sixteen* years, being chargeable to any such parish or union, who are orphans, or are deserted by their parents, or whose parents, or surviving parent or guardians, are consenting to the placing of such children in the school of such district; but the said commissioners shall not include in any such district, any parish, any part of which would be more than fifteen miles from any other part of such district." It is perhaps to be regretted that the last restriction was introduced into the statute, for it is mainly in thinly peopled and extensive country districts that the present workhouse of a single union furnishes the smallest means of training the pauper child; and perhaps it is also precisely in this class of unions that unwillingness to incur any risk of adding to the poor-rate for an educational purpose, is most likely to be found.

The powers thus conferred on the Poor Law Commissioners were found insufficient to bring about the establishment of school districts; and in 1848, a statute (11 & 12 Vict. c. 82.) was passed to extend those powers. But, down to January, 1849, no progress whatever seems to have been made in carrying out the law. In that month there occurred a great sacrifice of life among pauper children, who, farmed out by their respective parishes, were kept in an establishment of a Mr. Drouet, at Tooting, in Surrey. By this calamity, the condition of the metropolitan children was brought under the more immediate notice of the Poor Law Board, who "deemed it a fitting opportunity to make renewed efforts for the establishment of district schools."* But, even after the passing of the additional statute, and notwithstanding these renewed efforts, and the recorded opinion of so many competent authorities, that the ordinary workhouse is not a proper school for the young, and cannot be made one, the change introduced in the mode of educating these pauper children, has consisted rather in an endeavour to improve the workhouse school, than to carry out the real hope and intention of parliament. The First Report of the Poor Law Board, dated 31st December, 1848, informs us that "in many unions the boards of guardians have applied themselves with much energy to the industrial training of the children in the *workhouse* schools, and have taken active measures for their instruction in useful occupations, so far as the limited resources of a single union would allow;" but it goes on to state the belief of the Board, "that *a really effective system of education and industrial training can only be established in unions having a considerable population, or where several unions are combined for the purpose.*" And in the following year the Board at once avows the principle on which it has proceeded, and shows how little it has accomplished. "In dealing with this subject, we have been anxious to carry with us the convictions and feelings of the

* Second Annual Report of the Poor Law Board, p. 13.

guardians; and, although we are empowered to form school districts without the assent of the guardians, we deemed it important that their cordial co-operation should be secured. No school district has, therefore, been declared, without the express concurrence of the large majority of the guardians concerned in it being first obtained."

When the Poor Law Board thus abstains from moving at all, until it can carry with it, in each case, not merely the convictions, but even the feelings of the guardians, and only performs its own proper and exclusive function, when the express concurrence of the large majority of the guardians has been first obtained for its doing so, we really need not wonder at finding that, down to the end of the year 1849, so little progress was made in carrying out these important improvements in the poor law. Nor can it surprise any one to read, in the same Report, the avowal, by the Poor Law Board, that success in the establishment of district schools had not been so great as they could have desired; although, as they add, the efforts made were not altogether unavailing, "three very important school districts having, within the year, been formed in and near the metropolis." In addition to the three school districts thus constituted in and near London, three others were formed in the country; and, by the end of the year 1849, out of more than 15,000 places in England and Wales, separately maintaining their poor, 259 only, contained in twenty unions, had obtained the benefit of these educational provisions of the legislature, by being combined into six school districts. During the whole of the following year, no addition was made to this number, either in town or country. This is stated in the Third Annual Report of the Poor Law Board, in the following terms. "The importance of affording to the children in union workhouses, such an education as may best tend to raise them from the class of paupers to that of independent labourers and artizans, is becoming more and more felt, by boards of guardians. Still, little progress has been made during the year in the formation of school districts, under the provisions of the 7 & 8 Vict. c. 101.; and although the matter has, in some instances, repeatedly been brought before the board of guardians of the unions proposed to be included in districts, the number of those opposed to their formation has appeared to be such as to preclude the hope, at all events for the present, and especially in the rural unions, that the provisions of the law, in regard to such schools, can be made generally available."

The repeated attempts here alluded to are, I suppose, such as have been made, at the instance of the Poor Law Board, by Poor Law Inspectors, in the vain hope of persuading boards of guardians to adopt provisions of the law, which seem unavailing and nugatory, till the guardians think fit themselves to legislate, by so adopting them. The Poor Law Board is manifestly impotent to carry out its recorded conviction, of ten years standing, on this subject: and its progress, in the endeavour to do so, is such, that if continued, at its present rate, some generations must pass away, before the country will be properly supplied with district schools.

The enormous number of pauper children, so large a proportion of whom are inmates of workhouses, and the neglect of Parliament, or of the Poor Law Board, or of Boards of Guardians, effectually to organise district schools, tend strongly to connect juvenile crime with the pauperism of the country. To this subject I shall revert, in considering the relative pauperism of the agricultural and manufacturing districts. M. Ducpetiaux has well observed, that the recent increase, in criminality of juvenile delinquents, in Belgium, is explained by the statistics of indigence.

The Reports on Elementary Schools, recently published with the Minutes of the Committee of Council on Education, show how totally inadequate to the educational wants of the children of the working classes generally are the means of education now provided. And even those inadequate means exist, in many parts of the country, only for a small fraction of the population. In Wiltshire and Berkshire, agricultural counties which, probably, are on a level with others in this respect, less than half the children of the labouring classes go to school at all, and those who do go, leave for the most part at so very early an age, that their schooling does extremely little towards cultivating either their moral or their intellectual nature.* Moreover, the sort of education often furnished where there is a school for the children, may be judged of by the instance recorded by Mr. Moseley† of a school "of considerable reputation," even provided with a *master*, attended by children of farmers as well as of labourers, and having more than the usual proportion of big children. "Of the first class, composed of eleven children, four only could write the Belief on their slates correctly, as to the spelling; only two had any knowledge, however slight, of geography; and seven did not know the name of the country in which they live. When told, and asked, who governs our country, they were unable to tell, and appeared to attach no definite idea to the inquiry. Six children only, out of eighty-two, could read with tolerable ease and correctness, in books of general information, and seven others only could read in the Scriptures. One boy was learning the compound rules in arithmetic, four were in division, and twenty-six in addition, but not one in the first class could write in figures the number ten thousand and ten, and not one could multiply correctly 3*l.* 6*s.* 8*d.* by 6. The children of the second and every lower class were ignorant of the simplest facts in Scripture history; none of them could read correctly a simple sentence, or write in figures the number four hundred and seventy-eight, or tell the product of 4 by 9."

It has been said that "The State has awakened to the conviction, that it is bound both by duty and by necessity to take care that its whole population shall have such an education as promises to render them peaceable and orderly, and to fit them for the intelligent discharge of their functions as members of a free state."‡ If the State has not awakened to this conviction, its slumber will, ere long, be disturbed by

* Mr. Moseley's General Report, Minutes of the Committee of Council on Education, for 1850–51, vol. ii. p. 1.

† Mr. Moseley's Report, ibid. p. 8.

‡ Archdeacon Hare's Sermon, "Education the Necessity of Mankind." London, J. W. Parker, 1851.

the voice of the country crying out for the fulfilment of the great duty of the State, which has been so long and so sadly neglected. It is a cheering fact that men of different parties, and of different religious views, who have entered into controversy as to the mode in which the duty shall be performed, all agree that a vastly improved system of education, for the great body of the people, is become of paramount necessity to the well-being of the whole community. It is one of the many glories of Manchester to be the battle-field of this controversy*: and I rejoice to find, since the above sentences were written, that a bishop of the Church of England, "who has devoted the best years of his life to the work of education," is now urging on his clergy to employ their most strenuous exertions to obtain some settlement of the great question of education of the young.†

Now that 3,000,000 of our population, belonging to an ignorant, degraded, and miserable pauper class, actually receive parish relief in the course of every year, and indicate the existence of a still larger class to which they belong, and which is but little, if at all, less ignorant, degraded, and miserable than themselves, it becomes high time not merely for Christian philanthropists, but for practical statesmen, to turn their attention to effecting some elevation and improvement in the condition and instruction of the great masses of the people. The ignorance in which those masses are left, may be seen in some of Mr. Clay's valuable reports on the Preston House of Correction. The appalling ignorance of criminals is a proof, if proof be needed, of the total want of education of the whole class from which the bulk of criminals is supplied. In 1850, Mr. Clay says, "With reference to 1636 male prisoners, it is a fact that 674 were unable to read in the slightest degree; 646 were ignorant of the Saviour's name, and unable to repeat a word of intelligible prayer; and 1111

* See the Scheme of Secular Education proposed by the National Public Schools Association, compared with the Manchester and Salford Borough Education Bill. London, Longmans, 1851.

† Charge to the Clergy of the Diocese of Manchester, by James Prince, Lord Bishop of Manchester, p. 29. London, 1851.

were unable to name the months of the year in their proper order; while 713 were well acquainted with the exciting adventures and villanies of Turpin and Jack Sheppard, and admired them as friends and favourers of the poor, inasmuch as if they did rob, *they robbed the rich for the poor*."*

Sadly does the State neglect its duty, when such is the intellectual, moral, and religious condition of a numerous class of its children. The Pagans of the ancient world admitted the existence of this duty; and it has been justly observed, that "the philosophers of antiquity well knew what an important part of man's work it was to educate the young to become worthy active members of their civil commonwealths. Hence education was ever a main element in their scheme of polity, whether practical or ideal." But this duty we, who call ourselves Christians, and profess to follow the divine precept, "Love one another," entirely neglect to fulfil.

* The Rev. J. Clay's Report on the Preston House of Correction, for 1850, pp. 53, 54.

CHAP. II.

THE NUMBER, COST, AND CONDITION OF PAUPERS IN THE METROPOLIS.

Per me si va nella città dolente. DANTE.

THE great Babylon of the modern world now contains 2,361,640 inhabitants; a number far exceeding the population of many considerable kingdoms and countries of continental Europe, and nearly equalling that of the whole of Scotland.* The pauperism of the metropolis is, on many accounts, entitled to be considered by itself; and I shall therefore endeavour to overcome any difficulty which may be found in the way of so considering it, and at once proceed to lay before my reader the number and cost of maintaining that great division of the army of English pauperism which constitutes its metropolitan force.

Following the same order as was pursued in the first chapter, I begin with ancient charitable foundations, and will comprehend under the same head the rest of the organisation of public charity, so far as it is independent of relief under the poor law.

We have seen that, in the sixteenth century, it was thought fit to suppress the separate administration of relief to the poor as furnished by then existing charitable foundations; and that all income derived from such foundations was then, both in England and France, placed in the hands which administered relief under the "poor law" of the day.

Since the Reformation the legislature has always permitted the revenues of such property to be administered independently of the relief raised in parishes by compulsory

* The population of the kingdom of Hanover is 1,741,000; of Saxony, 1,770,000; of Wirtemberg, 1,645,000; that of Austria Proper is as follows. Lower Austria, 1,531,034; Upper Austria, 870,676; making a whole of 2,401,710; that of all Scotland is 2,870,784.

taxation under the poor law; and the benevolence of private founders has greatly added to the amount of parochial and other charities appropriated to the relief of the poor. Such charities now produce yearly, as we have seen, an income of 1,209,395*l.* 12*s.* 8*d.*

Among the principal of these charitable foundations are the royal hospitals of London. Two of them, St. Thomas's Hospital and Christ's Hospital, were founded by Edward VI., in order to provide, in some measure, for the sick and the impotent poor in and about the metropolis. At the present day the annual income of these two hospitals alone is about 85,000*l.*; and the number of persons annually cured and relieved, as in-patients and out-patients, at St. Thomas's Hospital, is 50,000.*

The summary of the Report of the Commissioners of Inquiry into Charities gives the following statement of the income from the property of charitable foundations, administered in the City of London, in Westminster, and in the County of Middlesex. All these foundations, whether in London, Westminster, or Middlesex, belong to our Metropolis; with the exception, probably, of a trifling part of the 31,440*l.* 16*s.* 11*d.*, attributed to the county of Middlesex.

		£	s.	d.
London	Royal Hospitals - - - -	128,763	15	5
	Chartered Companies - - -	85,685	18	8
	Parochial Charities - - -	38,703	8	6
Westminster - - - - - -		18,557	15	7
Middlesex - - - - - -		31,440	16	11
		£303,151	15	1

* The present annual revenue of St. Thomas's Hospital is 25,000*l.* See Low's Charities of London, p. 6. "During the past year there have been cured and discharged from this hospital, of sick and wounded, maimed and diseased persons, 4340 in-patients, and 51,996 medical and surgical out-patients, including casualties, some of whom have been relieved with money and necessaries at their departure, to accommodate and support them in their journeys to their several habitations. Buried from thence, 276. Remaining under care, in-patients, 398; out-patients and casualties, 2700. Total 59,710. The hospital has accommodation for 428 beds. The two wings were rebuilt upon the formation of the approaches to London Bridge, and they alone afford room for 160." The revenue of Christ's Hospital is 60,000*l.* a year: ibid. p. 322.

Mr. Sampson Low's Account of the Charities of London, recently published, shows that, omitting from the account all parochial charities, and such as are in the gift of the City companies, the metropolitan charities derive, yearly, from property, 1,022,864*l*., and, from voluntary contributions, 741,869*l*., making a total of 1,764,733*l*. But some of these charities cannot be said to relieve merely the indigent poor. Selecting, from Mr. Low's summary, the numerous hospitals and other establishments by which relief is constantly afforded, in the metropolis, to the indigent poor, we find that the following is their aggregate yearly income:

	£
Voluntary contributions - - - -	193,840
Property - - - - -	319,696
Total -	513,536

It is not easy to ascertain, exactly, among how many persons these charities distribute their aid. The result of Mr. Low's researches into the matter is, that, during the year 1848-9, the general medical hospitals alone relieved, as in-patients or as out-patients, no fewer than 329,608 persons*; and the fifty special medical charities, 105,997 persons.† Upon the whole, we may safely conclude that 500,000 poor persons receive assistance, either in medical or other relief, in the course of the year, from the sum of 513,536*l*., dispensed by the charities referred to.‡

Last of all comes the official pauperism with which relieving officers, overseers of the poor, boards of guardians, the Poor Law Board, and last, not least, the parochial rate-payers of the metropolis, have to deal. The following table shows the amount and distribution, in the Districts of the registrar-general, of the pauperism of the metropolis, in the years which ended on 25th March, 1847, and 25th March, 1850.§

* The Charities of London, p. 4. † Ibid. p. 20.

‡ For the details of these charities, see Appendix.

§ A Table in the Appendix will exhibit the pauperism of the several Unions and Parishes which constitute each of these Districts.

Districts.	Population, 1851.	Net rental of Property as assessed to the Poor Rate in 1847.	Amount expended for the Relief of the Poor in the Year ended	
			Lady-day, 1847.	Lady-day, 1850.
		£	£	£
Western - -	376,427	2,086,605	100,706	123,255
Northern - -	490,396	1,951,232	109,759	145,074
Central - -	393,256	1,877,714	156,735	172,424
Eastern - -	485,522	1,068,272	104,165	123,821
Southern - -	616,635	1,845,695	163,604	177,148
Total -	2,362,236	8,829,518	634,969	741,722

Among how many poor persons is the enormous sum of 634,369*l.*, or 715,680*l.*, the cost of the official pauperism of the metropolis, yearly distributed? How much is expended in in-door relief? how much in out-door? The questions are important, in several points of view, and do not admit of any direct answer. The Reports of the Poor Law Board, are really of no use whatever, towards determining the number of the metropolitan poor. The number of paupers relieved on the 1st of January, and the 1st of July, in each year, is, no doubt, given for Middlesex, Surrey, and Kent, as well as for other counties of England and Wales; but the great Metropolis, as defined by the registrar-general, does not appear at all in the Annual Report of the Poor Law Board as presented to Parliament. The troublesome operation of extracting the expenditure of each metropolitan union and parish, from the pages of the Annual Report, enables us to determine accurately the yearly sum expended in relief in the metropolis; but there are no details given from which to determine the number of paupers, among whom that relief is distributed.

In this want of published official information, it has been a matter of some difficulty, to determine the number of the metropolitan poor. One important fact is obtained from the census of 1841. The inmates of metropolitan workhouses on the night of June 6-7, 1841, was 19,496. Now, to ascertain the average number of such inmates from 1841 to 1850, we must take into account a small extension of area, as well as a considerable increase in population and in absolute pauperism, during the period; not forgetting that, in June, the number of paupers in workhouses is below the average of the whole year. All these things considered, I concluded, some time ago, that 21,500 might safely be taken as the average number in metropolitan workhouses, on each day of the last ten years. The absolute necessity which I was under, for other purposes, of obtaining a large number of actual returns from clerks to guardians and vestry clerks, has shown me that my estimate was too low.

In the year which ended on 25th March, 1851, metropolitan pauperism was much less than it was in 1849 or 1850. It may probably be taken, that pauperism in London, during the last year, has been rather under than above its average during the decennial period from 1841 to 1850. Actual returns, obtained from the greater part of the whole metropolitan district, show conclusively that, in the year ended on 25th March, 1851, the average number of inmates of workhouses was not less than 23,000. I therefore take 23,000 as the number of the metropolitan in-door poor. The corresponding average number of poor receiving out-door relief in the metropolis is 68,000. It will probably be found to have been somewhat less, during the year ended 25th March, 1851; but, notwithstanding the increase of population, its average during the last ten years may, I think, safely be taken at that number.

The daily receivers of pauper-relief in the metropolis, are, therefore,

In-door - - - -	23,000
Out-door - - - -	68,000
Total -	91,000

The whole number of persons receiving relief, in the metropolitan workhouses, for a longer or shorter period in each year, appears to be decidedly upwards of three times as many as, on the average, are receiving relief there, on any given day.* The number of in-door poor, of each year, is, therefore, $23{,}000 \times 3 = 69{,}000$.

* See the table in Appendix.

Each year brings from three to four times as many different claimants of out-door relief as the number, 68,000, who are receiving it daily. In the whole year the number is 68,000 $\times 3\frac{1}{2} = 238{,}000$. We obtain, therefore, as the number of paupers actually relieved in each year in the metropolis:

In-door	- - - -	69,000
Out-door	- - - -	238,000
	Total -	307,000

Metropolitan pauperism, so far as it is ascertained by the mere cost and number of its paupers, is now fully before us.

It is a curious coincidence that this number of paupers of our great metropolis should be nearly the same as that of the poor citizens who received relief, at the public expense, in ancient Rome. That most able administrator, Julius Cæsar, on his accession to power, found the number of Roman citizens relieved at the public expense to be 320,000: it was one of the acts of his short-lived administration to reduce their number to about 150,000, as appears by the testimony of Dio Cassius and Suetonius.*

This immense mass of pauperism is not equally diffused over the whole area of the metropolis, but prevails in very different degrees of intensity in different localities.

First, the comparison, even of entire Districts of the metropolis, shows a great difference in their pauperism. A reference to a preceding table† will enable us to compare the poverty and labour of the east with the wealth and luxury

* Dio, xliii. p. 224. D. (tom. p. 335. ed. Reim.): *Οὐ μέντοι καὶ ἁπλῶς ἐμεγαλοφρονεῖτο, ἀλλὰ τά τε ἄλλα διηκριβοῦτο, καὶ τοῦ πλήθους τοῦ τὸν σῖτον φέροντος, ἐπὶ μακρότατον οὐ κατὰ δίκην, ἀλλ' ὥς που ἐν ταῖς στάσεσιν εἴωθε γίγνεσθαι, ἐπαυξηθέντος, ἐξέτασιν ἐποίησατο, καὶ τούς γε ἡμίσεις δμοῦ τι αὐτῶν προαπήλειψε.* Suetonius, in vit. Jul. Cæs. c. 41.: "Ex viginti trecentisque millibus accipientium frumentum è publico ad centum quinquaginta retraxit." Augustus was at one time desirous that these "frumentationes publicæ" should be wholly abolished, but thought it prudent to preserve them. Sueton. in vit. August. c. 42.: "Ut tandem annona convaluit, *impetum se cepisse* scribit, *frumentationes publicas in perpetuum abolendi, quod earum fiduciâ cultura agrorum cessaret, neque tamen perseverasse, quia certum haberet posse per ambitionem quandoque restitui.*"

† Above, p. 35.

of the west. A much heavier burden appears to be borne, in the Eastern District, by property yielding a net rental of one million, than falls, in the Western District, on property of double the amount.

Next, the difference in this burden, as it falls on the smaller area of union or parish, in different localities, should be considered. In some of the wealthiest parishes of London the burden of pauperism is comparatively light, and is scarcely felt by the ratepayer, while in poorer parishes it is heavy, and is extremely oppressive. In the parish of St. George, Hanover Square, the net rental in 1847 was 661,552*l.**, and the amount expended in relief of the poor was 18,205*l.*, or only the sum of 6½*d.* in the pound upon the net rental. Now, taking an aggregate of several metropolitan unions and parishes, the net rental of property in which may nearly equal that of the parish of St. George, Hanover Square, and comparing such an aggregate with that parish, we shall see how glaring is the difference, in the burden of pauperism, as borne by property in different parts of the metropolis.

The inspection of a subjoined table †, shows, that the Holborn, and the East and West London unions, with the parishes of St. Matthew, Bethnal Green, and St. George, Southwark, expend in relief of the poor, 77,333*l.*, out of a net rental of 644,612*l.* And this net rental, though actually less than that of the single parish of St. George, Hanover Square, contributes, towards relieving the poor, a sum more than four times as great as that similarly contributed by the wealthy and aristocratic parish.

But, in truth, in order to judge of the grievous inequality in the distribution of this burden, it is not necessary to go into the distant east, and to compare the poverty of St. Matthew, Bethnal Green, or the East London union, with the affluence of St. George, Hanover Square. The Western District of the metropolis will, within its own limits, exhibit sufficient examples of the inequality in the present incidence

* In 1851 it is returned as 694,380*l.*, Parl. Pap. 674., Commons, Sess. 1851.

† See Appendix.

of the burden of pauperism. The extremes of wealth and indigence are found side by side: a few steps bring us from parks, and squares, and palaces, to the obscure lurking-places in which the most squalid misery and pauperism are found. Some evil genius of the place, powerful for ill as Mezentius himself, must have decreed this monstrous union:

> Corpora quinetiam jungebat mortua vivis,
> Conjungens manibusque manus atque oribus ora !

The parish of Chelsea has a rental of 147,932*l.* a year: its year's pauperism costs 18,205*l.*, or 2*s.* 7*d.* in the pound on the rental; and this parish, adjoining those of St. George and of Kensington, supports a pauperism from four to five times as great as is supported by either of its wealthier and more fortunate neighbours.

This instance of inequality of taxation, and some others of a similar kind, will be apparent on an inspection of the following table:

	Population in 1851.	Expended for Relief of the Poor in the Year ended at Lady-day, 1850.		Net Rental of Property assessed to the Poor Rate in 1847.	Sum expended for Relief of the Poor on each Pound of Net Rental.	
LONDON:						
West District.		£	*s.*	£	*s.*	*d.*
1. Kensington - -	119,990	18,048	12	518,191	0	8¼
2. Chelsea - - -	56,543	19,193	7	147,932	2	7
3. St. George, Hanover Square - - -	73,207	18,205	6	661,582	0	6½
4. St. Margaret and St. John, Westminster -	65,609	16,875	2	212,396	1	7
5. St. Martin-in-the-fields -	24,557	16,850	18	249,555	1	4
6. St. James, Westminster	36,426	14,182	14	296,949	0	11½
Total - -	376,332	103,355	19	2,086,605	0	11¾

There is a disproportion, between amount of population and value of property, which is sufficiently apparent in this table, and is at least equally striking in various other parts of the metropolitan district. The population of the City of London has been diminishing gradually for the last half century, as the dwellings of the working classes have made way for the warehouses of capitalists. Let us compare the City of London union, in respect of population and property, with its two neighbouring unions, the West London and the East London.

Nearly 700,000*l.* rental is charged, in the City of London, with the relief of destitution among a population of little more than 50,000 inhabitants; but in the East and West London unions, less than 300,000*l.* rental has to maintain the destitution found among a population of nearly 100,000 inhabitants.*

The inequality of burden is shown, still more strikingly, by comparing single parishes. St. Mildred, Bread Street, in the City, lays no poor-rate whatever; in St. Nicholas Olave, also in the City, the rates are 8*s.* in the pound, on the rateable value of the fifty-one houses which constitute the parish.†

In the City, public buildings, such as the Bank, occupying nearly the whole of the small parish of St. Christopher le Stock, the Royal Exchange, great warehouses and offices (into which former residences have been converted), now cover the ground in parishes where the poor can no longer reside.‡

The population of the City, which had gradually decreased from 1821 to 1841, is found still decreasing from 1841 to 1851.* Employment in the City is, however, much greater now than it was thirty, twenty, or even ten years ago; the demand for mere labourers has increased, as the resident population has diminished, and a large proportion of the working people of the City of London is now domiciled in the suburbs. The richer parishes have no place in which the poor can reside, and hence those of the working classes, who from sickness, or

* For the details, see Appendix.

† See Mr. Rowsell's Evidence, given in 1850, before the Select Committee of the House of Lords, on the Laws relating to Parochial Assessments, Nos. 663—812.

‡ The change in character of property in the City of London has been accompanied, in many parishes, by an enormous increase in rateable value. It appears that the annual value of houses, &c. in the City, increased only 49,671*l.*, or 10·85 per cent., from 1771 to 1801, but that between 1801 and 1831, the corresponding increased yearly value was 285,532*l.*, or 56·27 per cent.,— an increase during which the population of the City was diminishing.

age, or want of employment, are likely to have to demand relief out of the poor-rate of the parish in which they reside, are mainly found lodging in the poor parishes. It will be shown, in a subsequent chapter, that such evils of the inequality of burden as arise from the constrained congregation of the poor in pauperised localities, are greatly aggravated by recent changes in the poor law; and that the present provisions of the law tend to relieve, in great cities, those parishes where the property is of the greatest ratable value, from their share of providing for the relief and maintenance of the poor, "and at the same time throw a most unfair and oppressive burden on those parishes in which the houses are small, and where the poor can find a residence."*

It will also appear, hereafter, that a similar inequality in the distribution of the burden of pauperism is found in country districts, where it is denounced, even still more loudly than in great cities. Much of this inequality, justly complained of both in town and country, is the necessary consequence of ill-contrived and injudicious legislation, and may easily be redressed.

My returns show that the out-door poor of the metropolis are nearly three times as numerous as the in-door. The proportion between the two classes varies with the character of the parishes in which they are found. In the wealthy and aristocratic parish of St. George, Hanover Square, the average number of out-door poor is little more than that of the in-door; in St. James, Westminster, and St. Martin-in-the-Fields, parishes of like character with St. George, the number of out-door poor is even less than the number of in-door: but in what may be called parishes of the working classes, such as Shoreditch, Lambeth, Rotherhithe, and the East London union, the number of in-door poor being more than equal to those of the wealthier parishes, the out-door

* These are the very words of a resolution of the Court of Common Council of the City of London, dated the 8th of May, 1850; on which resolution a petition was, on the 21st March, 1851, drawn up and passed, on the motion of Alderman Sydney, seconded by Alderman Copeland, to be presented to both Houses of Parliament, praying for an alteration of the law of settlement and rating for the relief of the poor.

poor are about four times as numerous as the inmates of workhouses.*

As the proportion between the number of in-door and out-door poor varies thus greatly, so does the fluctuation in the whole mass of pauperism also vary greatly in different localities of the metropolis. In parishes inhabited mainly by the working classes, the paupers relieved in the course of the year are five times as many as receive relief on a given day.

The proportion between the numbers of the in-door and out-door poor, relieved at the same time, in the metropolitan district, is very different from that which, as we have already seen, prevails in the country at large; and especially from that which prevails in some of the manufacturing districts. And the proportion of relief administered in workhouses to out-door relief, is far greater in London than elsewhere.†

A much larger proportion of *able-bodied adult* paupers is relieved in the workhouses of the metropolis than in those of the country. This appears by the following table, taken from the Third Annual Report of the Poor Law Board, p. 142–3., in which Middlesex and Surrey must serve as a rude approximation to the truth respecting the metropolis.

	Adult able-bodied Paupers relieved on 1st January, 1851.	
	In-door.	Out-door.
Middlesex - - - - -	2,303	7,987
Surrey - - - - - -	1,607	4,557
Total of Middlesex and Surrey	3,910	12,544
Total of all England and Wales	22,822	121,355

Throughout England, on the 1st January, little more than five able-bodied adult paupers received out-door, where one received in-door, relief; but in Middlesex and Surrey, there is one able-bodied adult in-door pauper for little more than three out-door.

* See Appendix.

† Above, p. 12. and p. 36.

Some of the evils of the unequal distribution of pauperism through the metropolis fall even still more heavily on the poor than on the ratepayers.

The crowding together of inmates in workhouses, and in ill-ventilated and unhealthy private dwellings, are among the most obvious causes of the excessive mortality of the poor.

Undoubtedly one of the most appalling effects of pauperism is its destruction of human life. The accidents, disease, and bodily suffering to which the poor are specially subjected, make their existence everywhere much shorter than the average duration of life of the whole community amid which they dwell.

In the metropolis alone, the annual mortality of large districts in which indigent poor abound, approaches four per cent. on the whole population, while in wealthier districts, inhabited by fewer poor, it is only half that amount.*

The general mortality of London is somewhat higher than that of the country at large. The general proportion of 1 death in 45 inhabitants, becomes for London 1 in 40 only. This is well established, for there were 519,757 deaths in London during the ten years 1840–9; 51,975 was therefore the year's average. Looking at the population of London, which was

* Tables exhibiting the excessive mortality in workhouses, more especially in those of the metropolis, are found in Appendix to a Report by a Select Committee on the Poor Law Amendment Act (1838) "Medical Evidence," and in M'Culloch's British Empire, vol. ii. pp. 569—570. "Vital Statistics." The author of this valuable article (Mr. Farr) considers the immense mortality of the London workhouses an insuperable objection to the extension of the workhouse test so called. "The mortality of paupers, out of doors, has not been ascertained; the mortality is probably raised 50 per cent. by confinement in the workhouse." The Poor Law Board could easily furnish a very valuable return of the average number of inmates, and of the annual admissions, discharges, and deaths, in all metropolitan and country workhouses, for several years past. In 1841, there died 4282 persons in London workhouses (Fifth Annual Report of the Registrar-General, p. 228.), the average number receiving relief there having been, during that year, about 21,000, so that the year's deaths were 20 per cent. on the average number of inmates; a high rate of mortality, but much lower than prevailed in metropolitan workhouses seventy or eighty years ago, as will be apparent from the inspection of a table published by Sir Frederick Eden (*State of the Poor*, vol. ii. p. 441.), respecting the inmates of the workhouse of St. Martin-in-the-Fields for the ten years from 1785 to 1794.

on the average more than 2,000,000, during the same decennial period, we may safely say that the yearly deaths are one-fortieth of the whole population, or, in round numbers, that 50,000 persons died yearly in London, out of an average annual population of 2,000,000, during this decennial period.

But of these 50,000 annual deaths, there were about 9000, or rather more than one-sixth, which occurred in workhouses, hospitals, and lunatic asylums. These alone denote the existence of a class of indigent poor, who, if their mortality were not greater than that of other classes, would amount to 360,000: an awful number of the inhabitants of this great city, each of whom, as he passes through his life of toil and suffering, must look forward

> To draw the latest breath,
> Where all that's wretched, paves the way for death!

It must be observed, that the numerous class of poor persons, who, when on the lists of relieving officers, die at their own homes, are not here included; not even when their funerals are paid for, or their coffins provided, by their parishes. Taking, then, the number of out-door paupers relieved in London, in the course of a year, to be nearly 238,000, and assuming their mortality to be only the same as that of the rest of the metropolitan population, there would die, of this class, 5950, or 1 in 40 of the 238,000, in the year. Adding, therefore, 5950, the number of deaths of out-door paupers, to the 9000 who yearly die in hospitals, lunatic asylums, and workhouses, we obtain an aggregate of 14,950 as the number of deaths of paupers in a year in London.* The result is, that from one-third to one-fourth of the 50,000 who die annually, belong to the class of paupers, although some of them may not, at the time of their death, be receiving actual parish relief. So great, then, in this metropolis, is the mor-

* Some of the 238,000 out-door paupers die yearly in hospitals, but such deaths do not more than measure the excess of mortality of the out-door paupers, above the average of 1 in 40, which has been taken to represent it, although the average is that of the whole community, and is much lower than that of the out-door poor.

tality of the pauper class of society, that, while it forms only from one-seventh to one-eighth of the living population, it supplies from one-third to one-fourth of all the deaths.

It was not till lately that the mortality of paupers, in the manufacturing or agricultural districts of England, has been much considered or noticed: attention has recently been called to the actual number of deaths of paupers, in one year, in Glasgow. In 1850, when the population of that city was estimated at 367,800 inhabitants, and its gross rental was 1,017,362*l.*, the poor cost the sum of 47,787*l.* 7*s.* 10*d.*, or nearly 1*s.* in the pound on the rental, a close approximation to the measure of pauperism found in London. The pauper burials in Glasgow, during the year 1849, were 3577, being 26 per cent. on the whole burials there. By "pauper burials" is meant those, the expense of which is paid from parochial funds. The fact of their occurring in such numbers, certainly exhibits "a sad picture of the condition of the working classes,"* and seems to call loudly for inquiry into the causes and remedy for such a fearful amount of pauperism; but not more so than does the condition of London itself. It, moreover, painfully reminds us of the stern, but truthful, word of the moralist, uttered several years ago: "In thrifty Scotland itself, in Glasgow or Edinburgh city, in their dark lanes, hidden from all but the eye of God, and of rare benevolence, the minister of God, there are scenes of woe, and destitution, and desolation, such as, one may hope, the sun never saw before in the most barbarous regions where men dwelt. These things are not of this year, have no reference to a state of commercial stagnation, but only to the common state. Not in sharp fever-fits, but in chronic-gangrene of this kind, is Scotland suffering." †

This excessive mortality of the poor is, in part at least, owing to external evils, which may be removed, and which

* See Dr. Strang's Report on the Progress of Glasgow in Population, Wealth, Manufactures, &c. Transactions of the Sections, p. 163., in the Report of the Twentieth Meeting of the British Association, &c. 1850. Fever and cholera both prevailed in Glasgow, in 1848 and 1849. In 1848 the pauper burials had been 4042.

† Carlyle, "Midas."

ought not to be allowed any longer to exercise, on Christian man, in a Christian country, their demoralising and degrading influences.

On the visitation of the epidemic cholera of 1848 and 1849, its ravages were defined, not by a line drawn between one class of society and another, but by mere limits of locality, mainly the abode of poverty. It was a law of the epidemic, to attack only such parts of towns as were in a bad sanitary condition, and where the poor mainly dwelt, and to leave the healthy portions, where the poor had no dwellings, untouched, or nearly so. Dr. Sutherland informs us, that it "was no respecter of classes, but was a great respecter of localities;" the rich and poor suffering alike, or escaping alike, wherever both classes were found within the local limits of its activity.* That those local limits were almost wholly peopled by the poorest class is apparent, not only from the general observation of competent witnesses, but also from the proportion of the registered deaths of each class in districts where all equally suffered. The obscure and unhealthy lurking-places in which poverty hides itself in the Western District of the metropolis, yielded nearly as large a proportion of the working classes, in the sum total of their victims, as was found even in the region of labouring poverty in the East.†

The dwellings of the poor in the worse parts of London, and, as we shall see hereafter‡, in many of the agricultural counties, are not only unnecessarily unhealthy, but are wholly insufficient to enable their inmates to observe even the common decencies of human life. The sanitary condition of the more populous districts of London is fully disclosed in the reports of medical inspectors, employed during the epidemic cholera to which reference has been made. "The uniform evidence of every medical man engaged during that period,"

* Report, p. 42. in Appendix (A) to the Report of the General Board of Health on the Epidemic Cholera of the years 1848 and 1849.

† See the Appendix, for the tabular statement, extracted from the Report of the General Board of Health on the Epidemic Cholera of 1848 and 1849, p. 159.

‡ Chapter XIV.

says Mr. Grainger, in a recent Report on the present State of the Metropolis *, "whether, as an inspector, visitor, or poor law surgeon, showed that, in all parts of the metropolis, the dwellings of the industrious classes were in a most deplorable condition; that they were filthy, unwholesome, and neglected; that they were deficient in all the arrangements demanded for decency, comfort, and health; that there were, in many localities, houses utterly unfit for human habitation; that the water supply was miserable, both as to quantity and quality, the privies foul and overflowing, and the scavenging grossly neglected; and that, as the direct consequence of all this, there was extreme misery, sickness, and mortality." "The Report of the General Board of Health on the epidemical cholera," adds Mr. Grainger, with perfect truth, "abounds in proofs that this is a faithful picture of the poorer parts of London."

A Committee of the Statistical Society in January, 1848, examined and reported on the condition of the dwellings of the inhabitants of Church Lane, St. Giles's, London. That locality is truly called "a type of the miserable condition of masses of the community, whether located in the small, ill-ventilated rooms of manufacturing towns, or in many of the cottages of the agricultural peasantry.†"

The Committee found, in Church Lane, a population of 463 persons, using 90 bedsteads , there was an average, therefore, of above five human beings to each bed. Their report is truly said to present a picture of human wretchedness, filth, and degradation, the chief features of which are a disgrace to any civilized country. "In these wretched dwellings," add the Committee, "all ages and both sexes, fathers and daughters,

* Parl. Paper, No. 388. Comm. Sess. 1851, p. 3.

† The villages of Eagleton and Branston in Rutland, and of Dukenfield and Bury in Lancashire, have bed accommodation as follows: at Eagleton, in 14 per cent. of the families are more than 3 persons to a bed; at Branston, Dukenfield, and Bury, the corresponding proportions are 19 per cent., 33 per cent., and 25 per cent.: see Colonel Sykes's Account of the Labouring Population inhabiting the Buildings of St. Pancras, erected by the Metropolitan Society for Improving the Dwellings of the Poor, read before the Statistical Section of the British Association, at Birmingham, Sept. 1849; published among the Transactions of the Association, and also published in the Journal of the Statistical Society of London, vol. viii. p. 46.

mothers and sons, grown-up brothers and sisters, stranger adult males and females, and swarms of children, the sick, the dying, and the dead, are herded together, with a proximity and mutual pressure which brutes would resist,—where it is physically impossible to preserve the decencies of life,—where all sense of propriety and self-respect must be lost."

Something has been done, and is now doing, to remedy this dreadful state of things. It is to be hoped that, by some more effectual provision for carrying out sanitary improvements, and by a more ready perception, on the part of the owners of property in London, of their duty to their fellow-citizens, as well as by continued exertions of judicious benevolence, in erecting healthy buildings for the habitation of the industrious poor, that further and more rapid progress may be made in the direction of sanitary reform. Such reform, improving the physical condition, will also greatly improve the moral condition of those within its benefits. An immense task certainly remains to be performed, before all the metropolitan abodes of honest, industrious poverty, can be made fit for human habitation. For years to come, fever, and other diseases will probably continue, in London and elsewhere, to decimate the poor; and doing so, will no doubt add to the burden on rated inhabitants nearly in the same proportion in which they add to the sufferings of paupers. The ordinary *habitat* of fever is everywhere found in such spots as the cholera selected for its inroads; and it is to attacks of fever, that the poor, in their overcrowded and unhealthy dwellings, are especially liable.

To see how much remains still to be done, in every district of the metropolis, in order to render the dwellings of the poor fit for habitation, we have only to look around us. While this sheet is passing through the press, I observe, in weekly returns of births and deaths, published by the Registrar-General, during the present month of December, 1851, numerous testimonies from medical attendants, showing what a loss of life is daily occurring, in London, among the working classes, from causes, which, in the main, affect them alone. Every week, if not every day, proofs may be collected, by any one who cares to look for them, showing this daily operation, the causes of which might be removed, of "Typhus," "Scarlatina maligna," and "Fever," in increasing the mortality and pauperism of the metropolis. Fever, in its varied forms, still adds greatly, in parts of the metropolis, to all other pauperising influences, to which the working classes are exposed.*

Dr. Southwood Smith has well described the peculiar effect of fever, both on the health and happiness of those who are compelled to ask for parish relief, and on the pockets of those who are obliged to pay for it. "There is no disease which brings so much affliction into a poor man's family as fever. It most commonly attacks the heads of the family, those upon

* In the week ending December 6. 1851, occurs the death, from *typhus*, of a labourer's son, aged ten years, in Wink's Buildings, South Chelsea: the medical attendant states, that the building in which the child had died "is most pestiferous," and "has always been the *haunt of fever*, which from that point, as from a centre, has often *spread with great virulence*." In the following week several similar cases are recorded. "In Paddington, at 108. Praed Street, a cordwainer's son, aged two years, died on the 7th December, of *scarlatina maligna*, fourteen days. The deceased lived in a damp and ill-ventilated kitchen; this is the second death that has occurred, from *the same cause*, in this kitchen, within three weeks." Another entry, in the same week, is of the death, at 9. Ball's Gardens, Chelsea, from *fever*, of a child aged five years, the son of a labourer. "The Gardens are the most unhealthy part of the district: they have an open sewer running along the front of the whole." At Rhodes Cottages, Islington, on the 13th December, 1851, occurs the death of a child, which is entered with the statement: "These cottages are *in every respect unfit for habitation*." In the following week, on December 15th, at 4. Pleasant Place, St. James's, Bermondsey, a stonemason's daughter, aged five years, died of *scarlatina*, "the third death within the same house within thirteen days, the house consisting of two rooms and an out-house, ill drained and ventilated: the supply of water is insufficient." In Camberwell, at 61. Waterloo Street, on 10th December, a carpenter's daughter, aged eight years, died of *scarlatina maligna*; "an open sewer runs within a few yards of the house; the effluvium is said to be most offensive; the mother states that this was the cause of the disease." In the same week's list, several other similar entries are found, of deat s seemingly caused by deleterious atmospheric influences. In the week ending on 27th December, 1851, we find an equal proportion of similar entries of deaths from these preventible causes. One of them will serve as a specimen: it is found at 23. Lucy's Buildings, Vine Street, St. Andrew Holborn, in death by *typhus*. "Lucy's Buildings are very close, thickly inhabited by working people, and the greater part built over the old sewer; the inhabitants are very poor; there is a public pump, but the supply of water is scanty."

whose daily labour the subsistence of the family depends. The present returns afford melancholy evidence of the pauperising influence of this prevalent and fatal disease. They show that out of the total number of persons, in London, who received parochial relief during the last year, more than *one-fifth* were the subjects of fever. In Bethnal Green the proportion was one-third, in Whitechapel it was nearly one-half, and in St. George the Martyr it was 1276 out of 1467. Placing out of consideration the suffering of the individual attacked with fever, which is one of the most painful maladies to which the human being is subject,—placing out of view also the distress brought upon all the members of the family of the sick,—it is plain that this disease is one of the main causes of pressure upon the poor-rates. That pressure must continue, and the same large sums of money must be expended year after year, for the support of families afflicted with fever, as long as those dreadful sources of fever, which encompass the habitations of the poor, are allowed to remain." *

The very improvements which have taken place recently in Westminster and in New Oxford Street, beneficial as they may be to the upper and middle classes, have only served to aggravate the evils under which the wretched population of adjoining lanes and alleys suffer. "The public are little aware of the extent of ignorance, depravity, and vice, in which a large proportion of the population of these parishes (of St. Margaret's and St. John's, Westminster) is sunk." "There are wretched dwellings in these parishes, occupied principally by thieves, prostitutes, huxters, street-singers, and persons who gain their living by begging, and the gross depravity of these classes is indescribable. The state of many of the dwellings it is impossible to conceive. The grossest immorality is the necessary result of their promiscuously crowded habitations." "These places have become more crowded since the making of new streets, and other improvements in similar parts of the metropolis; and it is to be feared that the proposed improvement in Westminster will

* See Report on Fever in the Metropolis, in the Fifth Annual Report of the Poor Law Commissioners, p. 174.

tend in the same way to increase the evils in the dwellings that will be left standing; while part of the degraded population will be driven to other localities to propagate their vices amongst a less corrupted class."*

The returns of the census of the present year, 1851, show how such evils of these confined and unhealthy quarters must have been aggravated, in various parts of London, during the last ten years. The five unions, or parishes of Clerkenwell, East London, Holborn, St. Margaret and St. John Westminster, and Whitechapel, are found to have increased, in inhabitants, from 269,730, in 1841, to 301,048, in 1851: and their houses have increased, during the same period, from 31,618 to 32,040.† Upwards of 30,000 additional inhabitants in the last ten years, and only 422 additional houses for them to live in! Fewer than nine inhabitants to each house in 1841, and nearly ten in 1851!

Glasgow, distinguished, as we have just seen, by the great mortality of its pauper class, exhibits in its wynds, comprising a fluctuating population of from 15,000 to 30,000 persons, a labyrinth of lanes, out of which a number of entrances lead into small square courts, each with a dunghill reeking in the centre. In some of the lodging rooms, are found "a whole layer of human beings littered along the floor, sometimes fifteen and twenty; some clothed and some naked; men, women, and children, huddled promiscuously together:" their bed consisting of a layer of musty straw intermixed with rags.

Dr. Sutherland, in his Report to the General Board of Health, dated April 24. 1850, says that, in these frightful abodes of human wretchedness, which constitute the wynds of Glasgow, "all sanitary evils exist in perfection." It appears, moreover, that Glasgow is rapidly increasing its population, without making any corresponding increase in the number of its houses, and must, therefore, suffer, like

* London City Magazine, Jan. 1851, cited by Mr. Montague Gore, "On the Dwellings of the Poor, and the Means of improving them." London: Ridgway, 1851, p. 14.

† For the details, see Appendix.

London, more and more, from that over-crowding which is so great a cause of immorality, disease, and death, among the poorer classes, when they are

> In populous cities pent,
> Where houses thick, and sewers, annoy the air.

The indigent classes seem to suffer, in respect of their excessive mortality, in some parts of other great cities and towns much in the same way as in parts of London and Glasgow. Interesting inquiries, instituted by M. Villermé, first showed how great a difference, in the duration of life, is found in different parts of the same city. M. Villermé especially examined and ascertained the mortality of the different arrondissements of Paris. The average mortality in Paris is 1 in 36 44: the rate in the first, second, and third arrondissements, mainly inhabited by the wealthier classes, is only 1 in 52, 1 in 48, and 1 in 43; while in the seventh, eighth, and twelfth arrondissements, inhabited mainly by the labouring classes, the rate becomes 1 in 30, 1 in 23, and 1 in 20; in other words, the sons and daughters of labour among the poor inhabitants of the Faubourg St. Antoine die, on the average, at little more than half the age which is attained by those who are born in the wealthier quarter of the Faubourg St. Honoré.

Subsequent investigations have tended to show the difference in mortality in different parts of London, and in different parts of several of the principal cities and towns of England. The difference in mortality between the worst and best parts of London, seems to be quite as great as the corresponding difference in Paris. If the result be embodied in a statement of the different duration of life of three different classes into which we may divide our society, it appears as follows:

Classes.	Average Years of Age at Death, including Children.
Gentry - - - -	44
Tradesmen - - - -	25
Labourers - - - -	22

and in our other cities and towns the corresponding difference in mortality, in the different classes who mainly inhabit different localities, is equally great.

It is worth while to compare the amount of the pauperism of London with that of Paris. Throughout France the *in-door* relief of the poor is given in hospitals (hôpitaux) for the sick, and in almshouses (hospices) for the aged and infirm. The out-door relief (*secours à domicile*), in great part raised by a local tax, is wholly under the controul of Bureaux de Bienfaisance. Laws, passed chiefly in 1796 and 1798, still regulate the administration of these establishments.* It is manifest that such establishments include not only the relief corresponding to what is administered in England by boards of guardians, but also the whole of that which our numerous medical and other charities supply.

To compare the pauperism of the capitals of the two countries, it is therefore plain that we must either add to the English account of our workhouses and boards of guardians, the sums expended, and the persons cured and relieved, in hospitals and almshouses, or we must *omit* from our comparison all inmates of hospitals and almshouses on both sides of the Channel.

Adding the relief by hospitals and other charities, mentioned at the beginning of this chapter†, to the relief given under the Poor Law, we should obtain for the pauperism of the metropolis, an annual expenditure of upwards of 1,200,000*l.* distributed among about 800,000 indigent poor. The result would give an average of 30*s.* a head for each poor person relieved, and the pauperism, or poverty, so estimated, must

* It is hardly necessary to correct the vulgar error, that all contribution to the relief of the poor in France is voluntary. The hospitals and hospices, like many of our own hospitals and other charities, possess considerable funds of their own, in land and other property, bequeathed to them by the piety of former ages; and the Bureaux de Bienfaisance, though obtaining some supplies by collections from poor boxes in churches and otherwise, still have recourse to taxation for the whole residue of the moneys which they administer in relief to the poor. They obtain this residue from what we may term the "borough fund" of the municipality. In each city the municipal council is to supply the Bureaux de Bienfaisance with funds "pris sur les revenus de la ville."

† Above, pp. 32—34.

be owned to comprehend within its ranks nearly 1 in 3 of the whole population of the metropolis.

But no one considers any man as a pauper merely because he has obtained medical relief, for himself or members of his family, from a public dispensary; and the best comparison practicable between the pauperism, properly so called, of the capitals of France and England, will be made by contrasting the out relief of the one, with the *secours à domicile* alone, of the other. If, then, we omit the *administrations hôpitalières* from the Parisian account, and the medical, parochial, and other charities from the London account, we shall obtain this comparison.

It must be remembered that, in London, the destitution of the able-bodied poor is relieved, to a considerable extent, in workhouses, and that, in Paris, such destitution is only relieved by *secours à domicile;* so that the comparison of *secours à domicile* as administered in Paris, with out-door relief as administered in London, certainly much exaggerates the relative amount of the Parisian pauperism.

The amount raised and administered for some years past in Paris, as *secours à domicile,* has exceeded 2,000,000 francs annually. M. Vée, in his essay on the pauperism of Paris, explains how this sum is applied, and shows how much is received by each class of the indigent poor among whom it is divided. He deals with the figures of the year 1843, in which the whole sum raised was about 1,900,000 francs; and the indigent families among which it was divided, were about 30,000. Of that sum no less than 200,000 francs was appropriated to the expenses of administration, and of maintaining the buildings called maisons de secours.* Making this deduction, there remains a sum of 1,700,000 francs for distribution as out-door relief. Of this sum, about 500,000 francs receives a special and exclusive application. It is principally expended in relief of blind and paralytic persons, of men upwards of seventy-four years of age, and of sick persons supplied with relief in medicine at their own houses.†

* Vée, *Du Paupérisme et des Secours Publics dans la Ville de Paris,* p. 52. Paris, 1849.

† Vée, ib. p. 57.

This privileged class numbers from 5000 to 6000 families. The sum remaining for general distribution, and which, perhaps, upon the whole, is the fittest for comparison with our out-door relief of the poor, amounts, therefore, only to 1,200,000 francs, and this sum is to be divided among 24,000 families. It follows that a sum equal to only about 48,000*l.* is all that is yearly divided, by public charity, among at least four-fifths in number of those who receive out-door relief in Paris.*

In London the out-door relief of a single year is probably about 450,000*l.*, if we assume the in-door and out-door relief to be 741,722*l.*, as it was in 1850. The families among whom this out-door relief was divided, cannot be so many as 100,000: in all likelihood they are not more than 80,000, so that not less than from 4*l.* to 5*l.* must be received, on the average, by each family; instead of the much smaller sum, which, as M. Vée shows, is received by each of the pauper families constituting the vast majority of the receivers of out-door relief in Paris.

The data now before my reader, sufficiently furnish the means of estimating the relative burden of the relief thus administered in the two capitals.

If we go back sixty-five years, and compare the pauperism of London and Paris prior to the great social change which was produced in France by the Revolution, we shall find that "la bonne ville de Paris" suffered more from pauperism than London did at the same time. But it is probable that during the greater part of the last century, France suffered nearly, if not quite as much, from pauperism, as England did. The Dixme Royale of Marshal Vauban, published under Louis XIV., and the Travels of Arthur Young, published in 1794, include between them a period during which the pauperism and social misery of the French people had increased rather than diminished; and the extent of that

* Private charity unquestionably adds very largely in Paris, as it does in London, to the contributions of the ordinary relief given under public administration. M. Vée, p. 58. speaks of the amount distributed by the Bureaux de Bienfaisance, to each indigent family, as "des contributions dérisoires."

pauperism and misery, at the time when Vauban wrote, is conclusively shown by his own unimpeached testimony.

In London, the medium payment for the poor, by the parishes, which in 1783, 1784, and 1785, might be fairly said to constitute the metropolis, was 200,762*l.* 8*s.* 7*d.**, or less than one-third of what is now expended in mere relief to the poor, and the medium poor-rate paid by England and Wales was then 2,167,749*l.* 13*s.* 8*d.**; so that, at that time, the whole official pauperism of London was not more than one-tenth of the aggregate then found in the country at large. But, in 1788, in the single Parisian parish of St. Etienne du Mont, there were 21,000 indigent poor to relieve; and when, in 1791, the Municipal Commission de Bienfaisance first essayed to establish *la Charité administrative*, their relief-list contained the names of 120,000 indigent poor, out of the then 550,000 inhabitants of Paris. Since that time, Paris has doubled its population; and, in doing so, has reduced the absolute number of its official paupers by nearly one-half. It now contains a million of inhabitants, of whom less than 70,000 are persons receiving relief from the Bureaux de Bienfaisance †: 238,000 persons yearly receive out-door relief in London, and each of them receives such relief to an extent about three times as great as is bestowed on those who are relieved by the Bureaux de Bienfaisance in Paris.

Unfavourable to us as is the above contrast, we must remember that London does not stand in a similarly unenviable position, if compared with the rest of England. The average expenditure for relief of the poor throughout London, for the year ended 25th March, 1847, was 1*s.* 5¼*d.* in the pound, on the rated value of the property assessed; the corresponding average of England and Wales, during the same year, was 1*s.* 7*d.*; and, in number of poor, the official pauperism of London is only 1 in 8 on the population,

* These are the figures of Mr. Colquhoun, and of Sir Frederick Eden, *State of the Poor*, vol. i. pp. 459—464.

† The recipients of *secours à domicile* who, in 1831, had been 101,805, out of a population of 680,000, were reduced to 62,705 in 1826; were only 66,148 in 1844, and in 1847 were 65,000.

whereas that of the whole country appears to be at least 1 in 6 on the population.

Such, then, is the condition of a large portion of the society of London. Millions, who have visited the World's Exhibition, during the last summer, have gazed with admiration on the prodigious industry and opulence of this capital of the commercial world.

> Not Babylon,
> Nor great Alcairo, such magnificence
> Equall'd in all their glories!

But it has been only a few who, while in the very midst of all that wealth or luxury can seek, have known that they were constantly within a step of innumerable abodes of the most squalid destitution and misery; and that, nevertheless, the pauperism of London is not nearly so grievous as that which presses on a great part of the length and breadth of England.

CHAP. III.

PAUPERISM OF AGRICULTURAL AND MANUFACTURING DISTRICTS.

Strait mine eye hath caught new pleasures
While the landskip round it measures;
Russet lawns and fallows gray
Where the nibbling flocks do stray—
Tower'd cities please us then,
And the busy hum of men. MILTON.

BEFORE entering into the consideration of a proper remedy for the great and varied evils of the existing pauperism of England, it will be worth while carefully to ascertain the incidence of the burden on agricultural and manufacturing districts respectively. The result of such an inquiry may enable us the better to determine, whether or not a great part of those evils, may justly be attributed, exclusively, to the law of settlement and removal of the poor. I the more willingly enter on this task, from the conviction that the comparison has not, as yet, been satisfactorily instituted, and that a sincere and earnest endeavour, to find out the truth, will, at least, be of some use in enabling others to discover it, if I should myself fail in the attempt.

Unless there be something very rotten in our laws or institutions, something which directly tends to produce in England an anomalous and abnormal condition of its pauperism, it is on the densely peopled regions of manufacturing and commercial industry that the burden of relieving the poor will be found to press with the greatest weight. In countries, where our law of settlement and removal of the poor is unknown, whether destitution is provided for by compulsory legal relief, levied as a tax on ratepayers, or by some other organisation of public charity, the fair fields of agriculture enjoy a comparative exemption from the burden.

With the increase in density of population, and in development of commercial and manufacturing industry, exercised on that great scale which is its usual modern characteristic, a corresponding increase in the demands of pauperism seems generally to arise. The process of accumulation of wealth in a few hands, by the labour of a race of freemen who have no property, mainly produces the necessity for poor laws. While labour is performed by man in a state of slavery or serfdom, the absolute property of his master, poor laws are unnecessary: for the slave or serf is provided for by his master. And in the earliest stages of the society of freemen, the class of proprietors of land has usually been numerous, and the free labourers, in proportion to the number of proprietors, have been few. But, in a subsequent stage of society, an immense increase in the number of the proletarian class, living from hand to mouth, having no other property than their labour, has generally, and perhaps necessarily, accompanied a great accumulation of capital in the hands of a small number of proprietors. In the seeming conflict of interests which has ensued, capital has gained little more than a Cadmean victory; and has been compelled, ultimately, to share its rent with the labourer, in his character of pauper. It will appear, hereafter, that in nearly every country of Europe, society advanced up to this point, during the sixteenth century; and that poor laws, of some sort or other, were then generally established. This connexion between the masses of capital acquired by the few, and the mass of pauperism of the many, led an eminent and facetious lord of our own day, to describe one of the great factories, to which England owes so large a part of her wealth and power, and some of her progress towards freedom, as being "a contrivance for manufacturing two articles—cotton and paupers." We shall see, hereafter, by what class of our society this pauper producing power is mainly exercised. It is to be feared, that in the fatal growth of the raw produce of pauperism, the industry of the English agriculturist, is unrivalled throughout the world; but, as to other countries, the law of pauperism is such as has been mentioned, whatever it may be with us. Argument on the subject is unnecessary, for the fact is unquestionable. Scotland, and France, may be referred to as neighbouring countries, each an example of this, which may be called the normal distribution of pauperism.

As to France, it is observed by De Villeneuve Bargemont, that the number of the indigent poor is always less in the country than in towns*; and the fact is notorious among all persons who have any knowledge of the statistics of indigence in that country. In Scotland, the proportion of paupers to population in the densely peopled manufacturing and commercial counties of Edinburgh and Lanark, is as 1 in $17\frac{5}{9}$, and as 1 in $19\frac{6}{10}$: in the fertile but less densely peopled region of agricultural industry, which contains the East Lothians, the proportion is only 1 in 27; and in the remote and very thinly peopled Orkney and Shetland Islands, the proportion becomes only 1 in 40.†

A similar distribution of pauperism is found in the Protestant countries of the Continent, where, at the time of the Reformation, a compulsory system of relief, like that of our statute of Elizabeth, has been adopted. Thus, in Switzerland, the pauperism is great in some of the principal towns. In the town of Berne, for instance, the number of persons relieved by public charity is 1 in 4 of the population; a proportion nearly as great as, if we made our calculations in the same way in which they have sometimes been made for other countries, would appear in London: while in the agricultural districts, and among the numerous small proprietors of many cantons, there is so little pauperism that the mean number of persons relieved, for the whole of the twenty-two cantons of Switzerland, including their towns, is only 1 in 18 on the population.‡

In order to form a correct notion of the comparative pau-

* Villeneuve Bargemont, *Économie Politique Chrétienne*, tom. iii. p. 41. "Le nombre des malades et des indigens est toujours moins élevé dans les campagnes que dans les villes."

† See Appendix.

‡ The number of persons relieved annually, is about 130,000: Franscini, *Nuova Statistica della Svizzera*, Lugano, 1847, tom. ii. p. 213.

perism of two countries, we should not only know how many persons in each of the two countries are relieved as paupers, within the same period, but also how much money each of them received. In the case of Switzerland, the annual amount levied yearly, for the relief of the poor, in seven of the principal Cantons, is 946,595 francs, or 37,863*l.*: the population of these seven cantons is 1,600,000 souls. The charge is little more than 6*d.* a head on the whole population; and, since the proportion of paupers is only as 1 in 18 on that population, the sum received by each pauper will amount only to 4*s.* 6*d.* yearly. In every respect, therefore, the pauperism of Switzerland invites a contrast with the corresponding pauperism of England. In the year ended 25th March, 1850*, the sum actually expended in relief of our poor gives 6*s.* 1*d.* as the sum per head on the population: upwards of 6*s.* per head, therefore, in England, corresponds to the 6*d.* per head paid by a free protestant country, which has adopted, like ourselves, the principle of regulating by law the distribution of public charity, and which, like ourselves, uses compulsory taxation to raise funds for the purpose. A Swiss writer has contrasted the condition of the two countries in respect of the amount which they thus raise by taxation for relief of the poor.†

Similarly, in Würtemberg, also a country of compulsory relief for the poor, there are towns in which a large proportion of the whole population receives more or less of public relief, while in some of the country districts the proportion of persons relieved, to the population, is only 1 in 53 or 54.‡

* See Appendix.

† Franscini, *Nuova Statistica della Svizzera*, tom i. p. 216. He points out that the Swiss tax is about 610 French francs, on every 1000 inhabitants, and is equivalent to a contribution of 2*s.* 6*d.* (3 francs) from each non-pauper family: his contrast with England, at once the classic land of great riches and of pauperism, "la terra classica delle grandi richezze e in una del pauperismo," is made by selecting our outlay in 1833, when gigantic abuses of admistration had so fearfully increased all the evils of our pauperism. But the contrast is sufficiently striking, if we look at our population, and annual poor relief, for any year since 1840.

‡ Schmidlin, *Allegemeiner Umriss des Würtembergischen Armenwesens*; and De Gérando, *Bienfaisance Publique*. tom. i. p. 121.

The increase in the value of the agricultural parts of England, during the last sixty or seventy years, it is difficult to estimate accurately, but it has certainly been very great. And of this increase a large part is due to causes wholly independent of the landowner, the more obvious of which are found in the unparalled extension of population and wealth, in the great localities of our manufactures, and in the constant demand created for agricultural produce to supply the wants of the increasing millions of home consumers. Such causes are also found in the construction of navigable canals, more than 2000 miles in length; in the rendering available of many navigable rivers; in the making of 20,000 miles of turnpike roads, all the work of little more than half a century: and last, not least, they have been found in the construction of a net-work of railways, nearly 7000 miles in length, and spreading over the whole country. The companies who have constructed these railways, have usually paid, in the first instance, a very large tribute, in the shape of "purchase money" and "compensation" to the landowners*: and moreover, the railway companies, in 1848-9, when 2669 miles only of railway had been opened, paid as much as 270,000*l.* a year towards the parochial rates of the different parishes through which their railways passed.

The railway itself, as soon as opened, tends both to diminish the cost of production, and to increase the price of agricultural produce; and the railway company, though its line of railway cannot add a pauper to the inhabitants of a parish, is so heavily taxed, by the mode of rating railways which the Court of

* "Purchase money" and "compensation" thus paid by the different railway companies in England during the last fifteen years, appear to have amounted in the whole to millions upon millions sterling; and it is in respect of the purchase of cultivable land, that a large part of this payment has been made. The Manchester and Leeds railway, fifty-six miles in length, now part of the Lancashire and Yorkshire railway, cost, in this respect alone, the enormous sum of 513,946*l.*, and this same short line has been required to pay on the average of several recent years, an annual contribution of 8018*l.* to the poor rates of the several parishes through which it passes. The correctness of the figures given respecting this line, is ensured by their resting on a return furnished to me by Mr. Lawn, the accountant of the Lancashire and Yorkshire Railway Company, in which the Manchester and Leeds Railway Company has been merged.

Queen's Bench has established, as sometimes to pay one-fifth, or even one-fourth, of all the poor rates of an entire parish.*

These and other sources of benefit enjoyed by the owners of agricultural land in England† are greater, perhaps, than their class has obtained, during the same period, in any other country. Even if English landowners had abstained, as completely as the gods of Epicurus, from taking any part in the industrial struggle of the busy world, below or around them, still they must, for more than half a century, have seen the value of their broad acres increasing. Certainly, if any one of them, lord or squire, had fallen asleep at the outbreak of the great French Revolution, and had slept on for fifty years, like Epimenides in ancient Greece, or Rip Van Winckle more recently on the Western side of the Atlantic, he would hardly, on awakening, have recognised the face of his old inheritance, so "crescent in its faculty."

Nec longum tempus, et ingens
Exiit ad cœlum ramis felicibus arbos,
Miraturque novas frondes, et non sua poma !

---

* The 270,000*l.* of my text is obtained from Mr. Watkins's Table found in the "Minutes of Evidence given before the Select Committee of the House of Lords on the Law relating to Parochial Assessments," 1850.

POOR AND OTHER LOCAL RATES PAID BY THE FOLLOWING COMPANIES.

Length open in 1849.	Name of Railway.	Amount paid for Rates.	
		1848.	1849.
		£	£
477	London and North Western - -	58,649	55,812
225	Great Western - - - - -	38,555	29,303
		B. & E.	8,100
216	London and South Western - -	19,491	19,351
162	London, Brighton, and South Coast	22,834	23,354
148	South Eastern - - - - -	24,367	30,518
247	Eastern Counties - - - -	24,754	25,635
465	Midland - - - - - -	33,125	32,118
198	Lancashire and Yorkshire - -	16,793	18,071
260	York and North Midland - -	13,960	15,855
268	York, Newcastle and Berwick - -	14,513	14,816
2,666	Total - - -	267,041	272,933

† See the enumeration in Lord Monteagle's lucid Report, prepared for the adoption of the Committee of the House of Lords on Burdens and Exemptions of Real Property ; Parliamentary Paper, 449, Commons, Sess. 1846.

The landowners of England have not, however, been careless lookers-on, but have taken a considerable part in the industrial progress of their country. English agriculture is now, in some respects, in advance of that of most, if not of all, the countries of the European Continent. The rental of whole counties has been greatly increased by the intelligent employment of capital and skill: not only has the rental of the old estate of the landowner been increased, but open and uncultivated commons and wastes have been largely enclosed, and throughout extensive tracts of almost every county in England, two blades of grass now grow, where only one was formerly found.

Between 1790 and 1820, through a considerable part of the country, the rent of land rose from 8*s.* per acre, to 16*s.* per acre. An intelligent writer on the subject, to whose report on the agriculture of Norfolk the prize was recently awarded by the Royal Society of Agriculture, teaches us that, in 1843, the rents of the county of Norfolk, were estimated "to be fully equal to those of the highest and palmiest days of agriculture;" and the same author states, that "nothing but a period of alarming distress, in the struggle through which numbers will be swept off, will cause any reduction." *

These various considerations prepare us to expect that the burden of pauperism will fall lightly, at the present day, on the English agriculturist. If, when the facts are ascertained, such expectation should prove wholly unfounded,—if it should appear, that the agriculturist is paying, in poor-rate, nearly twice as much, on his rental, as the more fortunate ratepayer of a manufacturing district,—we may feel assured that, but for the various causes which, during the last sixty years, have added so largely to the wealth of the landowners of England, the pauper would, by this time, have been receiving the lion's share in the rental of the whole region of English agriculture.

In order closely to examine, and correctly to appreciate this pauperism of the agricultural and manufacturing districts

* Richard Noverre Bacon, Report on the Agriculture of Norfolk, 8vo. London, 1844, pp. 40. 96, and 97.

of England, it will be most convenient to select a certain number of counties, as representatives of each interest.

As representing the agricultural interest, probably ten counties will be thought a sufficient number to collate with the three populous manufacturing and commercial counties of Lancaster, Stafford, and the West Riding of Yorkshire. These three counties will manifestly give very distinct evidence of all such evil influences, connected with pauperism, as are necessarily exercised by commercial and manufacturing industry and enterprise, and the presence of a dense population. The only difficulty is in making a fair and unobjectionable choice of the agricultural counties. That we may obtain a district wholly free from natural causes of pauperism, we should select only counties in which the population, per acre, does not exceed the average of England, and in which the rental of real property gives at least an equal sum, per head, for the population, with that given by the average of the whole country. The accurate and instructive statistical tables of the Registrar-General's reports, should also be consulted, and any such unhealthy region as, by its very nature, may tend to aggravate the evils of the working man's condition, and to convert the labourer into a pauper, should be excluded from our list.

Moreover, we ought to choose counties in which what is generally considered as the best and most economical system of agriculture prevails; which seems to be the case where, property in land being but little divided, either in ownership or occupation, the landlord obtains a greater amount of rent, than he would be likely to get from a more numerous tenantry, employing the same amount only of tenants' capital as that now used. That our selected counties may therefore admittedly represent the most truly English condition and character of agricultural life, they must, taken as a whole, consist of large properties and extensive farms, constituting a noble domain, of what French writers usually call "la grande propriété" and "la grande culture." It would be improper to select any one of the few counties in which owners and occupiers of land are decidedly more numerous than they usually are in the counties of England.

All such conditions will be fully satisfied by our selecting the agricultural counties of Bedford, Berks, Bucks, Dorset, Essex, Norfolk, Oxford, Suffolk, Sussex, and Wilts:

Counties.	Area in English Statute Acres.	Population Census of 1851.	Annual Value of Property as assessed to the Poor Rate in 1847.	Annual Income from Real Estate, as valued in 1847, per Head, on Population in 1851.
			£	£ s. d.
Bedford -	297,632	129,789	433,347	3 6 11¼
Berks - -	473,920	199,154	768,050	3 16 11
Bucks - -	463,880	143,670	706,265	4 18 3¾
Dorset - -	627,220	177,597	799,342	4 10 0
Essex - -	979,000	343,916	1,655,540	4 16 3¼
Norfolk -	1,292,300	433,803	1,914,282	4 8 3
Oxford - -	467,230	170,286	718,465	4 4 4¼
Suffolk - -	918,760	335,991	1,407,413	4 6 9¼
Sussex - -	907,920	339,428	1,348,701	3 19 2
Wilts - -	868,060	241,003	1,243,902	5 3 2¾
Total -	7,295,922	2,514,637	10,995,307	" " "
Average -	729,592	251,463	1,099,530	4 7 5¼
Lancaster -	1,117,260	2,063,913	6,463,363	3 2 7½
Stafford -	736,290	630,506	1,971,266	3 2 6¼
W. R. York -	1,622,840	1,339,962	3,576,281	2 13 2¼
Total -	3,476,390	4,034,381	12,010,910	" " "
Average -	1,158,796	1,344,793	4,003,636	2 19 6½
Total: England and Wales -	36,522,615	17,922,768	67,320,587	3 15 1¼

In these ten counties, the occupiers employing labourers, the labourers so employed, and the occupiers not employing labourers, are as follows.*

Occupiers employing Labourers.	Occupiers not employing Labourers.	Labourers employed in Agriculture.
30,553	10,106	232,759

Grand total of agriculturists - - 273,418

* These numbers are obtained from the Occupation Abstract of the Census of 1831. In the Census of 1841, agricultural labourers are confounded with domestic servants.

For all England the corresponding numbers and proportions are:

Occupiers employing Labourers.	Occupiers not employing Labourers.	Labourers employed in Agriculture.
141,460	94,883	744,407

Grand total of agriculturists - - 980,750

The proportion between occupiers employing labourers, and their labourers, which is nearly 1 in 8 for the ten counties, is little more than 1 in 5 for the whole country. This alone would show how much larger is the average size of farms in the ten counties, than throughout the country at large. But we find, likewise, that the proportion to the whole labouring population of men occupying small holdings, and so "not employing labourers," which, in the country at large, is 1 in 8, is here only 1 in 23. The mere labourers are about three times as numerous here as they are elsewhere, if their number be estimated with reference to the occupiers of land who do not employ labourers. It is to be observed, that the mere labourers employed in agriculture, in these ten counties, amount to nearly one-third of those similarly employed in all England and Wales; for their number here is 232,759, while those of the whole country are only 744,407; but, at the same time, the ten counties, containing about one-fifth of the cultivated land of England and Wales, have a total agricultural population of 273,218, which very slightly exceeds the general average; for the agricultural population of the whole country is 980,750. It is only on subdividing the whole agricultural population, for the country at large, and for these ten counties, into its constituent parts, of occupiers and labourers, that we find in the ten counties this large excess of mere labourers. Such results, perhaps, necessarily follow from the great size of estates and farms in the ten counties in question.

The whole population of agriculturists in these ten counties, 273,218 persons, gives less than twenty-four persons who find employment on each square mile of land. The proportion of inhabitants, who live on and by the soil, in countries of more divided property, throughout Europe, seems generally to be much greater. In different parts of the valley of Nievole, in Tuscany, the number of persons supporting themselves as agriculturists, per square mile, varies from 300 to 700.*

It is not essential to this inquiry to determine exactly the number of landowners in these ten counties. Various considerations, beginning with Domesday Book, and ending with parliamentary returns of yesterday, all tend to show that the landlords of the 141,460 occupiers, who cultivate at least nine-tenths of the cultivated land of England and Wales, are more numerous than has sometimes been stated by foreign writers, though less so than has been assumed in England. It is a singular fact that, in the middle of the nineteenth century, there should be more difficulty in coming to a conclusion, as to the number of English landowners, than there is in determining their number in the reign of William the Conqueror. Professor Schlosser, in his "History of the Eighteenth Century," estimates their entire body at 7000. M. Moreau de Jonnès, and other French writers, have gone, perhaps, to somewhat of an opposite extreme, in raising their number up to 50,000. I have no doubt that the truth lies between these limits. Probably, even the 141,460 occupiers, who cultivate nine-tenths of all the cultivated land of England and Wales, pay rent to a considerably greater number of landlords, than Professor Schlosser gives for the whole country.

Whatever the exact number of such landowners may be, either in the whole of England or in our selected counties, it is quite apparent that those counties furnish a most ample and unobjectionable example of that system of occupation of land, which its advocates describe as, for various reasons, the best; "which," according to Mr. M'Culloch, "gives the greatest scope to improvement; which allows of the division of labour being carried to the farthest extent; and which puts it into the power of the occupier, to avail himself of every new improvement and increased facility of production:"†

* Sismondi, *Études sur l'Économie Politique*, tom. i. p. 144., in the essay, "De la Condition du Cultivateur de Race Gaelique, en Écosse, et de leur Expulsion."

† M'Culloch, *A Descriptive and Statistical Account of the British Empire*, vol. i. p. 454.

by means of which "population is increased, proportionably to the increased produce of the land, at the same time that labour is properly distributed, that indolence and apathy are banished, and that a provision is made for a successful prosecution of all those arts, that improve and embellish society."*

In all other respects the condition of these ten chosen counties seems likely to ensure their freedom from any pauperism exceeding that of the rest of the country.

It will appear, by consulting the Registrar-General's tables†, that the average mortality which, in London, is 1 in 40, and in some of the manufacturing towns is much higher, is for all England 1 in 45. In the ten selected agricultural counties, the general health and longevity is decidedly above the average of all England.‡ If, in estimating the burden of pauperism, we consider the proportion which the charge for poor-rate, or, more correctly, *for relief of the poor*, bears to the *rent* of the occupier,—in other words, the amount of rate in the pound on the net value of the property assessed,—it is manifest that those counties ought to have the lightest burden of pauperism where the real property is in excess in proportion to the population.§ Now the net rental of England and Wales, as assessed to the poor-rate in 1847, was 67,320,587*l.*, which, on the population of 1851, gives just 3*l.* 15*s.* 1¼*d.* per head, as we see by the foregoing table. The corresponding apportionment, given by the above ten counties, is 4*l.* 7*s.* 5¼*d.* per head, on the population, a sum which greatly exceeds the average of the whole country. The three manufacturing counties give only 2*l.* 19*s.* 6½*d.* per head on their population, and are therefore below the general average.

These ten agricultural counties furnish nearly three acres of land for each individual of their population; the three

* M'Culloch, *A Descriptive and Statistical Account of the British Empire*, vol. i. p. 456.

† See the Registrar-General's Ninth Annual Report, p. 183.

‡ Appendix.

§ In the second chapter, this has been seen to be the case in the wealthy parishes of the metropolis, as in the parish of St. George, Hanover Square, where the relief of the poor costs only about 6*d.* in the pound on the net rental.

manufacturing counties less than one acre of land of an inferior quality*: the specific density of population is, in truth, nearly four times as great in these three manufacturing counties as it is in the ten agricultural. The annual value of the whole property assessed to poor-rate is greater in the three counties than in the ten; but this excess, 1,015,603*l.*, amounts to only 5*s.* per head, on the manufacturing population of 4,034,381.

If it should appear that pauperism prevails extensively in counties endowed with so many advantages, we may feel satisfied that such pauperism must mainly be the work of man alone; and that, as legislation has produced, so it may remove, the evil. At present, however, it is enough for us to ascertain what is the condition, in respect of pauperism, of these agricultural counties: the consideration of the remedy must be postponed till we shall have observed the symptoms, traced the history, and understood the nature and extent of the disease.

Before we endeavour to ascertain how the burden of relieving pauperism is distributed throughout these counties, let us see what are their sources of relief for the poor, independently of the poor-rate.

The apportionment of the charitable endowments, reported on by the Commissioners of Inquiry into Public Charities, is found to be as follows:

	£	s.	d.
Bedford - - - -	13,720	15	6
Berks - - - -	21,392	5	5
Bucks - - - -	11,397	5	9
Dorset - - - -	9,356	14	6
Essex - - - -	21,572	7	8
Norfolk - - - -	37,243	9	11
Oxford - - - -	13,945	12	1
Suffolk - - - -	28,948	13	5
Sussex - - - -	10,178	0	0
Wilts - - - -	16,662	17	3
Total - -	£184,418	1	8

* Appendix.

	£	s.	d.
Lancaster - - - -	35,322	9	1
Stafford - - - -	20,392	19	10
W. R. York - - -	52,775	18	4
Total - -	£108,491	7	3
Total of England and Wales	£1,209,395	12	8*

Of these foundations, a certain proportion has been created, with the intention of promoting education. The wise benevolence of our forefathers, thought, the education of the young just as necessary a work of Christian duty, as the support of the old. The parish officers are very frequently trustees of the educational as well as of the pauper fund thus created; and the children of the poor are usually the peculiar objects of the founder's intended bounty. A general statutory measure for regulating the application of these educational funds is greatly needed. The necessity of such a measure had become manifest at least twenty years ago. The Commissioners for inquiring into the operation of the Poor Laws declared, in 1834, that many of the funds thus destined to the purposes of education, were applied in a manner unsuited to the present wants of society; and, from that day to the present, no attempt whatever has been made, to prevent such misapplication, or in any way to improve the administration of any part of these ample funds. The country is now reaping the fruits of this neglect. It is found that "in the midland and southern parts of England, and in the rural districts more particularly, where such endowments exist, they have become, in nine cases out of ten, a positive hindrance, rather than a benefit, to the object they were intended to promote."†

No single work brings into one view, for these various counties, as Mr. Low's work has done for the metropolis, the amount of the annual voluntary contribution to such

* See the Summary appended to the "Analytical Digest of the Reports made by the Commissioners of Inquiry into Charities," part ii. p. 828. (presented to Parliament, and published in 1842).

† The Dean of Hereford, (the late Vicar of King's Somborne), *Suggestive Hints towards Improved Secular Education*, Introduction, p. 23.

public charities, as are mainly appropriated to the use of the poor.

I know of no statistics on which, either the sums annually disbursed, in these counties, by organised public charity, or the number of persons among whom the disbursement is made, can be exactly determined. Into this *terra incognita* I shall, therefore, not attempt to enter. It matters little, for the inquiry into which it is proposed now to enter, what the exact amount of their charities, in each county, may be. Undoubtedly it is great as a whole; and, in many large places the number of persons, so relieved, considerably exceeds the number relieved, both in workhouses, and as out-door paupers, during the same period.

A single table of such charities, in one manufacturing town, I can present to my reader. It contains the public charities, in Birmingham, by which relief is afforded to the indigent.

Name of Hospital, &c.	Income from Voluntray Contributions in 1850.			Income from Property in 1850.			Number of Persons relieved.
	£	s.	d.	£	s.	d.	
General Hospital - -	2,297	0	0	796	0	0	23,745
Eye Infirmary - ..	182	2	3	33	18	0	3,354
Ear Infirmary - -	28	13	0	4	9	6	287
Lying-in-Hospital - -	748	9	7	Nil.			1,769
Queen's Hospital - -	2,485	14	0	Nil.			5,490
Blind School - -	599	11	6	Nil.			14 males
Invested for Building -	1,234	17	10	Nil.			13 females
Bodily Deformity Institution	58	16	0	Nil.			100
Totals - -	7,635	4	2	834	7	6	34,772

By comparison of this table with subjoined details *, it will be seen, that the sum expended in Birmingham, by public charities, is less than the corresponding amount of relief under the Poor Law; and that the number of persons, obtaining relief and assistance from the public charities, is greater than the number relieved under the Poor Law; just as is the case in the metropolis itself.†

* See Appendix. I am indebted to Mr. Corder, the clerk to the guardians of the Birmingham Union, for these details respecting the public charities of Birmingham.

† Above, p. 34.

It remains for us to ascertain and compare the burden of pauperism, as relieved under the Poor Law, throughout these agricultural and manufacturing districts respectively.

What then, in the first place, does the year's expenditure in relief of the poor amount to as a poundage on the rateable value of real property assessed to poor-rate in these counties? In the year 1847 it was as follows:

	s.	*d.*
Bedford - - - -	2	0½
Berks - - - -	2	2¾
Bucks - - - -	2	4¼
Dorset - - - -	2	2¾
Essex - - - -	2	1¾
Norfolk - - - -	2	2
Oxford - - - -	2	5
Suffolk - - - -	2	2
Sussex - - - -	2	1¾
Wilts - - - -	2	3¼
Average - -	2	2½

A much lighter burden falls on the manufacturing district:

	s.	*d.*
Lancaster - - - -	1	0¾
Stafford - - - -	1	1
West Riding of Yorkshire - -	1	5½
Average - -	1	2⅜

For all England and Wales, the sum expended in relief of the poor was, on the average, a pound-rate of 1*s.* 7*d.* on the net rateable value of the property assessed. It appears, therefore, that, in respect of this pound-rate, the agricultural district is greatly above, and the manufacturing far below, the general average.

The burden of pauperism, as pressing on ratepayers, or their landlords, is therefore demonstrated to be, in one important point of view, far heavier in the agricultural, than in the manufacturing, district.

Another contrast, equally unfavourable to the agricultural counties, is obtained by placing them in juxtaposition with the whole of London itself. The average expenditure for relief of the poor throughout the metropolitan district, for the year ended 25th March, 1847, was 1*s.* 5¼*d.* in the pound, which stands contrasted with the 2*s.* 2½*d.* of the foregoing table. If another year be taken, and a like comparison be made of the proportionate outlay, per head, of population in each district, a result equally unfavourable to the agricultural interest will be obtained. By using the Census of 1851, and the Third Annual Report of the Poor Law Board, the most recent information will be put together. The following is the result:—The metropolitan district contains 115½ square miles, and a population of 20,447 on the square mile. These agricultural counties contain 11,399 square miles, and a population of only 220 on the square mile.

Name of District.	Population in 1851.	Expended for Relief of the Poor in the Year ended at Lady-day, 1850.	Proportion per Head on Population.
		£ *s.* *d.*	*s.* *d.*
London* -	2,362,236	741,722 0 0	6 3¾
The ten agricultural counties - -	2,514,637	1,137,250 1 0†	9 0½

If, instead of taking the whole of these ten agricultural counties, we should select single unions, in the purer regions of agriculture in each of the same counties, and thus see what is, in each of such unions, the extent of pauperism, we should find it greatly, indeed, to exceed the average amount throughout England. And this would appear to be so, even in the

* Above, p. 35.

† The details are as follows:

	£	*s.*	*d.*		£	*s.*	*d.*
Bedford - -	43,382	4	0	Norfolk - -	190,942	4	0
Berks - -	77,423	9	0	Oxford - -	78,947	8	0
Bucks - -	77,458	18	0	Suffolk - -	135,295	10	0
Dorset - -	83,818	6	0	Sussex - -	149,617	7	0
Essex - -	167,597	11	0	Wilts - -	132,767	4	0

case of extensive unions, in which the population is thinly spread, and the average acreage per inhabitant is greatly above the like average of the whole of England and Wales. This fact is, perhaps, more decidedly conclusive than any other, standing alone, to show that there must be some strange vice in the laws which can bring about so unnatural a result.

With such a region of selected unions of the purest agriculture, it is proposed now to compare an industrial and populous quarter of the metropolis, the "Eastern District" of the Registrar-General: comprising Shoreditch, Bethnal Green, Whitechapel, St. George in the East, Stepney, and Poplar. A subjoined table will supply all statistical details needed for such a comparison.*

The following are some of the more striking results of the table. In the country district, the population gives only one family of four persons for 15½ acres of land; the town district affords, for such a family, less than the twentieth part of a single acre; in other words, the density of the population in the one district is more than three hundred times as great as it is in the other. The whole net rental of the country district is upwards of 2,000,000*l.*; that of the town, little more than 1,000,000*l.*; and these respective amounts of net rental give 4*l.* 10*s.* 0½*d.* per head on the whole population for the country district; a corresponding sum of only 2*l.* 4*s.* 0½*d.* for the London. Yet the pauperism of the working classes is so much more severe in the country than in the London district, that each of the 447,823 inhabitants of the fertile region of agriculture would receive from poor-rate, if it were divided equally among them all, a sum of more than 10*s.* yearly, almost double the 5*s.* 1*d.* each, which would be the corresponding sum for each inhabitant of the town district. Even the landlord suffers, to this extent, in the country district: his double amount of net rental (two millions yearly, as contrasted with the single million of the London district) has to pay almost as high a pound-rate for relief of the poor as is re-

* Appendix.

quired in the London district; the country paying 2*s.* 2½*d.* in the pound, and London 2*s.* 2¾*d.**

The conclusion seems irresistible, that the burden of pauperism, looked upon as a charge on property throughout these regions, so differently circumstanced, is equal in amount; and that, so far as the poor are concerned, the pauperism which is diffused, with its sufferings and its crimes, throughout the pure region of agriculture, is, in its intensity, just twice as great as prevails in a metropolitan district exposed to the operation of many pauperising influences, from which the country is comparatively exempt.

Perhaps enough has been already said on the inequality in the existing apportionment of the burdens of ratepayers: let us, therefore, now turn to contemplate the wretched paupers themselves, and see what is their distribution over the face of the land.

Counties.	Population of the *Unions* in 1841.	Number of Paupers relieved in *Unions* during the Quarter ending Lady-day, 1841.	Proportion of Paupers relieved in the single Quarter of a Year to the whole of the Inhabitants.
Bedford - - -	112,379	11,279	1 in $9\frac{3}{4}$
Berks - - -	190,367	18,472	1 in $10\frac{2}{7}$
Buckingham - -	140,352	18,624	1 in $7\frac{1}{2}$
Dorset - - -	167,874	21,549	1 in $7\frac{4}{5}$
Essex - - -	320,818	41,807	1 in $7\frac{2}{3}$
Norfolk - - -	343,277	33,034	1 in $10\frac{2}{5}$
Oxford - - -	141,330	16,360	1 in $8\frac{5}{8}$
Suffolk - - -	302,178	33,789	1 in $8\frac{15}{16}$
Sussex - - -	223,435	29,257	1 in $7\frac{19}{30}$
Wilts - - -	233,246	30,003	1 in $7\frac{4}{5}$
Totals - - -	2,175,256	254,174	1 in $8\frac{1}{2}$

The average proportion of the paupers relieved during the

* It may be observed, that, wherever the amount expended, in relieving the poor of a thinly peopled district, measured by its proportion to the net rental of the property assessed, equals the corresponding amount similarly expended in a more populous place, we may be sure, not that the owner is suffering, in either instance, for the burden may still be light on him, but that the working classes in the district where there is a comparative surplus of property, and a deficiency of population, are, and of necessity must be, in a state of a greater destitution than exists, at the same time, in the other district.

first *quarter* only of the year 1841, to the whole of the inhabitants of the Poor Law Unions in these agricultural counties, is 1 in $8\frac{1}{2}$.

The estimated total of paupers relieved in England and Wales during the same quarter is 1,299,048, which, among 15,906,829 inhabitants, gives 1 in $12\frac{1}{4}$ as the average of the whole country.

The corresponding destitution in the Poor Law Unions of the three principal manufacturing counties during the same period was widely different, having been as much below the general average of the country, as that of the agricultural counties was above that average.

Counties.	Population of the *Unions* in 1841.	Number of Paupers relieved in *Unions* during the Quarter ending Lady-day, 1841.	Proportion of Paupers relieved in the Quarter, to the whole of the Inhabitants.
Lancaster - -	994,474	67,078	1 in $14\frac{5}{6}$
Stafford - - -	442,348	19,995	1 in $22\frac{1}{4}$
West Riding, York -	790,751	54,216	1 in $12\frac{3}{4}$
Total - -	2,227,573	141,289	1 in 16

Mr. Fletcher has given a table of the pauperism of England and Wales, as indicated by the proportion to the whole population of the persons relieved in the quarter ended Lady-day, 1844.* It may be observed, that a comparison of the like proportion between the persons relieved and the whole population, if made for any year, or quarter of a year, between 1837 and 1851, would lead to a like result. The following is extracted from Mr. Fletcher's table: —

Name of County.	Proportion per Cent. above or below the Average of England and Wales.
Bedford - - - -	+26·9
Berks - - - - -	+19·0
Bucks - - - - -	+49·7
Dorset - - - - -	+43·0
Essex - - - - -	+50·0
Norfolk - - - - -	+29·6

* Moral and Educational Statistics, Plate XI. and corresponding letter-press.

Name of County.	Proportion per Cent. above or below the Average of England and Wales.
Oxford - - - - -	+46·9
Suffolk - - - - -	+36·2
Sussex - - - - -	+43·0
Wilts - - - - -	+67·7
Lancaster - - - -	−14·5
Stafford - - - -	−25·8
West Riding, York - - -	−19·6

The one set of counties is 40 per cent. above the average of the whole country; the other, 20 per cent. below it.

The number of paupers actually receiving relief in these agricultural counties on the 1st January, 1851, (excluding vagrants,) was 178,864; the number receiving relief in Lancashire, Staffordshire, and the West Riding of Yorkshire, on the same day, being only 130,391. The population of the ten agricultural counties, therefore, though much smaller than that of the three manufacturing counties, contains a far greater absolute number of paupers.

The apportionment of the paupers, in the agricultural counties, is as follows:

Counties.	Population in 1851.	Paupers relieved on 1st Jan. 1851 (Vagrants excluded).		
		In-door.	Out-door.	Total.
Bedford - - -	129,789	1,024	6,452	7,476
Berks - - -	199,154	2,359	10,828	13,187
Bucks - - -	143,670	1,372	10,394	11,766
Dorset - - -	177,597	1,629	13,826	15,455
Essex - - -	343,916	4,422	22,270	26,692
Norfolk - - -	433,803	3,393	23,181	26,574
Oxford - - -	170,286	1,485	10,335	11,820
Suffolk - - -	335,991	4,039	22,120	26,159
Sussex - - -	339,428	3,057	14,989	18,046
Wilts - - -	241,003	2,794	18,895	21,689
Total - - -	2,514,637	25,574	153,290	178,864

In the year which ended 25th March, 1850, the expenditure for the relief of the poor in these ten agricultural counties was 1,137,250*l.*, or 9*s.* 0½*d.* per head on the population of 2,514,637 (census of 1851); that of the metropolitan district for the same period 741,722*l.*, or only 6*s.* 3¾*d.* per head on its population of 2,362,236.

Although the ten counties above taken are unexceptionable samples of the interest which they represent, I will nevertheless compare, in respect of pauperism, two other purely agricultural counties, Cambridge and Huntingdon, with three great commercial and manufacturing towns, Liverpool, Birmingham, and Stockport. It will be seen, by inspecting a subjoined table*, that the sums expended are nearly equal, being 110,942*l.* for the two agricultural counties, and 109,721*l.* for the three towns: but the difference in intensity of the pauperism in the districts compared, is evidenced by the result, that the sum, per head, on the population, expended in them respectively, is 9*s.* 2½*d.* throughout Cambridgeshire and Huntingdonshire, while the corresponding sum in the towns, is only 5*s.* 1*d.* per head.

Not only, therefore, is the burden of pauperism sustained by agriculture greater than that of the three manufacturing counties, but it is found to be equally in excess, whether we compare it with the pauperism of the metropolitan district, or with that of the most densely peopled of our large commercial and manufacturing towns.

Other terms of comparison may be suggested, which will make the condition of the English agriculturist, whether payer or receiver of the poor-rate, still more odious than it already appears. In the following table the sum "expended" is, in Scotland, not wholly applied in relief, but includes "management, law expenses, poor-house buildings, and general sanitary measures," for all Scotland. The sum "expended" for the ten English counties, is expended in relief and maintenance of the poor.

* See Appendix.

District.	Expended.	Proportion per Head on the Population of 1851.	Proportion per cent. on Real Property according to the Returns of 1847.
Scotland - - -	£ s. d. 581,553 4 3½	s. d. 4 0½	£ s. d. 6 4 9½
The Ten English Counties* - -	1,137,250 0 0	9 0½	11 0 10

So that all Scotland, with a rental † nearly equal to that of these ten English counties ‡, pays, as the whole outlay of her Poor Law administration, little more than half the sum which the ten English counties pay for relief and maintenance of the poor alone.

The contrast with miserable Ireland, even while she is still suffering from the consequences of the famine and fever which so lately decimated her population, is still more remarkable. The annual value of property rated to the poor-rate in Ireland is 13,187,421*l.*§; and the expenditure, under the Poor Law of Ireland, in the year ended 29th September, 1850, was as follows: —

In-Maintenance.	Out-Maintenance.	Salaries and Rations of Officers.	Total.
£ 710,945	£ 120,789	£ 447,318	£ 1,403,108

The Poor Law Commissioners for Ireland published, in their Fourth Annual Report, a statement of the corresponding expenses incurred in the first half of the year 1851; and a Parliamentary Paper, published since most of these pages were written, gives an account of the third quarter's expenditure of the same year in Ireland. It appears from these data that, during the whole year, which has now ended, on 29th September, 1851, the sum expended in Ireland in relieving

* See above, p. 74.

† Of 9,320,784*l.* See Parl. Paper, 87. ii. Commons Sess. 1849.

‡ 10,995,307*l.*, above, p. 66.

§ It is now stated, for 1851, at 11,923,459*l.* Parl. Paper, 641. Sess. 1851.

the poor will have been about 1,102,359*l.* The pauperism of all Ireland, therefore, with her 6,515,794 inhabitants, costs less in 1851 than the pauperism of these ten agricultural English counties with only 2,514,637 inhabitants.*

And what is the proportion, in our English agricultural counties, as compared with either Scotland or Ireland, of those who are compelled to have recourse to parochial relief? Here the pauperism, as measured by the number of persons relieved on a single day, is exactly defined by Poor Law Returns. The Reports of the "Poor Law Board" in England, the "Poor Law Commissioners" in Ireland, and the "Board of Supervision for the Relief of the Poor" in Scotland, give us the means of an accurate comparison.

This favoured agricultural district of England, containing a population smaller than that of Scotland†, gives 178,864 persons, as its paupers relieved on the 1st January, 1851, or nearly 1 in 14 of its population. The day's pauperism of Scotland, as returned for the 14th May, 1851, consisted of 83,292 persons only, or 1 in 34·46 of its population.

If the number of Irish paupers in Ireland be compared

* Parliamentary Paper 641, Session 1851. The following is the summary of its contents:

Quarter ended.	Expenses incurred.				Poor-Rate lodged.
	For In-Maintenance.	For Out-Relief.	Other Expenses.	Total Expenses incurred.	
	£	£	£	£	£
28th Dec. 1850	118,479	915	127,877	247,271	353,775
29th March, 1851	160,401	2,462	141,719	304,582	263,073
28th June, 1851	165,608	4,705	132,912	303,225	223,538
Total, 9 months	444,488	8,082	402,508	855,078	840,386

If we assume the quarter ending on 29th Sept. 1851, to be as expensive as that which ended on 28th Dec. 1850, we must add to the 9 months' total - - - - - } £247,271

Total of the year - - - - - £1,102,349

† The population of the ten counties is 2,514,637; that of Scotland, in 1851, is 2,870,784.

with that of the paupers of agriculture in England, the result is equally unfavourable to us. All Ireland, on the 1st February, 1851, when not yet recovered from the desolation of her famine, was relieving only 250,000 paupers, or little more than 1 in 30 of her inhabitants. At the same time, Bedford, Bucks, and these other eight agricultural counties in England, were relieving, as paupers, nearly 1 in 14 of their inhabitants. For every Irishman, therefore, who, in famished and depopulated Ireland, is reduced to the dire necessity of applying to the union, there are two Englishmen under a corresponding necessity in most of these ten selected counties, the choicest region of our aristocracy and agriculture. Alas, that the truthful and honest and industrious Anglo-Saxon race should be degraded below the level of the Celt!

The foregoing considerations are, perhaps, sufficient to satisfy most men that the evils of our poor laws press much more heavily on the agricultural interest of England than they do on the manufacturing or the commercial. At all events now, as prior to the inquiry of 1833, it is in agricultural regions that the evils of pauperism, whether produced by our poor laws or not, are much more heavily felt than elsewhere.

To complete the picture of pauperism, in town and country, some additional touches are needed. Offences against property, constitute, with the fearful list of offences against the game laws, the greater part of all offences committed against the criminal law, by Englishmen. The proportion of commitments for such offences, in these agricultural counties, is greatly indeed above the average of the whole country.* It appears that the greater proportion of such criminals is amid the greater mass of pauperism.

The relative proportion of criminals, as ascertained by official returns, in respect of the total number of commitments

* See Mr. Fletcher's Tables, as appended to his General Report, published in the Minutes of the Committee of Council on Education, 1848-49-50, vol. ii. pp. 255—340.; and also in the Moral and Educational Statistics of England and Wales, by the same writer.

of males, to quarter sessions and assizes, on the average of the years 1845-6-7, is as follows*:

Agricultural Counties.	Proportion per cent. above and below the average of England and Wales, in the period 1845-6-7.
Bedford	+ 15·1
Berks	+ 14·8
Bucks	+ 44·2
Dorset	+ 2·7
Essex	+ 16·9
Norfolk	+ 19·2
Oxford	+ 16·0
Suffolk	+ 2·0
Sussex	+ 2·8
Wilts	+ 16·2
Manufacturing Counties.	
Lancaster	— 1·4
Stafford	— 6·9
York	— 39·9

Why is it that the crime of these agricultural counties should thus, in each of them, exceed that of the average of all England? Surely because, in each of them, the labouring man is degraded and pauperised far below the average of his condition throughout the country at large.

> Meagre were his looks,
> Sharp misery had worn him to the bones;
> Noting this penury, to myself I said—
> An if a man did need a poison now,
> Whose sale is present death in Mantua,
> Here lives a caitiff wretch would sell it him!

How contrary is it to the experience of other civilised countries, to find an excess of crime, not where men most do congregate, but under the open vault of heaven, in the wide and fertile fields of agriculture!

* These per centages are from Mr. Fletcher's *Moral and Educational Statistics.*

There is usually some difficulty in instituting an accurate comparison between the crime committed in one country, and that committed in another: the difference in the classification of offences, and in the modes of procedure adopted by different countries, often renders such a comparison almost impracticable, and the attempt to make it of little use. But there is, or ought to be, no difficulty in ascertaining accurately how the criminality of different portions of the same empire is distributed. It will, it is believed, be found that generally, in every country, the greater proportion of crime, at all events of offences against property, occurs in great cities. It is, for the most part, within their gates that "Malesuada Fames ac turpis Egestas" are found.

A satisfactory comparison of the amount of crime in different populations, according as the town or country element of society prevails in them, will be furnished by ascertaining the proportion of crime to population in each of several provinces of the Austrian empire. Official statistical tables enable us easily to see what is this proportion. We must be content with the German class of offences called *Verbrechen*, instead of our own middle-age description of *felony*. By ascertaining the proportion of this great class of crimes called *Verbrechen*, as committed in different provinces of Austria, we shall see where most crime is found, just as satisfactorily as, by a table of all commitments for *felony* or *misdemeanor*, to quarter sessions and assizes, we do so, for the same period, in respect of different parts of England. I set down provinces in the order of their criminality. The table is founded on the average number of offences committed during the three years 1845, 1846, and 1847, and the proportion is that ascertained by reference to the census of 1846.

	Proportion.
Lower Austria - - -	1 in 468
Upper Austria - - -	1 „ 792
Bohemia - - - -	1 „ 814
Moravia and Silesia - - -	1 „ 925
Tirol - - - - -	1 „ 939
Kuestenland - - - -	1 „ 1553

With slight exception, increase in proportion of crime seems simply to follow the increase in the town element of the population. The great preponderance of Lower Austria, and the capital which it contains, over every other part of the empire, draws a remark from the editor of the official tables, on which the above statement is founded. After observing that Lower Austria, with the capital, far exceeds every other province in its proportion of 1 accused person out of 468 inhabitants, he says, truly enough, that the phenomenon ought not to seem strange, for great cities are always the centre of "poverty and criminals," as well as of intelligence and persons in easy circumstances; and that this must especially be so in a place such as Vienna has of late become, and containing, as that city now does, a considerable manufacturing population, "depending on the accidents of commerce."* How unnatural a condition of society, then, is ours here in England, where a greater proportion of criminals is found in agricultural districts than in our most densely peopled commercial and manufacturing counties.

The experience of many years has shown that a large part of the crime which leads to trial at quarter sessions and assizes, is committed from the pressure of poverty alone. An increase in the physical well-being of the people is ever accompanied by a diminution of crime. Wages remaining the same, a diminution in the price of bread is a sure forerunner of a diminution in the number of criminal offences. This result has been manifest enough, in many counties, since the repeal of the corn laws. If, therefore, we compare different *agricultural* counties with one another, we may expect to find that the counties of the greatest amount of pauperism will be those of the greatest amount of crime. "My poverty, but not my will, consents," may, unhappily, be the plea of

* Kurze Statistische Darstellung der bisherigen Civil- und Criminal-Gerichtspflege in den Œsterreichischen Staaten (ohne Siebenbürgen, Ungarn und der Militär-gränze), ihrer Kosten, und des für die Umgestaltung beiläufig erforderlichen Aufwandes. Im Auftrage des Justizministers. Wien, 1848, aus der Kaiserlich-königlichen Hof- und Staats- druckerei.

many of the poverty-struck depredators on property, who are yearly imprisoned in gaols.

A few agricultural counties may be found in which the proportion of paupers to population is a little below the general average of the whole country. Among such counties are, Northumberland, Cumberland, and Westmoreland. The pauperism from which the great agricultural county of Lincoln suffers, if estimated with reference to its population, but little exceeds the general average.

Now the sum expended in relief of the poor throughout England and Wales, for the year which ended on 25th March, 1847, amounted to a contribution of 6*s.* 1½*d.* per head on the whole population. The amount for each of the ten agricultural counties was about 9*s.* 6*d.** The corresponding amount for the counties now selected, is as follows:

	s.	*d.*
Northumberland - - - -	5	7½
Westmoreland - - - -	5	4¾
Cumberland - - - -	4	3
Lincoln - - - - -	6	7¾

It may be added that these four counties constitute a district which, taken as a whole, is certainly much more divided, both in property and occupation, than our selected ten counties†; and that, in this smaller region, the landowners act with singular mildness in protecting their game. The criminal tables of the Home Office, and the census of 1851, give us the means of comparing the four counties with the ten in their most recent production of criminals. The details of the comparison will be best seen in a tabular form‡: the result is, that the average number of prisoners committed for trial, or bailed, in the ten agricultural counties, of the

* Parl. Pap. 735. Commons, Session of 1848.

† See the Statistical Investigations of Mr. Fletcher's *Moral and Educational Statistics of England*, and Mr. Barton's *Essay on the Influence of Subdivision of the Soil on the Moral and Physical Well-being of the People*, found in the "Journal of the Statistical Society," vol. xiii. p. 63.

‡ See Appendix.

greatest masses of wealth and the greatest pauperism, is 8½ on each 1000 of the population; while, in the four counties contrasted with them, the corresponding number of commitments, during the same period, is only 4½ in the 1000. The corresponding number of persons committed, or bailed, in England and Wales, is 7½ in the 1000 on the population. Again, therefore, this select region of agriculture sinks below the general average of the country. And in the smaller agricultural districts, where a less amount of pauperism is found, crime is also diminished in a like proportion. Without pausing to ascertain whether undetected crime is not probably a good deal greater in these ten counties than in England at large, it should be observed that, where there are great estates in agricultural counties, game is usually preserved with some strictness, and the game laws undoubtedly do something towards filling gaols with men, and workhouses with women and children, and so increasing local rates. The number of criminal offences is much lower in counties where there are more landowners and occupiers, and fewer partridges and pheasants.

The prisons of England, great as is the improvement recently introduced into many of them, still, by their influence on their inmates, add largely to the catalogue both of criminals and paupers; and great amelioration in the organisation of such establishments is still called for. It may safely be asserted, that many of our prisons constantly and largely degrade and corrupt the unhappy children and young offenders who are confined for short terms within their walls. When it is the head of the family who is imprisoned, and not his child, the consequence of such imprisonment is, in a vast number of cases, necessarily to throw wife and children on the parish. It is not likely that the child should escape the evil influence to which the parent is subjected; and that parent, if once convicted of larceny, or any other felony, is by an intendment of law, created by express statutory provision, always to be considered as actually chargeable to the parish in which he may reside, and is therefore always liable to removal to his place of settlement, even if in employment, and not in need of parish relief.* Moreover, a large proportion of children are found among the inmates of workhouses, to the evil and corrupting influence of which such children are usually exposed, and must remain exposed, until district schools shall be effectually organised. "The child is father of the man." We may, therefore, look for a great preponderance of juvenile, as we have already found a great preponderance of adult, criminal offenders in these pauperised agricultural counties. Mr. Clay, in his Report on the Preston House of Correction for the year 1848, has given a table from which the following is extracted. He does not give all our ten counties; but the proportion would be substantially the same in all.

Counties.	Proportion of Juvenile Offenders in 1846 to Population in 1841.
Berks - - -	- 1 to 4,132
Bucks - - -	- 1 ,, 5,571
Dorset - - -	- 1 ,, 4,376
Essex - - -	- 1 ,, 4,011
Suffolk - - -	- 1 ,, 4,376
Sussex - - -	- 1 ,, 4,163
Wilts - - -	- 1 ,, 5,073
Average - -	- 1 ,, 4,529
North Lancashire - -	- 1 ,, 15,487

Ignorance, so often the nurse, if not the parent, of immorality and crime, reigns supreme amid the pauperism of these agricultural counties. This ignorance exceeds that which generally prevails elsewhere, at least as much as its accompanying pauperism here exceeds the average pauperism of the rest of the country.

It appears that about 33 per cent. of the male population, throughout England and Wales, sign their marriage register with marks. In these agricultural counties, the proportion of such signatures very greatly exceeds the general average: in the majority of them, the excess of ignorance thus ascer-

* 35 Geo. III. c. 101. s. 5.

tained, is from 30 to 53 per cent. above the average.* And, in agricultural counties generally, the necessity of making some such general provision for education, as may embrace within its scope the children of the working classes, is even greater than it is elsewhere; although its necessity may justly be said to be paramount throughout the whole country.

The inspectors of schools bear testimony, and it is easy to observe, that there is now gradually developing in the minds of merchants and manufacturers, as well as among the working classes in our town population, "a deep and honest interest in the educational problem of the country;" † but it may be justly doubted, whether any such interest is, as yet, generally felt, among either the landowners or the labourers in agricultural counties.

It has been in cities that all great movements, tending towards civilisation, seem ever to have originated. It was in cities that the Christian proselytes first learned a higher wisdom than that of their ancestors. Gospel truth itself was still rejected throughout the greater part of the domains of a wealthy territorial aristocracy, cultivated by a degraded race of slaves and colons, long after it had been largely received in the chief cities of the Roman empire; and, when the glad tidings of salvation were welcomed in those cities, the deposed deities of a time-honoured superstition sought for refuge, and long found protection, on the hills and in the valleys, amidst the groves and at the fountains, of that country region, from which the very name of pagan, as used by Christians, is derived.‡ We need not wonder that this modern paganism

* The whole number of men who signed the marriage register with marks, in the year 1844, in the ten agricultural counties, was 6999. A table obtained from Mr. Fletcher's investigations (and published with the Minutes of the Committee of Council on Education, 1848, 1849, 1850, vol. ii. pp. 341, 342.) will be found in the Appendix. It shows the excess as it is found in each of the ten agricultural and three manufacturing counties, above the general average of the whole country.

† Mr. Morell, General Report for the Year 1850; Minutes of the Committee of Council on Education, 1850-51, vol. ii. p. 630.

‡ The term *pagan* was originally applied to the inhabitants of the country, who, on the first propagation of the Christian religion, "adhered to the worship

of ignorance, and love of ignorance, should be so difficult to overcome in its rural fastnesses. With respect to our own landowners, and their furtherance of education, the testimony of inspectors of schools has long tended to show that "the great and crying evil of all, is the absence of such sympathy on the part of the owners of property generally, in the education of the working classes, as to induce them to support, efficiently, the annual expense of schools already existing;" and, it appears, that complaints of this unwillingness are louder in the agricultural districts than elsewhere. A recent Report on Essex, Norfolk, Suffolk, and two other adjoining counties, gives many instances of such unwillingness and neglect. From one parish alone the owner of the soil derives a rental of some 4000*l.* per annum, and gives to the school the sum of 7*l.*, while "the principal owner of the adjacent parishes derives from them a rental of upwards of 3000*l.* per annum, and contributes 1*l.* to the support of the school." Yet, in the very same place, the legal rights of these owners of property are most rigorously enforced, to the great discomfort and injury of the poor *, though corresponding duties are thus neglected. "The parish is in the more miserable con-

of false gods, or refused to receive Christianity," after it had been received by the inhabitants of the cities. See Facciolati, v. *Paganus.* In like manner *heathen* signifies an inhabitant of the *heath.* Remarkable instances are found of the continued worship, in country districts, of the pagan deities, and of nymphs of groves and fountains, long after the general adoption of Christianity; some such instances are indicated in Pashley's "Travels in Crete," vol. i. p. 89. note 28., and traces of the ancient heathendom are very distinctly perceivable in many modern superstitions, in different countries of Europe. In England, such traces are found in the names of some country places: for instance, of *Thurs*fold in Norfolk, *Thurs*field in Stafford, *Thurs*ley in Sussex, and, probably, *Thur*leigh in Bedford, *Thur*low in Essex; as well as in the fuller form, *Thunders*field in Surrey, and *Thunders*ley in Essex: these all seem to be derived from the old god *Thunar*, *Thonar*, or *Thor*, just as we owe to him the name of *Thurs*day. Similarly *Hamer*ton, in the West Riding of Yorkshire, *Hammer*ingham, *Hammer*wick, and perhaps *Homer*ton elsewhere, are derived from *Hamar*, one of the names by which the same god Thunar or Thor was designated: see Kemble's *Saxons in England*, vol. i. c. xii. s 2.; so also Wanborough, formerly Wodnesbeorh, in Surrey and in Wilts, Wonston in Hants, Wonersh in Surrey, and many other names of places in England, seem to be derived from *Woden*: see ib. p. 340.

* See below, Ch. XIV.

dition, as the proprietors of neighbouring parishes have reduced the number of cottages on their estates, and driven in the labourers to occupy small tenements in this, thus increasing, beyond due proportion, the population of the working classes." Elsewhere, as a large landowner testifies, a noble earl is the lord of the manor, within which seven-tenths of all the poor children attend a school, built for the use of three adjoining parishes, but from his lordship "no assistance can be obtained, either for the building of the school, or for its maintenance. The tenant of the earl also refuses any assistance, either to the building or to its support:" and in this case a clergyman is, in reality, the only resident, besides the two already mentioned, capable of assisting it. In the third parish, "the lord of the manor, and his tenant, made a small donation to the building, but each has refused further support." *

Human nature can show itself to be as selfish and unchristian, in our own age and country, as it was in the moral darkness of heathendom itself; and any English poet who, in the nineteenth century, should follow the example of Virgil, or Dante, and people the doleful shades with men of his own age and country, might, perchance, exhibit English landowners, sharing the torments of the crowd of ancient Romans:

> Qui divitiis soli incubuere repertis,
> Nec partem posuere suis, quæ maxima turba est!

Such instances of selfishness and neglect of a duty, which cannot as yet be enforced, "according to the form of the statute, in such case made and provided," is so common, that unless further and more effectual means be provided, to maintain such schools for children of the working classes, many even of those now existing, will wholly fail. Mr. Mitchell avers, in speaking of part of the West Norfolk district, that unless further means be devised for this purpose, such schools

* General Report for 1850, by Her Majesty's Inspector of Schools; the Rev. M. Mitchell, on the schools inspected by him in the counties of Cambridge, Essex, Huntingdon, Norfolk, and Suffolk; Minutes of the Committee of Council on Education, vol. ii. pp. 249—252.

"must all fall to the ground." And, moreover, as to the existing schools in the last-mentioned five counties, the Inspector reports, that there is a class of them "in which the master is ignorant and slovenly, the school-room dirty and ill found, the children ill-disciplined, unwashed, uncombed, with clothes unbrushed and ill put on, slouching in person, uncleanly in habits, ungainly in figure, debased in character, and degraded in circumstances." The reason why the number of schools with inefficient, and even with totally incompetent instructors, in this district, was very great, is accounted for, partly, "by the deficiency in numbers of duly qualified teachers, and partly by the very low salaries which are offered, and *which would often hardly secure the services of a decently skilled day-labourer*. Hence persons, broken in character, health, or morals, of that class who, having attempted many things without success, at length decline to school-keeping as a last resource, are ultimately, for want of other applicants, forced as it were, upon reluctant managers."* Nor is it solely the selfishness of the landowner, or his indifference to the cause of education, that is in fault, in causing a failure of those necessary funds without which it is utterly impossible that competent teachers should be obtained. Throughout the agricultural district, it is to be feared, that, on this question, an enlightened benevolence has not as yet found its way into the mind of the farmer. In speaking of local rating, in support of education, the Dean of Hereford says, "At present, in our rural districts, it would be almost impossible to bring it into operation; the education of the labouring classes is the very last thing for which the farmer would think of voting parish money, and it might not be too much to say, that, not one rural parish in the South of England, would willingly rate itself for that purpose. Parishes in the North might, and in many towns such a plan would, probably, work well, and, in the end, lead to its general adoption."

It would be a grievous error to suppose, that the middle classes of England would not benefit, in a high degree, by

* The Rev. M. Mitchell's Report, ib. p. 250.

such a general provision insuring the education of all. Their children would always remain at school two or three years longer than the children of the working classes, and would receive a more complete education than their poorer neighbours. Each class would, in its respective place, receive a corresponding improvement and elevation.

That the want of education, among a large part of the middle class in England, is great, notwithstanding the increase in recent voluntary efforts to amend it, no one can dispute. That it would receive a greater impulse, by a provision for the education of all, than by any other means, seems also clear. By such public provision, a very much better education would be ensured than has ever yet been brought within the reach of many among the middle classes; and the expense of such education would be greatly diminished. It is worth while to pause for one moment, in order to contemplate the want of education which in many parts of the country is found, even among men of substance, who, under any rational scheme of representative government, must certainly enjoy the elective franchise, and who, in the administration of matters of local interest, even fill important municipal or parochial offices, in which large sums of money pass through their hands, and accounts ought to be kept. Let us take the "substantial householders" appointed to the office of overseers of the poor, now, in the middle of the nineteenth century, in civilised England. Such officers are required to *sign* various written documents. The legislature assumes that they can write. The assumption is very often falsified by the fact. The statement of grounds of appeal, which the law has long* peremptorily required to be "*under the hands*" of parish officers, are not uncommonly signed by marksmen. Instances of such signatures, ×, have frequently, during the last fourteen years, come under my own eye, in the course of my professional practice. In the year 1848, the legis-

* Since the statute 4 & 5 Will. IV. c. 76. s. 81., which enacts that the overseers who appeal against an order of removal, shall deliver to the overseers of the respondent parish, "a statement in writing, *under their hands*, of the grounds of such appeal."

lature for the first time required (by the statute 11 & 12 Vict. c. 31. s. 2.) that overseers, obtaining orders for the removal of poor persons, should send to the parish to be affected, a statement in writing, "under the hands of such overseers, setting forth the grounds of such removal." Since the passing of this statute, I have had papers before me, as counsel, containing a marksman's signature to grounds of appeal, while the corresponding statement, setting forth the grounds of removal, in the very same case, has been similarly signed by a marksman overseer. Ignorance thus evidenced by the inability to write, has been noticed by observers, who have been placed in various situations, enabling them accurately to judge of the matter; and it appears, in many parts of the country, to pervade, to a considerable extent, the whole class of overseers of the poor.

The inquiry of 1833, alone, showed how general must be the ignorance, how universal the want of proper education, of a great part of that class of society out of which parish officers are chosen. In a parish in Sussex, as the rector testifies, neither of the two overseers could read or write.* In the Pershore division, containing sixty-six parishes, in Worcestershire, some of the overseers, as we are informed by an active resident magistrate, "can scarcely write their names, and few can keep accounts (witness the returns made to parliament), and are so ignorant or inattentive to the magistrate's orders, wishing to slip through their half-year with as little trouble as possible, that many appeals against removals and other expenses are very unnecessarily incurred." "Although clear and often able replies" to the queries of the commissioners in 1833, were "received from the officers of the town parishes, some of the answers, *even from the metropolis*, were evidently written by illiterate and ignorant men." One of the population returns from Middlesex, to which the commissioners, in 1833, had occasion to refer, was attested by the mark of the returning officer. In some of the parishes of Cheshire and

* Report from Her Majesty's Commissioners for inquiring into the Administration and Practical Operation of the Poor Laws, 1834; Statement of Rev. R. Ellison, Rector of Slaugham, vol. i. p. 159. Folio edition.

Nottinghamshire, a × was found substituted for the overseer's signature, in the revising barrister's list of voters. On the revision of the list of voters for West Sussex and for North Essex, the revising barrister, in both counties, "met with many overseers apparently perfectly unable to comprehend, from reading the Reform Act, what they were required to do. Many were unable to write at all, and others could with difficulty affix their names to the lists. Some appeared unable to copy accurately the schedule of the act, according to the form there given. Those lists which had any pretension to correctness, had been invariably written out by the parish schoolmaster, or under the advice and direction of some resident gentleman. Few were capable of furnishing any information, or of understanding that any distinction existed between a freehold and a leasehold qualification." There were "few lists which did not require considerable alteration. Attempts at an alphabetical arrangement seemed to have completely failed." In North Leicester, the revising barrister says: "I found very great difficulty in revising the list of voters, owing to the illiterate character of the overseers of many of the parishes. In one instance, where there were two overseers, one had not acted, and did not sign the list, though he was able to write; and a mark ×, was substituted for the signature of the other. There were, I think, three or four lists unsigned, none of the overseers being able to write, and about the same number only signed by one overseer. In about sixteen or eighteen lists, the overseers had resorted to the assistance of the parish schoolmaster, or some other person, to assist them. In not more than ten parishes, did the overseers appear in the least to comprehend the duties they were required to perform. I found, however, the overseers of the parishes of Loughborough, Castle Donnington, Melton Mowbray, and Ashby-de-la-Zouch, exceedingly intelligent men, while in the eastern side of the county, *where the population is exclusively agricultural,* I met with a *degree of ignorance I was utterly unprepared to find in a civilised country.*" *

* Report, p. 160.

In North Devon, the revising barrister "found that *not less than one-fourth of the overseers were unable to read*," and he mentions one overseer who had not that qualification, and yet was intrusted with the distribution of rates to the amount of 7000*l.* per annum.*

When the ignorance of the small farmer is like the "slavery that hugs her chain," and renders him unwilling to incur any trouble or expense for the purposes of education, we need hardly wonder that there should be at least an equal want, on the part of the ignorant agricultural labourer, of all perception of the necessary tendency and value of education to those who can obtain it.

Utter want of education by the agricultural labourer, and his inability to perceive its use, is, in part, the cause of that comparative lukewarmness, which prevails in rural districts, respecting this great question of educating the rising generation. "It must have been observed by all who have inquired into, and are conversant with, the question," says the present Dean of Hereford, "that the feeling in favour of education is much less strong in the rural districts than in the towns: this in some measure arises from the agricultural labourer seeing so little inducement, in a worldly point of view, to educate his children, and having no knowledge, from experience, that it can in any way render his home a more happy or a more contented one."† The same author, was himself, for years, a labourer in this vineyard of education: and while promoting industrial pursuits, and instilling feelings of self-respect and self-dependence, and principles of truth and honesty, into the hearts and minds of the young, he saw constantly around him how much happier and better the whole rising generation is made by such an education; he saw "that it leads to greater propriety of conduct in all the relations of life, and that those who have remained longest at school, have generally turned out the best, and have given

* Report, p. 160.

† *Remarks occasioned by the present Crusade against the Educational Plans of the Committee of Council on Education*, by the Rev. Richard Dawes, Vicar of King's Somborne, Hants. London, 1850.

a proof that the longer they remain the greater is the security of their becoming, in their respective stations, what the friends of education expect them to be."*

That voluntary efforts are utterly insufficient to educate the children of the whole community, the most ample experience has served fully to demonstrate. We might just as reasonably leave it to voluntary efforts to provide for the maintenance of the poor, among the whole body of our labouring classes, as leave it to such efforts to provide for the moral, intellectual, and religious training of the young, among the same classes. What claims on the charity of Christians have higher sanction than those of the poor? None in this country have been more universally admitted, from the earliest times; and, if the voluntary principle has been found wholly insufficient to provide for keeping body and soul together, even in the case of the poor, how can we rationally expect it properly to provide for any educational training of *all* the children of those very poor?

It will be seen, in the course of these pages, with how much reluctance the claim of the poor to a compulsory provision was admitted, and how anxiously the legislature was employed, during the greater part of a century, in endeavouring to render efficient the voluntary efforts of the day towards providing maintenance for the poor. The inadequacy of all such efforts was finally, though reluctantly, admitted; and at last, towards the end of the reign of Queen Elizabeth, the relief of the poor was provided for by compulsory taxation. No sober English statesman denies the justice and wisdom of such a provision; its principle has lately been extended and enforced in Scotland, and, for the first time, introduced into Ireland. The impossibility of adequately providing, by voluntary efforts, for the educational wants of the country, is, surely, at least as clear now as it ever was clear, that voluntary efforts would prove unavailing to provide for the maintenance of the poor, and prevent their dying from starvation in the midst of plenty. It would in truth seem, that

* Dawes, *Suggestive Hints towards improved Secular Education*, Introduction.

of the two laws of compulsory taxation, the first, ensuring food for a pauper parent, though able-bodied and profligate, the other, providing for the education of his helpless and innocent child, the latter is especially commended, by the consideration that its outlay, would greatly diminish the probable future amount to be expended in relieving pauperism. Such an outlay would also rapidly diminish a heavy item in our annual national expenditure, by reducing the number of inmates of cages and lock-ups, of gaols and bridewells, of houses of detention and houses of correction, of penitentiaries and model prisons, of hulks and transports, and of penal colonies. In those colonies, such an outlay would prevent the further flow of the turbid stream of corruption through countries till of late unstained by the vices of civilisation; and, at home, it would equally benefit the ratepayers, whose burden it would alleviate, and the poorer classes, whose pauperism it would prevent. Certainly, adult pauperism has never held out any such promise as its childhood does, to induce the State to provide for its necessities: it has generally rather resembled Dante's wolf, that could never satisfy its ravenous will, and was more hungry after its meal than before.

Intemperance may be justly considered as one of the chief causes of both pauperism and crime in this country; and when the brutalising and brutal character of the intemperance which now prevails, is looked at, it can hardly be doubted, that an immediate consequence of educating all children, of all classes of the community, would be, a great diminution in the amount of such intemperance, and a corresponding diminution in the amount of that pauperism and crime to which it gives rise. On questions of this kind, the dear-bought experience of our neighbours, ought to be used by us as a lesson. It appears that in Holland, an increased consumption of ardent spirits, has been the cause of an increase in the prevailing pauperism of the people. The special attention of the Dutch legislature, has been recently given, to the steady and continuous increase of pauperism, which for some years has been going on in Holland. It appears, from a Report made to the Dutch House of Commons in 1849, that in 1841, the proportion of persons receiving public relief in Holland, was 106·00 out of every 1000 of the population. In 1845 it had risen from 106·00 to 142·58, and in 1847 to 160·82,— one of the chief causes assigned, being the increasing abuse of spirits.*

Certainly one of the worst accompaniments and consequences of the uneducated state of our own working classes, is found in the habit of drinking, and in the drunkenness by which they are characterised. Perhaps an Englishman who has dwelt among, and seen much of the superior sobriety of the natives of either the European or Asiatic continent, feels all the more strongly, that this vice is a national disgrace, which ought to be removed from the English name. 'Tis of long standing. Whether "first introduced into this kingdom by the Danes," or introduced at a later period, it has certainly been the darling sin of our working classes, for more than two centuries. It appears greatly to have increased after the accession of James I., and was first prohibited by statute, early in his reign. The act (4 James I. c. 5. A.D. 1606-7) was intended to put down *sin;* and Blackstone justly reckons drunkenness, as one of the offences against God and religion, which, in England, it has been thought fit to include within the range of repressive temporal legislation.† The title of the act is, "An Acte for repressinge the odious and loathsome synne of Drunckennes," and the penalty imposed for a single sinful act, is 5*s.*, or, in default of payment, six hours imprisonment in the stocks: liability to conviction arises at once, whenever any man "shall be drunk." Dalton, writing in 1635‡, suggests the following criterion to guide the judgment of the temporal magistrate in enforcing these penal provisions against sin: "Now for to know a drunken man the better, the Scripture describeth them to stagger and reel to

* See an article *On the Use and Abuse of Alcoholic Liquors,* in the "British and Foreign Medico-Chirurgical Review," vol. vii. pp. 46. 48.

† On this head of our English legislation, see Spangenberg, in his *Uebersicht der Religionsverbrechen nach Englischem Rechte,* published in Mittermaier und Zacharia's *Kritische Zeitschrift für Rechtswissenschaft und Gesetzgebung des Auslandes,* vol. i. pp. 112—128.

‡ Dalton, *The Countrey Justice,* p. 27. ed, London, 1635.

and fro (Iob, xii. 25.; Esay. xxiv. 20.). And so, where the same legs which carrie a man into the house, cannot bring him out againe, it is a sufficient signe of drunkennesse."

Not only is punishment for being drunk provided by this statute of James I.; but to use the words of Blackstone*, "There are many wholesome statutes, by way of prevention, which regulate the licensing of alehouses, and punish persons found tippling therein;" and it has been said†, "Thus we see the legislature hath taken *the utmost care,* not only to punish, but even to prevent, this vice of drunkenness." In more recent times, however, even the slight preventive check of the licensing control of justices of peace, has been removed, in the case of some of the houses for sale of intoxicating drink; and, however great the number of parishes unprovided with schools may be, there are probably none, in which there is not an ample supply of beer-houses, licensed by the Excise.

The recital of the statute is, "Whereas the loathsome and odyous synne of drunkennes is, of late, growen into comon use within this realme, beinge the roote and foundacion of many other enormious synnes, as bloodshed, stabbinge, murder, swearinge, fornicacion, adulterye, and such lyke, to the great dishonour of God and of our nacion, the overthrowe of many good artes and manuell trades, the disablinge of dyvers workmen, and the gen̄all ympov̄ishing of many good subjectꝭ, abusievely wasting the good creatures. of God." My own experience in courts of criminal justice, extending over a good many years, next following the commencement of my practice at the bar, enables me to say, that most of the consequences of drunkenness, as here described, probably prevail in England at the present day, about as generally, as they can have done, in any other age or country; and that, certainly, a large proportion of all the crime which is yearly prosecuted at quarter sessions and assizes, originates in this source. The experience of every one, whether judge, counsel, attorney, juryman, or witness, who has had to attend much

* Blackstone's Commentaries on the Laws of England, vol. iv. p. 64.

† By Fielding, Works, vol. x. p. 348.

in courts of criminal justice in England, must lead him to this conclusion. On a recent occasion, a question was put by a select committee of the House of Lords * to Her Majesty's judges: "How far may we hope that good education, including therein infant training, as well as sound religious and moral instruction, will, by its preventive effect, lessen considerably the prevalence of crimes?" Mr. Justice Wightman, in answering this question, states his hope, that the first effect of the general diffusion of education and infant training will be, "to change the habits of the people, in their recreations and mode of enjoying leisure, from frequenting public-houses, and drinking to excess, to rational and innocent occupation and amusement. I particularly mention this," the learned judge adds, "as, according to my experience, at least three-fourths of the criminal charges that are brought to trial at the assizes, originate in habits of intemperance, and the spending all leisure time in public-houses; the parties usually being totally ignorant, unable to read or write, and, as it would seem, incapable of appreciating any other mode of enjoyment, or occupation of their leisure. Until the national character is much changed in this respect, any very great decrease in the amount of crime is scarcely to be expected." A most important testimony to the necessity of a great change in the educational system hitherto adopted in this country! Mr. Justice Cresswell, on the same occasion, avowed the opinion, which, if it needed great authority for its reception, would receive it by such avowal, "that good education, including infant training, as well as sound religious and moral instruction, will do more to lessen the prevalence of crime, than any other mode of dealing with convicts that can be devised."

It may be worth while to give a single specimen of the number of a serious class of offences, robbery from the person, to the commission of which drinking and its haunts frequently give rise. Let Manchester be taken as the locality

* See the First Report from the Select Committee of the House of Lords appointed to inquire into the Criminal Law, especially respecting Juvenile Offenders and Transportation, Session 1847, Appendix, vol. i. pp. 3—176.

of our inquiries, and let the number of these robberies from the person committed there, in a single year, in public-houses and beer-houses alone, be ascertained. The number of public-houses in Manchester in 1848, was 475, of beer-houses, 1143: in that year, 74 *robberies from the person* took place in the public-houses; and in the beer-houses, during the same year, 52 *similar robberies* were committed.*

Statistical investigations, of which the above is a slight specimen, all serve to show the truth of the opinion now, I believe, very generally entertained by those who are conversant with the administration of criminal justice in England, "that crime, legally considered, and intemperance, in its ordinary acceptation, are the concomitants of each other."† Statutory penalties, like those held out by our legislature, are futile; and the moral improvement, by education, of the great mass of our countrymen, is the only sure preventive of such sin and its accompanying crimes. Hundreds of thousands of convictions have been made in this long period of nearly 250 years, since the passing of the statute of 4 Jac. I. c. 5., and yet each morning's work of metropolitan police magistrates, in dealing with the cases of men and women found "drunk," or "drunk and disorderly," during the previous night, is still a sad indication of the state of our civilisation. Fearful evidence to show the enormous extent of the vice of drunkenness among us, may be obtained by ascertaining the number of persons, who, when in a state of intoxication, are taken into custody by the police. Official documents show exactly how many of such cases occur in a single year in London alone.‡ For 1848, that number was as follows:

* Tables of the Revenue, Population, Commerce, &c., of the United Kingdom and its Dependencies, part xviii. sec. B. 1848, pp. 173, 174.

† Neison, *On the Rate of Mortality among Persons of Intemperate Habits*, in the "Journal of the Statistical Society," vol. xiv. pp. 200. 216.

‡ See the Statement of the Number, Sex, Offences, and Degree of Instruction of Persons taken into Custody by the Metropolitan Police in the year 1848, in part xviii. sec. B. p. 154. of the Tables of the Revenue, Population, Commerce &c. of the United Kingdom, 1850.

Offence.	Males.	Females.	Total.
Drunkenness - - - - -	4,816	3,576	8,392
Drunk and disorderly characters -	4,381	3,688	8,069
Totals - - - - - -	9,197	7,264	16,461

Of the whole number of these miserable creatures, the proportion who had received a little education, may be seen by the returns.

Offence.	Neither read nor write.		Read only, or read and write imperfectly.		Read and write well.	
	Male.	Female.	Male.	Female.	Male.	Female.
Drunkenness - - -	1,344	862	2,748	2,500	531	184
Drunk and disorderly -	1,482	1,394	2,292	2,118	428	157
Total - - -	2,826	2,256	5,040	4,618	959	341
Total male and female -	5,082		9,658		1,300	

So that the total of persons taken into custody, for these offences, in the metropolis, in one year, is to be classed as follows:

Persons who neither read nor write - -	5,082
Who read only, or read and write imperfectly -	9,658
Who read and write well - - - -	1,300
There are also of superior education - -	421
Making a grand total of - -	16,461

No reasonable doubt can be entertained respecting the probable effect of a universally diffused system of public education, in preventing the existence, in a great part at least, of this dense and corrupt mass of degradation and misery.

Great as is the number of such cases brought into police courts, it does not show anything like the full extent to which, among the body of our labouring classes, the vice of drunkenness prevails. It is only those whose drunkenness is such as to be manifestly dangerous, either to the public or to themselves, who are thus taken into custody. A man may be habitually a drunkard, and may walk home, along the streets of London, at least half-drunk every night of his life, without being in any danger of having to appear at a police office.

If any care had been taken to elevate the moral character of the people, by some provision for their education, instead of taking "the utmost care" of them by fine and the stocks, and at the same time giving them an abundant supply of public-houses licensed by justices of peace, and of beer-houses licensed by the Excise, better results would have followed.

At no time does the attempt of the legislature to put down drunkenness by a penalty, appear to have had any beneficial effect in diminishing the prevalence of the sin. The complaint of De Foe, in his "True-born Englishman," shows what was the pre-eminent characteristic of our poorer classes in the reign of William III.:

> The lab'ring poor, in spite of double pay,
> Are saucy, mutinous, and beggarly;
> Good drunken company is their delight,
> And what they get by day they spend by night;
> In English ale their dear enjoyment lies,
> For which they'll starve themselves and families.

English ale has long ceased to be the sole, or even the main cause of their improvidence and suffering. Gin in England, and whisky beyond the Tweed, have long been the favourite beverages of our British drunkards.

Careful investigations by Mr. Porter, have shown that "the self-imposed taxation of the working classes in the United Kingdom, in gin, whisky, and rum, is annually 28,810,208*l.*; in beer of all kinds, exclusive of that brewed in private families, 25,383,165*l.*; and in tobacco and snuff, 7,218,242*l.*; making a total, under these three heads, of 53,411,615*l.*, a sum fully equal to the whole annual public revenue of the United Kingdom." It would be fallacious to use this vast outlay as a measure of the prosperity of the people: it is rather a proof of their degradation. The greater part of this enormous sum, is spent, by men alone, heads of families, in mere sensual indulgence, in which their wives and children do not participate.

Men of intemperate habits often spend half their earnings, if of from 10*s.* to 15*s.* weekly, and as much as one-third of those earnings, if of from 20*s.* to 30*s.* weekly, in this sottish indulgence, apart from the other members of their families. It is well observed that such a state of things would not exist if the men were better brought up; as is made manifest by the case of such artizans as are employed in matters for which education is needed, and who earn only a similar amount of wages. In this better educated class, a husband or father, spending on his own personal gratification alone, full half or one-third of his earnings, is wholly unknown; and, if discovered, would be execrated as a monster of brutality. "Take even the case of a clerk," says Mr. Porter, "with a salary of 80*l.* a year, a small fraction beyond 30*s.* a week, and it would be considered quite exceptional, if anything approaching to a fourth part of the earnings were spent upon objects, in which the wife and children should have no share. The peer, the merchant, the clerk, the artizan, and the labourer, are all of the same nature, born with the same propensities, and subject to the like influences. It is true they are placed in very different circumstances, the chief difference being that of the early training—one, happily, which it is quite possible to remedy, and that by a means which would, in many ways, add to the sum of the nation's prosperity and respectability." *

The same excessive use of ardent spirits, and other intoxicating drinks, which characterises our uneducated and unthinking labourers at home, accompanies such of them as serve their country abroad, into every clime in which the British flag is unfurled, to brave the battle or the breeze. In both army and navy, the striking influence of intemperance, in producing crime, has long been manifest and noto-

* Porter, *On the Self-imposed Taxation of the Working Classes in the United Kingdom*, a Paper read before the British Association in 1849, and published in vol. xiii. of the "Journal of the Statistical Society."

rious. No one can spend a month, either on board a ship of war, or in a considerable place garrisoned by British troops, without having ample opportunity of satisfying himself of the deplorable fact. The effect of drunkenness on the mortality of British troops has also been long observed, more especially on foreign stations. During a considerable period spent in and near the Mediterranean more than sixteen years ago, it was my fortune to have frequent intercourse, with distinguished members of both branches of the service. It was also my fortune, when on board a ship of war, to witness the dreadful spectacle of a man's back receiving its laceration by the "cat," for the grave, and, on board ship, unpardonable offence, of drunkenness on duty. How refrain from specially considering whether want of early education was not, in truth, the main cause of a great part of the crime and punishment, as well as of the mortality, from which both army and navy suffer? That improved education of the young was the only safe substitute for the torture of the lash, and must precede the abolition of that torture, was the conclusion at which, most reluctantly, and after much inquiry and repeated discussion of the question with those whose professional experience entitled their opinions to respect, I was obliged to come. While your people are brutes, it is only such motives as influence brutes that can influence them.

That drunkenness is the cause of the greater part of the crime, and much of the mortality, of our troops on foreign stations, seems to be now indisputable. Recent statistical inquiries of great importance, embodied in an able and interesting paper by Colonel Sykes, have shown how large a proportion of the crime and mortality now prevailing among our troops is due to intemperance alone.* Great exertions have been made, in the Indian army, to improve the habits of the soldier in this respect, "by canteen re-

* Out of 294 European soldiers, tried and convicted during one year in the Bengal Presidency, the whole catalogue "had in almost every instance its origin more or less remote, in drunkenness."—Col. Sykes, *Mortality and Disease of the Troops under the Madras Government*, Journal of the Statistical Society, vol. xiv. pp. 109. 135.

gulations, by encouraging temperance societies, by supplying malt liquor to the men so cheap that they may prefer it to spirits, and also by affording them physical and intellectual amusements;" yet, notwithstanding these praiseworthy endeavours, it is still found that "the chief cause of crime and mortality is drunkenness." The twig might easily have been bent, though the full-grown tree withstands any attempt to give it a new and better direction. It is hoped that, in a very few years, proper educational training of the masses of the people, by diminishing drunkenness both in the army and navy, and elevating the character of the men employed, will lead to relieving the nation, and the officers of both branches of the service, from the necessity of inflicting on the men that dreadful and revolting torture, the terrors and anguish of which are still required for the maintenance of military and naval discipline.

Such are some of the chief social benefits which the proper discharge of a great and primary duty of the State will ensure to the most numerous class of its children.

That the diffusion of education would tend to prevent this pauperism, which degrades and presses down to the earth our labouring population, cannot surely be any longer doubted. In the United States of North America, "it is acknowledged by the rich that where the free schools have been *most improved*, the people have been *least addicted to intemperance*, are more provident, have more respect for property and the law, are more conservative, and are less led away by socialist or other revolutionary doctrines. They (the educated labouring classes of New England) make better pioneers when roughing it in a log-house in the back-woods, than the uneducated Highlander or Irishman."*

Independently of the vast sums which these spendthrift drunkards squander yearly, and of the pauperism which, in their own persons, and in the persons of others, they yearly produce, the country would, by their reformation, save a considerable part of its annual expenditure on criminals. In

* Lyell, *A Second Visit to the United States of North America*, vol i. p. 230.

Manchester and Salford, the following appears to have been the cost of pauperism and crime in a year, during a period of perfect repose and general prosperity.*

	£	s.	d.
Expenditure in relief of the poor for the year ended 25th March, 1850, for Manchester - -	55,626	1	11
That for Salford - - -	9,517	16	4
Pauperism - -	£65,143	18	3
Expense of detecting and punishing offenders in the two boroughs in the year 1849–50, about -	60,000	0	0
Total cost of crime and pauperism	£125,143	18	3

Such robberies from the person, as have been already mentioned, committed in public-houses and beer-houses, cause a large part of this outlay in the borough of Manchester; they necessarily involve the ratepayers, or the public, in the heavy expense of prosecuting and convicting offenders, as well as of apprehending them by policemen, and punishing them in gaol. The food and lodging of the criminal in his model palace, is always superior to that of the pauper in a workhouse; the attendants on the criminal, the officers of his staff, his governor or jailer, his wardens or turnkeys, (to say nothing of those who are in attendance on him when abroad, his *pedisequi* of the detective and ordinary police,) are even more costly than the official staff which attends on the pauper.

Let any one figure to himself the cost of a single criminal in the course of a long career of crime, generally undetected, but frequently punished by summary convictions, and occasionally by sentences of courts of quarter sessions or assizes, until at last he is removed, by transportation, to exercise his vocation in another land.† By this time, the public outlay

* See the Scheme of Secular Education compared with the Manchester and Salford Boroughs Education Bill. London, 1851.

† At times, at least, such has been the administration of the colonial affairs of this great empire, that the prospect, or chance, of transportation, has not always been likely powerfully to deter men from committing crimes.

upon him has been enough, if applied in education, perhaps to have actually saved some scores of such men from a like career of crime and suffering; and certainly enough to have raised many from those ranks of ignorance, and its accompanying pauperism and crime, in which they are now left. It must be borne in mind that the whole of the machinery necessarily kept in perpetual motion to repress crime, and relieve pauperism, is extremely costly; and that it is impossible to improve the moral condition of the working classes, without largely diminishing, in every way, the cost of that crime and pauperism. When in gaol each prisoner costs the community after the rate of 22*l.* yearly: a larger sum than the honest agricultural labourer, in many of our ten selected counties, can earn for the maintenance of himself and his family. In some gaols, higher rates of cost prevail; as at King's Lynn, in Norfolk, where the net average year's cost of each prisoner, exclusive of any charge for rent or repairs, is as much as 38*l.*, and where, at the same time, it is officially stated that "under the present arrangements, most of the prisoners must necessarily be injured, instead of being improved, by their confinement."* And the outlay on prisoners in gaols, is a small part of what they cost the country.

In addition to the above fiscal reasons for spending more in promoting education, and less in repressing crime, there is another motive peculiarly important, and also peculiarly applicable to the present condition of England, which deserves to be mentioned. It will not be possible for us much longer, by the annual transportation of so large a proportion of our worst criminals, to pour an everflowing tide of pollution over a distant land: we must come, sooner or later, to that system of penal legislation, which enlarged benevolence and true wisdom would perhaps have already arrived at, by determining to provide for the punishment in England, of most, if not all, grave offences committed here. Moreover, it may, perhaps, be expected and hoped, that imprisonment and the severe discipline which may be ordered in prisons, may, ere

* Fifteenth Report of Inspectors of Prisons, vol. ii. Northern and Eastern Districts, p. 33. (presented to Parliament in 1850).

long, be the only mode of inflicting bodily punishment, practically known to the administration of our criminal justice, and will be found a far more effectual preventive of crime than that threat of death which, although still preserved, is so seldom carried out. Now, whatever improvement may be effected in the discipline of prisons,—and it may safely be conceded that great improvement is needed, and may easily be made in that discipline,—yet it is nevertheless certain, that the letting loose, yearly, of a large number of prisoners, is always likely to have very serious social effects on the society in which they are let loose. Such tendency has recently been exemplified in a neighbouring country. The prospect of any diminution in the outlet which distant colonies have long supplied for the disposal of our criminals, certainly increases the importance of our diminishing their number, by adopting the safe and cheap prevention of education, and so saving men from becoming criminals, rather than by striving, expensively and in vain, as we have long done, and are still doing, to reform them, when they have been made such.

The enormous and increasing proportion of criminals to the whole population must be remembered. That increasing proportion gives as its number, for the nine years, 1839-1847, no fewer than 197,705 persons tried at assizes and sessions, and 456,051 summarily convicted, making a total of 653,756, or an average of 70,417 different criminals, convicted and imprisoned yearly, during the whole period. The number discharged from the gaols is nearly equal to the number admitted into the same gaols; for the average duration of imprisonment is short, and the number of deaths in gaol few: and, in round numbers, from 60,000 to 70,000 discharged prisoners are thus annually let loose upon society in England!*

If the considerations already put forward show that education alone can remove a great part of the most fruitful sources of pauperism and crime, we need not be alarmed at any amount which, in reason, the nation could be asked to

* Some of the discharges are cases of prisoners recommitted in the same year in which they have been discharged, so that each of these *habitués* of prisons is counted twice or oftener in the number of the text.

expend in education. It should be remembered that, for every million paid in education rate, there will be a large corresponding saving in our annual outlay on paupers, misdemeanants, and felons; and it must also be remembered that if England could, by any means, extinguish nine-tenths of the crime and pauperism, which now prevail throughout the land, it would matter comparatively little whether she applied yearly 3,000,000*l.* or 5,000,000*l.*, of her abundant, if not superfluous, wealth in doing so.

It can hardly be doubted, that the effects of education in preventing pauperism, would be as great as in preventing the commission of crime. The direct and necessary tendency of such an outlay among the young, will be to give them that prudence which, when they attain to a mature age, but are still in the full vigour of life, will enable them, by the exercise of more intelligence, and the practice of more virtue than they now possess, to avoid being added to a formidable list of "able-bodied paupers," such as we are constantly providing for by the poor-rate of England. One of the things which appears greatly to have struck a recent traveller in the United States of America, is, "the almost entire absence of pauperism, even in the large towns, except among the old and infirm."* Such a condition of society forms a striking contrast between the state of things in New England and the Mother Country; if, what is seen on the one side of the Atlantic, fills the mind with joy and thankfulness, the contrast exhibited on the other ought surely to excite a feeling of humiliation and shame.

One section, out of each 640 acres of land, is appropriated, in every township throughout the Union, for the perpetual benefit of the common schools. The late Mr. Sydney Smith, in 1824, after stating that 14,500,000 acres of land had been then appropriated for educational purposes, in the different states of the Union, adds, "It is impossible to speak too highly of the value and importance of these facts: they quite put in the background every thing that has been done in the old

* See Sir Charles Lyell, *A Second Visit to the United States of North America*, vol. i. p. 187.

world for the improvement of the lower orders, and confer deservedly upon the Americans, the character of a wise, a reflecting, and a virtuous people."

But beyond the public education stock of these appropriated sections of land, the citizens of the different states of the Union have made large pecuniary sacrifices, if an excellent investment can be called a sacrifice, in providing for the public education of every citizen. In "New England," especially, the struggle has been earnest and continuous, to elevate the condition of the great body of the people, by making large and generous provision for the instruction of their childhood; and so, by fostering a virtuous prudence, and creating a cultivated intelligence in the mind and understanding of every citizen, furnishing him with the best safeguard against his ever burdening the state as a criminal or a pauper.

It is of the great spectacle of human happiness exhibited by the United States of North America, that one of us, now no more*, whose wisdom and benevolence were hardly exceeded by his hilarity and wit, has said, that he "could never think of it without considering it as a great lesson to the people of England."

"The number of public or free schools in Massachusets," says Sir Charles Lyell, in his recent book†, "in 1845-6, for a population of 800,000 souls, was about 3500, and the number of male teachers 2585, and of female 5000, which would allow a teacher for each twenty five, or thirty children, as many as they can well attend to. The sum raised by direct taxation, for the wages and board of the tutors, and for fuel for the schools, is upwards of 600,000 dollars, or 120,000 guineas; but this is exclusive of all expenditure for school-houses, libraries, and apparatus, for which other funds are appropriated, and every year a great number of new and finer buildings are erected. The sums expended on private instruction in Boston, are supposed to be equal to the money levied by taxes for the free schools, or 260,800 dollars

* The Rev. Sydney Smith.

† *A Second Visit to the United States of North America*, vol. i. p. 190.

(55,000*l.*)." "If we were to enforce a school rate in Great Britain, bearing the same proportion to our population of twenty-eight millions, the tax would amount annually to more than *seven millions sterling*, and would then be far less effective, owing to the higher cost of living, and the comparative average standard of incomes among professional and official men."

That the moral elevation of the masses of the people was sure to arise from educating them, must have been strongly felt by our brethren who formerly crossed the Atlantic, to carry the blessings of Christian freedom to a great part of a new hemisphere. The Puritans, early in the seventeenth century, provided by law, "that none of the brethren should suffer so much barbarism in their families as not to teach their children and apprentices so much learning as may enable them perfectly to read the English tongue." "To the end that learning may not be buried in the graves of our forefathers," it was ordered, in all the Puritan colonies, "that *every township*, after the Lord hath increased them to the number of *fifty householders, shall appoint one to teach all children to write and read;* and where any town shall increase to the number of one hundred families, they shall set up a grammar school, the master thereof being obliged to instruct youth so far as they may be fitted for the University."*

It is now felt by the most eminent of the sons of New England that this public provision for the education of every citizen, has made their country the truly classic ground of human freedom, intelligence, and happiness. "In these measures," says Mr. Bancroft†, "especially in the laws establishing common schools, lies the secret of the success and character of New England. Every child, as it was born into the world, was lifted from the earth, by the genius of the country; and in the statutes of the land, received, as its birthright, a pledge of the public care for its morals and its mind." Let the parent country follow the noble-hearted and generous example set by the child!

* Bancroft, *History of the Colonization of the United States*, vol. i. p. 459.
† Ibid.

Every visitor who treads on the soil of the United States, is constrained at once to adopt the opinion of all around him, as to the universality of the blessings which public education diffuses throughout the community. When, in order to enable the Magyar race again to rise from the grave in which they have been interred alive, the greatest of living orators sought but yesterday* to win sympathy and aid from the citizens of the United States, the first title of their country to the approval and admiration of mankind, of which he reminded those citizens, was this, that on one allotment, in every place marked to become a township, "even in territories where the sound of human step had never yet mixed with the murmurs by which virginal nature adores the Lord," the officers of the States of the Union always place a pole, with the glorious inscription, *Popular Education Stock!* "This," exclaimed Kossuth, to citizens of the Union, "is your proudest monument." And what topic did the representative of the true-hearted Hungarian nation select, as the chief glory of the city of New York, in which he was speaking? That out of a population of little more than 500,000 inhabitants, there were then nearly 100,000 children annually receiving their education in public schools. Kossuth declared to his generous hosts, that it was not their geographical situation, not their material power, not the bold enterprising spirit of their people, which he considered to be the guarantee of their country's future,—but *the universalit of education!*

Let us now depart from the land of extreme republican freedom, and see whether even the monarchical governments of the European continent have not done their duty better than England has done her's, in providing for the public education of all classes. We shall find, if we look into the statistics of education, crime, and pauperism, throughout the states of Europe, that great and wealthy England, unapproached by any nation on the face of the earth, in the millions of her annual outlay, for repressing crime and relieving pauperism, does less annually by education, towards

* On 15th December, 1851, at New York.

preventing the existence of these causes of misery, than any other civilised Christian land.

Englishmen, little as they admire the political institutions, or great centralised administration, of the Austrian empire, may well do honour to the solicitude, which, during the last forty or fifty years, has been manifested by the Austrian government, to provide education for the whole body of the rising generation, at least in her German provinces. The subjoined statement *, extracted from official tables, gives the educational statistics of a great part of the Austrian empire. It is manifest that, throughout the provinces contained in the table, after allowing for cases of necessary absences from sickness or accident, the *whole number* of the children, of an age to attend school, are actually attending it. The State has, therefore, performed, even in absolute Austria, one of its highest and most important duties. Political freedom is wanting in Austria; but from the example of Austria, as well as that of other absolute states on the Continent, we may certainly learn, that the blessings of education are not necessarily confined to the citizens of a great republic, but may be allowed to spread among the subjects of a monarchy.

Inquiries recently made, at the instance of the Committee of Council on Education, by Her Majesty's principal Secretary of State for foreign affairs, respecting public education as carried on in other countries; and the result of such inquiries, founded on communications received from the principal states of Europe and America, has been printed under the title, "State of Education in Foreign Parts."† This published account shows plainly, how very far we are behind the rest of the world in this most important national work. All the nationalities reported on, whether Sclavonic or German, Scandinavian or Celtic, leave the European branch of the Anglo-Saxon race far behind them. In Prussia, out of a less population than that of England, there are 2,433,333 children in constant attendance on the elementary schools; and if the

* See Appendix.

† Minutes of the Committee of Council on Education, 1847–1848, vol. ii. pp. 546—580.

attendance in gymnasia, or grammar schools, be added, the whole number of the young, receiving education, is 2,542,961, or 1 in 6 of the whole population of 16,000,000. "*School-money*" has long been levied, as a rate, incumbent on all who have children; and we are not surprised to read that "*poor-rates*" have *not* been generally exacted in any part of the kingdom.* The communal arrangement of Prussia would be a parochial one in England; subject always, like the administration of relief to the poor, to a limited central control, in order that neglect and abuse may be prevented.

Important and interesting as is the information conveyed by this paper on the State of Education in Foreign Parts, there is one remarkable omission in it: Switzerland is not named. This omission may, in few words, be supplied. No country presents a nobler example of national wisdom and virtue, in respect of its provision for the public education of its people, than does Switzerland. In every canton such provision is gladly made; school-buildings, and salaries of teachers are provided, and the children of the poorest classes have an education ensured to them in 5500 primary communal schools, which, during the greater part of the year, are frequented by about 350,000 pupils, or about 1 in 7 of the whole population of the country. An attendance of six hours a day is given, except during part of the summer, when three hours alone is required. A small payment is made by the parents of each child; and *all* classes, the children of high and low, rich and poor, equally attend in these people's schools, *Volksschule.* The principle on which the Swiss schools are organised, seems to be nearly the same as has received so high a recommendation, both in word and deed, by the example of the King's Somborne school in Hampshire, to which reference has already been made.†

Singing in concert is an occasional relaxation of the whole

* A fuller account of the system of public education of Prussia, will be found in an article by Mr. Wyse, in the second publication of the Central Society of Education (pp. 375—428.), and in Mr. Kay's work, *The Social Condition and Education of the People in England and Europe*, vol. ii. ch. viii.

† See also Dawes, *Hints on an improved and self-paying System of National Education, suggested from the working of the King's Somborne School.*

school; "Grütli" and "Wilhelm Tell," "Vaterland," "Patria," and other patriotic strains, occupy a prominent place in such printed collections of words and music as the school children use. Such strains remind the children of their country, which so carefully prepares them rightly to discharge in life their duty both to God and man. We need not wonder that, in return for this parental care, the Swiss should love their country, with affection as prodigal as that of the industrious and intelligent peasant of the neighbouring Tirol for his fatherland. But the neglected children of ancient Albion have no more idea than a horse or an ox has, of what it is to have a country; and thousands upon thousands of them have not even heard of the name of the Queen who presides over the destinies of England.*

A Swiss gentleman, who, in the prime of manhood, visits the people's school in which he has received his earliest training, has his heart filled with gratitude and pride, that his country possesses such institutions, and he anticipates with joyous confidence her future destinies.†

The annual outlay of Switzerland, in respect of education, on a population, in 1844, of 2,320,000 inhabitants, was 2,506,175 francs‡, which is 1 franc, 6 centimes, or $10\frac{1}{2}$*d.* per head on the population. No doubt this is a considerable

* See above, p. 29. and Dr. Lyon Playfair's Report on the Sanatory Condition of Large Towns in Lancashire, at p. 70, of the Appendix to Second Report of Commissioners of Inquiry into the State of Large Towns and Populous Districts. Dr. Playfair's, or rather Mr. Clay's tables, show that in the whole of a gaol population of the year 1844, "about 40 *per cent.* of the prisoners were ignorant of the Sovereign's name;" and their civil ignorance was equalled by their religious, for "about 40 *per cent.* of the prisoners were unacquainted with the Saviour's name." Ib. p. 71. What, for such poor creatures, is the blessing of life itself?

† Franscini's words, on such an occasion, are, "Usciva egli profundamente commosso di quelle scuole, e in una superbo delle istituzioni del suo paese, e pieno di liete speranze per l'avvenire della patria." — *Statistica della Svizzera* tom. i. p. 217.

‡ This sum does not by any means include all the sums annually appropriated to educational purposes in Switzerland: it leaves out of consideration, the foundations for educational purposes, which, in several cantons, are administered by ecclesiastics, and the rich endowment of the college of the Jesuits, in the canton of Freiburg.

charge, — one which, if we make allowance for the difference of prices and manners in Switzerland and England, would not probably be exceeded by a charge of 2*s.* 6*d.* or 3*s.* per head on the population with us, but one which does much towards making it sure that the outlay on crime and pauperism will be reduced within the narrowest possible limits.

The Swiss cantons spend annually, in this public provision for ensuring the education of every citizen, about twice as much as it costs them to repress crime and to relieve pauperism. Well may the patriotism of every citizen of Switzerland become more fervent, when he contemplates so great and successful an effort of his country, by enlarging the sphere of education, to ameliorate the condition of each successive generation of her citizens.

It appears, therefore, that it is not only among our own kith and kin, across the Atlantic, that a people, jealous of their freedom, and fully alive to the advantage of local government, can make a great pecuniary sacrifice for the purpose of ensuring a competent amount of education to every citizen; but we also find a similar example for our instruction and imitation, among the hardy, frugal, and industrious sons of freedom in Switzerland; and even in the great monarchies of Europe, among subjects of an absolute Emperor, or a little less absolute King, great exertions have of late years been made, to ensure the general education of the people. It is only in aristocratical England that the education of the people has been wholly neglected by their rulers. Here is the land where generation after generation has been allowed to pass away, each equally ignorant and degraded with that which preceded it; and has lived and died, destitute alike of physical comfort and moral training, elevated but little above the quadruped companions of their daily toil.

Mr. Porter, in a temperate and able article, contained in his work on the "Progress of the Nation,"* mentions how totally the rulers of England have neglected the education of the people. After laying down that it is the duty of government to provide for the security of all, by seeing that its sub-

* Porter, *Progress of the Nation*, p. 684. ed. 1851.

jects are taught their duty, as men and as citizens, Mr. Porter adds: "Lessons to this end have indeed been taught by the government of England, but to whom have they been imparted, and by what agency have they been enforced? To be adopted as a scholar a man must—at least up to a comparatively recent period—have qualified himself to appear as a criminal at the bar of justice, and his chief schoolmaster would have been—the hangman! If one tithe of the expense that has been incurred, to so little purpose, during the present century, in punishing criminals, had been employed in preventing crime, by means of education, what a different country would England have been to that which our own criminal records show it to have been!"

Down to our own time, no inconsiderable part of the upper classes has harboured a rooted distrust, which seems, happily, now to be disappearing, of any plan for the education of the people; and many a time has it been asked, among those who are deemed exclusively to constitute "society," and beyond whose sphere nothing but a wide world of nobodies exists, What can be the possible use of education to a mere labourer? Even a merchant in a seaport town has been found to participate in this feeling of those who are above him in our social scale; and could gravely assure a poor law commissioner, a few years ago, not only that an agricultural labourer was very little above a brute, which might, perhaps, have been conceded, but that, "to educate him, would merely have the effect of rendering him dissatisfied with his situation in life."* When the Government, in 1839, first had the courage to constitute, by Order in Council, a Board of Education, the unwillingness pervading the great body of the ruling class of this country, to elevate the people from their state of ignorance, was such, that, even in the House of Commons, the Government had only a majority of 275 to 273 votes in support of the Order which they had issued. So hard a matter was it to take the first step towards providing, at all, for the education of the people, and to apply a paltry sum of 30,000*l.*

* Mr. Twistleton, in the Seventh Annual Report of the Poor Law Commissioners, p. 211.: cited by Mr. Porter, *Progress of the Nation*, p. 694.

for that purpose! And yet there was no lack of money in the country; and, at the same time, larger sums were easily given towards objects of comparatively trifling importance. When the Order had been made by the Government, (and notwithstanding the favourable vote of the people's House,) the more exclusively aristocratical branch of the legislature, on the motion of an archbishop, supported by the speeches of two bishops, of the Church of England, at once carried an address to the foot of the throne, praying that the Order in Council might be rescinded! But, although ecclesiastical intolerance was thus placed in the van of the aristocratical force opposed to the Government, and rendered the hostility of that force still more formidable and dangerous, yet the Government was firm enough to persevere in its honourable career. The sphere of action, created by the first Order in Council, has since been gradually enlarged; but is now found to be, in its very nature, wholly inadequate to the necessities of the country.

Illegitimate births among the poor may be compared, as another indication of the moral condition of these agricultural and manufacturing districts respectively. Tables in the Appendix to this chapter show, that, on the average of three years, 1849, 1850, and 1851, the number of poor relieved in the workhouses of our ten agricultural counties, on the 1st day of January, was 28,355, among whom 2601 were illegitimate children. The illegitimate children so relieved are, therefore, in the agricultural counties, 1 in $10\frac{1}{2}$ of the whole number of chargeable paupers. In the manufacturing district, the corresponding total of paupers relieved was 13,687, of whom 741 only, or 1 in $19\frac{4}{5}$, were illegitimate. The proportion of illegitimate births among the poor who receive parish relief is, therefore, nearly twice as great in the agricultural as in the manufacturing districts.

But the proportion of illegitimate to legitimate births, if we take all classes of society into account, is lower in these agricultural counties than it is in the manufacturing; and it is not very much higher in these ten agricultural counties than the general average for all England. Notwithstanding the large number of persons belonging to the class of paupers in the agricultural counties, and the excess of such births among that class, it still appears that if the whole number of illegitimate births be looked at, the agricultural counties are not very much worse, in this respect, than the average of the whole country. This result, which will be apparent from a subjoined table*, might, perhaps, have been expected: and makes some, at least, of the social effects of the agricultural pauperism the more manifest and glaring.

The causes of an excess of illegitimate births, among births in populous manufacturing counties, are, perhaps, sufficiently obvious. Such causes are abundantly pointed out and exemplified by M. Villermé, in his "Picture of the Physical and Moral Condition of the Workmen employed in the Cotton, Woollen, and Silk Manufacture;"† and M. Moreau de Jonnès, in his excellent little book, "Eléments de Statistique,"‡ has given our three counties of Lancaster, Stafford, and the West Riding, as exhibiting the contrast between manufacturing and agricultural districts, in respect of the proportion of illegitimate births.

In other countries the region of agriculture is almost exempt from this scourge of capital cities and of great and populous towns, whether manufacturing or commercial. Throughout many of the provinces of the Austrian monarchy, the proportion of illegitimate births diminishes, just as the rural and agricultural elements of society increase. Lower Austria contains the great imperial city, Vienna, and, therefore, stands on a "bad eminence," and heads the list with a

* See Appendix.

† Villermé, *Tableau de l'Etat Physique et Moral des Ouvriers employés dans les Manufactures de Coton, de Laine, et de Soie.*

‡ *Eléments de Statistique*, ch. x. p. 258. Here he states, as one of the causes of illegitimate births, "Le rapprochement intime ou la promiscuité que produisent forcément, entre les deux sexes, les travaux des manufactures." He subjoins, as a proof, a short table of illegitimate births in England.

In Manufacturing Counties.		In Agricultural Counties.	
Lancaster - - -	1 in 13	Bedford - - -	1 in 30
Stafford - - -	1 „ 17	Hertford - - -	1 „ 28
York, W. R. - -	1 „ 18	Cornwall - - -	1 „ 32

fearful proportion of more than one illegitimate to three legitimate births.*

Countries.	The Illegitimate are to the Legitimate Births in the proportion of 1 to
Lower Austria - - -	2·8
Upper Austria - - -	4·4
Bohemia - - - -	5·4
Moravia and Silesia - - -	6·2
Kuestenland - - - -	14·7
Tirol - - - - -	22·6

In France, also, it is mainly in towns that illegitimate births occur. The country there is comparatively free from this great social evil. The proportion of illegitimate births to the whole population is, in the towns, 1 for 161 inhabitants; and, in the country, 1 for 870 inhabitants.† In Sweden, the pro-

* The table is calculated to one place of decimals only; it is found in the official "Tafeln zur Statistik der Oesterreichischen Monarchie, für die Jahre 1845 und 1846." Wien, 1850.

† The legitimate and illegitimate births in France, in 1846, were as follows:

	Legitimate.	Illegitimate.	Total.
Country - - -	781,841	34,410	816,251
Town - - -	131,999	35,223	167,222
France - - -	913,840	69,633	983,473

See Moreau de Jonnès, *Annuaire de l'Economie Politique, &c. pour* 1849.

The following table is for 1846, in England, and for 1845 in Austria:

	Legitimate.	Illegitimate.	Total.
England - - -	534,096	38,529	572,625
Austria (excluding Lombardy, Venice, Hungary, Transylvania, and the military frontier) -	594,476	97,280	691,756

These figures, for Austria, are taken from the official "Tafeln zur Statistik der Oesterreichischen Monarchie," published at Vienna in 1850.

portion of illegitimate births is three times as great in towns as in the country; and, in the Netherlands, the difference in the proportion, in favour of the country district, is nearly as great.*

In Lancashire, Staffordshire, and the West Riding of Yorkshire, not only is there this necessary preponderance of the town element of society; but such causes of illegitimate births as arise from the exercise of manufacturing industry, on the grand scale, are also in full operation.

Some of the causes of this excessive immorality of the pauper class in our agricultural counties will, probably, be fully explained, when we see what has been the effect of the law of settlement and removal on the cottage accommodation of the poor in the agricultural districts of England.

Additional historical causes of a low standard of female virtue may, perhaps, be found in the injurious influences of the bastardy law, which, with a little occasional mitigation or change, has been in force in this country from the reign of Queen Elizabeth to that of Queen Victoria. Those injurious influences will probably have been the more deeply felt in the more pauperised districts. Greatly, indeed, is it to be deplored that, throughout this agricultural district, such should be the condition and character of women, among a numerous class, in the society of the Anglo-Saxon race; among descendants of a people, with whom the domestic hearth was something sacred, and who based every legal right on the family relations; with whom, as with their

If London be compared with Paris, or rather the metropolitan district with the department of the Seine, there is obtained:

	Total of Births in 1844.	Of which Total the Illegitimate were	Proportion of Births.	
			Legitimate.	Illegitimate.
Metropolitan District -	60,240	1,925	96·80	3·20
Department of the Seine	40,005	11,527	59·30	40·70

See the Registrar General's Sixth Annual Report.

* Moreau de Jonnès, *Eléments de Statistique*, p. 258.

kindred races, the only crime that virtue could not forgive, was want of chastity*; with whom, even freedom itself was forfeited by unchasteness†, and whose women could, one and all, submit to death rather than to dishonour.‡

A proverb used by our kinsmen in Germany, shows that the feeling entertained respecting the value of female chastity, by the forefathers of the German race, still prevails among their descendants.§

Another painful characteristic of the pauper classes of England is, the enormous amount of insanity and idiocy which is found to exist among them. The proportion of insane persons and idiots to the whole population in the favoured region of agricultural industry is truly frightful.

That the physical suffering of the poor exceeds that of the other classes of society will be admitted; and physical suffering is a most powerful agent in producing disease of the brain and insanity. It is the poor, likewise, who are peculiarly exposed to the operation of some, at least, of the moral causes of insanity.

Poverty alone directly produces a very large proportion of the whole number of cases of insanity which occur among the

* Tacitus, *Germania,* xix. "Septâ pudicitiâ agunt—publicatæ pudicitiæ nulla venia; non forma, non ætate, non opibus maritum invenerit—plusque ibi boni mores quam alibi bonæ leges, valent."

† J Grimm, *Deutsche Rechts Alterthümer*, p. 329. "Richilda, quæ libertatem suam *fornicando* polluit, amisit . . . filiæ illorum *liberæ* permaneant . . nisi forte *adulterior* vel *fornicatione* polluantur." Here, in England, our old Anglo-Saxon laws provided, among other things, on this subject, that any man having illicit intercourse, should forfeit communion with the Church, and that foreigners, for such misconduct, should depart from the land, "with their goods, and with their sins." Laws of Wihtraed, 3, 4. Thorpe, vol. i. p. 39.

‡ All the women who had shared in the danger of the great battle, and became captives on the defeat of the Cimbrians, by Marius, sought of the conqueror, to have their chastity respected, and to be assigned as serfs, to the Vestal Virgins: on the rejection of their petition, they all put themselves to death. Orosius v. 16., Florus, iii. 3., and Valerius Maximus.

§ "Wer wissentlich eine Geschändete nimmt, ist entweder ein Schelm, oder will einer werden." See Hertius, *De Paræmiis Juriis,* i. 12. (in his Opuscula, vol. ii. p. 273.) A curious Academical Dissertation was published in the year 1717, entitled "Dissertatio Juridica qua Doctrina Vulgaris Maiorem a Feminis, quam a Viris, requirens castitatem, sub examen reuocatur."

indigent poor. The fatal link between poverty and insanity, was noticed long ago, and by no less profound an observer of all causes of human happiness and misery, than Shakspeare: "My lord, this is a poor *mad* soul: she hath been in good case; and the truth is, *poverty* hath distracted her."* A greater number of the inmates of the county asylums, at Wakefield, in the West Riding of Yorkshire, and at Hanwell, in Middlesex, says Sir William Ellis†, are sent there from distressed circumstances, than from any other moral cause. "These cases generally occur amongst married persons. Parents, in addition to their own personal sufferings, from want of the common necessaries of life, are continually enduring the most painful anxiety, from seeing their children, who look up to them for support, undergoing the same privations, without being able to afford them any relief. It is a lamentable fact, that the most frequent instances of insanity, from this cause, are amongst the honest and industrious. A poor man, who has been in the habit of maintaining his family in respectability, has been, from depression in trade or some untoward circumstances, thrown out of employment, or not able, with his utmost exertions, to earn what has been sufficient for the bare sustenance of his wife and children. He has been unwilling to apply to the parish for assistance; or, when driven there by absolute necessity, has received such a scanty pittance from a harsh and unfeeling overseer, as barely to enable him to drag on a miserable existence with a body emaciated from want. The brain, participating in this general weakness, is no longer able to endure the high state of action into which it is thrown by anxiety, without having its functions injured." It appears that exposure to cold, which, in most constitutions, produces inflammation of the lungs, or rheumatism, is, not unfrequently, the immediate cause of insanity, in those who have a great predisposition to disease of the brain. "Much of the insanity amongst the

* Shakspeare's *King Henry IV.*, part ii. act ii. sc. 1.

† *A Treatise on the Nature, Symptoms, Causes, and Treatment of Insanity*, by Sir W. C. Ellis, M.D. 8vo. London, 1838.

agricultural labourers," adds the same author, "is to be traced to their exposure to cold, and to the vicissitudes of the weather, combined with their poverty and their indifferent diet. Not only do we find that the exposure to partial cold, and checked perspiration, are causes of insanity, but such a sympathy seems to exist between the brain and the skin, that, in some individuals, when a cutaneous eruption has been repelled, a seton or an issue dried up, or an old ulcer healed too rapidly, the disease has been transferred to that organ, and has produced insanity in some cases, paralysis in others." "This state of poverty, too, is not only a source from which the disease first originates, but it very frequently is the cause of relapses. Removal from the scenes of misery which have been so painfully felt, and occupying the mind with other objects, aided by the influence of good diet, have often produced very salutary effects in a short time, and ultimately restored the patients to sanity. A return to the poverty which they had left, has, however, in many instances, brought on fresh attacks almost immediately."

The number of insane and idiot paupers in these agricultural and manufacturing counties respectively will be found in the Appendix to this chapter. On the 1st January, 1847, the whole number in England and Wales was 18,065, or 1 in 880 on the population of 15,906,741; in the manufacturing counties the number was only 2717, or 1 in 1112 on the population of 3,031,699; while on the same day, in the ten agricultural counties, the number was actually 3107 on a population of 2,330,944, or 1 in 740; a proportion far above the average of all England, and exceeding that of the manufacturing counties by nearly 50 per cent.

What a picture is this of the social condition of a wealthy agricultural region, unrivalled in its fertility!

In florid beauty groves and fields appear,
Man seems the only growth that dwindles here!

Again, it will be found, there is a striking contrast between the labouring agriculturist in England and in France. In the latter country, in the year 1844, the whole number of the insane poor, out of a population of 35,401,761, was 12,286.* The six departments of the Seine, Seine Inférieure, Bouches du Rhône, Rhône, Nord and Calvados (including, as they do, not only Paris and its neighbourhood, but the chief districts of manufacturing and commercial industry), with a dense population of 4,714,703 inhabitants, supply no less than 4124, or nearly one-third of the whole number of the 12,286 insane poor of all France; in the remaining departments of agricultural industry, with their 30,687,058 inhabitants, are found only 8162, as the corresponding number of their insane poor.† In the region of great cities and commerce, the insane are, therefore, nearly as 1 in 1000, while in a like region in England, they are only 1 in 1112. But in the fields of agriculture in France, the insane poor are no more than 1 in 3759, while our corresponding English proportion is 1 in 740. It follows, therefore, that a great commercial district with us, suffers less from insanity, than a like district of France; but the proportion of our agricultural population, as subjected to this greatest of all human sufferings, is five times as great as that of the agricultural population of France. And yet the physical organization of the human race is much the same in France, as it is in England; and the aspect of nature, cultivated by the hand of man here, is, at least, as pleasing to look on as it is across the Channel.

It is impossible not to see, or fear, that the unequal distribution of landed property, the progressive extinction of the class of small proprietors, the creation of a vast proletarian population, and the neglect of the State to make public provision for the education of all members of the community, as well as the law of settlement of the poor, may have been connected with the development of pauperism, and the other social evils which are so rife in the agricultural districts of England.

* Of this number 10,621 were lodged in public establishments: in "asiles publics" 6060, and in "quartiers des les hospices" 4621; and only 1605 in private houses.

† See table in Appendix; it is founded on figures which have the stamp of official authority, and are to be found in the *Annuare du Bureau des Longitudes for* 1851, and De Watteville, *Établissements de Bienfaisance.*

It must be owned that most of the land throughout these ten agricultural counties is the property of a small number of proprietors, and is cultivated by farmers, each of whom occupies a large holding. In these "happy fields" there are nearly nine agricultural labourers for every occupier of land*, and "la grande propriété," throughout the whole district, seeks to obtain for itself all the pecuniary benefit which can be derived from "la grande culture." These most pauperised regions of the land are unquestionably those in respect of which it may be said that the consolidation of farms here, just like the establishment of great manufactories elsewhere, indicates an improvement in the economy of labour; that, in the country of great farms, with a given amount of labour, a larger quantity of food and other commodities is now brought to market than formerly: and that such economy of labour somewhat lessens the cost of production. Be it so. "And let the economy of labour be valued at what it is worth; but "let us not omit to inquire at the same time, whether other and higher considerations are not involved in the question."†

Perhaps it is of little use to look at the condition of the labouring classes in other countries, with a view to judging of our own. In France, Belgium, and Switzerland, and in many other parts of Europe, the peasant proprietor largely occupies the place of our labourer as a tiller of the soil. In the vast agricultural region of France, our miserable proletarian class can hardly be said to exist; for the length and breadth of the land is cultivated by its four millions of proprietors, aided by their families. More self-respect, more prudence, later marriages, and a very slow increase of population, are there the characteristics of that great change in their social condition, which was effected some sixty years ago;

* See the Occupation Abstract of the census of 1831. Much fuller information than has heretofore been given, respecting the occupation of land in England, and other relations of the land to those who live on it, is to be expected from the able hands to which the returns of the census of 1851 are confided.

† See Mr. Barton's essay, *On the Influence of the Subdivision of the Soil on the Moral and Physical Well-being of the People of England and Wales*, published in the "Journal of the Statistical Society of London," March, 1850.

and, with trifling exceptions, it may be said, that, throughout France, it is only in *towns* that it has been found necessary to organise any substantial administration of public relief to the poor.

The result of an inquiry into the condition of the labouring classes, and the provision for the relief of the poor in Holland and Belgium, instituted by direction of the English Government in 1838, threw additional light on the condition of peasant proprietors and occupiers of small farms.

The various duties cast on the small cultivators call for the constant exercise of industry, skill, and foresight; "and to these qualities," says Mr. Nicholls *, "they add a rigid economy, habitual sobriety, and a contented spirit, which finds its chief gratification beneath the domestic roof, from which the father of the family rarely wanders in search of excitement abroad. It was most gratifying to observe the comfort displayed in the whole economy of the households of these small cultivators, and the respectability in which they lived. As far as I could learn, there is no tendency to the subdivision of the small holdings." Mr. Senior also, in his able and compendious survey of the provision for the poor, and of the condition of the labouring classes †, points out the striking contrast between the economical situation of the labouring population in England and in most other countries of Europe in which the English principle of acknowledging a right in every person to support at the public expense has been adopted. While, with us, the class of labourers without property, as Mr. Senior justly observes, constitutes the bulk of English society, it forms the small minority of that of the North of Europe. After pointing out that a very large portion of the whole labouring population in Norway, Denmark, Schleswig-Holstein, Sweden, Wurtemburg and Bavaria, consists of landowners, Mr. Senior concludes (p. 87.), "It is probable, therefore, that the class of persons who, in the

* Third Report of G. Nicholls, Esq., containing the Result of Enquiries, &c. dated 5th May, 1838, p. 167.

† Senior, *Statement of the Provision for the Poor and of the Condition of the Labouring Classes in a considerable Portion of America and Europe.* London, 1835.

North of Europe and Germany, would be exposed to the temptation of applying for public relief, if it were granted on the same terms as in England, would be a small minority, and would be, perhaps, a seventh or a fifth, or at most a third, instead of three-fourths, or even a larger proportion of the whole community."

M. Chateauvieux, in his valuable paper communicated to the Commissioners of Inquiry into the poor law in 1833, points out very forcibly the wide difference in the condition of the French agricultural labourer, generally a proprietor of land, and that miserable class of men in England.*

The late Dr. Channing also seems to have looked on our plutocratical institutions as the cause of much of the social evil of our present condition. In his "Duty of Free States" he dwells largely on the deep-seated evils of English pauperism. "To a man who looks with sympathy and brotherly regard on the mass of the people, who is chiefly interested in the 'lower classes,' England must present much which is repulsive. The condition of the lower orders at the present moment is a mournful commentary on English institutions and civilisation. The multitude are depressed in that country to a degree of ignorance, want, and misery, that must touch every heart not made of stone. In the civilised world there are few sadder spectacles than the contrast now presented in Great Britain, of unbounded wealth and luxury with the starvation of thousands and ten thousands, crowded into cellars and dens without ventilation or light, compared with which the wigwam of the Indian is a palace. Misery, famine, brutal degradation in the neighbourhood and presence of stately mansions, which ring with gaiety and dazzle with pomp and unbounded profusion, shock us as no other wretchedness does; and this is not an accidental, but an almost necessary, effect of the spirit of aristocracy and the spirit of trade acting intensely together. It is a striking fact that the private charity of England, though almost incredible, makes little impression on this mass of misery; thus teaching the rich and titled to

* F. L. de Chateauvieux, *Recherches sur la Situation Comparative des Pauvres en France et en Angleterre.* Foreign Communications, p. 21. F.

be 'just before being generous,' and not to look to private munificence as a remedy for the evils of selfish institutions."

Nothing certainly can be more utterly desperate than the condition of the English agricultural labourer: to him, "hope never comes, that comes to all." Mr. Twisleton, an Assistant Poor Law Commissioner, says of him, "Even if he has transcendant abilities, he has scarcely any prospect of rising in the world, and of becoming a small farmer. He commences his career as a weekly labourer, and the probability is, whatever may be his talents and industry, that as a weekly labourer he will end his days. If he cherishes the ambition of becoming a small farmer, his wisest course is to emigrate to Canada or New South Wales, or some other of the colonies, where alone he can put forth his energies, for the attainment of that object, with a reasonable prospect of success." *

The writer of an able article in a leading periodical, hopeful enough in his view of the condition and prospects of the rest of our society, admits and deplores the distressed and impoverished condition of the agricultural labourer over many parts of England; and justly looks upon this feature in our social state "with almost more anxiety than any other," because "an air of wretchedness and of inability to rise would here appear to be a characteristic of a whole section of our population."†

There is an utter want of all provision for a rainy day among the whole of this unhappy class of our community; they live literally from hand to mouth; their immediate and general recurrence to the poor-rate equally arises with a season of drought in the summer and with one of frost in the winter. On the 1st May, 1845, the Poor Law Commissioners state, "The year since the 1st May, 1844, has, on the whole, been favourable to the poorer classes of this country. In the manufacturing districts, the demand for labour has been extensive and constant; and even the iron and coal districts, which were the last to recover from the general depression, were prosperous during the last twelve months. The drought

* Sanitary Inquiry, England, "Local Reports," 1842, p. 142.

† Edinburgh Review, vol. xciii. p. 323.

of last summer, and the length and severity of the cold during the last winter, were unfavourable to the employment of agricultural labourers; but we rejoice to say, that the number of rural unions in which difficulty arose from the applications of unemployed able-bodied men, was not considerable."* Though the difficulty alluded to was not considerable, and though the relief of the poor throughout England and Wales for the parochial year, 1845, scarcely differed from that of the previous year, yet there was a wide contrast in the effects of the excessive heat and cold on the working classes of the manufacturing and the agricultural counties. A table containing six manufacturing and twelve agricultural counties, published in the Twelfth Annual Report of the Poor Law Commissioners, exhibits some of the results of the season, 1844–5.

The decrease in expenditure, for the second year, in the manufacturing counties, varies from 5 to 12½ per cent., and the corresponding *increase*, in the agricultural counties, was just as great.

The Poor Law Commissioners observe†, "It will be perceived, upon an inspection of this table, that the diminution has chiefly occurred in the manufacturing, and the increase in the agricultural districts. Thus, whilst in the West Riding of York, an important seat of manufacture, there was a decrease of 11 per cent., in the East Riding, which is purely agricultural, there was an increase of 1 per cent. This difference was mainly owing to the fact stated in our last Annual Report (par. 23.), that whereas the demand for labour in the manufacturing districts was extensive and constant during the parochial year, 1845, an interruption in the employment of the agricultural labourers was caused by the drought in the summer of 1844, and the length and severity of the cold during the winter of 1844–5."

A subjoined table‡ exhibits the contrast between the parochial years 1844 and 1845 in our ten agricultural counties, and

* Eleventh Annual Report of the Poor Law Commissioners, 1845, p. 9.

† Twelfth Annual Report of the Poor Law Commissioners, 1846, p. 2.

‡ See Appendix.

shows the effect produced there, under the influence of these alternations of excessive heat in the summer, and cold in the winter, in the latter year. It is distressing to see how soon the wretched agricultural labourer is withered up by the drought, and frozen by the cold.

Assuming that the laws preventing the alienation and division of real property, have had some share in inflicting on England the evils of its existing pauperism, there is no doubt on my mind, and I think it may be shown to demonstration, that all those evils have been greatly aggravated by the law of settlement and removal of the poor, and will be greatly mitigated by the repeal of that law.

My reader has now before him the whole of a very imperfect sketch of the pauperism of England, as it exists in the middle of the nineteenth century, and of some of the causes by which it has been produced.

CHAP. IV.

ECCLESIASTICAL PROVISION FOR THE POOR TILL THE REFORMATION.

Est dives, inquit, non nego,
Habetque nostra Ecclesia
Opumque et auri plurimum,
Nec quisquam in orbe est ditior—
Ventum ad sacratam januam:
Stabant catervæ pauperum,
Inculta visu examina:
Fragor rogantum tollitur. PRUDENTIUS.

AMONG the many great changes, which the spread of Christianity, introduced into the manners and laws of the Roman world, that which concerned the relief and support of the poor, holds a prominent place. What is now emphatically called Christian charity, man's love of his neighbour, may be said to have been unknown, in ancient Rome, until Christianity became, under Constantine, the avowed public religion of the State. The light so long shining in darkness, that at first comprehended it not, at length enabled men to see the deformity of some parts of that system of law and manners, which prevailed. Scarcely had Constantine assumed the imperial purple, when he issued the first of a series of legislative provisions, destined soon to form the poor law of the empire.*

* The earliest poor law of ancient Rome may be said to have been the *lex frumentaria* of the younger Gracchus, which lasted much longer than the agrarian law of Tiberius Gracchus, but, as it seems, was ultimately repealed, and a more limited provision made, by a law of M. Octavius, passed A. U. C. 687. Great abuses, however, crept into the administration of this latter law, as is likely to be the case with any *national* provision, and as was found to occur, on a grand scale, under our own frumentarian law, passed a few years ago, for the relief of starving Ireland, and in the *ateliers nationaux* of 1848, in Paris. It is only after the accession of Constantine that the provision for the relief of the poor, at Rome, becomes fit for comparison with modern legislation on the subject. The previous Roman poor law had merely ensured rations of food to *idle citizens*, who looked down on all industrial pursuits, and left them to be followed by slaves.

This duty of providing and administering relief for the poor, was, in the first instance, undertaken by the Christian State; but was soon transferred to the Church; and the very ample endowment of the clergy seems, to a great extent, to have been bestowed for the purpose of enabling them to perform this primary and paramount duty. The administration of relief to the poor, which, at first, had been superintended by the civil officers of the State, was now placed wholly in the hands of bishops and priests. In this transfer is to be found one of many sources of that immense wealth, which, in the course of a few centuries, the clergy accumulated throughout both the Eastern and the Western Empire; and in this source, too, appears also to be found the chief origin of that payment of tithes which, after being received for a few centuries, by the clergy, as a gift, was ultimately converted into a legal burden on the laity; and which, at one period, was claimed not only in respect of land, but of the annual income derived from every art, trade, or profession, that man or woman could exercise. *

From the age of Constantine, we find an organisation of public charity, in which Church and State united their efforts, to provide for pauperism; hospitals, poor-houses, orphan-houses, and other similar establishments, were erected, and richly endowed, in all the chief cities of the empire, and the

* "De militia, de negotio, de artificio redde decimas," were the words of St. Augustine (see below, p. 143.); and, according to Fra Paolo, in his Treatise delle Materie Beneficiarie, the Canonists say that the beggar is bound to pay tithe of all that he receives: "e che la meretrice è tenuta a pagar la decima del guadagno meretricio!" So much for clerical aggression, as manifested by the Canonists. The attempt of the clerical titheowner to tax mere income, was never generally allowed. A somewhat similar claim has been brought forward in the middle of the nineteenth century, on behalf of the lay landowners, for whom it is sought now, in England, to throw the burden of maintaining their poor from off their own shoulders. Impotent and miserable is this endeavour, to convert local poor-rates into a general burden; and by imposing a new tax on the industry of the producing classes of the community, to keep up, on a level with war prices, the rental of landowners. Such a scheme for relieving landowners from the burden of pauperism (to whatever extent the proposed change of system might increase the absolute amount of that burden), needs no refutation or comment. Its advocates have chosen their position.

"Non ragionam di lor, ma guarda e passa!"

clergy everywhere became overseers and relieving officers of the poor.

To write the history of the poor, to give an account of the mode of their support, for about a thousand years after the establishment, under Constantine, of Christianity, as the public religion of the State, would be little less than to write a continuous chapter in the history of the Church itself. Such a chapter would show how constantly it was deemed to be the duty, and was the practice of the Church, to administer all the relief, that was administered to the destitute poor during this long period.

An attempt will be made to state some of the more prominent facts of this history, in itself highly interesting to the student, both of ecclesiastical and legal antiquities: and the attempt, it is thought, will also serve to give a clearer idea of the principle which lies at the basis of all our pauper legislation.*

The two constitutions of Constantine, with which the imperial legislation on this subject commences, are contained in a title of the Theodosian Code, "De alimentis quæ inopes parentes de publico petere debent." They are deserving of consideration. The first, promulgated A. D. 315, relates to Italy; the second, promulgated seven years later, relates to Africa. Shortly before the issuing of each law, calamities, likely to have produced much poverty and distress in those respective regions, had occurred. The prevalence of unusual destitution and suffering in Ireland a few years ago, facilitated, if it did not cause, the adoption of a poor law for that country. Similar destitution and suffering, caused or aggravated by bad harvests and a high price of corn, led to great changes in the poor law of England, first under Charles II., in 1662, and, afterwards, under George III., in 1795.

The first of these imperial provisions was limited to the

* The familiar provision of the statute of Elizabeth, under which, in England, churchwardens are, by virtue of their office, overseers of the poor of the ecclesiastical district, the parish, and the common application of statutory penalties to the relief of the poor, are existing effects of this principle.

case of parents whose children were a burden to them. In the downward progress of the Empire, indigence, which became very general, and often made it difficult, and sometimes impossible, for the parent to support his child, had led to the continuance of that practice of infanticide, which, before the spread of Christianity, so largely prevailed in the ancient world. * The State now provided food and clothing for the child, which its parent was unable to bring up.†

An absolute state provision was thus made, for saving the life, and ensuring the maintenance, of every poor and helpless infant, that, but for the humanity of the law, would, in the then degradation and pauperism of the proletarian class, have been put to death, or exposed on the soil of a wealthy territorial aristocracy. The learned Gothofredus reminds his reader that the practice against which provision was then made, is earnestly denounced by Christian writers, especially by Tertullian; and appropriately adds, that Lactantius, the preceptor of the heir-apparent to the empire, was inscribing to Constantine, at the very time of the publication of this law, the work which has come down to us. In the sixth book of that work, we find a passage deserving of being compared with the very words of the Emperor. ‡

* Perhaps the infanticide which so long prevailed in ancient Rome was in the mind of the poet when he described the voice and cry which first attracted the attention of Æneas on his descent into the pagan Orcus:

"Continuo auditæ voces, vagitus et ingens,
Infantumque animæ flentes in limine primo,
Quos dulcis vitæ exsortes, et ab ubere raptos,
Abstulit atra dies, et funere mersit acerbo."

† Cod. Theod. xi. 27. 1. "Per omnes civitates Italiæ proponatur lex, quæ parentum manus a parricidio arceat, votumque vertat in melius—ut si quis parens adferat subolem, quam pro paupertate educare non possit, nec in alimentis, nec in veste inpertienda tardetur, cum educatio nascentis infantis moras ferre non possit: *ad quam rem et fiscum nostrum et rem privatam indiscreta jussimus præbere obsequia.*"

‡ Lactantius, Div. Inst. vi. 20. "Ergo, inquit, ne illud quidem concedi aliquis existimet, ut recens natos liceat *oblidere*, quæ vel maxima est impietas.—Non possunt innocentes existimari, qui viscera sua in prædam canibus objiciunt, et quantum in ipsis est, crudelius necant, quam si strangulassent.—Tam igitur nefarium est exponere quam necare. At enim *Parricidæ* facultatum augustias

In the year 322, the same Emperor extended his benevolent solicitude to the cause of children of more mature age, and provided, for such as were in danger of being sold by their parents, that those who had no property, and could not support their children, should receive, from the local authorities, such an allowance as might be requisite. The Emperor thought it repugnant to Christian morals that any man should be permitted by the State either to die or to commit a crime from starvation.*

It is greatly to be feared that in the present day, in our own country, the practice of infanticide, so justly denounced by the first Christian emperor as repugnant to every Christian principle and feeling, has again, from the degradation and poverty of our poorer classes, become a very prevalent crime. It occurred to me to be engaged as counsel, at the York assizes, a few years ago, in prosecuting a man charged with the murder of his infant child; the only motive for the deed was the prospect of obtaining, on the child's death, a small sum of money from a burial club. The death of two other children, of the same unhappy father, had been previously brought about, probably in a similar way and from a like motive, without any suspicion being excited against him. Within the last few years, similar cases have been the subject of criminal prosecution in other counties. It appears also to be quite clear that, at the present day, the average mortality of such children of the poorer classes, as are members of burial clubs, is decidedly higher than the average mortality of all other children in their neighbourhoods. A mournful proof this of the necessity of some provision in England for imparting the blessings of education to the now wholly uneducated classes of the community, and

conqueruntur, nec se *pluribus liberis educandis sufficere posse* prætendunt, quasi vero aut facultates in potestate sint possidentium, aut non quotidie Deus ex divitibus pauperes, et ex pauperibus divites faciat."

* Cod. Theod. xi. 27. 2. "Universis quos adverterint in egestate miserabili constitutos, *stipem necessariam largiantur:* atque ex horreis substantiam protinus tribuant conpetentem. *Abhorret enim nostris moribus ut quemquam fame confici, vel ad indignum facinus prorumpere, concedamus.*"

for doing something, at the same time, towards improving the physical conditions of their existence.*

The Roman jurisprudence regarded, with some jealousy, the acquisition of property by ecclesiastical and other corporations†; and, in the case of dispositions to take effect after death, it was only the privileged priesthood of certain pre-eminently honoured gods and goddesses, to whom the piety or superstition of a dying man was permitted to make any bequest of his property.‡ As early as the year 321, the Emperor Constantine granted a similar permission in favour of the Church: it could hardly be thought unreasonable to grant to the Christian clergy the same privilege which had been long enjoyed by a considerable class of the heathen priesthood.§ But when the ancient temple of Didymean Apollo, or Ephesian Diana, was now replaced by the church of St. Sebastian, or the Blessed Virgin, the Christian ecclesiastics became mere stewards of their temporal possessions; all of which were intended by the State to be administered in relieving the poor. And if a clergyman, either by the exercise of parsimony, or industry of his own, or by any other provision, became possessed of property,

* Dr. Lyon Playfair's valuable Report on the Sanatory Condition of large Towns in Lancashire, contains ample evidence of the general prevalence of practical infanticide among the large class of children, whose deaths ensure payments from burial clubs. A great part of the present excessive low average of duration of the life of our working classes, is owing to the vast number of deaths, in infancy, which occur among their children. In the town of Liverpool alone upwards of one thousand coffins are provided yearly for the *pauper burials* of young children: see Dr. Playfair's Report, p. 76.; Appendix to Second Report of Commissioners for Inquiry, &c. 1848.

† Diocletian and Maximian, l. 8. C. vi. 24. "Collegium, si nullo speciali privilegio subnixum sit, hereditatem capere non posse, dubium non est."

‡ Ulpian, Fr. Tit. xxi. 86. "Deos heredes instituere non possumus, præter eos, quos senatusconsulto, constitutionibus principum, instituere concessum est: sicuti Jovem Tarpeium, Apollinem Didymæum, Martem in Galliâ, Minervam Iliensem, Herculem Gaditanum, Dianam Ephesiam, Matrem Deorum Sipylensem, quæ Smynæ colitur, et Cælestèm Salinensem Carthaginis."

§ Constantinus, l. i. C. de Sacrosanctis Ecclesiis. "Habeat unus quisque licentiam sanctissimo venerabilique concilio, decedens bonorum quod optaverit relinquere, et non sint cassa judicia ejus." The same law is preserved in the Theodosian Code, xvi. 2. 4., where see the judicious and learned commentations of Gothofredus.

the law expressly required it to be applied *to the use of the poor.**

In the legislation of the Christian emperors, strictly ecclesiastical institutions were soon associated with poor-houses (ptochotrophia, ptochia), hospitals (xenodochia), infirmaries (nosocomia), and orphan-houses (orphanotrophia), as objects of the imperial solicitude; and it appears, by the Code of Justinian, that the charitable provision for the poor, and for orphans, under ecclesiastical management, was invested with the same privileges, as guarded bequests, or endowments, in favour of Holy Church herself.† The immediate government of all such institutions being entrusted to the inferior clergy, the due performance of the resulting duties, which must have been both varied and important, was provided for by the control of the bishop, to whom the administrators of every form of public charity were made accountable by Justinian.‡

The claims of charity, when its administration was thus wholly confided to the ecclesiastical hierarchy, could hardly

* This was established, A.D. 357, by Constantius and Julian: the imperial constitution, addressed to "Felix, Bishop of Rome," is preserved in the Theodosian Code, xvi. 2. 14. "Si quid enim, vel parsimonia, vel provisione, vel mercaturâ, honestati tamen conscia, congesserint (clerici), *in usum pauperum atque egentium ministrari oportet:* aut id quod ex eorundem Ergasteriis, vel Tabernis conquiri potuerit, et colligi, collectum id religionis æstiment lucrum." Another Constitution (l. 10. of the same title) provides, that the clergy should not carry on any gainful *trade:* "Cum *certum sit,* quæstus, quos ex tabernaculis atque ergasteriis colligunt, *pauperibus profuturos.*"

† C. i. 3. De Episcopis et Clericis, l. 35. "Omnibus privilegiis, quæ eadem sancta ecclesia, vel nunc adipiscitur, vel postea merebitur, perpetuo potiri pietatis intuitu decernimus." A constitution of the Emperor Justinian, authorises certain donations to be made in favour of Holy Church, and of poor-houses, orphan-houses, foundling hospitals, infirmaries, and the indigent poor, without the observance of those legal forms which were needed in other cases. Cod. i. 2. De Sacrosanctis Ecclesiis xix. "Vel in sanctam ecclesiam, vel in *xenodochium,* vel in *nosocomium,* vel in *orphanotrophium,* vel in *ptochotrophium,* vel in *gerontocorinium,* vel in *brephotrophium,* vel in *ipsos pauperes.*"

‡ Justin. Novell. cxxxiv. De Sanctissimis Episcopis, c. 23. "Œconomos autem, et xenodochos, et nosocomos, et *ptochotrophos,* et *aliorum venerabilium locorum* gubernatores, et *alios* omnes clericos jubemus, pro creditis sibi gubernationibus, apud proprium episcopum, cui subjacent conveniri, et rationem suæ gubernationis facere," &c.

fail to acquire some additional influence on the feelings and liberality of the public; and the Church probably found its power increased in various ways by the great addition to its temporal possessions which this trusteeship soon facilitated. The Novels of Justinian show, that the State was willing to open the door as wide as possible to the influx of wealth into the Church. If any pious testator left all his worldly possessions "to Christ," without designating who, in the world, was to enjoy their temporal proceeds, the imperial legislator provided that the bequest should belong to the church of the testator's place of domicile. But here, again, we are reminded of the condition on which Church property was held, namely, that the proceeds should be distributed among the poor, "ea tamen lege, ut totum illud, quod inde consequatur, *pauperibus eroget.*"

The Emperor Anastasius imposed restrictions on the alienation of real property or income, by churches, monasteries, and the various establishments for the relief of the poor.* These provisions show that such establishments had not only grown up along with the Church, by which they were protected and governed, but had acquired fixed property, sufficient to make them, equally with the Church itself, an object of legislation.

According to the law of the Roman Empire, as it seems to have existed for many centuries after Christianity became the established religion of the State, all fines imposed on the clergy, and even on lay offenders in causes ecclesiastical, were applied exclusively to the relief of the poor. The first occasion which appears to have given rise to the general provision, substituting the poor in the place of the imperial treasury, was that of an appeal by the Bishop Chronopius, under

* Anastasius, C. i. 2. De Sacrosanctis Ecclesiis, xvii. In the case of monasteries, the alienation could not be allowed without the consent of the abbots and the monks; they were to be present (*πάρειναι*); and in the case of the poor-houses, the governor, officials, *and the poor* were to be present, so that that might prevail which pleased the majority, *ὥστε κρατεῖν τὸ τοῖς πλείοσιν ἄρεσκον*, with the consent of the bishop, *συναινοῦντος καὶ τοῦ ἐπισκόπου τῶν τόπων, ἐν οἷς τοῦτα σύνηθές ἐστι γίνεσθαι.*

Valentinian, Valerius, and Gratian, A.D. 369. The bishop failed in his appeal, and was condemned in the ordinary fine; and "Chronopius's case" gave rise to the general law, which is still preserved in the Theodosian Code*, and which was also inserted, in a mutilated form, by Tribonian, in his compilation under Justinian.†

The collection of ecclesiastical constitutions, published by Justellus, contains several Greek texts, which show the prevalence, throughout the Eastern Empire, of this application of fines imposed on the clergy.‡ And the poor appear to have received the proceeds of such fines under barbarian kings in the West of Europe, as well as under the emperors in the East. Athalaric, remitting to ecclesiastical authority the decision of all causes in which a clergyman was concerned, and visiting the contempt of that authority by a heavy penalty, expressly subjoins that the penalty is to be distributed among the poor.§

Enough has been said to give a general notion of the course of the imperial legislation, both in the West and in the East, during many centuries. Let us now turn, for a moment, to the origin of tithes, and see to what extent, according to the language of fathers and councils of the Church, the receipt of tithes by the clergy, was intended, throughout all Christen-

* Codex Theodos. xi. 36. 20. "Quoniam Chronopius, ex Antistite idem fuit in tuo, qui fuerat in Septuaginta Episcoporum ante judicio, et eam sententiam provocatione suspendit, a qua non oportuit provocare, argentariam multam, quam hujusmodi facto sanctio generalis inponit, cogatur expendere. Hoc autem, *non fisco nostro volumus accedere*, sed *his qui indigent* fideliter *erogari*. Quod in hac causa, et ceteris Ecclesiasticis, fiat."

† C. i. 4. (De Episcopali audientia) 2.

‡ Justelli, Bibliotheca Juris Canonici Veteris, tom. ii. p. 1273. Ἐὰν πρὸ τελείας ψήφου κληρικὸς ἐκκαλέσεται, τὴν ὡρισμένην τούτου ποινὴν ὁ φίσκος οὐ λαμβάνει παρ' αὐτοῦ ἀλλὰ τοῖς πένησι διανέμεται: the fisc does not receive the fine from him (the clergyman), but it is distributed to the poor. The other passages are at p. 1270. and p. 1273. of the same volume. They are all indicated by Gothofredus, in his commentary on the text above cited from the Theodosian Code.

§ Cassiodorus, Var. viii. 24. p. 136. "Decem librarum auri dispendio feriatur; quæ a Palatinis Sacrarum Largitionum protinus exactæ, per manus sæpe memorati Antistitis pauperibus erogentur."

dom, to be subservient to the performance of their office of relieving the poor.

Tithe, itself, in its original institution among Christians, appears to have been, not so much a tribute to the clergy, as a charitable offering to the poor. St. Jerome, writing from Palestine to Pope Damasus at Rome, about the year 382, speaks of the possessions of the clergy as belonging wholly to the poor; and shows that tithes and oblations were, in part, appropriated to maintaining hospitals, *xenodochia*. He says, expressly, that such clergymen as cannot support themselves, from property of parents or relations, may be maintained out of the property of the Church; but that those clergymen who are under no such necessity, are guilty of sacrilege, if they consume the substance of the poor, for whom the Church seems to have been considered as a mere trustee.*

Another father of the Church, St. Augustine, more than once makes the clear and undisputed duty of the Church to relieve the poor, the ground of his earnest appeals to the laity to give tithes to the clergy. The misery and starvation of the poor, sure to ensue from any failure in the relief fund, which the Church administered, are sometimes put forward by St. Augustine, as the only ground of his appeal to the laity for the payment of tithe.†

* B. Hieronymus. "Quoniam *quidquid habent clerici, pauperum est*, et domus illorum omnibus debent esse communes; susceptioni peregrinorum, et hospitum invigilare debent; maximé curandum est illis, ut de *decimis, et oblationibus*. Cœnobiis et *Xenodochiis*, qualem voluerint, et potuerint, *sustentationem impendant.* Clericos autem illos convenit Ecclesiæ stipendiis sustentari, quibus parentum, et propinquorum nulla suffragantur. *Qui autem bonis parentum et opibus sustentari possint* si *quod pauperum est* accipiunt, *sacrilegium profecto committunt.*"

† St. Augustine's homily on the subject is referred to, and cited, by Selden, *History of Tythes*, c. iv. s. 4. The saint says: "Decimæ tributa sunt egentium animarum, redde ergo tributa *pauperibus*, offer libamina sacerdotibus;" and he admonishes that if they have no fruit of the earth, they should pay tithe of whatsoever they live by, "de militia de negotio de artificio redde decimas." Again: "Decimæ ex debito requiruntur, et qui eas dare noluerit, res alienas invasit, et quanti *pauperes*, in locis ubi ipse habitat, illo decimas non dante, fame mortui fuerint, tantorum homicidiorum reus, ante tribunal æterni judicis apparebit; quia a domino *pauperibus delegatum* suis usibus reservavit."

Such solicitation by pious fathers, bishops, and priests, urged in the name of the poor, produced its natural effect on the laity.* The demand of the Church, made on behalf of suffering humanity, and in the very words of Holy Scripture, was liberally complied with. Ample funds were henceforward bestowed on the clerical trustees of the poor, and in a little while, even before the end of the sixth century, the true origin of the layman's charitable offering was forgotten, or denied; and the Church took upon itself to claim as a right, what had been a mere gift on the part of the laity. Still, even the very canon which thus claims the tithe as due by ancient custom, and divine right, expressly states the object of the payment to the clergy, which is "for *the use of the poor*, for *the redemption of captives*, and that the clergy may not, by any necessity of labour, be prevented from performing their spiritual ministrations at the lawful hours." †

It was not until the year 779 that the union of "Church and State" was close enough to produce the fruit of a capitulary, by which the State imposed a legal duty of paying tithes to be distributed "per jussionem pontificis," ‡ a phrase

* Other instances of the precepts or practice of the Fathers, in receiving and distributing alms, are found in Erasmus, and in Pascal, *Provinciales*, the 12th letter, "Réfutation des Chicanes des Jésuites sur l'Aumône et sur la Simonie." The passage of Erasmus, De Ratione Concionandi, lib. i. p. 843. (Opp. vol. v. ed. Lugd. Bat. 1704), is as follows: "Insignis ille Evangelista qui dicit: Volo omnes vos esse sicut ego sum; qui toties gloriatur quod manibus suis sibi pararit victum ut gratuito diceret Evangelium, vix ullum reperit imitatorem.—Posterioribus sæculis Episcopi quidam accipiebant quæ offerebantur, sed *ut dispensaturi in subsidium egenorum*, quod sobrio victui superesset. At D. Cyprianus de suo jubet subveniri pauperibus; D. Basilius e propriis facultatibus aluit pauperes. Augustinus ab apostolica libertate minime recessit, nihil sibi ferens obtrudi, nisi quod in communem rerum transire non posset. Quibus porro verbis mendicat a populo? Fratres, non habeo *quod dem pauperibus*, subveniat illis caritas vestra."

† The words of the Canon are: "Unde statuimus et decernimus, ut mos antiquus a fidelibus reparetur, et decimas ecclesiasticis famulantibus ceremoniis populus omnis inferat; quas sacerdotes aut *in pauperum usum*, aut in captivorum redemtionum prærogantes, suis orationibus pacem populo et salutem impetrent. Si quis autem contumax nostris statutis saluberrimis fuerit, a membris ecclesiæ omni tempore separetur."

‡ Capit. a. 779. cap. 7. "De decimis, ut unusquisque decimam donet, atque per jussionem pontificis dispensentur." See Eichhorn, *Deutsche Staats- und Rechtsgeschichte*, vol. i. s. 186.

which, perhaps, indicates a little of clerical as well as of papal aggression.

That during the whole period of middle-age barbarism and oppression, the clergy were *bound* to relieve and provide for the poor, may be satisfactorily established. In the lists of the children of misfortune, whom it was the especial duty and practice of the Church to relieve, the impotent, whether old or young, as well as widows and orphans, formed as large a proportion as they do in the relief lists of our modern poor law. It was the province of the clergy, also, to extend the administration of their charitable funds far beyond the limits within which the reason of modern times justly restricts relief of the poor, when its means are provided from year to year, not from ample endowments of land and tithes, but by constant taxation of almost all the non-pauper classes of the community. Immense sums were frequently applied by the Church to effecting the redemption of "prisoners and captives." Such redemption was expressly enjoined on the clergy by the canons of several councils, and for this purpose it was allowed to pledge even the sacred vessels of the Church.* Charity, in all its forms, was ever one of the leading characteristics of those great and numerous retreats, which the Church, in its ample wealth, possessed in England and throughout Europe, scattered here and there "among the huts of a miserable peasantry, and the castles of a ferocious aristocracy;" and without which society would, for many centuries, have consisted merely "of beasts of burden, and of beasts of prey."†

By the Apostolical Canons, every bishop is to have the management of the pecuniary affairs of the Church, "for when the souls of men are entrusted to him, much more may their moneys be committed to him;" and is, by his priests

* Concil. Aurel. ann. 511. c. 5. Concil. Aquisgran, ann. 816. c. 13. The canon of the Church became a capitulary of the temporal power, and is found in the collection of Baluze. "De sacris vasis Ecclesiæ, quæ in pignus à nonnullis in quibusdam locis dari comperimus, inhibitum est ne deinceps à quoquam fieri præsumatur, *nisi solummodò necessitate redimendorum captivorum compellente.*"

† Macaulay, *History of England*, vol. i. p. 8.

and deacons, to administer relief to those who are destitute; and, so far as is requisite, may also take a portion for his own necessities, and for the purposes of hospitality.* The Council of Antioch, held A. D. 341, seems to show that bishops had proved unfaithful stewards of the fund for the relief of the poor, and the necessity for an official audit of the episcopal accounts, was admitted. Although a bishop was concerned in the abuse, yet the democratical character of the ancient organisation of the Church, did not fail to provide a remedy for such an evil. In more recent times, abuses of a similar character in the administration of funds intended, like those of the Church in ancient times, to relieve the poor, had become general, in this country, in the reign of William and Mary. And as the statute, passed in the year 1691 †, shows that the modern administrators of relief for the poor had misapplied their funds, "chiefly for their own private ends," and proceeds to provide a small measure of redress for a great offence, so the Council of Antioch, in the year 341, provided that in the case of like misapplication, by any bishop, of the then pauper relief fund, "to his private uses," he should render an account to the synod. ‡

The fifth canon of the Council of Orleans, A.D. 511, enumerates, as the objects to which the property of the Church was applied, "the reparation of churches, the maintenance of the clergy *and the poor*, and the redemption of captives." The general control of the bishop, over every source and application of ecclesiastical income, is confirmed (Canon XV.): and by an additional Canon (XVI.), the bishop is required to supply *food and clothing to the poor*, or infirm, who were unable to work.

* Can. Apostol. xli. "Ut in ejus sit facultate omnia administrare, et iis qui egent per Presbyteros et Diaconos subministrare cum Dei timore et omni Religione; etiam (*si sit opus*) in necessarium suum usum accipere, et fratrum, qui hospitio excipiuntur, ita ut ipse nullo modo egeat."

† 3 & 4 W. & M. c. 11. s. 11.

‡ Concil. Antioch. Can. xxv. "Episcopus si non sit contentus iis quæ illi sufficiunt, verum res ac redditus ecclesiæ, absque cleri consilio, in alienos usus transfert, pœnæ ab eo coram synodo exigantur. Si vero quæ pauperibus debita sunt, in proprios usus converterit, sic etiam synodo rationes reddat."

A fourfold appropriation of the income of the Church, one part for the maintenance of the bishop, another for the maintenance of the clergy, a third for the *maintenance of the poor*, and a fourth for repairing the fabric of the church, was, during many centuries, a matter of frequent precept by the highest ecclesiastical authority.* The language used by one of these authorities, directing the division among the four classes according to the claims of each, *pro singulorum meritis*, shows, plainly enough, that the division was not into four *equal* shares; and shows also how completely the maintenance of the poor was provided for out of the revenues of the Church.†

It is said that the resident or *settled* parochial poor were entitled to the above share, and that *casual* relief to wayfarers fell on the episcopal fund.‡

Theological writers trace this practice of the Church, in taking upon herself the relief of the poor, up to the time of the Apostles, by whom distribution was made unto every man according to his need.§

By the general law of the Church, therefore, as well as by

* One of them is Pope Gelasius, c. vobis 23. c. 12. q. 2. "Unam sibi tollat Antistes, aliam clericis, pro suo judicio et electione, faciat erogari, *tertium pauperibus, sub omni conscientia, faciat erogari;* fabricis vero quartam." See J. H. Boehmer, *Jus Parochiale*, vol. ii. p. 11.; Selden, *Works*, vol. iii. p. 1120.

† Fra Paolo has made the observation, *Trattato delle Materie Beneficiarie*, s. viii. "Non si del però credere che questa divisione fosse in quattro parti aritmetiche, e uguali, ma con proporzione, poichè in alcune chiese il numero de Cherici ricercava che più fosse speso per loro, che per i poveri: in altri, il gran numero de' poveri e picciolo de' Cherici, ricercava altrimenti."

‡ Fra Paolo, *Trattato delle Materie Beneficiarie*, s. vii. "La quarta (parte) per li poveri, ma questi poveri nella maggior parte delle chiese, come S. Gregorio narra, *non s' intendevano se non i poveri del luogo;* imperocchè l' ospitalità tutta toccava al Vescovo, che a spese della sua porzione era obbligato ad alloggiare i clerici forestieri, e *spesare i poveri che di fuori venivano.*"

§ Acts, iv. 35. See Boehmer, *Jus Parochiale*, vi. 1. 5. and *Sarpi, ubi sup.* s. iii. A Roman Catholic prelate, D. Carlo Luigi Morichini, Degl' Instituti di Pubblica Carità, etc., in Roma, vol. i. p. 239., says, "Cessata la comunion de' beni che ebbero i primi fedeli quando la chiesa era nascente, furono le offerte de' pii fondatori che *alimentavano i poveri, e si amministravano miste e confuse ai beni del clero e della chiesa stessa.*" He refers to a work which I have not seen, *Richerche sulle pie fondazioni, e sull' uffizio loro a sollievo de' poveri, ec.* del cav. P. Magentu; Pavia, 1838.

that of the State, each Christian bishop, throughout the chief part of Europe, was emphatically the overseer and relieving-officer of the poor of the diocese, or *parish*, as dioceses were for some centuries usually called. The Council of Orleans, A. D. 511, enforced on all bishops the duty of relieving the impotent poor*; and such duty was frequently recognised and enforced by the sanction of other Councils. The Canon Law adopted, in its fullest terms, the principle, that it is the duty of bishops to provide needful maintenance "for the poor, and for those who are unable to work."† And we find, even in the sixteenth century, that a decree of the Council of Trent still imposes on every bishop, by virtue of his office, the oversight and control of the administration of relief to the poor.‡

The Penitentials, Confessionals, and other compilations of the Anglo-Saxon prelates, afford ample testimony to the full and unvarying recognition by the Church of England, from the earliest times, of its duty to provide for the poor.

The Confessional of Archbishop Ecgberht, directs the priest to exhort his penitent, to be "gentle and charitable to the poor, zealous in almsgiving, in attendance at church, and in the giving of *tithe to God's church and the poor*."§ And in the canons enacted under Eadgar, it is said to be right "that one part be delivered to the priests, a second part for the need of the Church, and the third part for the poor."

It has been seen that hospitals, *xenodochia*, before the time of Justinian, were placed wholly under the care of the clergy; we find them in the same hands in England, as early as the seventh century. An ecclesiastical regulation is found in the "Capitula et Fragmenta" of Archbishop Theodore, respecting those who administer the xenodochia of the poor, or receive tithes, and convert any portion thereof to their own use.

* "Episcopus pauperibus vel infirmis, qui debilitate faciente non possunt suis manibus laborare, victum et vestitum in quantum sibi possibile fuerit largiatur."

† Gratian, Decret. i. Pars. Dist. lxxxii.

‡ Concil. Trident. sess. 22. cap. viii. "Episcopi omnia quæ ad Dei cultum aut animarum salutem seu *pauperes sustentandos* instituta sunt, ipsi *ex officio suo* juxta Sacrorum Canonum statuta cognoscent et exequantur."

§ *Confessionale Ecgberhti.* Thorpe, vol. ii. p. 132.

The practice of the Anglo-Saxon Church seems to have fully carried out the principle, already mentioned as sanctioned by the authority of St. Jerome.* Every clerk was required, under the penalty of excommunication, to bestow all his superfluous possessions on the poor†; the laity were counselled by the Church to do the same thing, but the Church could not, even in the plenitude of its authority, denounce against the layman, who declined so to abandon his superfluities, the same penalty of excommunication as enforced clerical obedience to the ecclesiastical decree.‡

The ecclesiastical institutes of the early Anglo-Saxon Church, show that the clergy were required "at the hours when they left off the reading of holy books and prayers," to undertake some useful secular work. "By handywork," says the law, addressing the clergy alone, "ye may control your bodies, that they be the slower to vices, and also ye may provide so; by that work, that with your goods ye may help poor men, who have not themselves, and have not the power to work."§

Fasts and penances, prescribed by the Church or the clergy, were made subservient to the relief of the poor. The canons of Eadgar provide that, "When a man fasts, then let the dishes that would have been eaten be all distributed to God's poor; and the three days that a man fasts, let him abandon every worldly occupation, and by day and by night, the oftenest that he can, let him remain in church, and then feed, those three days, as many of God's poor as he possibly can; and, on the fourth day, bathe them all, and shelter them, and distribute money." And, according to the Ecclesiastical Institutes, "Holy writings inform us, that sins are

* Above, p. 143.

† *Pœnitentiale Theodori*, xxv. 6. "Clericus habens superflua, *donet ea pauperibus;* sin autem *excommunicetur.*"

‡ Ibid. xxv. 7. "Si quis laicus thesaurizat sibi superflua in crastinum tempus, *tribuat illa pauperibus;* si autem hoc non vult, audiat quod scriptum est: 'Thesaurizat, et ignorat qui congregabit ea.' Talis, si ad pœnitentiam conversus fuerit, primitus ea quæ thesaurizavit *pauperibus tribuat*, deinde, judicio sacerdotis iii. annos pœniteat."

§ *Eccles. Instit.*, vol. ii. pp. 404-5. ed. Thorpe.

forgiven in seven ways:" the third of which is, that "they are redeemed by alms, of which Daniel said to Nebuchadnezzar the king, 'Redeem thy sins with alms in money to the poor;' and that, 'as water extinguisheth fire, so alms extinguish sin.' And the Lord said in the Gospel, 'Give your alms, that ye may through that be pure.'" Again, "It is daily needful for every man that he give his alms to poor men; but yet, when we fast, then ought we to give greater alms than on other days, because the meat and drink which we should then drink, if we did not fast, we ought to distribute to the poor;—many men, when they fast, as soon as they hear the none-bell, take to meat, but it is right that after none-song, mass be heard, and after the mass, even-song at the time, and after the even-song, let every one give his alms, so as his means will permit him, and after that take to meat."

Several express provisions of the Penitential of Theodore *, require such persons as, through infirmity, cannot fast, to give, by way of commutation, alms to the poor; and a third part, even of the spoils taken in war, is appropriated to the same purpose.†

Some centuries later, when an indulgence not to fast was obtained from a "foreign prince, prelate, or potentate," the poor seem to have been remembered. In the reign of Henry III., the festival of St. Edward, king and confessor, used in London to be ushered in by a great *procession*, in which the City magnates were included, and which seems to have far outshone the magnificence of lord-mayor's day of our own age. This festival was solemnly celebrated in the two halls of Westminster; the king himself usually attending, and partaking in a banquet on the occasion. Now King Henry III. had made a vow never to eat meat on a Saturday, and, with the revolution of years, an approaching St. Edward's day was, in the year 1255, to fall on a Saturday. The king knew not how to abstain from honouring such a day by feasting, but still he must keep his vow. He turned, like a dutiful son, to him whom he looked up to as his spiritual father and

* *Pœnitent. Theodor.*, ed. Thorpe, vol. ii. pp. 61. 68.

† *Pœnitent. Ecgb.*, ed. Thorpe, vol. ii. p. 232.

guide, and was relieved from his conflict of duties by a papal bull, in which "the servant of the servants of God," permitted "his Excellency, the illustrious King of England," to eat meat on St. Edward's day of that year; but only on condition of the king's feeding *one hundred poor* on the same day.*

It appears to have been the usual custom for the king's "two halls of Westminster," on the celebration of the festival in question, to be filled with poor people, who were there fed. On one occasion Henry III. was absent in Scotland, and feared that he should not be able, personally, to be present at the metropolitan celebration of St. Edward's day. He therefore invited and commissioned the lord treasurer, and the bishops of Salisbury, Norwich, Bath, and Chichester, with neighbouring abbots and priors, to celebrate the festival in his absence, and expressly requires them to take care that his two halls at Westminster be filled with poor people, who are to be there fed, "as had been accustomed" on the occasion.† Such instances as these show how relief of the poor, whether for good or for evil, was wrought into the daily habits of society, and was the never-ceasing theme and object of the ministration of the Church.

Other instances of royal and episcopal almsgiving, on a grand scale, are recorded. St. Louis of France, the celebrated contemporary of Henry III. of England, seems always to have made it his especial care liberally to give alms to the poor. It is said, that by doing so, he showed an especial regard for the interests of agriculture; he caused relief lists

* Rymer, *Fœdera*, tom. i. par. xi. p. 15. ed. Hag. Com. prints the bull: "Alexander Episcopus, servus servorum Dei, carissimo in Christo filio Henrico, illustri Regi Angliæ, salutem et Apostolicam benedictionem. Cum, sicut ex parte tua nobis extitit intimatum, tu abstinere a carnibus, diebus Sabbati, tenearis ex voto; nos tuis precibus annuentes, Excellentiæ Tuæ, ut, si contigerit Festum translationis Sancti Edwardi in die Sabbati celebrari, liceat tibi (non obstante voto hujusmodi), necnon et convivis tuis, qui tali voto se nullatenus obstrinxerunt, *carnes comedere*, auctoritate præsentium *indulgemus*. Volumus autem quod propter hoc *centum pauperes eodem die pascere* tenearis."

† Rymer, *Fœdera*, tom. i. pt. 2. p. 4. "Et duas aulas Regis Westm. *impleri pauperibus* in dicto Festo, et eos pasci faciant, sicut fieri consuevit."

to be prepared of the agricultural labourers, who, in each province of France, were unable to work, whether from disease or age, and charged himself with their maintenance.* Joinville speaks of St. Louis as having been more fortunate than Titus, in having never passed a day without bestowing such frequent alms on the poor, who, by old age or sickness, could not work, that the number could hardly be told. †

Prelates rivalled kings in this display of eleemosynary munificence. Contemporary history has recorded such acts of St. Eloi, of St. Epiphanius, and of Gregory the Great. At one time 2000 modii of wheat were distributed to the poor; at another, 6000 captives of war were redeemed from slavery; and an English archbishop, Robert of Winchester, when filling the see of Canterbury, used, on Sundays and festivals, to distribute food to poor people, to the number of 3000; and in times of scarcity, even to the number of 4000. ‡

It appears, by the Excerpts of Ecgberht, Archbishop of York §, and by the laws of King Ethelred ‖, that the obli-

* *Chroniques de France*, tom. ii. f. 80. Beugnot, *Essai sur les Institutions de Saint Louis*, p. 261. M. Beugnot says, "Ce qui preuve le mieux, tout l'intérêt que Saint Louis prenait à l'agriculture, c'est," &c.

† Joinville, p. 151. cited by M. Beugnot, *Essai sur les Institutions de Saint Louis*, p. 261. "Par dessus toutes choses, le Roy donnoit chascun jours si grans et si larges aumosnes, aus poures qui par vieillesce ou par maladie no pooient labourer ne maintenir leur meistier, que à peinne porroit l'en raconter le nombre; dont nous poon bien dire que il fu plus bienaeureus que Titus l'empereur de Rome, dont les anciennes escriptures racontent que trop se dolut, et fu desconforté, d'un jour que il n'avoit donné nul benefice."

‡ Wharton, *Anglia Sacra*, p. 12. "In eleemosynæ largitione *pauperibus* hostiatim *mendicantibus* debilibus et ægrotis, tantum tribuit quod *prælatos alios excellebat;* unde quolibet die Dominico, et feria quinta, per annum *cuilibet pauperi venienti* fecit dari, quorum numerus, tempore carestiæ quatuor millia vel circiter, et fertilitatis tempore, ad tria millia extendebat."

§ Ecgberht, *Excerpt.* v. "Ad ornamentum ecclesiæ primam eligant partem; secundam autem *ad usum pauperum* atque peregrinorum, per eorum manus cum omni humilitate dispensent; tertiam vero sibimetipsis sacerdotes reservent." Ibid. lvi. Canon Aurelianensis. "Episcopus pauperibus et infirmis qui, debilitate faciente, non possunt suis manibus laborare, victum et vestimentum, in quantum possibilitas fuerit, largiatur."

‖ Ethel. ix. 6. "And respecting tithe, the king and his 'witan' have chosen and decreed, as is just, that one-third part of the tithe which belongs to the Church go to the reparation of the church, and a second part to the servants of God; and the third to God's poor, and to needy ones in thraldom." The bishop's

gation of the Church to maintain the poor, in this country, did not rest solely on the doctrines of theologians, whether contained in precepts of the early fathers, or in decrees of popes or general councils; but was expressly adopted by the Church, and established by the State of England, at a very early period, as an absolute duty of the Anglican clergy.

The free barbarians of the west of Europe seem to have adopted provisions like those of our own Anglo-Saxon forefathers, in respect of the fourfold division of tithes. Everywhere the poor were to have one of the portions. The law of the Lombards required four parts: "the first for the bishop, the second for the clergy, the third for the poor, the fourth for the fabric of the church."*

Similar, and equally absolute, provisions were made by the early rulers of the Frank monarchy †; and it is laid down in the Capitularies, that those who rob the Church of any of her possessions, are to be considered as homicides in the sight of God, for they deprive of needful sustenance the poor, whom the Church ought to feed.‡ Again, the clergy are not to

share is not mentioned in this threefold division. The fourfold division was earlier in point of time. Selden, *Works*, vol. iii. p. 1120. "Neither had the parochial priests at first such a particular interest in the profits received in oblations, as of later time. All that was received, wheresoever in the bishopric, was as a common treasury, to be so dispensed. One part was allowed to the maintenance of the ministery, out of which every parochial minister had his salary;—another to the relief of the poor, sick, and strangers; a third to the reparation of churches; and a fourth to the bishop." See also Phillips, *Angel-Sächsisches Recht*, p. 251.

* Canciani, *Barbarorum Leges Antiquæ*, tom. i. pp. 160—161. "Ut decimæ populi in quatuor partes, dividantur. Prima pars Episcopis detur; alia Clericis; tertia *Pauperibus*; quarta in fabrica ipsius ecclesiæ."

† Baluze, *Capitular. Reg. Franc.* tom i. p. 1105. (lib. vii. c. 375.). "Instruendi sunt presbyteri pariterque admonendi quatenùs noverint *decimas et oblationes* quas à fidelibus accipiunt, pauperum et hospitum et peregrinorum esse stipendia, his non quasi suis sed quasi commendatis uti debere; de quibus omnibus sciant se rationem reddituros in conspectu divinæ majestatis, et nisi eas fideliter *pauperibus*, et his quibus præmissum est administraverint, condemnationem patiendos. Qualiter verò dispensari debeant, canones sacri instituunt: scilicet ut quatuor partes ex omnibus fiant, una ad fabricam Ecclesiæ relevandam, altera *pauperibus* distribuenda, tertia Presbytero cum suis Clericis habenda, quarto Episcopo reservanda. Et quicquid exindè Pontifex jusserit, prudenti consilio est faciendum."

‡ Baluze, *Capit. Reg. Franc.* tom. i. p. 1009. (lib. vi. c. 430.). "Volumus omnes scire quod qui Christi et Ecclesiæ pecunias auferunt, resque ejus fraudant,

presume to sell tithes, bestowed for the use as well of the poor as of the Church. It is stated that the clergy had sometimes sold the tithes of a former year, when stored in barns; and the law alleges, that many poor who died on such occasions, would be required at the hands of the clergy.*

Louis the Debonnaire made a somewhat different provision in certain cases. His law, issued in the year 818, directs that, of all voluntary gifts to the Church, *two-thirds*, in rich places, should be applied to the use of the poor, and the third part only should be retained by the clergy; in lesser places, the division was to be equal between the poor and the clergy.†

In France, even during the eighteenth century, and so late as shortly before the revolution of 1789, cases occasionally occurred of great ecclesiastics being compelled, by legal proceedings, to apply, to their original purposes of relieving the poor, a part of the revenues of their lands.‡

At the end of two centuries after the Conquest, we find, in the language of the Church in England, a strong recognition of that duty of the clergy in respect of relieving the poor, which in the Anglo-Saxon age had been so fully recognised and performed. It is required, by a canon of the year 1281 (9 Edward I.), that non-resident rectors should at least provide for the necessities of pauper parishioners; and many archbishops of Canterbury appear to have inserted in dispensations for non-residence, an express provision for distribution of a portion of the proceeds of the benefice *among the poor*.§

rapiunt, vastant vel diripiunt, homicidæ ante Deum deputantur, quia *res pauperum*, quas Ecclesia *pascere debet*, diripiunt.

* Baluze, vol. i. p. 1212. Addit. 4ta. c. 89. "Ut non præsumant presbyteri decimas vendere, quæ *in pauperum* et in Ecclesiarum usibus dantur, sicut hactenus mirabile dictu, in horreis veteratæ, ad thesaurorum cumulum. In cujus rei testimonio multi pauperum de manibus sacerdotum requirendi moriuntur."

† *Capit. Reg. Franc.* vol. i. p. 718. ed. Baluze (lib. i. c. 80.). "Statutum est ut quicquid tempore imperii nostri à fidelibus Ecclesiæ sponte conlatum fuerit, in ditioribus locis duas partes in usus pauperum, tertiam in stipendia cedere Clericorum aut Monachorum, in minoribus vero locis æque inter clerum et pauperes fore dividendum; nisi forte a datoribus ubi specialiter dandæ sint, constitutum fuerit." Found also, ib. tom. i. p. 564.

‡ Merlin, *Dictionnaire de Jurisprudence*, v. *Aumône*.

§ Lyndwood, p. 132.; Bishop Gibson's *Codex*, vol. ii. p. 885. Archbishop

When tithes and oblations became payable to rectors of parishes, the relief of the poor, continuing an ecclesiastical, became a parochial burden; and hence it is that an ancient ordinance, preserved in the "Myrror of Justice," expressly lays down that the poor are to be sustained "by the parsons, rectors of the church, and by the parishioners, so that none of them die of default of sustenance."* The "parishioners" would sustain the poor by paying their tithe, and making their oblations to the Church. The duty of providing for parochial poor was, moreover, enforced by an act of parliament, passed in the reign of Richard II.†, which requires that in every license of impropriation of any parish church, it should be expressed, that the diocesan shall ordain, according to the value of such church, a convenient sum of money to be distributed yearly of the fruits thereof *to the poor.*

The word used in middle-age Latin to denote the giving, *in alms,* when the proceeds of land were to be applied for the benefit of the poor, is "*eleemosynare;*" and the appropriate explanation of the word by Ducange, is "Dare in eleemosynam, *ecclesiæ, monasterio,* vel *pauperi:*" the giving to the Church was equivalent to a giving directly to the poor. Certainly the very tenure by which the monasteries in England held their land, in frankalmoigne, or *free alms,* sufficiently in-

Hubert gives a dispensation "Taxatione tamen moderatæ distributionis inter *Egenos Parochianos* annuatim, prout in absentiam Parochiis nostræ Diœceseos secundum Juris Exigentiam et *antiquam consuetudinem* observatur, communiter faciendæ, nobis specialiter reservata." In the time of Archbishop Reynolds, the non-resident's oath was to make a distribution "inter *pauperes parochianos;*" and the *Langham Register* contains a dispensation with the clause, "Quod absentiæ suæ damnum recompensetur, *Eleemosynarum largitione in Parochiâ suâ* facienda; de qua fiet fides Domino (Archiepiscopo) in eventu."

* *Myrror of Justice,* cap. i. s. 3. "Ordeiné fuit que les povres fuissent sustenus par les persunes, rectors de Esglise, et per les parochians, cy que null ne morust per défaut de sustenance." The duty of the Church, or State, to prevent its members from dying of starvation, when once acknowledged, seems to give a right to enact laws for repressing vagrancy. Lord Coke places in juxtaposition, without comment, the ordinance of the Myrror, and "an ancient ordinance of 50 Edw. III. concerning ribauds and sturdy beggars, that they be driven to their occupations or services, or to the place from whence they came." 3 Inst. 103.

† 15 R. II. c. 6.

dicated the share of the poor in the grant.* Each monastery appears, in the various parts of Europe, to have had a *poor-house* or *almshouse*, in or adjoining to the building of the monastery.† Each monastery had also a relieving officer, the eleemosinarius or almoner, and his duties have been defined by middle-age writers with as much precision as could be desired in a document emanating from a Poor Law Board in our own days.‡ He was not obliged to apply the *almshouse test* by refusing *out-door relief*, but was to visit the sick and infirm at their houses, and to relieve them there.§ Nor was this duty and practice of relieving the poor confined to the regular clergy. The Council of Oxford directed every bishop to have almoners‖; "for reading and prayer sufficeth not in a bishop, unless he also give alms."¶

Even the king had his almoner, like the abbot and bishop, and the importance of the duties of the office of king's almoner, or, perhaps, his constant official attendance on the king's person, may have been a reason why the *grand aumonier* of the king of France became so great a functionary, and acquired the command of such enormous wealth and patronage. With us, the more modest king's almoner, the "lord almoner"

* Scriptor ap. Ducange, v. *Eleemosyna.* "Res Domino jure *Eleemosynarum* legitime conservatæ sunt; Ecclesiæ ejus sunt, quia *suis pauperibus* et specialiter sibi servientibus datæ sunt."

† Ducange, 3 Eleemosyna. "Domus monasterio vel ecclesiis adjuncta, in qua eleemosynæ pauperibus erogabantur ab eleemosynario."

‡ Ducange, v. Eleemosynarius, who transcribes a long fragment of a chapter, *De Officio Eleemosynarii.* In the register of Spalding Priory is a short account of an almoner in the thirteenth century. "Non est autem silendum qualiter se gesserit in officio Eleemosinarii permissione Prioris emit terras, ædificavit domus et capellum, fecit ortum, plantavit vineam et pomaria, *congregavit miseros, prebens eis necessaria alimenta.*" MS. Cole, Brit. Mus. vol. xliii. p. 93., and Sir H. Ellis, *General Introduction to Domesday Book*, vol. i. p. 120. note (2).

§ Lanfrancus in Decretis pro Ord. S. Benedicti, c. 8. s. 5. (ap. Ducange, l. c.). "Eleemosynarius aut per se perquirat, aut per veraces et fideles homines cum multa sollicitudine perquiri faciat, ubi ægri et debiles jaceant, qui non habeant, unde se sustinere valeant, et ingressus domum blande consoletur ægrum, et offerat ei, quod melius habet, et sibi intelligit esse necessarium," &c.

‖ Lyndwood, vol. i. p. 12. Ducange, v. Eleemosynarii Episcoporum.

¶ Lyndwood, ubi sup. "Non enim sufficit episcopo lectio et oratio, nisi adsit eleemosynæ largitio."

as he is sometimes called, still exists; and the duties of his place in distributing relief, both in money and kind, to the poor, have not been transferred to any other overseer, but are still performed by himself, and exhibit yearly a trace of that almsgiving which, in former times, was of daily occurrence.*

* It is said by Sir Edward Coke (1 Inst. 94 a.), that the duties of king's almoner are excellently described in ancient authors. Fleta (ii. 23.) is the chief of those ancient authors. The almoner was to collect, daily, the fragments from the royal table, and to distribute them to the poor: he was charitably to visit the sick and lepers, prisoners, and poor widows, and other indigent poor persons, and wanderers; and whatever the king gave, whether in horses, clothes, or money, the almoner was to receive, and faithfully to distribute in alms. He was also, by frequent admonitions, chiefly on saints' days, to stimulate the king to give alms; and he was to ask of the king to order that the contents of the royal wardrobe "quæ magni sunt pretii," should be given, not to stage-players, flatterers, or minstrels, but to the increase of the alms which the almoner administered.

A contrast between the ancient duties thus described, and their modern discharge, will be furnished by the following, which is the substance of a contemporary account of the lord almoner's distribution of relief to the poor in 1851. *Passion Week.*—On Monday and Tuesday in this week the customary bounties were issued to the aged and meritorious poor, at the Almonry in Whitehall, under the direction of the Lord High Almoner and the Sub-Almoner. The recipients included numerous cases of blindness and other infirmities. *Maundy Thursday.*—These ancient and royal charities were distributed yesterday to 32 aged men and 32 aged women, with the usual formalities, in Whitehall Chapel. At two o'clock in the afternoon a *procession* proceeded to the chapel. The *procession* was joined by the Rev. Dr. Wesley, sub-dean of the Chapels Royal; also by the priests, gentlemen, and choristers. The Church service appointed for the afternoon was read. The 41st Psalm (the grand chant) was sung, and was followed by the first lesson. Then followed the first anthem (41st Psalm)—"Blessed is he that considereth the poor and needy, the Lord shall deliver him in the time of trouble." *The sum of 1l. 15s. was then distributed to each woman; and to each man was given shoes and stockings.* The second anthem (a prayer) was then sung. *Woollen and linen cloths were then distributed.* After which the third anthem (61st Psalm and the 18th verse of the 132d Psalm) were sung. *The purses, containing the Maundy money, were then distributed.* The second lesson was then read, which was followed by the 4th anthem. Two prayers, composed for the occasion, followed, the first of which was: "O Lord, the Sovereign of the world, we acknowledge that Thine is the greatness, the power, and the glory, and the victory, and the majesty; for all that is in the heaven and in the earth is Thine. Thine is the kingdom, O Lord, and thou art exalted as Head above all; both riches and honour come of Thee, and Thou reignest over all. In Thy hand is power and might, and in Thy hand it is to make great, and to give strength unto all. Now, therefore, our God, we thank Thee

During several centuries, it was usual, in England, for the king to grant all goods of persons felons of themselves, and all deodands (both which matters were regarded as of an ecclesiastical nature), to his almoner.* The grant was by writ of privy seal. Henry VIII., in the first year of his reign, on 8th November, 1509, so grants "to our dear clerk and councillor, Master Thomas Wolsey, our almoner," this augmentation of the almoner's means of relieving the poor.†

Moreover, lands appear, in some cases, to have been held directly of the Crown by its eleemosynary officers, for the purposes of their office. Among the tenants *in capite,* whose names are preserved in Domesday Book, are several "king's

and praise Thy glorious name, that Thou hast not only bestowed greatness and majesty upon our Sovereign Lady Queen Victoria, but hast given her a heart also to take compassion on them that are below her, and show mercy unto the poor and needy. Accept, Most Gracious God, of this tribute, which she pays unto Thee, the giver of all good things, and make her still more fruitful and abundant in these, and all other good works, that, by mercy and truth she may be preserved, and her throne upholden by mercy. And stir up the hearts of all those who have now been partakers of her bounty, to be truly thankful unto Thee for it, and both to bless and praise Thee continually for setting such a pious princess over us, and also pray most earnestly that Thou wouldst reward her charity with a long and prosperous reign in this world, and with a heavenly kingdom in the world to come; through Jesus Christ, our Lord and only Saviour. Amen." The usual prayers followed, which concluded the service. The Lord Bishop of Oxford, Lord High Almoner, who usually officiates in person, was this year unavoidably absent through indisposition. Sir George Smart presided at the organ.

* Many instances of these grants are found in Rymer's *Fœdera,* and are collected in the *Index rerum præcipuarum,* under the title "Eleemosynarius regis;" in the Hague edition of 1741.

† Rymer, *Fœdera,* tom. vi. par. i. p. 8. ed. Hag. Com. 1741. "Rex omnibus ad quos &c. salutem, Sciatis nos concessisse Dilecto Clerico et Consiliario nostro Magistro Thomæ Wolsey Eleemosinario nostro, in Augmentationem Elimosinæ, tam omnia et omnimodo Bona et Catalla quarumcumque personarum Felonum de Se et cujuslibet Personæ Felonis de Se, infra Regnum Nostrum Angliæ inventa et invenienda, forisfacta et forisfacienda, aut Nobis tàm nunc quàm in futurum quovis modo pertinentia, quàm omnia deodandia quæ Nobis infra Regnum nostrum Angliæ prædictum tàm infra Libertates quàm extra pertinent, aut unquam post primum Diem Regni, nostri Nobis pertinuerunt aut pertinere debebunt aut contingent ullo modo, quamdiu ipsum Thomam Elimosiniarium fore contigerit."

almoners," some of whom appear to have so held their lands from the time of Edward the Confessor.*

Still further provision of this kind was made in ancient times. Many branches of the king's revenue were charged with alms. "This alms was called *eleemosyna constituta,* the *settled alms.* To this may be added the *decimæ constitutæ.* These the accountant constantly paid out of the revenue within his receipt to which they were affixed, and had an allowance thereof upon his account."†

Substantially, however, provision for the poor seems to have been a charge on the revenue of the Church from very remote times till the reign of Henry VIII.

The early fourfold division, which has been mentioned, extended to the *oblations,* or *offerings,* of the parishioners as well as to their tithes ‡; and the Church of England has retained, both in her Book of Common Prayer and her Rubric, manifest traces of the ancient right of the poor to a share in this part of the parochial income of the clergy.

The Sentences exhort us to relieve the poor: "Give alms of thy goods, and never turn thy face from any poor man; and then the face of the Lord shall not be turned away from thee." "He that hath pity upon the poor, lendeth to the Lord." "Blessed is the man that provideth for the sick and needy; the Lord shall deliver him in the time of trouble." And, according to the Rubric, "while these sentences are in reading, the deacons, *churchwardens,* or other fit persons, are to receive the *alms for the poor,* and other devotions of the people." By "other devotions of the people" is supposed to be indicated the share of the clergy in these offerings.§

The Church in England, therefore, from the first conversion of the pagan Anglo-Saxons to Christianity, during a long

* *Domesday Book:* Elemosinæ Regis, Midd. 130 b., Leic. 231., Warw. 244. Elemosinarii Regis, Dors. 79., Midd. 130 b., Bedf. 218 b., Northampt. 222 b.

† Madox, *History of the Exchequer,* vol. i. p. 348. ed. 1769.

‡ Such a division is confirmed by Innocent III., in 1199, ap. Harduin, tom. ii. Concil. p. 1010. "Decernimus ut decimæ seu *oblationes* fidelium tam pro vivis quam pro defunctis in quatuor partes dividantur: quorum una sit episcopi, alia ecclesiarum, *tertia pauperum,* quarta clericorum."

§ Wheatly on the Common Prayer, vi. 10. 1.

course of centuries, was not only accustomed, but *bound*, to provide for the maintenance of the poor. Although, by some means or other, the Church of England, at an early period, was relieved from the duty of repairing the fabric of the church, and that burden thrown on the laity, yet, for centuries, both before and after the Conquest, ample provision for the poor was still found in the rich and splendid endowment of the clergy. It was only when the country had made great progress towards emancipation from feudal servitude and oppression, and when great changes in population had already taken place, accompanying the growth of new towns and boroughs, and the decay of old ones, that the "patrimony of the poor," as the Church revenue was called, failed to effect the great object of charity which it was originally intended to fulfil. The pauperism and vagrancy which thus spread throughout England, had frequently, in the latter part of the fifteenth, and the early part of the sixteenth, century, attracted the attention of the legislature, before the suppression of the monasteries. To whatever extent the secular clergy may have ceased to administer any definite part of their income as relief for the poor, there can be no doubt that the suppression of the monasteries would add greatly to the claims made on the laity, charitably to contribute to the relief of destitution. And it is equally certain that provision for the maintenance of all the sick, aged, and otherwise impotent poor, was still largely made out of the vast possessions of the monasteries, down to the very day of their confiscation by an arbitrary and rapacious monarch.

CHAP. V.

PAUPER LEGISLATION BEFORE THE REIGN OF ELIZABETH.

Il y a deux sortes de peuples pauvres: ceux que la dureté du gouvernement a rendus tels; et ces gens-là sont incapables de presque aucune vertu, parceque leur pauvreté fait une partie de leur servitude: les autres ne sont pauvres que parcequ'ils ont dédaigné ou parcequ'ils n'ont pas connu les commodités de la vie; et ceux-ci peuvent faire de grandes choses, parceque cette pauvreté fait une partie de leur liberté. — MONTESQUIEU.

It is highly probable that, from the time of the Conquest till the reign of Edward III., England was little troubled with either vagrant beggars or paupers. The "patrimony of the poor" was found in the possessions of the Church; and each lord maintained his serfs or villeins much as each proprietor of a West India sugar plantation, in more recent times, has maintained his slaves. It is not till after Edward III.'s wars in France, and after the industry and wealth of towns came into existence, that we first notice traces of any considerable class of free labourers.

The destructive plague, which ravaged Europe in the year 1348 *, greatly thinned the ranks of these free labourers in

* This pestilence is mentioned in a poem, entitled *Les Adventures advenues en France:*

> "En l'autre année advint si grant mortalité
> Qu'il mouru bien le tiers de la Crestienté!—
> Après le mortuaire, fu le temps si très chier,
> Que poures gens n'avoient pas grantment à mengier."

Probably the number, "there died at least *the third* of Christendom," is not a poetical exaggeration, at all events, so far as the labouring population is concerned. We are told, in more recent times, that an ordinary visitation of the plague used to carry off one-fifth of the inhabitants of a great city: see Sir William Petty, *Political Arithmetic*, p. 118. ed. Dublin, 1769. And Boccaccio's immortal description of this very plague of 1348, as it devastated Florence, shows that it visited the poor with far greater destruction than fell on any other

England. Hence the demand for labour became greater than the supply, and the result was that its wages rose. This was natural and just, but between the lords and their, villeins, very shortly before, there had been "no judge but God;" and the lords seem now to have determined to retain the free labourer in a state of permanent subjection, which would render his condition not a whit better than that of the slavery from which he had been freed. The Statute of Labourers, promulgated in 1350 (25 Edward III.), and frequently confirmed and extended by subsequent statutes, furnished the machinery by which the wages of labour were arbitrarily defined for upwards of two centuries.

The excess of demand over supply in the labour market, the natural consequence of pestilence and depopulation, produced inconvenience to the employers of labour; and they obtained a very full measure of protection to their own interests, at the expense of the interests of others, by an enactment that every one should serve "at the wages which were accustomed to be given, in the place where he cometh to serve," in the twentieth year of the king's reign, or five or six common years next before. The "lords" were to be

class of society. "*Della minuta gente,*—era il ragguardamento di *molto maggior miseria* pieno: perciocchè essi *il più*—ritenuti nelle lor case,—*a migliaja per giorno* infermavano; e non essendo nè serviti, nè atati d'alcuna cosa, quasi *senza alcuna redenzione tutti* morivano: ed *assai* n' erano, che *nella strada pubblica*, o di dì, o di notte *finivano.*" De Foe, in his *History of the Plague of London*, tells us that "it was chiefly among the poor," and that, where the poor could get employment, "they pushed into any kind of business, the most dangerous, and most liable to infection; and if they were spoken to, their answer would be,—I cannot starve, I had as good have the plague as perish for want.—This adventurous conduct of the poor, was that which brought the plague among them in the most furious manner; and this, joined to the distress of their circumstances, when taken, was the reason why they died so *by heaps.*" A parallel to the proportion of one-third, as given by the middle-age poet, is furnished by statistical investigation of the recent diminution in the population of Ireland. During the latter half of the decennial period ending in 1851, about *one-third* of the whole population of the province of Connaught has been swept away; and a large proportion of that desolation has been due to the ravages of famine, and the disease which followed in its train. This has happened notwithstanding the gigantic benevolence of the imperial legislature, and the noble efforts of Christian charity, to relieve Irish suffering, made by the British people.

preferred before other claimants for such services, and a refusal, &c. to serve, was punished by imprisonment till surety was found to serve as required.

Wearisome and painful would be the task of examining the oppression exercised over the whole class of labourers from the early part of the fourteenth century till the end of the fifteenth. The legislation on the subject of these poor helots, seems throughout to be selfish and unjust. The labourer was never to better his condition. Imprisonment and branding on the forehead with a hot iron was the lot of the fugitive servant, although he had never *consented* to enter into the service of his lord, and had been compelled to do so for wages less than he was justly entitled to receive. Even "artificers, and people of mysteries," were liable to be *pressed* by the lord to get in his harvest*, and if a poor labourer's unmarried daughter of eighteen or twenty years of age, had been "required to serve" any master, she must, under the statutory provisions, either have gone into the service, or have been committed to gaol for refusing. No child could be apprenticed to any useful craft, unless its parents were owners of land yielding a certain amount of yearly rent; and the compulsory service, such as has been described, paid for by a rate of wages below the just level, would be a perpetual cause why servants should have endeavoured to free themselves from their bondage, and why the "valiant beggars," of whom we read, should have so greatly increased throughout the country.

It has been observed†, that we cannot be surprised, that the lords should have endeavoured to preserve some affinity between the new class of villeins, whose earnings they tried to limit, and the old ones, whose persons they had before controlled. "All the restrictions of the legislature on personal industry, evince a disposition of this kind; and various statutes to regulate wages, dress, and apparel, seem to have been framed with the same view, namely, to curb the aspiring exertions of industry and independency." ‡

* 13 Rich. II. c. 3.

† Eden, *State of the Poor*, vol. i. p. 41.

‡ Eden, vol. i. p. 42.

Spread of commerce and increase of towns, ultimately extinguished the predial slavery, which had so long pressed down the agricultural population. As the development of our manufacturing industry, in more recent times, has served to attract to its great centres, the ill-paid, ill-fed, ill-clothed, and ill-lodged agricultural labourer and his family, and has thus absorbed a considerable portion of the increasing agricultural population, so in the thirteenth and fourteenth centuries, an analogous, but much more active movement, must have been going on, in the same direction. We see the jealousy with which it was then regarded by the landowners, and it must be remembered that they were likely to lose their property, by the then change. If the villein fled into any privileged town, "or other place enfranchised," and remained there a year and a day, without being seized by his lord, the lord could not, after that time, enter the franchise to retake him.

Leases for life, and for terms of years, frequently reserving a fixed money rent, had become common, even during the thirteenth century, and numerous instances of such leases are found in the collection of Madox. Their existence indicates the progress of agriculture. The mere serf, or villein proper, could never have entered into any such contract. The pure tenure of villenage imported, that the tenant was to do "all that the lord should him command;" and the lord, according to the precise language of the law, "may rob, beat, and chastise his villein, at his will, save only that he may not *maim* him, for then he shall have an appeal of maihem against him."* He might have cut off his villein's ears, perhaps his nose, with impunity; although he could not have knocked out a foretooth, or cut off a forefinger. I know not that the villein's condition was worse in England than in other countries of Europe. Froissart certainly speaks of this wretched serfdom as embracing a more numerous population in England than elsewhere.†

* Termes de la Ley, "Villain" and "Villainage."

† Froissart, ed. Buchon, tom. viii. c. vi. "Un usage est en Angleterre, aussi est-il en plusiers pays, que les nobles ont grands franchises sur leurs hommes, et les tiennent en servage, c'est à entendre que ils doivent de droit et

Pierre de Fontaines, in the twenty-first chapter of his "Conseil," speaking of the old French jurisprudence, says, that if the lord plunder his villein, he will act contrary to the will of God, and will peril his soul "as a robber;"* but, he adds absolutely, "between villein and lord there is no judge whatever, except God."†

The reign of Henry VII. is, in many respects, an important and interesting epoch in English history. Among the various causes, which would be likely then to increase the number of paupers and vagrants, is to be reckoned the effect of the civil wars, between the houses of York and Lancaster. Maimed and crippled veterans, and widows with fatherless children, would especially stand in need of public or private charity. So at later periods we find these incidents of war made the ground of a specific charge on parishes; as in the reign of Queen Elizabeth, soon after the defeat of the Spanish Armada‡, and under Cromwell.§

par coutume labourer la terre, &c. et doivent iceux hommes tout ce faire par servage aux seigneurs ; et *trop plus, grand foison a de tels gens en Angleterre quē ailleurs.*"

* Pierre de Fontaines, *Conseil*, ch. xxi. § 8. p. 224. ed. Marnier. "Saches bien que, selon Deu, tu n'a mie plenière poesté sor ton vilein ; dont, se tu prens dou suen fors les droites recevances qu'il te doit, tu les prens contre Deu et sor le péril de t'ame, come robierres."

† "Mes par nostre usage n'a-il, entre toi et ton vilein, juge fors Deu," &c. Beaumanoir, *Coutumes de Beauvoisis*, ch. xlv. s. 36. (tom. ii. p. 237. ed. Beugnot):—"Plus cortoise est nostre coustume envers les sers que en autre païs, car li segneur poent penre de lor sers, et à mort et à vie, toutes les fois qu'il lor plest et tant qu'il lor plet." See also De Lauriere, *Glossaire*, v. Droits Seigneuriaux. A slight modification of the lord's power of life and death over his serf is supplied by "Li Livres de Jostice et de Plet," s. 9. p. 57. ed Par. 1850. "Li sires a poer sor son serf, et quanquez li serf conquiert, il est au seignor. Mès ore—cil qui aucit *son serf* sanz cause, ne doit pas meins estre puniz que sil avoit ocis *autrui serf*." He who kills his own *serf* is not to be less punished than if he had killed the *serf* of another man ; and, in that case, he is punished, not so much as having killed a man, but rather as having deprived another lord of the use of a chattel. Ibelin, in the *Assises de Jerusalem*, vol. i. p. 496. ed. Beugnot, says but little of the civil condition of serfs. M. Beugnot, his editor, observes that the power of lord over serf had no legal limits ; and after referring to Beaumanoir (c. xlv.), justly adds, "Quel commentaire pouvait, on faire sur des lois aussi claires et aussi dures ?"

‡ See 35 Eliz. c. 4., 39 Eliz. c. 21., 43 Eliz. c. 3.

§ Many acts and ordinances for the relief of maimed soldiers, and of the

But another circumstance in the condition of society in England at this period, probably contributed much more to increasing the numbers of the poor, than the maimed soldiers and their widows and orphans had done.

The reign of Henry VII. is the period of great progress in the breaking up of the feudal system, and of great consequent change in the mutual relations of all the different classes of society, living on and by the cultivation of the soil. With that change, and the increase of free labourers, which preceded and accompanied it, there would probably arise an additional number of vagrant poor. From some one or other of these causes, a need for fresh provisions against vagrancy and mendicancy, would be felt in the latter part of the fifteenth century.

Two statutes of Henry VII. (11 Henry VII. c. 2., and 19 Henry VII. c. 12.), prescribe severe punishment for vagrancy, and put some restraint on beggars not able to work.

The first of these statutes (passed in 1495), is entitled "An Acte agaynst Vacabounds and Beggers;" it provided (s. 1.) that all such vagabonds are to be taken and "sette in stokkes, ther to remayne by the space of 3 daies and 3 nyghtes, and ther to have noon other sustenaunce but brede and water, and after the seid 3 daies and 3 nyghtes to be had oute and

widows and orphans of persons slain *in the Parliament's service*, are found in Scobell's "Collection." The first Act of the series begins as follows (1642, cap. 3. p. 37.): "Whereas divers well-affected persons have gone forth in the army raised by the Parliament, for the defence of the Parliament, religion, laws, and liberties of the subjects of England, and in fight have received divers wounds and maims in their bodies, whereby they are disabled to relieve themselves by their usual labour, and divers others have lost their lives in the said service, whereby they have left their wives and children destitute of relief to support and sustain them: the Lords and Commons assembled in Parliament, taking the same into their pious and charitable consideration, and having relieved divers of them here at London with some small relief for their present subsistence, but finding that that course cannot be held for any continuance of time without many inconveniences, have thought fit and do hereby ordain, that in every parish within the kingdome of England, wherein any such persons, either now maimed or slain, did last inhabit afore their going forth to the aforesaid service, shall raise a competent stock of money, by way of assessment upon the inhabitants of the said several parishes, for the relief of the said maimed souldiers, and the widdows and fatherless children of the said slain persons."

set at large, and then to be comaunded to avoide the towen." If again taken "in such defaute in the same town or township, then he to be sette in the like wise in stokks by the space of 6 daies with like diete as is before reherced." Section 2. provides that "all man of beggers not able to werke, goe rest and abide in his hundred where he last dwelled, or ther where he is best knowen or born, ther to remayne or abide without begging out of the said hundred."

It was thought necessary, therefore, to restrain the practice of mendicancy, even of the infirm poor, within the somewhat large limits of hundreds thus loosely defined.

In 1503–4, the statute 19 Henry VII. c. 12. was passed. Although its title is merely "De *Validis* Mendicantibȝ repellend," yet it contains a provision for the infirm poor, "that all man of beggers not able to werk, goo rest and abide in his cite, towne, or hundred wher they were borne, or els to the place where they last made their abode the space of 3 yeres, ther to remayne or abide without beggynge oute of the seid cite, towne, hundred, or place."

The frequent enfranchisement of slaves in the Roman empire, which took place soon after Christianity became the religion of the State, has been said to have filled many towns with freemen, who possessed nothing but their liberty. Hence in part arose the necessity of that frequent legislation and provision for pauperism and mendicity, which is met with in the monuments of the Lower Empire. As the statutes of our Tudor Princes contained penalties on able-bodied mendicity, "*valiant beggers*,"* and that of Henry VII. is entitled "De Validis Mendicantibus repellendis," so the Code of Justinian has a title "De Mendicantibus Validis." Such mendicants were punished by the loss of their liberty, and by being reduced to the condition of *coloni*, who may be called the serfs of the Lower Empire, who could not be severed from the land even by the proprietor, and whose unhappy condition has recently been illustrated in a learned dissertation by one of the most eminent of living jurists.†

* First mentioned in statute 23 Edw. III. c. 7. See Reeves, vol. v. p. 14.

† Von Savigny, *Ueber den Römischen Colonat*, Vermischte Schriften, vol. ii.

From the latter part of the fifteenth century to the end of the sixteenth, an ever-increasing pauperism characterises the reigns of Henry VII., his son, and his grandchildren. A further cause of this spread of pauperism may probably be found in the historical fact, that many of the great landowners thought fit, during this period, to clear a good part of their estates, by pulling down houses, and turning tillage land into pasture. The statutory provisions on this subject, towards the end of the fifteenth and during the sixteenth century, at least establish the fact that this course was perseveringly and extensively pursued.

Moreover, the accumulation of wealth in few hands, seems to have led, during the same epoch, to a great change in the distribution and enjoyment of ownership, as well as occupation of landed property, and to have largely diminished that great number of landed proprietors, which, shortly before the accession of Henry VII., had justly formed a main ground of England's claim to superiority, in social condition, over many other countries.

Fortescue, in his celebrated treatise, tells his prince, "England is so thick spread and filled with rich and landed men, that there is scarce a small village in which you may not find a *knight*, an *esquire*, or some substantial householder, commonly called a *frankleyne*, all men of considerable estates. There are others who are called freeholders, and many yeomen, of estates sufficient to make a substantial jury, within the description before observed. There are several of those yeomen in England who are able to dispend by the year a hundred pounds and more; juries are very often made up of such." "Other countries, my prince, are not in such a happy situation, are not so well stored with inhabitants. Tho' there be in other parts of the world persons of rank and distinction, men of great estates and possessions, yet they are not so frequent, and so near situated one to another, as in England. *There is nowhere else so great a number of landowners.* In a

pp. 1—66. See also E. Laboulaye, *Histoire du Droit de Propriété foncière en Occident*, liv. ii. ch. xviii.

whole town, in any other country, you can scarce find a man of sufficiency enough to be put upon a jury."

The first of the statutes just alluded to, passed to prevent the conversion of tillage lands into pasture, was 4 Henry VII. c. 19. (1488). It prohibits the pulling down farm-houses, "to which twenty acres of land lying in tillage or husbandry" were annexed. Similar provisions were frequently repeated during the next 150 years, a fact which, as has been observed, strongly indicates that these legislative provisions were disregarded. The same statute of 1488, in its recital, distinctly states the existing evils, which it was intended to check. "Great inconvenyences daily doth encreace by desolacion, and pulling down and wilfull waste of houses and townes within this his realme, and leyeng to pasture londes whyche custumeably have been used in tilthe, wherby ydilnes, grounde and begynnyng of all myschefes, daily doo encreace; for where in some townes two hundred psones were occupied and lived by their lawfull labours, nowe ben there occupied two or three herdemen, and the residue fall in ydelnes, — the husbondrie, whiche is one of the grettest comodities of this realme, is gretly decaied." It is quite possible that the number of lords and squires who were owners of land in England, may have been more numerous at the death of Henry VIII., than they were at the accession of Henry VII.; but whether the class of the *larger* proprietors increased or diminished in that interval, there can be no doubt that the old "franklin" and the "yeoman" were gradually disappearing. Sir Frederick Eden adverts to the fact as one naturally arising from the improvement in agriculture. "The race of cottagers was going fast to decay: this must ever be the case in *an improved state of agriculture;* the half-starved proprietor of ten or twenty acres will often be persuaded to part with his land to a rich neighbour, who farms on an extensive scale."*

It was surely rather a mere increase of wealth unequally distributed, than any improvement in agriculture, that tended

* Eden, *State of the Poor*, vol. i. p. 115.

thus to extinguish the race of small proprietors. Before the end of the Roman Commonwealth, men like the Camilli and Curii, and other "half-starved proprietors of ten or twenty acres," had similarly ceased to exist; for when great masses of wealth were accumulated in few hands, the small proprietor was easily "persuaded to part with his land to his rich neighbour." Instances were not wanting in Imperial Rome, in which districts, even larger than the county of Sutherland, became a single estate; and thus it happened, that the Roman aristocracy never farmed on so extensive a scale as during the long period of the decline of the Empire.* Poets, historians, and philosophers have all agreed in deploring the very condition of society which Sir Frederick Eden here seems to approve; and which, however extensive its farms and estates may be, must certainly deprive itself of an important element in the constitution of every rightly ordered commonwealth, when it absorbs and extinguishes

> The happy man, whose wish and care
> A few paternal acres bound,
> Content to breathe his native air,
> In his own ground!

The statute, 25 Henry VIII. c. 13., prohibits the keeping of more than 2000 sheep by any one person. The prohibition is preceded by a recital that "sundry persons, within fewe years, had practised and invented ways and means how they might accumulate, and gather together into few hands, as well great multitude of farms as great plentitude of cattle, and in especial sheep, putting such lands as they can get to pasture, and not to tillage;" and as it was thought that the greatest occasion of this was "only the great profit that cometh of sheep, which now be come to a few persons' hands of this realm, in respect of the whole number of the king's subjects, that some have four-and-twenty thousand, some twenty thousand, some ten thousand, some six thousand, some five thou-

* The result of this downward progress was apparent to Pliny, N. H. xviii. 7. 3. "Verumque confitentibus Latifundia perdidere Italiam, imo et provincias." The chief stages of the same progress are indicated by passages of Livy, Sallust, Tacitus, and Appian.

sand, some more, and some less;" therefore the enactment was made. Contemporary writers bear testimony to the historical fact. Sir Thomas More*, in describing the cause of the increase of the offence of stealing, which characterised a great part of the reign of his royal master, mentions "the increase of pasture, by which sheep, mild and tractable, may now be said *to devour men*, and *unpeople towns and villages.* For, when an insatiate wretch, the plague of his country, resolves to enclose many thousand acres, landlords as well as tenants are turned out of possession by tricks or main force, or, wearied by ill-usage, they sell at last. Thus, men and women, married and single, old and young, with their poor and numerous families (for farming requireth many hands), are compelled to change their residence, and know not whither to go; when no tillage remaineth, there is no need of the labour they have been bred to. One shepherd can tend a flock which will graze acres, that would employ many hands were they in tillage...... Banish these evils; command those who have dispeopled so many acres to rebuild the villages they have destroyed, or to let their lands to those that will do so. Restrain those engrossings of the rich, nearly as bad as monopolies. If you find not a remedy for these ills, it is in vain to boast of your severity in punishing theft, which, though it may wear the appearance of justice, is neither just nor salutary. *For if you educate your people ill, and corrupt their manners from their infancy, and then punish them for crimes to which they are disposed by education, what is it but to make thieves and then punish them for being such?*"

So far that great and excellent man, Sir Thomas More, in the celebrated work which, according to the testimony of a distinguished living author †, "abounds in lessons of practical wisdom," and "would of itself have made his name immortal."

* In his "Utopia," which I quote from Cayley's *Memoirs of Sir Thomas More*, vol. ii. p. 24.

† Lord Campbell, *Lives of the Chancellors*, vol. i. p. 593., where it is justly observed that the work referred to in the text shows "what law reforms Sir Thomas More would have introduced when Lord Chancellor, had he not been three centuries in advance of his age."

"Depopulation," says Harrison *, "is growing;" and he speaks of the "inhabitants of manie places of our countrie as being devoured and eaten up, and their houses either altogether pulled down, or suffered to decaie by litle and litle." He speaks of "tenements fallen down, or into the lord's hands, or brought and united together by other men, so that in some one manor seventeen or eighteen or nineteen houses are shrunk;" and he even says, "that he could say somewhat of towns pulled down for sheep walks, and no more but the lordships (manor houses) now standing in them."

A statute passed in the reign of Henry VIII., in the year 1531, long before the dissolution of the monasteries, is a slight indication of the poor law legislation which was to follow. By this statute, 22 Henry VIII. c. 12., "An Acte concerning Punysshement of Beggers and Vacabunds," justices of peace in every county, dividing themselves, are to make diligent search and inquiry of all aged poor and impotent persons which live by alms, and, upon such search made, may authorise to beg within their divisions "such of the said impotent persons, which they shall think most convenient, to live of the charity and almes of the people." And the justices are to deliver "to every such impotent person, by them enabled to beg," a letter under hand, and sealed with such a seal as shall be engraved with the name of the limit wherein such impotent person shall be appointed to beg. If such impotent person so authorised to beg, "do beg in any other place than within the limit he shall be assigned unto," the justices are to punish him by imprisoning him in the stocks for two days and two nights, "giving him only brede and water;" and after that he is to be sworn to return to the limit within which he is authorised to beg.

Any one "who shall be a vagarant and go a begging having no such letter under seal," is to be stripped naked from the middle upwards, and whipped, if it shall seem to the justice of peace, or high constable, before whom he is taken, "that it be convenient so to punish such beggar;" if not, the vagrant beggar is to be set, by the space of three days and three nights,

* Cited in Eden, vol. i. p. 118.

in the stocks, there to have only bread and water; and thereupon the justice or constable is required, absolutely, "to limit to him a place to beg in," and to give him a letter, under seal, in due form, authorising him to beg, and to swear him to depart and repair thither immediately after his punishment.

It is manifest that every impotent person might, within the parish of his residence, after the passing of this act, still beg, without obtaining any licence, and live on the alms and charity which he could obtain by begging, in such his parish. It is only begging elsewhere than in "the limit he shall be assigned unto," that is prohibited; but even the impotent are punished for vagrant mendicancy, unless a permission to exercise the vocation of a vagrant be first obtained, in due form, under the statute.

Section 3. of the statute provides that, "if any one, being whole and mightie in body, and able to labour, having no land, or master, and using no lawful merchandize, craft, or mystery, whereby he might get his living, be vagarant, and can give none rekening how he do the lawfully get his living," he is to be taken to the next market town, there to be tied to the end of a cart, *naked*, and beaten with whips throughout the said market town, "till his body be bloody by reason of such whipping;" and his punishment had, he shall be enjoined, upon his oath, to return, "like as a true man ought to doo." He is to have, by way of passport, a letter, under seal, giving an account of his punishment, and prescribing a term during which he may beg, on his way to the place to which he is to return.

This statute is the first which can be said to make any provision for the relief of poverty; the previous legislation is wholly directed against vagrancy alone. The present authorises vagrancy, when its limits are once defined by a justice of peace; but, nevertheless, vagrancy is only authorised as a mode of relieving the impotent poor, each of whom may now levy his contributions on a wider district than his own proper parish, by way of rate in aid, in ease of his fellow parishioners. This certainly is a curious and most unsatisfactory mode of providing for the relief of destitution. The mendicancy which it has been the object of so many statutes to repress, is now expressly sanctioned; and the vagrant beggar may hold up his head, and avow his calling, if he can obtain, from any justice of peace, a license for its exercise.

In the session of parliament held in 1535-6, when this law had been in force about five years, it was repealed, by a statute which introduced a system of compulsory charity for relieving the poor. This important step in the progress of the legislature towards that mode of providing for the pauperism of the country, which was finally sanctioned towards the close of the reign of Queen Elizabeth, was made by the statute 27 Henry VIII. c. 25.: it is entitled, "An Act for Punishment of sturdye Vacabundes and Beggers;" and, after reciting the law last mentioned, it states that, forasmuch as it was not therein provided "how the said pore people and sturdie vacabundes should be ordered at their repaire and at theyr comyne into their countries, nor how the inhabitants of every hundred should be charged for the relief of the same pore people, nor yet for the setting and keping in work and labour of the aforesaid valiaunt vacabundes, at their said repaire into every hundred in this realme;" it therefore enacts, that the head officers and ministers of every city or parish, "at the repaire and comyng thider of suche poore creature or sturdie vacabund as is conteyned in the said acte, shall moost charitably receyve the same, and order the same in mann and forme followyng, that is to sey, that all the goṽnours and ministers of evy of the same cities, shires, towns, hundreds, wapentakes, lathes, rapes, rydinges, tythinges, hamlettes and parisshes, aswell within libties as without, shall not oonly socour, fynde, and keepe all and eṽy the same poore people, by way of voluntarie and charitable almes," in such wise "as none of them of verie necessitie shall be compelled to wander idly and go openly in begging to ask almes" in any of the same cities, &c., "but also to cause and to compell the said sturdie vacabund and valeant beggers to be sett and kepte to continuall labour, in suchewise as by their seid labours they and every of them may get their own living with the contynuall labour of their own hands;" this is to be done "on pain that every *parish* making default shall forfeit twenty shillings a month."

Section 3. of the statute enacts, that every "idell personne and personns, ruffelers, calling themselves servingmen, having no master, shall be entreated, used, and ordered," as specified in the act.

The fourth section directs that the head officers of corporate towns, and the *churchwardens,* or *two others* of every *parish,* shall, in good and charitable wise, take order "by gathering and pcuring of suche charitable and voluntarie almes of the good Christen people *within the same,* with boxes evy sonday, holyday, and other festivall day, or otherwise amonge themselffs, in such good and discrete wise as the pore, impotent, lame, feble, syke, and disseased people, beyng not able to worke, may be pvded, holpen, and relieved, so that in no wise they nor none of them be suffered to go openly in begging; and that such as be lustie, or havyng their lymmes stronge ynough to labour, may be daily kepte to contynuall labour, wherby evy one of them may gette their own substaunce and lyving, with their own hands, uppon peyne that officers of cities, parishes, &c. shall forfeit twenty shillings for evy month that it is omitted."

By the same statute (s. 9.), "evy preacher, pson, vicar and curate, as well in all and evy their smons, collacions, biddynges of the beads, as in time of all confessions, and at the making of the willes or testamentes of any psonnes at all times of the yere, shall exhorte, move, stirre, and pvoke people to be liball, and bountefully to extende their good and charitable almes and contribucions from tyme to tyme, for and toward the comforte and reliefe of the said pore, impotent, decrepite, indigent, and nedie people, as for the setting and keping to continuall worke and labour of the forsaid ruffelers, sturdie vacabundes, and valiaunt beggers."

The money collected is (s. 18.) to be kept in the "comen coffre or boxe standing in the churche of every parisshe," or else it is to be committed to the custody of such "good and substantiall trustie man" as they can agree upon, to be delivered as necessity should require. Almsgiving, otherwise than to these common boxes or gatherings, is prohibited on forfeiture of ten times the amount given.* "The overplus" of the collection of wealthy parishes is to be applied, by s. 23., in aid of other parishes within the same city, borough, town, hundred, lathe, rape, or wapentake.

Accounts of the produce and application of alms in every parish are, according to s. 5., to be kept by the "*parson*, vicar, or parish priest, or some other honest man of every *parish* of this realm, without taking or demanding any thing for the same."

Section 10. provides that any sturdy beggar, once convicted and whipped, which is the first appointed punishment, upon due proof of his continuing to wander in idleness, "shalbe eftsones not onely whipped ageyne, and sent into the citie, warde, towne, hundred, or parisshe, wherunto he was first appoynted, but also shall have the upper parte of the gristell of his right eare clene cutt of, so as it may appere for a pctuall token after that tyme that he hath ben a contemmour of the good order of the Cōmon welth."

By sect. 11. any sturdy beggar, "not havyng the upper parte of the right eare, and being cutt of as is aforesaid," is to be sent to the quarter sessions, and there to be indicted "for wandering, loitering, and idelnes," and, if convicted, is to have judgment, "to suffer peynes and execucion of dethe as a felon and as enmies of the Cōmen welthe." A proviso, s. 27., exempting mendicant friars from the penalties of the statute, will be referred to hereafter.†

The provisions of this statute of Henry VIII., passed in 1536, deserve to be compared with contemporaneous provisions found in an ordinance of Henry II. of France, issued at Saint-Germain-en-Laye, on the 9th July, 1547.‡ Poor boxes were to be placed in the churches and parishes of Paris, to receive the alms of the charitable people of that

* See the clause, sect. 13.; the substance of it is set out above, p. 3. Sect. 21. of the statute allows of almsgiving to fellow parishioners and prisoners.

† Below, p. 185.

‡ One of the provisions of this ordinance has already been compared with a contemporary clause of the English statute, above, p. 3. note †, where, the reference to Chapter IV. is meant for this place.

city; and every Sunday, the work of almsgiving was to be commended, not only by the curés or their vicars, but also, "*par les prescheurs en leur sermons et prédications.*" Mendicants were to be punished by the whip and the galleys.

Such was the existing legislation of England, respecting the poor, at the time when the monasteries were finally suppressed, in 1539, by "our most dread sovereign lord, Henry the Eighth, by the grace of God King of England and of France, defender of the faith, lord of Ireland, and in earth, immediately under Christ, supreme head of the Church of England."

Bishop Burnet, in his "History of the Reformation," estimates the clear yearly value of all the suppressed houses which then came into the king's hand, as at least 1,131,607*l.* 6*s.* 4*d.* That estimate has been said to be too high; although some have put the whole annual value of the property confiscated by the royal reformer at 1,600,000*l.*

It cannot be doubted that the aggregate amount was an enormous sum, and it seems to have been not less than one-fifth of the real property of the whole kingdom.* By reason of long leases then existing, the value, at the moment of confiscation, would perhaps not exceed one-tenth of that of the whole kingdom.† In any point of view, the rental of the property taken would have been more than sufficient to provide for all the pauperism of England, year by year, from the reign of King Henry VIII. down to that of Queen Victoria.

The king at first gave out, and "seemed to design, noble foundations;" but the result was, that either "out of policy, to give a general content to the gentry, by selling to them at low rates, or out of easiness to his courtiers, or out of an unmeasured lavishness in his expense, it came far short of what he had given out he would do."

Selden, who cannot be looked on as an over-zealous defender of the temporalities of the Church, has an interesting

* See Burn, *Ecclesiastical Law*, title *Monasteries*, x. 2., where data are stated for estimating, at different periods, the revenues of the *Church*: they appear to have been from one-fourth to one-third of those of the whole kingdom.

† Hallam, *Constitutional History of England*, vol. i. p. 104, *note*.

passage on this subject. It is found in the "Review," added to his "History of Tythes:"* "I doubt not but that every good man wishes that at our dissolution of monasteries, both the lands and impropriated tythes and churches possessed by them, (that is, things sacred to the service of God, although abused by such as had them,) had been bestowed rather for the advancement of the Church, to a better maintenance of the labouring and deserving ministry, to the fostering of good arts, *relief of the poor*, and other such good uses, as might retain in them, for the benefit of the Church or Commonwealth, a character of the wishes of those who first, with devotion, dedicated them (as in some other countries†, upon the Reformation, was religiously done), than conferred with such a prodigal dispensation, as it happened, on those who stood ready to devour what was sanctified, and have (in no small number) since found such inheritances thence derived to them, but as *Sejus* his horse, or the gold of *Tholouse*. But I abstain from censure, and add here, by the way, a complaint made to the parliament not long after the dissolution, touching the abuse that followed in the Church, through laymen's possessing of appropriated churches and tythes."

The author of the complaint‡, after speaking of the alms that the abbeys dealt, and the hospitality that they kept, proceeds: "But now that all the abbaies, with their lands, goods, and impropred parsonages, be in temporal mens hands; I do not here tell that one half penie worth of almes, or any other profit, cometh unto the people of those parishes. Your pretence of putting down abbeys, was to amend that was amiss in them. It was farr amiss, that a great part of the lands of

* Works, vol. iii. col. 1338.

† As in Wurtemburg, where a large proportion of the parishes possess a fund called *pium corpus*, arising principally "from funds which, previously to the Reformation, had been employed for the purposes of the Roman Catholic worship, and instead of being confiscated by the government, as was the case in England, were directed to be employed for charitable purposes." See Senior, *Statement of the Provision for the Poor*, p. 54. Bishop Latimer, on the seizure of the abbeys, moved that two or three might thus be left in every county, for pious uses. See Bishop Kennett's *Parochial Antiquities*, vol. ii. p. 48.

‡ Selden, ib. col. 1339.

the abbeys (which were given to bring up learned men, that might be preachers, to keep hospitalitie, and to give almesse to the poore) should be spent upon a few superstitious monks, which gave not forty pounds in almesse, when they should have given two hundred. It was amisse that the monks should have parsonages in their hands, and dealt but the twentieth part thereof to the poor, and preached but ones in a yeer to them that paid the tythes of the parsonages. It was amiss, that they scarcely, among twenty, set not one sufficient vicar to preach, for the tythes that they received. But se now how it that was amisse is amended, for all the godly pretence. It is amended even as the devil amended his dames legge (as it is in the proverb), when he should have set it right, he bracke it quite in peices. The monks gave to little almesse;—but now, where twenty pounds was geven yerely to the poore, in more than in a hundred places in Ingelande, is not one meales meat given. This is a fair amendment."

There can be no rational doubt that the poor would be placed in a far worse condition, by the dissolution of the monasteries under Henry the Eighth*, and that an immense accession would be made to the number of destitute vagrants who infested the country. The dissolution directly involved the great majority of some 50,000 persons in utter ruin, and many of them were compelled to swell the numbers of the unemployed wandering population of the day. When mendicant monks thus reinforced the ranks of merely lay vagrants and beggars, it would seem as if the edge of the sword of legislation was made sharper than ever. In the first year of the reign of Edward VI., a statute was passed full of provisions against vagrants, characterised by a barbarous and ruthless severity wholly unworthy of the legislation of any Christian people. By this statute, 1 Edw. VI. c. 3., "for the punishment of vagabondes, and for the relief of the poore and impotent parsons," it is recited, that "idlenes and vagabundrye is the mother and roote of all theftes, robberyes, and all evill actes and other mischiefe;" that "godlie lawes"

* Compare Mr. Hallam's idea, vol. i. pp. 108-109, with the facts and authorities of Brodie's *Introduction* to his *History of the British Empire*.

had been previously passed for repressing this "idlenes and vagabundrye," but that "ptelie by folische pitie and mercie of them which shoulde have seen the said godlie lawes executed, ptelie by the pverse nature and longe accustumed idleness of the parsons given to loytringe, the saide godlie statutes hitherto hath had small effecte, and idle and vagabounde psons, being unprofitable membres, or rather ennemyes, of the Comen wealthe, hath byn suffred to remayne and encreace and yet so doo, who, *yf thei should be punished by deathe, whippinge, emprysonement, or wth other corporall payne, it were not withowt their desertę*, for thexample of others and to the benefitt of the Cōmenwealth." And then the statute proceeds to enact, after repealing all former acts on the subject, that "any person so living idelye and loyteringlie," may be branded with a hot iron with the letter "V," and to be adjudged to be the slave for two years of the person who brings him to justice; and the master is to order the said slave "as followethe, that is to saie: to take such persone adjudged a slave with him, and onelye giving the saide slave breade and water, or small dryncke, and such refuse of meate as he shall thincke mete, cawse the said slave to worke, by beating, cheyninge, *or otherwise,* in such worke and labor, how vyle so ever it be, as he shall putt him unto." The slave's absence from his master for fourteen days during his term of slavery, is to be followed by a second branding, *and slavery for life;* and, if he run away a second time, he is to be *a felon;* "and such loiterer and runaway, thereof being lawfullie indicted and attaynted, or otherwise condempned, *to suffer paynes of death,* as other fellons ought to doo."

The very framers of the statute seem to have felt that there might not be found, among the humane and generous people of England, men who would be willing to desecrate their hearths by the presence of a domestic slave. If no Englishman would submit to the degradation of becoming the owner of a slave, the above stated clauses of the statute would be futile. Provision was therefore made for this anticipated practical difficulty in executing the statute: "Allthoughe there be no man wch shall demaunde suche loyterer or loyterers, as before expressed, into their svice, yet, nevertheless, any justice of peace, dwelling in that place or country, *by his or their offices*, shallbe hereafter bounde, by virtewe of this acte, not onelie to enquire of all suche idle psons, *but allso, if thei doo espie any suche vacaboundes or idle parsone, or yf anny suche be detected unto them, to examyn him or her of the tyme of their vagaboundrye*, and yf it shall appear, to anny justice of peaxe, any suche man or woman to have been a vagraunte and vacabound, or ydle parson, by the space as is aforesaid, to cawse the same to be marcked on the brest with an V, made with a hote iron,"—"*and then to be delivered to the hedd officer or constable*" of the place, "*there to be nourished and kepte of the same citie, towne, or village, in chaynes or otherwise,*—to be *slave* to the corporacon of the citie, or to the inhabitaunte of the towne or village, that he or she were borne in, after all suche same condition, space of yeres, orders, punishments for runninge awaie, and all others, as are expressed of a comen or private person to whom any such loyterer is adjudged a slave." Another clause, s. 8., is, "that if it fortune, when the saide vacabounde is brought to the said citie, towne, or village, where the saide parsone *said* he was borne, to appere and be manifest, that he or she was *not* there borne, that then, *for suche lye*, the said vagraunte *shalbe marked on the face* with an S, and *be slave* to the inhabitants or corporation of the citie, towne, or vyllage, where the saide vagraunt said he was borne, *for ever*."

A penalty was imposed (by s. 6.) on any city or town for the default of such slave being allowed "to live idellye—by the space of three wóking daies to gither." The slave's employment was to be "in chaynes at the comen wókes, in amending high waies or other comen wóke, or from man to man." And by s. 16., any master might put a ring of iron about the neck, arm, or leg of his slave, and any one helping such bond of iron from such slave was to forfeit 10*l*.

This outline of the law of absolute slavery thus introduced among a nation of freemen, would be incomplete if the 13th clause were omitted. Among other things, it provided that if any such slave shall be "warde, or bondeman, or neif of bloode," to any one, then he "to whome anny suche warde, bondeman, or neif shall apptayne," may seize and take such wards, bondsmen, or neifs, and they were "discharged of the saide slaverie."

This provision leads us to suppose that the number of *serfs*, who are here designated, and the rights of whose lords were thus jealously protected by the legislature, must at this time have been still considerable. In England the law had always, from the time of the Conquest, not only treated the serf as himself the mere property of his lord, but even held that all which the serf gained, or saved, by his industry, likewise belonged to his lord. Hence the rule that no serf could purchase his own freedom, for all that he possessed was his lord's already.* The 13th section of this statute is therefore meant as a measure of "protection" to the lords, in the enjoyment of their ancient right of property; and shows that the very legislature, which professed to protect the public from vagrant mendicancy, by visiting every such offence with so severe a punishment, was yet willing to condone any number of such offences, rather than, by punishing them, to obstruct the enjoyment by any lord, of his right of property in his serf.

It may be added, that these serfs were still found in England as late as the reign of James I.; but ultimately, though the legislature never did any thing to emancipate them, they somehow obtained their freedom. Such of them as still belonged to the Crown in Queen Elizabeth's time, were enfranchised by her in 1574, and the instrument of their manumission is deserving of perusal. The Church, which had alone stood, for centuries, between them and their oppressors, and had largely contributed to their emancipation from the bondage in which they were held by lay lords, was, herself, still a little slow to emancipate them, when they were

* Glanville, v. 5. "Illud tamen notandum est, quod non potest aliquis in Villenagio positus, libertatem suam propriis denariis suis quærere. Posset enim tunc à Domino suo secundum jus et Consuetudinem Regni ad Villenagium revocari, quia omnia Catalla cujuslibet Nativi, ita intelliguntur esse in potestate Domini sui, quod *propriis denariis versus Dominum suum à Villenagio se redimere, non poterit.*"

found on Church lands. It seems to have been a harder task to practise than to preach. Sir Thomas Smith says, that "the holy fathers had convinced the laity how dangerous a practice it was for one Christian man to hold another in bondage, so that temporal men were glad to manumit all their villeins. But the said holy fathers, with the abbots and priors, did not in like sort by theirs; for they also had a scruple in conscience to impoverish and despoil the Church, and so kept their villeins still."*

Serfs of the Church were, however, not only in a far better condition than that of the serfs of private lords, but during the greater part of a rude and barbarous age, serfdom under the Church was often preferred to liberty itself. Instances are found in which, by the very instrument of manumission, the serf of a private lord, as the first and only act of his brief freedom, voluntarily made himself the serf of the Church."† The same superiority in condition of the ecclesiastical serf is also evidenced by an old German proverb.‡

This statute of 1 Edw. VI. c. 3., which contains so many severe and cruel provisions, for repressing vagrancy, gives considerable powers for the relief and control of the impotent poor.

Section 9. of the statute prohibits the *impotent* poor from begging anywhere except in the places where they were born, or had resided three years. These impotent poor persons, having this domicile of birth or residence, are all to be "bestowed and provided for of the tenauntries, cotages, or other convenient howses, to be lodged in at the costes and charges of the saide cities, townes, boroughes, and villages, there to be relieved and cured by the devočon of the good people of the saide citie," &c. By s. 10., all aged and other impotent poor were, once a month, to be removed from

* Smith, *Commonwealth of England*, vol. iii. p. 10., quoted by Blackstone, *Commentaries*, vol. ii. p. 96.

† M. Guerard, *Prolegomènes* to the Cartulaire de l'abbaye de Saint Pierre de Chartres, p. 56, and the charter of Gibuin and Gualand, A.D. 1061, p. 189. of the same Chartulary, "Testes Gibuini, vice Sancti Petri, *cui se sponte subdidit* Ulgerius major," &c.

‡ *Unter dem Krummstabe ist gut wohnen.*

places in which they were found begging, if they had not been born in such places, or had not resided there three years. The removal was to be to their places of birth, or of residence for three years, "there to be provided for, kepte and nourished of almes." A proviso of the act authorises a discretionary punishment for the idleness of all impotent poor persons, who were not so impotent as that they could not do *some* manner of work; and this punishment was to be "with chayninge, beating, or *otherwise*," as should seem convenient.

For the great purpose of relieving "suche which ar in unfayned miserie, and to whome charitie ought to be extended," it is enacted that, every Sunday and holyday, after the reading of the Gospel, "the curate of every pishe doo mak, according to suche tallent as God hath given him, a godlie and brief exhortac̃on to his pishoners, moving and exciting them to remembre the poore people, and the dewtie of Xp̃ian charitie in reliving of them which be *their brethrene in Christe, borne in the same pishe, and neding their helpe.*"

Rapin gives us an account of the real occasion of passing this statute, which, so far as one class of its provisions is concerned, may properly be called, a "very remarkable act against vagabonds." He says: "This law was thought very severe in a country like England, where slavery seems inconsistent with the privileges of the people. But herein the Court, by whom the Parliament was governed, had an eye only to the monks, who being gone from their monasteries, little inured to labour, could not think of working for their livelihood. Those men spent their time in going from house to house to cabal against the Government, and inspire the people with the spirit of rebellion. So the Court judging it to be an effect of their idleness, and that if they betook themselves to some employment, they would at length lose this habit, resolved to make them work, how loth soever they might be. Meanwhile, as the law was general, it occasioned great murmurings among the people. Wherefore it was never rigourously executed, and another parliament repealed it." *

* Rapin's *History of England*, book xvi. vol. viii. p. 34. London, 1732.

Bishop Burnet has also observed of this statute *, that "it was chiefly levelled at the monks and friars," who, their occupation now gone, went up and down the country and found the people "apt to have compassion on them." This repressive legislation was, perhaps, none the milder, because it proceeded in good part from those who had got possession of the lands of the wandering monks, and from ecclesiastics of the new establishment.

This savage and inhuman law, as we have already seen, did not remain long on the statute book. Some of its cruel penalties against vagrants were repealed, and its other provisions modified, by 3 & 4 Edw. VI. c. 16.

The character of Henry the Eighth's legislation to repress vagrancy, was, certainly, severe enough; but it becomes humanity itself if compared with the law before us. It would be a mistake to suppose that the legislature, in the first year of the reign of Edward VI., intended to diminish the severity of the previous penalties against vagrancy.† The statute of 27 Henry VIII. c. 25., against vagrants, passed just before the statute for the dissolution of the lesser monasteries (27 Henry VIII. c. 28.), contained an express provision, in favour of the very men who were so soon to be made wanderers, and who were now, in the reign of Edward VI., to be hunted down, like so many wild beasts. A mild and humane provision, of the former statute, enacted, on the very eve of the dissolution of the smaller monasteries that, "In as moche as friers mendiantes have litle or nothing to lyve uppon, but onely by the charitie and almes of Christien people, this acte therefore, ne any thing therin conteyned, shalbe pjudiciall or hurtfull unto any psonne or psonnes, for gyving of theym in genal or pticular any man almes in money, vitaile, or other thing, ne also to theym or any of them, for beyng or remaynyng out of theyr places where they were

* *History of the Reformation*, pt. ii. bk. i. p. 83.

† Report from the Commissioners for Inquiring into the Poor Laws, in 1834, p. 7. "It appears that the severity of this act (27 Henry VIII. c. 25.) prevented its execution. Such, at least, is the reason assigned for its repeal by the 1 Edw. VI. c. 3., which recites, &c., *and as a milder punishment*, enacts," &c.

borne or had their last habitacion, or for passing abrode to gather the almes and charitie of Christen people, or for contynuance of theyr religion as they have been accustomed to do."

The provision for the poor, under 3 & 4 Edw. VI. c. 16., was still a charitable voluntary contribution, made by the devotion of the good people of the city, town, or place, where the poor were born, or had dwelt for three years.

So far the voluntary principle alone was appealed to, and the appeal, seemingly, was not successful; for by 5 & 6 Edw. VI. c. 2., collectors appointed under the statute are enjoined, on the Sunday next, or next but one, after Whitsunday, gently to ask every man and woman, what they of their charity will give eekly towards the relief of the poor, to write the same in a book, and to distribute what they collect weekly to the poor and impotent. If any one able to further the charitable work, do obstinately and frowardly refuse to give, or do discourage others, the minister and churchwardens are gently to exhort him; if he will not be so persuaded, the bishop is to send for him, and induce and persuade him, by charitable ways and means, and so according to his discretion, take order for the reformation thereof.

This statute (5 & 6 Edw. VI. c. 2.), passed in 1551, seems, like those which preceded it, to have been ineffectual for the adequate relief of the poor. It was thought necessary to repeat its preamble and enactments in the statute, 2 & 3 Philip & Mary, c. 5., passed in 1555. But under the Roman Catholic, as under the Protestant reign, the gentle askings of the collectors, the gentle exhortations of the ministers and churchwardens, and the charitable ways and means of the bishop, failed "to induce and persuade" the parishioners to "give weekly of their charity," as it was intended they should, towards the relief of the poor.

Religious feelings, and ecclesiastical authority, were in vain invoked, to enforce on the people the performance of their Christian duty. The Reformation had taken away from the Church, before Queen Mary's accession, a large part of its wealth; and lay impropriators, whether under a Roman

Catholic or a Protestant sovereign, felt no such obligation as had certainly attached on the clerical holders of tithes and other possessions.

It cannot be doubted, that during eight or nine hundred years, a large part of what had been given to the Church, for the use and benefit of the poor, was applied, by the Church, to the purposes for which it was given. But, the statute book, throughout the reigns of Henry VIII., Edward VI., and Mary, bears ample testimony to the magnitude of the evil of an increasing pauperism, with which society, and not the Church alone, had then to deal; and which, towards the close of Elizabeth's reign, ended in the casting of a burden on property, locally situated in each ecclesiastical district, the parish; and in authorising the taxation of the occupiers and inhabitants of each parish, for the relief of its poor.

CHAP. VI.

PAUPER LEGISLATION OF THE REIGN OF ELIZABETH.

Magnus ab integro sæclorum nascitur ordo.—VIRGIL.

IT appears that, during the whole of the long and glorious reign of Queen Elizabeth, the statesmen by whom she was served made the condition of the poorer classes of her subjects an especial object of their attention and care. Legislative provisions, for a pauperism which seemed to grow with the very growth of the country itself, were slowly and gradually adopted.

"Pauper ubique jacet!" is said to have been a frequent exclamation of the Queen in her various progresses, as she beheld the immense numbers of destitute poor people who, in every part of the country, flocked to see her. It is said that she made it a continued study how to release her people from the poverty which was so widely diffused, and to make their labour more profitable to themselves and the nation. It is therefore probable, that the personal feelings of the Queen may have been interested in such acts of her parliaments as related to the poor. She may thus have striven to make compensation for sternness and cruelty to some, even of her own sex, by that long course of benevolent legislation in behalf of the most helpless classes of her subjects, which characterises her reign, and was closed by the celebrated statute, passed shortly before her death, under the provisions of which all relief of the poor of England and Wales has now been administered for 250 years.

We shall best understand the grounds of that statute, the 43 Eliz. c. 2., and the intention of its framers, if, in the first instance, we take a survey of the series of provisions which had previously been made by parliaments of Queen Elizabeth, respecting the relief of the poor. This survey will not only make us acquainted with the care and attention then bestowed on a subject which was felt to be important, but will be most instructive in exemplifying the result of the various remedies applied in succession to the great and growing evil of pauperism. It will be found that, by one of these remedies, the parochial tie, which in England had connected the Church and the poor for at least a thousand years, was wholly done away; a district for the settlement of the poor was created, quite independent of parochial boundary; a power of removing the poor to and from such district was given, wholly independent of parochial control; and the wants of the poor were to be relieved by the compulsory taxation of the whole district. This completely new organisation of relief of the poor, had a fair and full trial; for the statute by which it was created, remained in force more than twenty years. This provision, having been repealed, no longer appears in ordinary editions of the statutes; and it is believed that the resuscitation of this important page in the history of the Poor Law, will be effected, for the first time, in the present chapter.

The first great measure of reform of the Poor Laws, under Queen Elizabeth, is the statute 5 Eliz. c. 3. (A.D. 1562-3), "An Acte for the Reliefe of the Poore," passed "to thintent that idell and loytering ꝑsons, and valiant beggers, may be avoyded, and thimpotent, feble, and lame, w[ch] are the poore in very dede, should bee hereafter relieved and well provided for." This statute, after confirming 22 Hen. VIII. c. 12., and 3 & 4 Edw. IV. c. 16., contains a series of provisions, corresponding to those of former statutes, for the appointment of collectors of charitable alms for the relief of the poor *in parishes.* It superadds, however, a very important section to those contained in former statutes, for it enacts (s. 7.) that if any person "of his or their frowarde or wilfull minde, shall obstinatly refuse to gyve weekly to the releef of the poore, according to his or their habilitees, that then the bishoppe or ordinarie of the dyoces, chauncellours, or their cōmissaries," shall have power to bind him to appear at the next sessions. If he refuse to be so bound, the bishop is authorised to commit him to prison, there to remain until he shall become bound as aforesaid; and at the sessions (s. 8.) the justices, "if the said obstinate ꝑson doo appeare before them, shall charitably and gentelly perswade and move the said obstinate psons textende his or their charitee towardes the relief of the poore of the ꝑishe where he or she inhabitethe and dwelleth; and yf he or she shall obstinatly and wilfully stande in the same, and will not bee ꝑswaded therin by the sayd justices, maio^{r}, bailiefes, or other heade officers, that then yt shall and may be laufull to and for the sayd justices,—wth the churchewardens wher the sayd obstinate ꝑson shall inhabite, or one of them, to cesse, taxe, and lymit upon every suche obstinate ꝑson so refusing, according to their good discretions, what sōme the said obstinate ꝑson shall pay, weekly, towardes the relief of the poore wthin the sayde ꝑishe where he or she shall inhabyte and dwell." If he refuse to pay, the justices are, "upon complaynte and certificate to them by the collectoures and churchwardens of the same ꝑshe wher the sayd obstinate ꝑson shall dwell, to cōmit the said obstinate ꝑson and ꝑsons so refusing to pay, to pryson, to the next gaole, there to remaine wthout bayle or maineprise till he or they have payde the sayd sōme so appointed, taxed, and limited, together wth tharrerages therof, yf any suche shall fortune to bee."

Some other clauses of the statute can only be carried out by the action of the bishop, and he is, to a considerable extent, invested with the duty of an administrator of relief to the poor. One of these clauses (s. 10.) imposes heavy penalties on justices of the peace for disobedience to the statute, and the money levied on any of them is to be employed to the use of the poor "of any *ꝑishe* or *ꝑishes* wthin the said countie where the said justices dwell, at the oversight and appointment of the bishoppe, or his chauncellour, of the same diocesse." Another clause (s. 9.) directs that "the bishoppe of the diocesse shall—examyne howe and after what maner ys bestowed," any sum of money which any person had, by his foundation, appointed to the use of the poor, or for the repairing of highways or bridges. The bishops are to call to account the parties which claim the said money, "and thereupon to take suche order as the same from thensfoorthe be distributed to the poore."

Queen Elizabeth, or her statesmen, seem to have been most anxious to ensure the performance by the bishop of these important functions, touching the administration of relief to the poor, with which they now invested him. The penalty for neglect to perform this ancient episcopal duty, now enforced by a statutory sanction, was fixed at 20*l.* "to be employed to thuse of the poore." Next, it is provided, by sec. 10., that, if any parish, city, or town, have in it "mo poore and impotet folkes, not hable to labo^{r}, then the said pishe ys able to relief," on certificate thereof, justices are to examine the certificate, and, finding the same true, "shall then grante unto suche and as many of the said poore folkes, as by their discretion they shall thinck good, a sufficient licence under the seale appointed for the limit, to go abrode, to begge, get, and receyve the charitable almes of thinhabitantes of the countrey, *out of the sayd parishes, cities, and townes so surchardged.*" If the poor person, so licensed, transgress the appointed limits, and beg elsewhere, he is to be taken for a "valiant beggar," and punished accordingly.

Compulsory taxation of any parishioner, by merely *secular* authority, for the relief of the poor, is now for the first time authorised by this statute of 5 Eliz. c. 3.; but it is only in the case of obstinate refusal to comply with exhortations of ministers and churchwardens, followed by obstinate refusal to yield to the persuasions of the bishop, that the perverse recusant can be handed over to the secular arm.

The parochial principle is, therefore, strengthened by this statute, and the ministrations of the Church and its parochial officers are preserved. At the same time, that which had been, heretofore, more or less, a contribution of Christian charity, is now, in substance, converted into a compulsory assessment, depending on the amount of each parishioner's property, and, in strictness of law, equally due from each parishioner, whether Christian, Jew, or Heathen.

The 5 Eliz. c. 3. remained in force, and the parochial administration of relief to the poor, was carried out under it, for a period of about nine years.

Corresponding with this first statute of Elizabeth, relating to the relief of the poor, but preceding it by a few years, we find an Ordinance of Henry II., king of France, issued on 13th February, 1551. After reciting that beggars had become "quasi *innumerables*" at Paris, and that "the collects and alms which it was endeavoured to collect weekly in each parish, had so much diminished, and the charity of the residents in easy circumstances, was so much cooled, that it was impossible to continue to the poor, the alms that had been weekly distributed to them:" therefore the parliament was authorised to name commissioners, who were to collect what every one of their charity would weekly give, for the support of the indigent poor. This ordinance was issued fifteen years later than that of Francis I., which first provided for the giving of parochial relief to the impotent poor at their dwellings.

But the pauperism and mendicity which prevailed in Paris, appeared to need an absolute tax for the relief of the poor, and ample provision was made, by the same ordinance, for compulsory taxation of every one, in proportion to his means rather than to the extent of his charitable disposition. The ordinance requires the commissioners to make a list of the sums which every inhabitant was willing to contribute, and to submit it to the parliament, which is thereupon to tax every inhabitant "weekly, according to his offers and means: *par sepmaine, à raison des ses offres et facultés.*" *

In 1561, an ordinance, dated at Fontainebleau, and prepared by the illustrious De l'Hôpital, was issued in the name of Charles IX., reforming various abuses which prevailed in the administration of the hospitals of France; and in 1566 another royal ordinance, dated at Moulins, also the work of

* The Ordinance proceeds: "Voulant, que chacun manant et habitant de quelque qualité qu'il soit, qui sera refusant payer la taxe à laquelle il aura esté cottisé et imposé par nostre dite cour, ou ses commis et députés, soit exécutés et contraints payer ladite taxe pour l'advenir, sans préjudice des restes qu'il pourrait devoir pour le passé."

the same great chancellor, provided for the repression of mendicity and vagabondage, and completely adopted the principle of compelling each parish to provide for the relief of its poor. The Ordinance of Moulins, which is almost an anticipation of what was enacted in England under Elizabeth, some thirty years later, completed the body of legislation, respecting the poor, of which De l'Hôpital appears to have been the author.*

In 1572, the statute 14 Eliz. c. 5. effected a great alteration in the poor law of England. It is entitled, "An Acte for the Punishement of Vacabondes, and for Relief of the Poore and Impotent," and begins by reciting that all parts of the realm were "with roges, vacabonde, and sturdy beggers exceedinglye pestred," and, "for avoydinge cōfusion by reason of numbers of lawes concerninge the ꝑmisses standing in force togeather," proceeds to enact that the statutes 22 Hen. VIII. c. 12., 3 & 4 Edw. VI. c. 16., and 5 Eliz. c. 3., "shalbee, from and after the feaste of Saincte Bartholomewe thapostell next comynge, utterly void, frustrate, and of none effect."

Among the provisions which the new statute substitutes for those of the previous law, we may pass rapidly over the series of regulations, still of much severity, for the repression of vagrancy and mendicancy. A long clause gives a very comprehensive definition, or description, of the persons to be considered as vagrants, within the penalties of the act.

The provision of the 14 Eliz. c. 5. s. 16., for the relief of the impotent poor, is deserving of a closer attention. "For-

* M. De Watteville, *Législation Charitable*, pref. p. viii., speaks of this last-named ordinance, and of De l'Hôpital, as follows: "L'Ordonnance de Moulins en 1566, plus souvent citée quoiqu'elle soit, à notre avis, moins remarquable, renouvelle l'ordre aux villes, bourgs et villages de secourir leurs pauvres, et défend à ces derniers de demander l'aumône hors du lieu de leur domicile: '*et, à ces fins, seront les habitants tenus de contribuer à la nourriture des dits pauvres, selon leur facultés, à la diligence des maires, echevins, consuls et marguilliers des paroisses.*' Cette ordonnance complète l'ensemble de la législation charitable, que nous a léguée un des plus grands hommes d'état, une des gloires les plus pures dont s'honore la France. On trouve dans ces lois justes, bienveillantes et ternes, l'homme vertueux qui, sur le declin d'une vie glorieuse, pouvait dire avec un noble orgueil: *J'ai soutenu les affligés contre ceux qui les voulaient opprimer, les pauvres contre les riches, et les faibles contre les forts.*"

asmuch as charitye would that poore, aged, and ympotent ꝑsones should, as necessarylye be provided for, as the said roges, vacabondes, and sturdye beggers repressed, and that the said aged, ympotent, and poore people, should have convenient habitacõns and *abydinge places* throughout this realme, to *settle* themselves uppon, to the end that they, nor any of them, should hereafter begge or wander about." It is therefore enacted that all justices of the peace, &c., "shall-devide themselves, and so being devided, shall, within every of their severall divisions and aucthorities, make diligent searche and enquierye of all aged poore, ympotent, and decayed persons, *borne within their said divisions and lymittes,* or whiche were *there dwelling within three yeres next before* this ꝑsent parliament, which lyve, or of necessitye be compelled to lyve, by almes of the charytye of the people," and shall make a register containing the names of all such aged, decayed, and impotent poor people; and when their number is thus known, the justices are to "devise and appointe, within evrye there said severall divisions, meete and convenient places by their dyscretions, to *settle* the same poore people for their habitacõns and abydynges, yf the ꝑishe within the whiche they shalbe founde, shall not or wyll not provide for them; and shall also, within lyke convenient tyme, number all the said poore people within there said severall lymytes;" and that done, *the justices* shall, by their good discretion, *tax* the inhabitants of such *division** "to suche weekely charge, as they and everye of them shall weekely contribute towardes the releef of the said poore people."

Section 21. of the statute enacts that, "Yf any ꝑson or ꝑsons, beinge able to further this charitable worcke, will obstinatly refuse to geve, towardes the helpe and relief of

* Reeves, *History of English Law,* vol. v. p. 21., after mentioning the statute, 5 Eliz. c. 3., says, "This led to the taxation of every *parishioner,* by 14 Eliz. c. 5." This is very inaccurate, and must have been taken, like the rest of the page in which it is found, from a reference to some common edition of the Statutes at Large, in which none of the statutes, 5 Eliz. c. 3., 14 Eliz. c. 5., and 39 Eliz. c. 3., are printed at length. My extracts are from the "Statutes of the Realm," as printed by order of King George III.: folio, London, 1810-1828.

the said poore people, or doo wylfully discourage others from so charitable a deede, the said obstinate ꝑson or wylfull dyscourager shall ꝓsently be brought before two justices, to shewe the cause of his obstinate refusall or wilfull discouragement, and to abyde suche order therein as the said justices shall appointe; yf hee refuse so to doo, then to be cōmitted to the next gaole," "ther to remayne untyll hee be contented with their said order, and doo ꝑfourme the same."

Provision is made, by section 23., that the justices, out of the surplus of such collections (the impotent being first provided for), "shall place and settle to worcke the roges and vacabondꝭ—borne within there said countyes, or there abydinge for the moste parte wthin the said three yeers, there to be holden to worck—to get their livinges, & *to lyve and to bee sustayned onely upon their labour and travayle.*" And by section 27., "the justices in sessions—within any of the countyes, cyties, or townes, where collection of mone cannot ꝓsentlye bee had," are "to graunt—to suche and so manye of the said poore and ympotent, or diseased ꝑsons, to aske, geather, and receve, within suche other towne, paryshe, or ꝑishes of the said countye, as the said justices shall especyallye name," charitable devotions and alms at the houses of the inhabitants, such towns or parishes being within the division of the same justices. "And the inhabitauntes of every such ꝑishe or ꝑishes, to the whiche suche poore or ympotent ꝑsons shalbee so appoineted as ys aforesaid, shalbe coacted and bound by vertue of this acte, under such payne as to the dyscretion of the said justices shall seeme convenient, to releve the said poore and ympotent ꝑsons in suche sorte as the said justices shall appoint."

This statute, 14 Eliz. c. 5., certainly effected a very sweeping and radical change in the poor law. The previous power of taxation was conferred on the quarter sessions, to be exercised only in the exceptional case of an obstinate person, complained against by the minister and churchwardens, and the bishop. Now, a discretionary power is conferred on justices of peace, out of sessions, to tax every person dwelling in their division, and to direct the application of the money which they are thus authorised to levy.

The previous legislation of Henry VIII. and Edward VI., and of Elizabeth herself, seems always to have treated the relief of the poor as a parochial burden, in raising and distributing which the churchwardens, overseers, minister, and bishop, were respectively concerned. But now, by 14 Eliz. c. 5., the parochial system is abandoned, and the charge is wholly thrown on the inhabitants of the division within the jurisdiction of the assessing justices.

Birth, or a three years residence, even in the case of the impotent poor, seems to have been the necessary title to relief of any one residing in a division; and the words of the seventeenth clause of the statute clearly authorise the removal of any impotent poor person from his dwelling-place, in any division, in which he had not either been born, or resided during three years, to the division in which he had been born or had so resided.*

Poverty, therefore, even when arising from old age, sickness, or accident, now renders a man, who has committed no crime, liable to be taken by the constable of the hundred in which he is dwelling, "on horsebacke, in carte, or otherwyse, as shall seeme best to their discretions, to the next counstable, and so from counstable to counstable — tyll the said ꝑson be brought to the place," perhaps at the extremity of the kingdom, in which, according to the statute, he is to be settled.†

* The substance of the clause is contained in Lambarde, *The Duties of Constables*, p. 30.

† The statute of 1 & 2 Edw. VI. c. 3. s. 10., and 3 & 4 Edw. VI. c. 16. s. 5., had only authorised the monthly clearance and removal of all "aged impotent and lame persons, *beggars*," from places where they had not been born, and had not resided for three years. The statute 5 Eliz. c. 3. confirmed the 3 & 4 Edw. VI. c. 16. in this respect, and otherwise; but the 14 Eliz. c. 5. has no limitation whatever, on the generality of its words, to restrict them to *beggars*. It may, however, be, that practically, the removal would take place under the 14 Eliz., just as it had done under the 3 & 4 Edw. VI. c. 16. Possibly some act of begging in a parish would, by a lawyer looking at other clauses of the act of 14 Eliz., be considered necessary, to bring a man within the meaning of its 17th section; the *words* of that section do not, however, require the man to be a beggar, or to have begged, to render him removable, but merely to be poor, and non-settled.

By sect. 40., if any one should refuse to be bestowed in the said abiding places, and should depart and beg elsewhere, he is to be accompted a rogue and vagabond, within the penalties of the statute. Whenever any city or town corporate shall chance to have in it "moore poore folkes then the inhabitauntes thereof shalbe able to releve," justices in sessions are to provide for this surplus of paupers "by gevinge of lycense to begge" in other places of the county, "out of suche cytie or towne corporate so surchardged." A similar provision was found in the statute 5 Eliz. c. 3.* But in the present statute, 14 Eliz. c. 5., other licensed vagrants and beggars are named besides these sanctioned by justices of peace. Severe as are these penalties on unauthorised mendicancy, the statute preserved the existing practice, in other cases, as in the instance of "schollers of the universityes of Oxford or Cambridge" authorised under the seal of the university, by the commissary, chancellor, or vice-chancellor, of the same (s. 5.); and in that of persons licensed by the lord chancellor or keeper of the great seal of England for the time being (s. 12.).

Sect. 33. of the statute gives protection by the imposition of a penalty against the bringing from either Ireland or the Isle of Man, of "any vacabond, roge, or beggar, *or any suche as shalbe forced, or very lyke to lyve by begging,* within the realme of England or Wales, being borne in the realme of Ireland or in the said Isle of Manne." The penalty is to be "to the use of the poore *of the same parishe* in whiche they were sett on land:" a provision which, if it had existed, and could have been enforced, during the recent famine and desolation of Ireland, might have saved an immense expenditure to the parish of Liverpool, then inundated by Irish pauperism.

The statute, 18 Eliz. c. 3. (1575), "An Acte for the setting of the Poore on worke, and for the avoȳding of Ydleness," purports to be passed "for some better explanac̃on, and for some needfull addic̃on" to the statute of 14 Eliz. c. 5.

* See the tenth section.

It contains two classes of provisions, each of which now appears for the first time in our pauper legislation, and the principle of each of which has since greatly divided the opinions of men, both in England and elsewhere. "To the intente yowthe maye be accustomed and brought up in laboure and worke,—and *that other poore and needye ꝑsons, being willinge to worcke, maye bee set on worcke,*" it is enacted, that "in everye cyttye and towne corporate w^th^in this realme, a competent store and stocke of woole, hempe, flaxe, iron, or other stufe, by thappoinetemente and order of the maior, bayliffꝭ, justicꝭ, or other head officers having rule in the said cityes or townes," shall be provided, the said stores and stocks, to be committed to the custody of the collectors and governors of the poor, "to thentente everye suche poore and needye ꝑson, olde or younge, able to doe any worcke, standing in necessitye of releife, shall not, for want of worcke, goe abrode, eyther begginge, or committinge pilfringes, or other misdemeano^r^, lyvinge in idlenes." The object of the legislature is solemnly to inaugurate that right, respecting which, under the name of *droit au travail*, so much has been heard, in a neighbouring country, in more modern times; and the parliament of Queen Elizabeth, now guarantees employment to all those members of the community, who cannot find it for themselves. The provision is worthy of being compared with the declarations of the Constituent Assembly of France, made in 1790, and of the subsequent Convention, in 1793, neither of which oversteps the proper province of legislation further than is done by this statute of Elizabeth.*

* The Assemblée Constituante, 12 Août, 1790, "Instruction," &c. ch. viii. (Recueil, tom. i. p. 216.). "Il faut que l'indigent soit secouru, non seulement dans la faiblesse de l'enfance, et dans les infirmités de la vieillesse, mais même lorsque, dans l'âge de la force, le défaut de travail l'expose à manquer de subsistance: ce n'est pas seulement à la sensibilité de l'homme, c'est à la prévoyance du moraliste, c'est à la sagesse du législateur, que ces devoirs se recommandent." The Déclaration des Droits de l'Homme et du Citoyen, made on 24th June, 1793, by the Convention Nationale, was, on this point, as follows: "Art. 21. Les secours publics sont une dette sacrée. La societé doit la subsistence aux citoyens malheureux: soit en leur procurant du travail, soit en assurant les moyens d'existence à ceux qui sont hors de l'état de travailler." Montesquieu, *De l'Esprit des Lois*, liv. xxii. ch. xxix., had laid down the duty of the State in

The other new feature of the statute of 18 Eliz. c. 3., is "concerning bastards, begotten and born out of lawful matrimony (an offence against God's law and man's law), the said bastards being now left to be kept at the charges of the parish where they be born, to the great burden of the same parish, and in defrauding of the relief of the impotent and aged, *true poor* of the same *parish*, and to evil example and encouragement of lewd life: It is ordained and enacted, by authority aforesaid, that two justices of the peace,—upon examination of the cause and circumstance, shall,—by their discretion, take order, as well for the punishment of the mother and reputed father, as also for the better relief of every such parish in part or in all; and for the keeping of every such child, by charging such mother or reputed father with the payment of money weekly, or other sustentation for the relief of such child in such wise as they shall think meet and convenient: and if, after the same order by them subscribed under their hands, the said persons, viz., mother or reputed father, upon notice thereof, shall not, for their part, observe and perform the said order, every such party so making default, to be committed to gaol, there to remain, except he, she, or they, shall put in sufficient surety to perform the said order, or else personally to appear at the next general sessions of the peace, and also to abide such order as the justices of the peace then and there shall take in that behalf."

This clause, and the long train of subsequent legislative provisions, on the same subject, have contributed greatly to aggravate the demoralising influences of our poor laws. Any detailed notice of the subsequent legislation, or discussion of the principles involved in it, would be out of place here; but I cannot leave the subject without quoting the view and recommendation of the Commissioners of Inquiry in 1833, in

terms at least equally extensive: "Quelques aumônes que l'on fait à un homme nu dans les rues ne remplissent point les obligations de l'état, qui doit à tous les citoyens une subsistance assurée, la nourriture, un vêtement convenable, et un genre de vie qui ne soit point contraire à la santé."

respect of this important question, and expressing my own regret, that that recommendation should have been disregarded, and that our statute book should still be disgraced by provisions directly tending to injure both female virtue and public morals.

"We recommend that the second section of the 18 Eliz. c. 3., and all other acts which punish *or charge* the putative father of a bastard, shall, as to all bastards born after the passing of the intended act, be repealed.

"Cases will, no doubt, occur, of much hardship and cruelty, and it will often be regretted that these are not punishable, at least by fine, on the offender. But the object of law is not to punish, but to prevent, and if the existing law does not prevent, as is too clear, it must not be maintained against its proper design with a view to punishment, still less must it be maintained if it acts as an incentive. It must be remembered, too, that we do not propose to deprive either the woman or her parents of their direct means of redress; she may still bring her action for breach of promise of marriage, and her parents may still bring theirs for the loss of their daughter's service.

"One objection, however, may be made to our plan, which deserves an answer, in deference, not to its force, but to the religious and moral feelings in which it originates. It may be said that throwing upon the woman the expense of maintaining the child, will promote infanticide. It appears from Mr. Walcott's Report, that infanticide, and in one of its worst forms, is promoted by the existing law: but we do not, in fact, believe that we have to choose between the two dangers; we do not believe that infanticide arises from any calculation as to expense. We believe that in no civilised country, and scarcely in any barbarous country, has such a thing ever been heard of, as a mother killing her child in order to save the expense of feeding it."*

* The Report is dated 20th Feb. 1834, and is signed "C. J. London" (Dr. Blomfield, still Lord Bishop of London), "J. B. Chester" (Dr. Sumner, the present Primate of all England), W. Sturges Bourne, Nassau W. Senior, Henry Bishop, Henry Gawler, W. Coulson, James Traill, Edwin Chadwick.'

The House of Lords inserted a string of bastardy clauses in the Poor Law Amendment Bill, which, founded on this Report, had, in 1834, passed the Commons without any such stain upon it*; and the very last Bastardy Act seems to have passed through Parliament against the opinion of almost every one who had given much attention to, and was competent to form a judgment upon, the principle and tendency of the measure. It was said, at the time, that all the noble lords who were chairmen of boards of guardians, were in the minority.†

Under the statute, 14 Eliz. c. 5. (1572), thus explained and extended by 18 Eliz. c. 3. (1576), vagrancy was repressed, and pauperism relieved, at the cost of the newly constituted districts. The ample and ever increasing text of English law, which is confided to the administration of justices of the peace, received illustration in the reign of Elizabeth, from the learned Lambarde, a commentator whose works have lived and are still quoted in Westminster Hall. His "Eirenarcha, or, Of the Office of Justices of the Peace," was published in 1581, only five years after the passing of the statute, 18 Eliz. c. 3. In the third book, "containing the Practique of two or more Justices of the Peace out of the Sessions," various duties of justices, under 5 Eliz. c. 4., 14 Eliz. c. 5., and 18 Eliz. c. 3., are enumerated.

* The introduction of these clauses was greatly promoted, if not mainly caused, by the ill-directed benevolence of a few ladies of quality. They were drawn by a noble Baron, now no more, and moved by the Duke of Wellington.

† According to the *Code Civil* of France, art. 340., "La recherche de la paternité est interdite." There is much interesting matter to be found on the subject, in the valuable publication of Locré, *Législation de la France*, tom. i. especially in the "*Procès-verbaux du Conseil d'État*, which had no less than seven different discussions on the important and difficult question of "*La paternité et la filiation.*" Duranton, *Cours de Droit Français suivant le Code Civil*, tom. iii. p. 188., observes, "On a pensé qu'il était plus juste, plus moral et plus conforme à l'ordre social, de laisser à un individu la liberté de manifester son opinion personnelle sur un fait de cette nature et de s'en constituer le juge souverain." Rogron, *On the Code Civil*, art. 340. "Le législateur ne devait pas souffrir qu'une mère éhontée pût faire tomber à son gré une odieuse paternité sur la tête la plus innocente. Il fallait mettre l'homme honnête et d'une conduite pure à l'abri des attaques d'une femme impudente et d'enfants qui lui sont étrangers ; il fallait aussi tarir la source d'une foule d'actions scandaleuses, et dont le résultat était toujours arbitraire."

The same author, in 1583, published his book, "The Duties of Constables,"* along with which is a chapter on "The Office and Duetie of the Collectors and Overseers for the Poor, settled in their abiding Places;" another on "The Office of the Collectors and Governors of the Poore;" and a third on "The Duties of the Censors or Wardens, and of the Collectors for the House of Correction.

One of the Harleian MSS. in the British Museum, cited by Eden†, contains a code of orders and rules agreed on by the justices of Suffolk at their general sessions, holden at Bury on May 31. 1589, "for the punishinge and suppressinge of roags, vacabonds, idle, loyteringe, and lewde persons; which doe or shall hereafter wander and goe aboute" within certain hundreds in that county. The justices state, in the preamble of their code, that "yt appeareth by dayly experience, that the nomber of idle, vagraunte, loyteringe, sturdye roags, masterless men, lewde and yll disposed persons, arre exceedingly encreased and multiplied, committinge many grevious and outeragious disorders and offences;—for remedy of theis and suche lyke enormities, which hereafter shall happen to arise or growe within the hundreths and lymits aforesaid," they order the building of "one convenient house, which shal be called the house of correction," within the town of Bury, and that "all persons offendinge or livinge contrary to the tenor of the said twoe acts within the hundreths and lymitts aforesaid, shal be, by the warrante of any justice of peace, dwellinge in the same hundreths or lymitts, committed thether, and there be releived, punished, sett to worke, and ordered."

The justices descend to very minute regulations concerning the reformatory discipline which is to be administered to the inmates, the amount of work which is to be required from them, and the very prayers, in which, "reverently kneeling down upon their knees, they are to join."‡

* *The Duties of Constables, Borsholders, Tithingmen, and such other low Ministers of the Peace.* London, 1583.

† *State of the Poor*, vol. iii. Appendix, pp. cxxxvi—cxlvi.

‡ P. cxliii. "They shall saie and pronounce distinctly and modestly, after one that shall be appointed to read, the confession sett downe in the begynninge of the book of Common Praier, the Lords praier, the articles of our beleffe, the x

Probably the orders and regulations made by the Suffolk justices, are a fair indication of the mode in which the statute of 14 Eliz. c. 5. was administered, throughout England, for the greater part of the time while it remained in force.* During this period, it would seem that the parochial tie, which had so long connected the interests of the impotent poor, with those of their wealthier neighbours, was not wholly severed. The habits of centuries could not be changed by the legislation of a day. The feelings of Christian charity, which had always been appealed to on behalf of the poor, would still operate, and many of the poor would still be relieved by their fellow parishioners, even after parliament had organised a sort of district settlement, and had given power to justices of peace to tax the inhabitants of each of the new districts for the relief of the district poor.

A phrase in the 18 Eliz. c. 3. itself, tends strongly to show that this parochial tie, though abrogated by the previous

commaundements, and a short gyvinge of thanks for benefitts receyved, and after that the praier that is entituled For the whole estate of Christs church militante here on yearth; and this order of praier to be kept every eveninge, also at the leavinge of theire worke, and so every daye contynually."

* The following are specimens of the regulations made by the Suffolk justices of peace. "All unrulie and stubborne persons shal be corrected oft'ner, and used both with *harder cloggs*, *shackles*, *irons*, or both, and with *thinner diett* and harder labour, untyll he or she shal be brought to reasonable obedience and submission to the keper of the said house; and that every person that shall stubbornely refuse to labour and worke, as he or she shal be appointed by the keper of the said house, or shall not be quiett or obedient to his commaundement, to be ordered accordinge to the rules of the said house," shall be flogged. If so flogged three times, then he is "to be committed to the next gayle, there to be punished as a roage according to the statute." What further punishment he received in the gaol we need not inquire. His first reception in this house of correction, built and ordered by the Suffolk justices, had been regulated by several clauses, one of which is as follows: "Item, it is ordered and agreed uppon, that every stronge or sturdie roag, at his or her fyrst enterance into the said house, shall have xij stripes uppon his beare skynne, with the said whipp provided for the said house; and every yong roage, or idle loyterer, vj stripes with the said whipp in forme aforesaid. And that every one of them, withowte fayle, at theire fyrst comminge into the said house, shall have putt uppon hym, her, or them, some clogge, cheine, collers of iron, ringle, or manacle, such as the keper of the said house shall thinke meete, so as he maie answere for every one, as well for his forth comminge, as also that they shall be quiett, and doe noe hurte for the tyme they shall contynue in the said house."

law of 14 Eliz. c. 3., still existed in fact, four years after the 14 Eliz. c. 5. had been enacted. The phrase is in s. 2. of 18 Eliz. c. 3., where mention is made of defrauding of their relief "the impotent and aged, *true poor of the same parish.*" And the statute 14 Eliz. c. 5. itself, making provision for the "habitations and abidings of the poor in the new district," expressly subjoins the remarkable phrase, "yf the pishe within the whiche they shalbee founde, shall not, or wyll not, *provide for them;*" as if parliament retained the hope that the joint persuasions of ministers of the Gospel and of the law, might still induce parishioners to relieve destitution in members of the parochial family.

The curate of each *parish* had been directed, by the statute 1 Edw. VI. c. 3., to exhort his *parishioners* to relieve those *born in the same parish,* and needing their help; and even as early as the year 1536, the statute of 27 Henry VIII. c. 25., imposing a fine "on the *parish* in which the impotent poor should not be relieved," directed the surplus collections of rich *parishes* to be applied for the relief of poor *parishes* within the same hundred. Under 5 & 6 Edw. VI. c. 2., the charitable contributions of the parishioners were asked for in the *church,* and the administration of the charitable relief of the poor was placed in the hands of ministers and churchwardens of each *parish.* One of the first acts of parliament passed on the accession of Elizabeth*, provided that every one should resort to his parish church upon every Sunday and holiday, "upon pain of punishment by the censures of the Church, and also upon pain that every person so offending shall forfeit, for every such offence, twelve pence, *to be levied by the churchwardens of the parish* where such offence shall be done, to the use *of the poor of the same parish.*"

Among the penalties imposed on the clergy and applied to the use of the poor, must also be mentioned that which was created by the statute 13 Eliz. c. 20., "An Act touching Leases of Benefices and other ecclesiastical Livings with Cure." Any incumbent non-resident above eighty days in a year, is to lose one year's profits of his benefice, "to be dis-

* 1 Eliz. c. 2. s. 14.

tributed by the ordinary *among the poor of the parish.*" The intent of the statute was, "that the cure might be well served, and that poor people might be well relieved."*

By 23 Eliz. c. 1., "An Act to retain the Queen's Majestie's Subjects in their due Obedience," it was provided that forfeitures which it imposed, for instance, those on Roman Catholics for attending the celebration of the rites of their own religion, and for omitting to attend the public services of the Establishment, should be given, one-third to the informer, one-third to the Queen, for her own use, and one-third to the Queen, *for the poor of the parish* in which the offence was committed.†

Laws for preventing tippling, swearing, disorderly conduct on the Lord's day, and other similar offences, usually classed as offences "against God and religion,"‡ were visited with pecuniary forfeitures, which were, in part, applied towards the relief of the poor of the parish where the offence was committed. A similar class of provisions has continued to be approved of by the legislature, and to be inserted in acts of parliament, down to our own day. But this modern parliamentary parody of the course formerly pursued at Rome§, and afterwards by the Church, throughout Christendom‖, has probably yielded but little relief to the ratepayers, who alone, and not the poor, derive any benefit from such clauses, since relief of the poor is equally administered by overseers, whether they receive their funds from fines, or from poor-rate.

In the olden time, doubtless, the *penalties* of *penance*, imposed by the Church, served largely to relieve the poor, as well as to redeem the captive, and to emancipate the serf or slave.¶

* In the case of *Canning against Doctor Newman*, 2 Brownlow and Goldsborough, p. 54. (decided in 1610), it is said, that two causes of making the statute of 21 Henry VIII. c. 13. (requiring incumbents to reside on their benefices), were, first, hospitality, and second, *the relief of the poor*; and "these are to be done *in the parsonage house*, which is the free alms of the Church."

† 23 Eliz. c. 1. s. 8. By 23 Eliz. c. 10., "An Act for the preservation of Pheasants and Partridges," one-half of certain penalties (s. 3.) shall be *to the poor of the parish* where the pheasants or partridges were taken, to be recovered by any one of the churchwardens of the parish.

‡ Above, p. 99.

§ Above, pp. 141, 142.

‖ Above, pp. 149, 150.

¶ Above, pp. 145. 152.

The statute 39 Eliz. c. 3., which reverted to and established, that parochial principle of administration of relief of the poor, which has ever since prevailed, is the third of a series of six acts of parliament, passed together, and forming a body of legislation on several kindred subjects, which may well be looked on as a connected whole. The titles of these several acts will sufficiently indicate their connection with the relief of the poor, and the repression of vagrancy. They are as follows:

39 Eliz. c. 1., An Act against the decaying of Towns and Houses of Husbandry.

39 Eliz. c. 2., An Act for the maintenance of Husbandry and Tillage.

39 Eliz. c. 3., An Act for the Relief of the Poor.

39 Eliz. c. 4., An Act for Punishment of Rogues, Vagabonds, and Sturdy Beggars.

39 Eliz. c. 5., An Act for erecting of Hospitals, or abiding and Working Houses, for the Poor.

39 Eliz. c. 6., An Act to reform Deceipts, and Breaches of Trust, touching Lands to charitable Uses.

It seems unnecessary to advert to the provisions of the statute 39 Eliz. c. 3., for they were, in substance, re-enacted, with such addition and amendment as experience had suggested, by the 43 Eliz. c. 2.

Before stating the chief provision of this statute, under which our annual millions are still raised for the relief of pauperism, other facts of importance and interest, respecting the condition of the poor, and the state of society during the reign of Queen Elizabeth, deserve consideration.

Causes similar to those which produced so great an increase in pauperism, vagrancy, and mendicancy in England, in the sixteenth century, were simultaneously operating, and produced like results, throughout most of the countries of Europe. These like results occurred in countries where no monasteries were suppressed, as, for instance, in France *, Holland, the Netherlands, Spain, and even in Rome itself.

* Above, pp. 3. 176, 177. 192, 193.

It is said that, among the Dutch, in the sixteenth century, the poor requiring alms were chiefly "the sick, maimed, and aged, since the varied and extensive demands for labour, and the industrious and careful habits of the working classes, enabled them generally to support themselves in plenty and independence." A complete system of poor relief was, however, organised, in Holland, in the early part of the sixteenth century. Hospitals, and other eleemosynary establishments, were open for the sick and aged; relief for the poor was administered, even at their homes; and it appears that the benevolent Dutchmen did much the same thing as had been done by the Emperor Constantine, more than a thousand years before *, and "the children of *such as were too poor to support them,* were brought up, until a certain age, at the public expense;" this was done under the inspection of the burgomasters, who bound such children apprentices to some trade or manufacture, "and they seldom failed to reward the care thus taken of them by their country, by becoming worthy and industrious members of society." †

The contemporaneous repression of vagrancy and mendicancy, and provision for the relief of the poor, in Spain and the Netherlands, was effected, without recourse being had to compulsory taxation. ‡

Many were the attempts made in Rome during the sixteenth century, to suppress an ever-increasing mendicancy and vagabondage. Numerous charitable establishments were founded for relief of the poor, and the papal remedies for repressing mendicancy, may almost be compared, in point of severity, with those of our own legislation at the same epoch. The series of bulls and apostolical letters, respecting pauperism and mendicancy, seems to have commenced with Pope Pius V., who filled the chair of St. Peter from 1566 to 1577, and to have been continued by Gregory XIII.; but the most

* Above, p. 137.

† Davies, *The History of Holland and the Dutch Nation.* vol. i. p. 488. See also vol. iii. p. 383.

‡ Guarinos, *Biblioteca Española Economico Politico,* and *Ed. Rev.* vol. xxii. pp. 188, 189.

remarkable documents of the series are two bulls, issued in 1587 and 1588, by Sixtus V., which show that an increasing pauperism and mendicancy were then causing as much anxiety to the State in unreformed Rome, as they seem to have been producing, at the same time, in reformed England.

Bishop Morichini has observed, that in thus making public provision for this social evil, Rome preceded all other cultivated nations *; but we have already seen, that England and France had somewhat the precedence of her.

The Bull of Sixtus V. (1587), *Quamvis infirma*, founds a great hospital, and shows, by its recital, the extent of the pauperism then existing in Rome.† It also shows, that even in that stronghold of the temporal wealth, as well as spiritual power of the Church, the demands of pauperism, under Sixtus V., were no longer met by the Church alone; but, as in England, laymen had been subjected to gentle persuasions of the clergy and bishops, to induce them charitably to relieve the poor, so in Rome herself, where no Reformation had confiscated any part of the revenue of ecclesiastics, the laity were reminded of some decree of an ecclesiastical synod, according to which they, the laity, not alone, but in conjunction with the clergy, were to perform the charitable work of relieving the poor.‡

* Morichini, *Degli Instituti de pubblica carità in Roma*, tom. ii. p. 10. "Fece pertanto (Sisto V.) una costituzione la quale onora il pontificato, e da a vedere come presto i Papi pensassero a medicar la piaga sociale *della miseria*, e *come ancora in ciò Roma precedesse tutte la altre più colte nazioni*."

† After premising the religious grounds on which provision ought to be made for the poor, the Bull proceeds, 61 (Magni Bullarii Romani, tom. ii. p. 625.): "Quæ quidem nos attentius considerantes, simulque *egenorum calamitates, quorum ingens quotidie numerus nobis ante oculos versatur;* paterna charitate miserati, tum Christianæ pietati tum etiam nostro pastorali officio consentaneum esse duximus, in hac Alma Urbe *ad quam, plurimi pauperes*, fame, frigore, nuditate, rerumque omniam inopia conflicti, ac variis morbis et incommodis conflictati, *se recipiunt*, Domum *Hospitalem* instruere, &c., ne ulterius mendici per vias et plateas tota urbe dispersi ac vagantes, victum quæritando, defatigarentur, ne non modò publica loca, aut privatarum ædium vestibula, sed ipsa quoque templa gemitibus et ejulationibus compleant, ne suis clamoribus obstrepant fidelibus dum divinis officiis, aut missæ sacrificio, intenti-sunt," &c.

‡ The Bull of Pope Sixtus V. l. c. "Considerantes ac revolventes in quâdam aliquando Synodo piè constitutum fuisse, ut unaquæque civitas pauperes et

The second Bull of Pope Sixtus V. on this subject (*Postulat ratio*), issued in 1588, contains severe provisions for repressing the vagrancy then prevalent at Rome, although there had been no dissolution of monasteries there, to furnish an additional supply to the ranks of pauperism.*

It must be remembered that, according to one of the decrees of the Council of Trent, the pope, even if his episcopal power only equalled that of other bishops, would, as bishop of Rome, have the special control of all institutions for the relief of the poor of that city.† A system of out-door relief, and of public workhouses for the able-bodied poor, was afterwards established by Pius VII. and Leo XII.‡

We may well compare the foundation, by Sixtus V., of a great hospital at Rome, and his Holiness's stringent prohibition of mendicancy, with the nearly contemporary legislation of Edward VI. here, and his foundation of hospitals in London. "To provide," says Blackstone§, "in some measure for both these poor," (the sick and impotent who were unable to work, and the idle and sturdy who were unwilling to do so,) "in and about the metropolis, Edward VI. founded three royal hospitals: Christ's and St. Thomas's‖, for the relief of the impotent through infancy or sickness; and Bridewell for the

egenos incolas suas alimentis congruentibus pasceret, secundum vires, et *tam vicini presbyteri, quam cives omnes, suum pauperem pascerent,* quò fieret, ne pauperes ipsi per alienas civitates vagarentur."

* Magni Bullarii Romani, tom. ii. p. 699. "Quoniam verò ea est perditorum quorumdam hominum impudentia, ut quamvis validi et robusti sint, tamen interdùm ficta aut simulata infirmitate, aut alio prætextu, per segnitiam et socordiam malint *incertis sedibus,* huc illuc vagando, mendicitate quam ex honestis laboribus et industria victum sibi comparare, eisdem Hospitalis præfati administratoribus, contrà eos omnes, qui mendicare per Urbem præsument, Edicta et Banna proponendi et publicandi, et inobedientes pœnis *tam pecuniariis quam etiam corporis afflictivis, et triennium, vel aliis eorum* arbitrio (*non tamen ultimi supplicii*), puniendi planam et liberam tribuimus potestatem."

† Concil. Trid. Sess. xxii. Cap. viii. "Episcopi Eleemosynas Montis pietatis sive charitatis, et pia loca omnia, quæ ad Dei cultum seu *pauperes sustentendas,* instituta sunt, ipsi ex officio suo, juxta sacrorum canonum statuta, cognoscant et exequantur."

‡ Chamborant, *Du Paupérisme,* p. 154.

§ Blackstone's *Commentaries on the Laws of England,* vol. i. p. 360.

‖ Above, p. 33.

punishment and employment of the vigorous and idle. But these were far from being sufficient for the care of the poor throughout the kingdom at large."

But, in England, the dissolution of monasteries, and the confiscation of ecclesiastical property, by Henry VIII., though it did not create the necessity of providing for the poor, yet it certainly increased that necessity for doing so which already existed.

Royal proclamations and commissions, issued by Queen Elizabeth, throw additional light on the condition of the poor, and of society in England, during the latter part of her reign. In 1574, the emancipation from their bondage of all the serfs of the Crown was effected.* This was done under a royal commission, directed to "Sir William Cecill, of the Garter Knighte, Lord Burghley, and Highe Treasorer of England," and to Sir Walter Mildmay, Knight, Chancellor and Under Treasurer of the Queen's Exchequer. The commission recites, "Whereas divers and sundrie of our poore, faithfull, and loyal subjects, beinge borne *bonde in blode*, and regardaunt to divers and sundre our mannors and possessions within our realme of England, have made humble suyte unto us to be *manumysed*, *enfraunchised*, and *made free*, with theire children and sequells, by reason whereof they, theire children, and sequells, may become more apte and fitte members for the service of us and of our common wealthe," and after reciting that the Queen, "having tender consideration of their said sute, and well consideringe the same to be acceptable unto Almightie God, who, in the beginninge, made all mankinde free," proceeds to appoint commissioners, and to authorise them to compound with these serfs, as to the commissioners should seem meet, for such sums of money as the commissioners and the serfs might agree on. The enfranchisement is to be under the Great Seal, on paying "for all manner of fees, at the Great Seal, twenty-six shillings eight pence, and not above." †

* Above, p. 182.

† The commission is set out in Rymer, *Fœdera*, tom. vi. pt. iii. p. 158. ed. Hag. Com.

The very language of the Queen in this commission deserves to be compared with some of the expressions attributed, by Froissart, to the serfs themselves, when, in the reign of Richard II., they vainly asked for manumission. The reform which Queen Elizabeth now voluntarily granted, seems in the main, to have been that which it was the object of the insurrection under Wat Tyler to effect.

Stow, in his "Survey of the Cities of London and Westminster,"* sets forth inconveniences, to prevent which a royal proclamation was issued on 7th July, 1580 (22nd Elizabeth). Among the "many inconveniences" enumerated as occasioned by "the daily access of people to the metropolis," it is mentioned that "it was thought to tend to the rendering of the city more sickly, and to bring in a mortality, the preservation of the people in health seeming impossible to continue, where such numbers were brought to dwell in small rooms; whereof a great part were very poor, and such as must *live of begging*, or worse means, and they heaped up together, and in a sort smothered, with many families of children and servants in one house."

It also appears from Stow†, that, in 1583, another proclamation was issued, and that certain proceedings took place in the Star Chamber, touching the vagrancy which then prevailed, in and near the City of London.‡ Rymer's Collection contains a very remarkable commission, granted by Queen Elizabeth, in 1595, in consequence of previous tumults, some of the offenders in which had already been punished, by the Lord Mayor's Court, and by the Star Chamber. The instrument certainly seems to show that the monarchy of England, under the Tudors, could, at times, overturn, with a high hand, the ordinary administration of law and justice.§

* Vol. ii. p. 34. ed. 1755. † Ibid. p. 35.

‡ In Maitland, *History of London*, vol. i. pp. 275, 276. ed. 1775, are set out a proclamation of Elizabeth, dated 21st Feb. 1593, and an Order of the Privy Council, dated 17th April, 1593, for repressing vagrancy, in and about the city of London.

§ The Queen's Commission, by writ of Privy Seal, directed to Sir Thomas Wyllford, Knight, and dated the 18th July, 1595, after reciting that of late there

Some illustration of the social changes which, about this time, were taking place in England, may also be found in the proceedings of Parliament. In the discussion which took place in the House of Commons before the passing of the Statute of Tillage, in 1597*, "Mr. Francis Bacon" made a motion, "against inclosures and depopulation of towns and houses of husbandry and tillage." The substance of his speech is preserved in Dewes's Journal†: "And because former laws are medicines of our understandings, he said, that he had

had been "sundry great unlawful assemblies of a nomber of base people, in riotous sort, both in our Citie of London, and in the suburbs of the same and in some other partes near to our said Citie, for the suppression whereof, although there hathe been some proceedings in ordinarye manner by the Maior of the said Cittie, and sundry offenders committed to severall prysons; and have also receaved corporall punyshment by direction and order of our counsell in the Starr Chamber at Westminster,—yet," proceeds the Queen, "for that the insolencye of many of the kynde of desperate offenders is suche, as they care not for any ordynerye punishment, by ymprisonment and other severe punishment inflicted on them, therfore; We fynde yt necessarye to have *some* suche notable, rebellious, and incorrigible persons to be speedily suppressed by execution of *death*, according to the justice of our marshal law; and therefore we have made choice of you, upon speciall trust of your wisdome, discretion, and other qualities mete for this purpose, to be our provost marshall, gevinge you aucthority, and so we comand you, upon signification geven to you by our justices of peace in our Cittie of London, or of any place neare to our said Cittie, in our counties of Middlesex, Surrey, Kent, and Essexe, of such notable, rebellious, and incorrigible offenders worthely to be speedily executed by martial law, to attache and take the same persons, and in the presence of the said justices, according to justice of marshal law, to execute them uppon the gallowes or gibbet openly, or neare to suche place where the said rebellious and incorrigible offenders shall be founde tu have committed the said greate offences. And furthermore, we aucthorice you to repair with a convenient company into all comon high wayes neare tour said Cittie, vehere you shall understand that any vagrant persons do haunt, and callinge to your assistance some convenient nomber of our justices and constables abidinge about the said places, to apprehend all suche vagrant and suspected persons, and them to deliver to the said justices, by them to be committed and examined of the causes of their wandringe, and finding them notoriously culpable in the unlauful manner of life, as incorrigible, and so certified to you by the said justices, you shall by our lawe martiall cause to be executed upon the gallows or gibbet, some of them that are so found moste notorious and incorrigible offenders, and some suche also of them as have manifestly broken the peace, sithence they have bene judged and condamned to death for former offences, and have had our pardon for the same."

* Above, p. 206.

† Sir Simon Dewes, *Journal*, p. 551.

perused the preambles of former statutes, and by them did see the inconveniences of this matter, being then scarce out of the shell, to be now full ripened.—And though it may be thought ill, and *very prejudicial to Lords, that have enclosed great grounds, and pulled down even whole towns, and converted them to sheep pastures*, yet, considering the increase of people, and the benefit of the commonwealth, I doubt not but every man will deem the revival of former moth-eaten laws in this point, a praiseworthy thing. For in matters of policy ill is not to be thought ill, which bringeth forth good. For inclosure of grounds brings depopulation, which brings, first, idleness; secondly, decay of tillage; thirdly, subversion of houses, and decay of charity, and *charges to the poor;* fourthly, impoverishing the state of the realm. A law for the taking away of such inconveniences is not to be thought ill or hurtful unto the general state, and I would be sorry to see within this kingdom, that piece of Ovid's verse prove true, *Jam seges ubi Troja fuit*, instead of a whole town full of people, nought but green fields,—but a shepherd and a dog."

After much discussion, the Statute of Tillage passed. Its repeal was moved in 1601 (43 Eliz.). Bacon supported the statute, and spoke of the policy of supporting agriculture. Sir Walter Raleigh made a strong speech in favour of free trade in corn: among other things, he urged that "the Low-Country man, and the Hollander, which never soweth corn, hath by his industry such plenty, that they will serve other nations;—and therefore I think, the best course is to set it at liberty, and leave every man free, which is the desire of a true Englishman." Mr. Secretary Cecil supported the law, on the ground of the pulling down of cottages which would ensue if each landowner were permitted, in the language of one of their class in our own days, to do as he liked with his own.*

* Dewes, *Journal*, p. 674. "If," said Cecil, "we debar tillage" (that is, if the statute were repealed), "we give scope to the *depopulator;* and then if the poor, being thrust out of their houses, go to dwell with others, straight we catch them with the statute of inmates; if they wander abroad, they are within the danger of the statute of the poor, to be whipt. So by this means undo this statute, and

Lord Bacon's attention was much bestowed on this point of the magnitude of estates in England; and, in his works, he more than once speaks of the good and evil resulting from the law of entail, which prevented the accumulations of one generation from being re-distributed in another. In one place he deplores the condition of the English landowners, "tied to the stake by these perpetuities of entails, and restrained from disposing of their land to their own or to their children's good;" and concludes that "it is worthy of consideration, whether it be better, for the subject and sovereign, to have the lands secured to men's names and bloods by perpetuities, with all the inconveniences above mentioned, or to be in hazard of undoing his house by unthrifty posterity." *

That Bacon's judgment was mainly in favour of the free transfer of property in land, and against the power of entailing, is manifest from other passages of his works. He observes, in his Essays, that "above all things, good policy is to be used that the treasure and monies of a state be not gathered into few hands. For, otherwise, a state may have a great stock, and yet starve; and money is like muck, not good except it be spread." Again, "The advice of King Henry VII. (whereof I have spoken largely in the history of his life), was profound and admirable in making farms and houses of husbandry of a standard; that is, maintained with such a proportion of land unto them, as may breed a subject to live in convenient plenty, and no servile condition, and to keep the plough in the hands of the owners, and not mere hirelings. And thus, indeed, you shall attain to Virgil's character, which he gives to ancient Italy:

'Terra potens armis atque ubere glebæ.' "†

In the same parliament, which was so much occupied in legislating for the poor, the ancient application of Church

you indanger many thousands. *Posterior dies discipulus prioris.* If former times have made us wise to make a law, let these latter times warn us to preserve so good a law."

* Bacon, *Use of the Law*, in Law Tracts, p. 146. 2nd ed.

† Bacon, *Essays*, *Greatness of Kingdoms and Estates*, p. 108. ed. B. Montagu, 1836.

property seems to have been made the ground of a proposed statute. In the session of 39 & 40 Elizabeth, a bill "for the Relief of the Poor, out of Impropriations and other Church Livings," was read a second time, in the House of Commons, but was lost on motion for going into committee, by a majority of 146 against 117.*

A learned writer of Queen Anne's time, suggested, as an amendment in the poor law, that the poor should again be put upon the Church lands and tithes. To obviate the probable objections of lay impropriators, it was proposed, in effect, to purchase their property; and then "the poor to be thrown altogether and entirely on the clergy, together with such restored lands and tithes." Sir Frederick Eden observes, truly enough, that the nation would have effected a considerable saving, if the legislature of the day had listened to the proposal.†

Two years before the end of the reign of Queen Elizabeth, the provisions of the statute of 39 Eliz. c. 3. were superseded by the 43 Eliz. c. 2. A statement of the chief provision of this statute, with which every one acquainted with the administration of the poor law is familiar, and under which the funds needed for the relief of the poor, throughout England, are still raised, may properly conclude this long chapter. The first section directs, that the churchwardens of every parish "and fower, three, or two substanciall householders there," to be nominated yearly, "shalbe called overseers of the poore of the same parishe, and they or the greater parte of them, shall take order from tyme to tyme, by and withe the consent of two or more suche justices of peace as is aforesaide, *for settinge to worke* of the children of all suche whose parentes shall not, by the saide churchwardens and overseers, or the greater parte of them, bee thoughte able to keepe and maintaine theire children. And alsoe *for settinge to worke* all such ꝑsons, maried or unmaried, havinge no meanes to maintaine them, use no ordinarie and dailie trade of lief to get their livinge by; and also *to raise weekelie* or otherwise, *by*

* Sir Simon Dewes, *Journal*, p. 561.

† Eden, *State of the Poor*, vol. i. p. 264.

taxac̄on of every inhabitant, parson, vicar, and other, and of ev̄y occupier of landes, houses, tithes impropriate, or propriac̄ons of tythes, colemynes, or saleable underwoods, in the saide parishe, in such competent sume and sumes of money as they shall thincke fytt, *a convenient stocke* of flaxe, hampe, wooll, threed, iron, and other necessarie ware and stuffe *to sett the poore on worke*; and alsoe *competent sum̄es of money* for and towardes the *necessarie reliefe* of the lame, impotente, olde, blinde, and suche other amonge them, *beinge poore and not able to work*, and alsoe for the putting out of suche children to be apprentices, to be gathered out of the same parishe accordinge to the abilitie of the same parishe; and to doe and execute all other thinges, aswell for the disposinge of the saide stocke as otherwise conc̄ninge the p̄misses as to them shall seeme convenient."

CHAP. VII.

RELIEF OF THE POOR FROM THE REIGN OF ELIZABETH TILL THE RESTORATION OF CHARLES THE SECOND.

Defluit saxis agitatus humor,
Concidunt venti, fugiuntque nubes.— HORACE.

NO provision was made by the statute of 43 Eliz. c. 2., either for ascertaining a place of settlement by which the indigent poor were to be maintained, or for removing them to any such place. The memory of the great evil which had arisen, and the prospect of the little advantage likely to accrue from any such attempt, had prevented the insertion of removal or settlement clauses in this great statute. The experience of four years passed under the 39 Eliz. c. 3., which contained no such clauses, must have been favourably contrasted with the practice under the whole series of provisions contained in a former act of parliament.*

For a long period after the passing of the statute of 43rd Elizabeth, its humane and reasonable provisions were carried out without its being necessary to remove any poor people from one part of the kingdom to another, in order that they might be relieved. Throughout the whole of this period, that is, from 1601 to 1662, all poor persons were entitled to needful relief, wheresoever they were residing; and it was only the rogue or vagrant that was liable to any removal to his place of birth, or last three years' habitation. Perhaps place of *domicile*, by birth or residence, would be the most intelligible and appropriate description of the place to which, under the final legislation of Queen Elizabeth, the rogue or vagrant was by law to be removed. Destitution was supported wheresoever it was found, without any such

* 14 Eliz. c. 5.

interference with the labour of the poor, and with their personal freedom, as it was reserved for the restoration of Charles II. to sanction, and for subsequent ages to deplore. By 3 Car. I. c. 5. the statute of 43 Eliz. was continued in its integrity; probably it had been found not inadequate to the two great purposes expected of it, the relief of the aged and impotent, and the extension of charitable support to the able-bodied, by means of industry, imposed as the peremptory condition on which alone relief of the able-bodied could be bestowed.

It does not appear that during the reigns of James I. or Charles I., any evil or inconvenience arose to the community, from thus conferring on the destitute poor an absolute right to relief at the expense of their richer neighbours. King James and his son appear equally to have admonished their subjects to attend to the providing of workhouses, and to requiring labour from such able-bodied poor persons as were relieved.* The complaints which we meet with in the reigns of James I. and Charles I., are complaints of neglect to carry out the statute, and not complaints of its operation.

That removal of the destitute poor was no part of the machinery for relieving them, under the statute of Elizabeth, may be collected from legal writers of the period which followed the passing of the statute. The illegality of removing any person who was not a vagrant, is manifest from several passages from Dalton, an accurate author of the reign of Charles I. "*Young children*, whose parents are dead, are to be set on worke, relieved, or maintained, at the charge of the toune where they were dwelling at the time of the death of their parents, and are not to be sent to their place of birth, &c. For if the parents were not rogues, wee may not make the children rogues, except they wander abroad and beg. This was the direction of Flemming, Chiefe Justice, in a case between *Weston* and *Cowledge*, An. 11 Jac. Regis."† Lambarde‡ also states that, by resolution of the judges, only

* Daines Barrington, *Observations on the more Ancient Statutes*, p. 538.

† *The Countrey Justice*, ed. London, 1635, pp. 98, 99. & 101. c. 40. "Poor."

‡ *Duties of Constables*, p. 51. ed. 1619.

rogues, that is, persons liable to be convicted as criminals, could be removed. Mere poverty was not punished by the severe sentence of removal.

Dalton shows that mendicity was steadily repressed under the statute of Elizabeth; that the merely indigent poor were protected from being sent, as vagrant rogues might be, from the place of their destitution to any place of settlement; and that the impotent were at once relieved, while the able-bodied were set to labour. "None may be suffered to take reliefe at any man's doore, though within the same parish, unlesse it be by the order of the overseers; neither may any be suffered to beg by the highwaies, though in their own parish. *No man is to be put out of the towne where hee dwelleth*, nor to be sent to their place of birth (or last habitation), *but a vagrant rogue;* nor to be found by the towne, except the partie be impotent; but ought to set themselves to labour, if they be able, and can get worke, *if they cannot get worke, the overseers must set them to labour.*"

"Sir Francis Harvey, at the summer assizes at Cambridge, An. 1629, did deliver it, that the justices of peace (especially out of their sessions), were not *to meddle either with the removing, or settling, of any poor*, but *only of rogues.*"

Carew, in his "Survey of Cornwall," published soon after the accession of James I., and dedicated to Sir Walter Raleigh, speaks of the last Vagrant Act of Queen Elizabeth*, as the "late most beneficial statute;"† and King James, in one of his speeches to parliament, says, "Look to the houses of correction; remember that in the time of Chief Justice Popham, there was not a wandering beggar to be found in all Somersetshire, being his native country."‡

Dalton, in speaking of the "thriftlesse poore," divides them into five classes, and says, that for all of them the

* Above, p. 206.

† Carew, *Survey of Cornwall*, p. 185. ed. Lond. 1811.

‡ Daines Barrington, *Observations on the more Ancient Statutes*, p. 538. On the early life of Popham, C. J., in part spent by him in the vocation of highwayman, and on his severity as a "hanging judge," see his life in Lord Campbell's *Lives of the Chief Justices of England*, vol. i. ch. vi. Popham was Chief Justice from 1592, till his death in 1607.

House of Correction is fittest; and he refers also to the rule of the Apostle, "That such as would not work should not eat" (2 Thes. iii. 10.); and adds that, "for overseers to suffer such persons (or any other persons, which can live of their labours or otherwise) to be chargeable to the towne, or to relieve suche, were a meanes to nourish them in their lewdnesse or idlenesse which take it, and to rob others of relief that want it, to wrong those of their money that pay it, and to condemne them of oversight which dispose it."*

It appears probable, however, that the proper carrying out of the provisions of this statute was greatly neglected, and that, for twenty, thirty, or forty years after its passing, there were many parishes in which no such poor-rates as it required to be laid were ever made at all; it is even said that many poor people perished for want.†

It cannot be questioned that the statute of 43 Eliz. c. 2. contemplated the direct relief, by money or maintenance, of the impotent poor only; and that the direction, as to the raising of a convenient stock, on which the able-bodied poor might be set to work, shows that neither money nor maintenance was to be bestowed on the able-bodied, except in return for labour. And it seems clear that, before the restoration of Charles II., the unpaid annual officers, under whose care the poor were placed by the statute of Elizabeth, had not only failed to raise proper funds for relieving the impotent, but still more had neglected to carry out the parochial organisation of labour, which the statute contemplated. Able-bodied applicants for relief obtained some allowance in money, without being put to work at all. That this was the state of things in the interval between 1601 (43 Eliz. c. 2.) and 1662 (14 Car. II. c. 12.), is manifest from the language of Sir Matthew Hale in the second chapter of his "Discourse touching Provision for the Poor," in which, after observing that the statute of Elizabeth makes two provisions,—1. For the impotent poor, that are not able to work; 2. For those poor that are able to work, "in reference to whom it gives power

* Dalton, *The Countrey Justice*, p. 101.

† Eden, *State of the Poor*, vol. i. p. 144.

to raise stocks by rating the parishioners and setting the poor on work," he states in terms that there was a defect in the execution of the statute; "for let any man look over most of the populous parishes in England; indeed, there are rates made for the relief of the impotent poor, and it may be the same relief is also given *in a narrow measure* unto some others that have great families, and upon this they live miserably, and at best from hand to mouth; and, if they cannot get work to make out their livelihood, they and their children set up a trade of begging at best. But it *is rare to see any provision of a stock in any parish for the relief of the poor*."*

The author of "Greevous Grones for the Poore," published in 1622†, states that there had been no collection for the poor, "no not these seven yeares, in many parishes of this land, especiallie in countrie townes; but many of those parishes turneth forth their poore, yea, and their lustie labourers that will not worke, or for any misdemeenor want worke, to begge, filtch, and steale for their maintenance, so that the country is pittifully pestered with them; yea, and the maimed souldiours that have ventured their lives, and lost their limbes in our behalfe, are also thus requited; for, when they return home to live by some labour in their naturall countrey, though they can worke well in some kinde of labour, everie man sayeth, wee will not bee troubled with their service, but make other shifte for our businesse. So are they turned forth to travaile in idlenesse (the highway to hell), and seeke their meate uppon meares (as the proverbe goeth), with begging, filching, and stealing, for their maintenance, untill the law bring them unto the fearfull end of hanging." The author of "Stanleye's Remedy," who wrote in 1646, bears similar testimony.‡ "The generall rule of all England is to whip and punish the wandring beggars, and to brande them according to the forme of the new statute, and

* *A Discourse touching Provisions for the Poor*, written by Sir Matthew Hale, Knt., late Lord Chief Justice of the King's Bench: ed. London, 1716, c. ii. p. 119.

† Eden, *State of the Poor*, vol. i. p. 155.

‡ Ibid. vol. i. p. 168.

so mark them with such a note of infamie, as they may be assured no man will set them on work; and so, many justices execute one branch of that good statute (which is the point of justice); but as for the point of charitie they leave undone, which is to provide houses and convenient places to set the poore to work, which ought to be done in equitie and justice, as well as the other."

Sir Matthew Hale points out some undoubted defects of the original statute of 43 Eliz. c. 2., one of which is, that it gave no power to parish officers to purchase or hire any workhouse. This eminent judge proposed to remedy the omission by establishing workhouses as places in which labour should always be provided for the able-bodied indigent poor; not to serve as a mere test of destitution, but rather amounting to an organisation of labour by the State, which, as he imagined, would be productive of the greatest benefit to the whole of society. Neither *phalanstère*, nor *atelier national*, have held out brighter prospects, in the eyes of modern enthusiasts, than Sir Matthew Hale beheld in his own scheme of the organisation of labour, by incorporating workhouses, and making ample provision that the State should always supply the means of labour to all those who could not find it for themselves.

He sets down in his treatise, some of the "very many and great benefits that would come by this method." A subjoined extract will show the author's sanguine expectation that great social advantages would ensue from the adoption of his plan.*

* "1. By incorporating of these workhouses, which are the best kind of hospitals, charitable minded persons would have, as it were, a pillar whereunto to fasten their charity, which would prevent many difficulties in the faithful administration thereof, and would invite benefactors. 2. Whereas hospitals provide for some few poor impotent people, this would *prevent poverty*, and in a little tract of time bring up hundreds to be able to gain their livelihoods. 3. Whereas in that state that things are, populousness, which is the greatest blessing a kingdom can have, becomes the burden of the kingdom, by breeding up whole races and families, and successive generations in a mere trade of idleness, thieving, begging, and a barbarous kind of life, which must in time prodigiously increase and overgrow the whole face of the kingdom, and eat out the heart of it. This course, within one seven years, alters the whole state of this disorder, and brings people and their children after them into a regular, orderly,

But sounder views on the subject of the real use and advantage of workhouses soon spread, and, after the erection of such buildings under numerous local acts, in various cities and populous towns, during the interval between the reigns of Charles II. and George I., the public statute, called Sir Edward Knatchbull's Act, was passed in 1722 (9 Geo. I. c. 7.), giving authority to parish officers to purchase or hire workhouses in which they might employ all poor persons; and it was declared, that persons refusing to be maintained in them were not entitled to relief. The workhouse therefore, in 1722, became strictly a test of destitution, which parish officers might always apply before giving relief.

The neglect fully to carry out the provision of the statute of Elizabeth, during the interval between 1601 and 1662, would be likely to produce a considerable difference in the burden of pauperism in different parts of the country. Probably the parishes which gave relief in money, without exercising a very vigilant care in scrutinising the actual destitution in each case, would be likely to suffer much more from pauperism than such as applied the disagreeable test of requiring labour by every able-bodied applicant, in return for the relief bestowed on him. Thus, neglect in the administration of this statute produced evils corresponding to those which followed from a like neglect in the administration of

and industrious course of life, which will be as natural to them as now idleness, and begging, and thieving is. 4. By this means the wealth of the nation will be increased, manufactures advanced, and every body put into a capacity of eating his own bread; for upon what imaginable account can we think, that we should not be as able to improve our populousness to our wealth, as well as Holland, and Flanders, and Barbadoes, if we had but their industry and orderly management. 5. By this means there would soon be an improvement of the several manufactures of the kingdom, both for the necessary consumption of the kingdom, and for exportation; whereby our trade outward would exceed our trade inward, which outward trade is the basis and foundation of all our trade inward; and the excess and overballance of our trade outward, to our trade inward, is the only means not only to keep our money at home, but to gain an increase of money, and so advance the true intrinsick wealth of the kingdom." Lord Campbell (*Lives of the Chief Justices*, vol. i. p. 582.) adverts to the pamphlet which Sir Matthew Hale had written "in ignorance of the elements of political economy, and amiably led away by communist doctrines."

the Vagrant Act, passed shortly before the end of Elizabeth's reign.* Lord Coke informs us that, on the making of this last mentioned statute, "and a good space after, whilest justices of peace and other officers were diligent and industrious, there was not a rogue to be seen in any part of England; but when justices and other officers became *tepidi*, or *trepidi*, rogues swarmed againe."†

* Above, p. 206.

† Lord Coke, *Second Institute*, p. 729.

CHAP. VIII.

STATUTE OF CHARLES II. FOR THE REMOVAL OF THE POOR.

Così quel fiato gli spiriti mali,
Di qua, di là, di giù di su gli mena:
Nulla speranza gli conforta mai,
Non che di posa, ma di minor pena. — DANTE.

So hither, thither, upward, downward driven,
Like evil spirits, in the tempest's blast,
To them relief nor settlement is given,
Nor hope, that this remove will be the last.

THE origin of a great part of those evils which the poor laws have entailed on the country, is to be found in the statute passed about two years after the restoration of Charles II., and in the 14th year of his constructive reign. This statute gave an arbitrary power of removing a poor man from the place of his residence, to what is called the place of his settlement; and thus again adopted a principle which had met with a long trial in the reigns of Edward VI. and Elizabeth, and was finally rejected by the statute under which the poor had now been relieved for more than sixty years.

The recital of this statute, passed in 1662, is diffuse in explanation of alleged grounds for its enactment. The number of the poor, throughout England and Wales, is stated to have increased, and to be "very great and exceeding burdensome, being occasioned by reason of some defects in the law concerning the settling of the poor, and for want of a due provision of the regulations of relief and employment in such parishes or places where they are legally settled, which doth enforce many to turn incorrigible rogues, and others to perish for want." This recital involves two historical facts, and one legislatorial conjecture. The two facts are, 1st, That from neglect of the provisions of the statute of Elizabeth, many poor people had been enforced to turn incorrigible rogues, and others to perish for want: 2nd, That the number of the poor had greatly increased. The conjecture is, That the evil described was, in part, due to some "defects in the law concerning the settling of the poor," and, in part only, to the neglect to carry out the statute of Elizabeth.

It is highly probable that the whole grievance complained of, arose from the neglect conscientiously and strictly to administer the statute of Elizabeth; and the best remedy would, in all likelihood, have been found, in enforcing the then existing law, and certainly is not found in the statute of 14 Charles II. c. 12.

Only a few years ago, we saw, even under the superintendence and control of a Central Board (constantly endeavouring to prevent any gross mal-administration of relief to the poor), that a temporary want of proper vigilance and discrimination in administering that relief, aided by other accidents, very rapidly produced an alarming increase in the number of the vagrant poor. In 1847 and 1848, the evil was general, and "no part of the country was exempt from the infliction."* Vagrancy had suddenly become a plague which could scarcely be exaggerated. "The vagrants," says a poor law inspector†, "are described by the relieving officers and masters of workhouses as coming in hordes towards evening, asking for food and lodging as a right. They are said to be dirty, ragged, and abusive. They circulate in rounds of from thirty to fifty miles radius. They live by begging and vagabondage. They have no intention of ever doing a turn of work. They use the workhouse as their inn, avoiding any, where the discipline is troublesome, or administration of relief difficult." "They roam about in bands consisting of large numbers of women and children, to whom it is almost impossible to refuse relief, and from whom it is difficult to exact any work. The men belonging to them often have money, and remain outside the workhouse, sleep-

* First Annual Report of the Poor Law Board, 1848, pp. 5, 6.

† Captain Robinson, R. N., Report on the Counties of Surrey and Sussex, dated July, 1848, p. 86. of Reports to the Poor Law Board, &c. 1850.

ing, at this season, in the open air, and sending their women and children into the house for food and shelter." "The extraordinary number of the applicants almost precludes any examination into their case; and except where the relieving officers have been persons of great firmness and nerve, the abuse has been permitted to extend to a most alarming height." "*The whole matter is well worthy of the attention o the legislature.*"

Happily, no act of parliament was passed! An excellent Minute of the Poor Law Board, dated Aug. 4. 1848, prepared by the late Mr. Charles Buller, pointed out and explained that a sound and vigilant discrimination in respect of the objects of relief, and the steady " refusal of aid to all who are not ascertained to be in a state of destitution, are obviously the most effectual remedies against the increase of vagrancy and mendicancy." This minute was communicated to Boards of Guardians in the summer of 1848, and the adoption of its advice was at once followed by a great diminution of the number of vagrant poor applying for relief.*

The legislature of Charles II., instead of confining itself to the task of thus providing a simple and efficacious remedy for a temporary grievance, by improving the administration of the relief given under the statute of Elizabeth, devised and established a new and stringent code of pauper legislation containing an arbitrary and unjust law of settlement and removal, the effects of which have been felt down to the present day.

At the time of the restoration of Charles II., a period of more than half a century had passed since the enactment of the great statute of Elizabeth; and during the whole of that period, the only complaint respecting the law which appears to have been made was, that it was not in all places sufficiently acted on; that parishes were slow and reluctant to perform their duty of making proper provision for the relief

* Second Annual Report of the Poor Law Board, 1849, p. 11. "The recommendations of this minute were very generally adopted, the consequence of which was a marked decrease of the number of vagrants applying for relief. It will be noticed that the number relieved on the 1st July, 1848, before the issuing of the minute, was 13,714, but the number relieved in July, 1849, was only 5662, being a decrease of 8052, or 58·7 per cent."

of their poor. No one, either in parliament or out of parliament, proposed to repeal that statute; and we may be sure that a compulsory law, imposing a direct tax, such as the poor-rate is, would not have been submitted to by the landed interest of England, silently, and without any attempt to get rid of it or to amend it, had it not been thought just, and found to work well. The governments of James I., of Charles I., and of Cromwell, equally acquiesced in the Elizabethan poor law. The owners of real estate, by whom in substance, the poor-rate, under the statute of Elizabeth, has ever been borne*, were probably as little likely to remain silent, under any supposed grievance, in the seventeenth century, as they prove themselves to be in the nineteenth.

Political events which preceded the restoration of Charles II., render it highly probable that an efficient administration of a vagrant law was then called for. A temporary evil seems to have led to the passing of this permanent measure, and that temporary evil seems, even from the recital of the statute, to have consisted, in neglect to provide relief in some parishes, and to administer it in others, under the statute of Elizabeth.

The price of wheat at the time of the passing of the statute of 14 Charles II., and for some years previously, deserves to be noticed.

Year.	Wheat per Quarter. £	s.	d.
1654	1	6	0
1655	1	13	4
1656	2	3	0
1657	2	6	8
1658	3	5	0
1659	3	6	0
1660	2	16	6
1661	3	10	0
1662	3	14	0

* The power, which the statute was held to give, of assessing inhabitants in respect of their visible personal property, locally situated within the parish, must always have been inconvenient, and, except in a small class of places, impracticable to act on.

This steady increase in the price of wheat for so many continuous years, undoubtedly would not be accompanied by any equal rise in the wages of labour, and great distress would be felt by the poorer classes. Hence, an increase of pauperism from this temporary cause, probably made the landowners uneasy; and led them to seek relief in the arbitrary experiment of the statute. So hard is the wisdom of abstaining from legislation, and so easy is it for those who wield an almost absolute power, to apply an ill-contrived and inadequate remedy to an evil, the pressure of which is severely felt, though its cause may not be understood.

It cannot reasonably be doubted that the new statute was solely the work of the landowners of the day, and was adopted exclusively on a mistaken view of their own interests. The first parliament of the Restoration was not likely to be greatly swayed by any strong sense of right or justice, or to be prevented from disregarding the welfare of the poor and destitute members of the community.* It was easy for such a parliament to adopt the pernicious idea of reverting to a principle which had received an ample trial, and had been found injurious, and rejected, so long before.† This was done by restricting a man's labour to a single parish, and so restoring, as nearly as could be effected, that relation

* In endeavouring to ascertain the motives for this retrograde legislation, it should be remembered that in the time of James I., it had been proposed to commute the feudal services (by which lands were held from the time of the Conquest to that of the Commonwealth), for a money payment, to be made by the landowner to the Crown ; but it was reserved to Charles II. to adopt the abolition in fact of these services. This had been already effected by Cromwell, and Charles II. received in exchange for them, from the same parliament which passed this statute for removal of the poor, a tax, levied, not on the lands from which it ought in justice to have issued, but on the industry and commerce of the country. The hereditary excise duty, on various articles of general consumption, was granted by the landowners to the Crown in lieu of all these services ; and thus landed estates were relieved from a permanent heavy charge, by the levying of a new and perpetual tax on every consumer throughout the kingdom. When injustice such as this towards the whole industry and commerce of England, could be committed by Charles II. and his first parliament, the observation in the text is justified.

† Above, pp. 193, 194. 206.

which had existed, in a bygone and barbarous age, between the mere land and the labourer who renders it productive.

The statute of Charles II. enacts, "that whereas, by reason of some defects in the law, poor people are *not restrained from going from one parish to another*, and, therefore, do endeavour to settle themselves in those parishes *where there is the best stock*, the largest commons and wastes to build cottages, and the most woods for them to burn and destroy, and when they have consumed it then to another parish, and at last become rogues and vagabonds, to the *great discouragement of parishes to provide stocks*, where it is liable to be devoured *by strangers*; be it therefore enacted,—that it shall and may be lawful, upon the complaint of churchwardens or overseers, within forty days after any such person coming to settle in any tenement under the yearly value of 10*l.*, for any two justices of the peace—of the division where any person *likely to be chargeable* shall come to inhabit, by their warrant, to remove and convey such person or persons to such parish where he or they were last legally *settled*, either as a *native*, *householder*, *sojourner*, *apprentice*, *or servant*, for the space of forty days at the least:"

Little consideration of the jumble of recital and enactment which constitutes this main provision of the statute of Charles II. is needed, to satisfy any one that it is founded on hypotheses which, if true in the reign of King Charles, are so no longer in that of Queen Victoria.

Before adverting to the several grievances, which the statute was intended to redress, it may be observed that a house worth 10*l.* a year in 1662, the occupation of which is the sole protection against the arbitrary power of the parish officer to interfere with any man's liberty, would be worth about 50*l.* a year of our present currency; and that the labouring classes do not usually occupy houses worth as much as 10*l.* a year, even at the present day.* The statute

* Rents are a good deal higher in large towns than in the country; yet in 1847 there were nearly 17,000 houses in Leeds worth less than 10*l.* a year each, and only 6269 worth more. Sixth Report of the Commons' Committee on the Law of Settlement and Removal, 1847 (4253, 4254, and 4255.).

was, therefore, nearly as great a restriction on the free circulation of mere labour, as it would have been if its ban had been pronounced against all who had not 100*l.* a year of real estate.

The first grievance recited, as a ground for the enactment, is, that men endeavour to settle themselves where there is the best "stock." Probably the "stock" alluded to is the stock of materials to work up, provided under the statute of Elizabeth. Now, whatever danger and difficulty there is found in organising labour by the State, there can be no doubt that as soon as the opportunity of honest labour is furnished, whether by parish officers, or by any other employer of labour, the poor man does nothing more than is natural and reasonable, in migrating from the place where he cannot obtain work, to the place where he can obtain it. His migration seems to have been merely to such places as offered him the prospect of employment, from parishes, the overseers of which neglected to do so; and hard indeed would it be, if the poor man, who can only live by his labour, should not be allowed to remove to the place where he can find labour to live by.

Perhaps the recital of the statute might, with equal truth, have been differently worded, and have alleged, that whereas the neglect by overseers, to carry out the statute of Elizabeth, had compelled poor persons to leave their own parishes, and to seek, in other parishes, for overseers who obeyed the law; and that, as a remedy for the evil, some additional provision ought to be made for compelling all overseers to perform their statutory duties, and so forth.

Commons and wastes are spoken of, and the legislature is anxious, in 1662, to protect them from intrusion; in 1851, they have long since been enclosed, and, for the most part, are no longer to be seen as commons and wastes. The burning and destruction of "woods" has also ceased to call, if it ever called, for special legislation directed solely against the indigent poor; and although incendiaries have been found in England, during the last twenty or thirty years, yet they have not been found specially among parish paupers; and no one has ever imagined that during the last half century, the power of removing a pauper to his place of settlement, has been of any use in preventing the commission of these acts of "burning and destruction."

It was a little hard, even when the statute of Charles II. passed, that the merely indigent poor should be punished, by liability to removal, because the country possessed no adequate police for repressing crime: but, at the present day, there is an efficient police in every county in which it has been thought fit to adopt the provisions of the law by establishing one, and we need not continue to punish the innocent pauper for the offences of the guilty misdemeanant.

Moreover, under the Poor Law Amendment Act of 1834, the country has gained, at least, some approach to uniformity in the administration of relief to the poor. The guardians of the poor in every union raise whatever funds are needed, and the whole of what is raised is equally administered under the orders and control of the same central authority, the Poor Law Board. If by "stock," in the statute of Charles II., were merely meant the fund for the relief of the poor, it is plain, that the suggestion of the legislature is no longer applicable to the conditions under which relief, by boards of guardians, under the supervision of a central authority, is now bestowed.

There is no doubt that, before 1834, the poor, in many instances, were accustomed, and had been led, in part by the vicious administration of relief under the statute of Elizabeth, in part by the necessary effect of the statute of Charles II., to look for parish relief as their absolute and sole patrimony; as entitling them to increase and multiply at their own pleasure, and at the expense of their more provident and richer neighbours. In those days, the character of the parish, from which the poor were entitled to receive this their inheritance of relief, made a great difference in its value. The provision for the poor, and the mode of dealing with them, varied greatly in different parishes; but no one has yet dreamed that since 1834, in the eyes of those who may be in need of relief, one union board, or union workhouse, is very much more attractive than another.

It may safely be alleged, that all the very special inducements, which appear to have influenced the Restoration Parliament, in imposing these most injurious and unjust restrictions on the free circulation of labour, long since ceased to exist; so that if there ever existed any reasonable ground or justification for passing such a statute, it exists no longer.

By this statute, however, fetters are imposed on the labourer, under which his race has suffered for five or six generations. The free exercise of his industry is denied him; he once more becomes *adscriptus glebæ*, and from the chain which binds him to the spot where he was born, or otherwise became settled, he can only free himself by performing some statutory condition, which shall rivet on him similar bonds in another place. Man, only nominally free, again becomes the mere slave of the land, and the agricultural labourer has hardly had a better place assigned him, in the political and social organisation of England, for the last two centuries, than that which he possessed, throughout the greater part of Europe, during the feudal age.* The name of serf or villein has, it is true, fallen into disuse; but the spirit of serfdom and villenage has been preserved, by the legislation of Charle II., the practical effect of which, from the very first, has been to retain every labouring man within the parish where accident may have given him a settlement. The serf or villein of feudal barbarism, effectually acquired his freedom

* From the age of Constantine, the *colonus*, though nominally *free*, like the settled parishioner of our pauper code, really existed in a serfdom, that was little better than slavery itself he was *servus terræ*, bound for ever to the land on which he was born. Every able-bodied beggar had a place of settlement assigned to him, where he was to cultivate the land: so in our law of settlement, every man who has to ask an overseer of the parish of his residence for a loaf of bread, or a shilling, is at once liable to removal to any distant part of the kingdom, where, by derivation from any ancestor, or by any act of his own, he may be "settled." Moreover, a mere residence of forty days in any of the characters specified in the statute of Charles II., impressed this character of the ancient serfdom. *Die Luft macht leibeigen* was the familiar rule of what may be called serfdom *by settlement* in the feudal law. See Hertius, *De Hominibus Propriis*, iii. s. 3., and Loysel, *Institutes Coutumières*, liv. i. c. xxi.

if, escaping from the bondage of his original settlement, he resided for a year and a day within the walls of a town*; but no term of mere residence, even if it endured from generation to generation, could, under the statute of Charles II., destroy the poor man's liability to removal to the original place of his derivative settlement.

No attempt to mitigate or qualify the effect of this legislation appears to have been made, until after the revolution of 1688.† During the long period of misgovernment by the two brothers of the Stuart race, the necessary evil of the law of settlement and removal, its tendency to injure every labourer in the country by restricting the exercise of his industry, and arbitrarily interfering with his personal freedom, remained in full operation.

* Above, p. 164. Houard, *Traité sur les Coutumes Anglo-Normandes*, tom. ii. p. 389. Coke on Littleton, p. 137. b. Brussel, *Usage de Fiefs*, p. 902. De Laurière, *Glossaire du Droit Français*, v. Bourgeois de parcours.

† An act of James II. (1 Jac. II. c. 17.) had merely revived and continued the statute of Charles II.

CHAP. IX.

PAUPERISM FROM THE REIGN OF CHARLES II. TILL THE END OF THE SEVENTEENTH CENTURY.

Ætas parentum, pejor avis, tulit
Nos nequiores, mox daturos
Progeniem vitiosiorem. HORACE.

IN the interval between the reign of Charles II. and the end of the seventeenth century, the pauperism of England appears to have increased greatly; and it frequently found a place in royal speeches to parliament, as well as in discussions at the council board, and in provisions of the legislature. Among other eminent names of those whose attention was attracted to the condition of the poor, and the state of the poor law, under William III., is found that of the celebrated John Locke: his views were embodied in a Report from the Board of Trade, of which he was a member, to the Lords Justices of the kingdom. This Report bears ample testimony to the increase of pauperism, under the law of settlement and removal, which had been in force during the two preceding reigns of Charles II. and James II. "The multiplying of the poor, and the increase of the tax for their maintenance," says Locke, in his Report of the year 1696, "is so general an observation and complaint, that it cannot be doubted of, nor has it been only since the last war that the evil has come upon us; it has been a growing burden on the kingdom these many-years; and *the two last reigns felt the increase of it as well as the present.*" He observes, that "the evil has proceeded neither from scarcity of provisions, nor from want of employment for the poor; since God has blessed these times with plenty not less than the former." He concludes that the growth of the poor could only be caused by "the relaxation of discipline and corruption of manners."*

* Cited by Eden, *State of the Poor*, vol. i. pp. 244, 245.

In the session of parliament next after this Report was presented, the speech from the throne contained the following passage:—"I think it would be happy if some effectual expedient could be found for employing the poor, which might tend to the increase of our manufactures as well as remove a heavy burden from the people." This suggestion, however, led to no result; and in the next session, William III., in addressing his parliament, again adverted to the poor law:—"The increase of the poor is become a burden to the kingdom; and their loose and idle life does in some measure contribute to that depravation of manners, which is complained of, I fear with too much reason. Whether the grounds of this evil be from *defects in the laws already made, or in the execution of them,* deserves your consideration." The king's suggestion seems not to have been acted on, or noticed; and in the following session he again recurred to the subject:—"If you can find proper means of setting the poor at work, you will ease yourselves of a very great burden, and at the same time add so many useful hands to be employed in our manufactures and other public occasions."* We need not wonder that William III. should not have known enough of political economy to be aware, that for the State to undertake to find work for such of its citizens as may be unable to find it for themselves, is going a little beyond its proper duty and province. The statute of Elizabeth having sanctioned the principle of finding every one in work, who could not find himself, these speeches of William III. seem rather to show the then opinion, that the statute of Elizabeth worked well, but was imperfectly carried out.

It is highly probable that the neglect to carry out the statute of Elizabeth, would be as great, after the passing of the statute of Charles II., as we have already seen that it was, during the earlier part of the century. And it seems certain that the pauperism of England greatly increased in the latter part of the seventeenth century. A statute passed in 1691, speaks of the rates for the poor as being "daily

* Eden, *State of the Poor*, vol. i. pp. 247, 248.

increased;"* and in a pamphlet, published at Exeter in 1698, entitled, "Bread for the Poor,"† it is stated, in a kind of introduction, that the charge of maintaining the poor of the county of Devon "is most-wheres double within twenty years past, and like to double again in a short time."

During the latter part of the seventeenth century, the annual produce of the poor-rate of England and Wales, is estimated to have been from 600,000*l.* to 840,000*l.*, which was probably bestowed on 250,000 to 300,000 persons, that is, on between 1 in 20 and 1 in 24 of the then population.

That it was absolutely necessary to introduce some mitigation into the law of settlement and removal, seems to have been admitted early in the reign of William III. A statute passed in 1692 (3 W. & M. c. 11.), indicates that the law of Charles II. had been found unduly to restrict the circulation of labour. Several new heads of settlement were created, each of which would have the effect of making a forty days' residence, under the conditions defined by the statute, a protection against that very removal which the statute of Charles II. had authorised. Forty days' residence, and payment of a tax, as a rated tax-payer, in the parish, and the executing a public annual office for a year, were added to the catalogue of the heads of settlement. But, on the other hand, the acquisition of a settlement was impeded by various provisions; among others by one, that the forty days of residence should, in numerous cases, be counted from the publication of a notice to be delivered to the parish officers. Under such a state of law it is manifest that no working man could ordinarily have a chance of acquiring a settlement, except with the full consent of the parish officers.

One of the clauses of this statute shows, by a recital, the existence of administrative abuse, which probably called for much more effectual redress than it met with, and must have served to suggest to reflecting minds how great is the danger of abuse to which the administration of any poor law, and most of all one confided to irresponsible annual officers, must

* 3 W. & M. c. 11. s. 11.

† Eden, vol. i. pp. 248–9.; Ruggles, Letter xiv. p. 165.

necessarily be liable. The recital referred to shows that the money of ratepayers was misapplied by overseers, "chiefly for their own private ends;" and that the overseers, "by reason of their unlimited power," could give relief "to what persons and number they thought fit;" by which means, as the statute informs us, the rates of the poor were daily increased. All that was done to remedy this evil was, by requiring overseers to keep a register of the names of persons relieved, "with the day and year when they were first admitted to have relief, and the occasion which brought them to that necessity;" provision being also made for a revision, once a year, of this register, by the parishioners in vestry, and relief being limited to persons on the register, unless "*by authority under the hand of one justice of peace* residing within or near the parish, or by order of justices in quarter sessions." This concluding provision, introducing justices of peace to aid in the administration of relief in each particular case, ultimately proved a great evil, and was finally abrogated in 1834.

Five years later, a second statute of King William (8 & 9 Will. III. c. 30.) was passed; the recital of which shows incontrovertibly, how injurious the statute of Charles II. had proved in its influence on the distribution of labour. The language of this recital is remarkable: "Forasmuch," says the legislature, "as many poor persons, chargeable to the parish, township, or place where they live, merely for want of work, would, in any other place, where sufficient employment is to be had, maintain themselves and families without being burthensome to any parish, township, or place;" but, "they are for the most part *confined to live in their own parishes*, townships, or places, and *not permitted to inhabit elsewhere*, though their labour *is wanted in many other places*, where the increase of manufactures would employ more hands." Having thus clearly stated the existence of a great and crying evil, the legislature proceeds to provide a small and most inadequate remedy.

The puny enactment ushered in by this ample preamble is, that if any person should bring a *certificate* from the parish where he was last legally settled, subscribed by the church-wardens and overseers, and allowed by two justices, every parish should be *obliged to receive him*, and he should *not be removable* merely upon account of his being likely to become chargeable, but only upon his becoming actually chargeable.

It is remarkable that the injury, both to the poor, and to the rest of the community, arising from the law of settlement and removal, should be so solemnly recognised, and that yet, no more vigorous attempt should be made to redress it. The parish of settlement is put under no obligation whatever, in any case, of giving any such certificate as is thus elsewhere to protect from removal. The parish officers may give or refuse, as they think fit. If the settled inhabitant, who needed such certificate, had been authorised by the statute to require its delivery to him by the overseer, such a provision might have caused some relaxation in the parochial imprisonment of the working classes: but as the law remained, under the Certificate Act, it amounted to this, that no working man could leave his parish of settlement for the purpose of exercising his industry elsewhere, without a *passport*, called a certificate, which passport the overseer was authorised, at his own mere caprice, to give or withhold.

It is difficult to discover any rational ground for the continuance, by the legislature in William III.'s time, of the arbitrary power of removal by parish officers. One would have thought that, when the necessity of qualifying the practical effect of the statute of Charles II. was understood, and avowed, and acted on, actual destitution, and a claim on the parish funds, would at once have been made the necessary condition of each removal.

Dr. Burn has observed, that "there is somewhat of hardship in this matter of certificates, by putting it into the power of a parish officer to imprison a man, as it were, for life, however inconvenient it may be for him to continue at that place where he has had the misfortune to acquire what is called a settlement, or whatever advantage he may propose to himself by living elsewhere."

The injustice of leaving it at the option of the parish officers to refuse such a certificate as would prevent the poor man from being removed till actually chargeable, was pointed out and urged on the consideration of the public, a century ago*, by a member of the House of Commons, who appears to have laboured earnestly, but in vain, both in Parliament and in print, to reform the poor law.

The system of certificates, though at times considered, and though seemingly intended, as some slight mitigation of the rigour of the pauper code, appears in truth, to have done little more than increase the power of parish officers over the poor.

But this small contingent of freedom which the statute *permitted* each "churchwarden stern, or kingly overseer," to bestow on the poor labourer, by granting him a certificate, was accompanied by other provisions calculated to embitter the bread of poverty. One enactment was, that every person receiving relief in a parish, should wear a badge, consisting of a large roman P. on the right sleeve of his uppermost garment, "in an open and visible manner," on pain of having his allowance withdrawn, or of being imprisoned, and kept to hard labour, and whipt; and even the overseer who relieved unbadged paupers, was subjected to a penalty.†

The late Mr. Sydney Smith speaks of treatment sometimes bestowed on inmates of gaols, in terms which may be well applied to this indiscriminate badging of the poor. Substitute the word "workhouse" for "prison," and his words become,

* Hay's *Remarks on the Poor Law Question*, quoted by Eden, *State of the Poor*, vol. i. p. 296.

† See Dean Swift's Works, vol. vii. p. 574. "On giving Badges to the Poor," and "Considerations about maintaining the poor," showing certainly that a scheme of badging the poor, was not very likely to be effectual. About the year 1839, in several union workhouses in England and Wales, single women, mothers of children, or pregnant, were compelled to wear a dress of a peculiar colour, as a mark of disgrace: but the practice was at once repressed, by a minute of the poor law commissioners: Sixth Annual Report, p. 98. With the *badging* of the poor of the eighteenth century in England, we may contrast the treatment of the class of *Poveri vergognosi*, at Rome, as described by Bishop Morichini, in his work, *Degl' Istituti di pubblica Carità*, etc. *in Roma*, and with a similar provision in Holland.

"The substance of this way of thinking is, that when a fellow-creature is in the frying-pan, there is no harm in pushing him into the fire; that a little more misery, a little more infamy, a few more links, are of no sort of consequence in a *workhouse* life. If this monstrous style of reasoning extended to hospitals as well as *workhouses*, there would be no harm in breaking the small bone of a man's leg, because the large one was fractured; or in peppering with small shot, a person who was wounded with a cannon ball." *

Various provisions are contained in the same statute, respecting the trial at quarter sessions, of appeals against orders of removal. The statute of Charles II. had given the appeal to quarter sessions. Specific legislation was now needed for the *costs* of such appeals. The antagonism of interest between parishes, created by the statute of Charles II., with its various heads of settlement, had already produced a very natural result in the fruitful and expensive crop of parochial litigation, of which the annual growth, subject to considerable variations, has continued down to our own time.†

As if to aggravate the hardship to the poor, and to increase the expense to the litigating parishes, the powers of removal and of appeal were so given, that as soon as the *ex parte* order of justices was made, the poor man and his family were instantly removed to the parish of his alleged settlement, which, upon so receiving the pauper, became entitled to appeal. This parish, if successful in quashing the order on appeal, obtained from justices of the county into which the provisional removal had been made, a sort of retrograde order; and, thereupon, they re-removed the pauper to the place from which he had been removed to them. Even when an order was quashed, on appeal, for any technical slip or informality, all this oppressive and expensive procedure took place before the parish officers, who originally removed the pauper, could

* Sydney Smith's Works, vol. ii. p. 205.

† The expenditure of poor-rate in this single matter of litigation respectiny settlements, amounted to between 200,000*l.* and 300,000*l.* per annum, during many years after the peace in 1815. Since the passing of the Poor Law Amendment Act, in 1834, the amount thus expended yearly, on the average, has been less than 100,000*l.*

commence a second attempt to obtain a valid order of removal.

It must be owned, that but little was done during the latter part of the seventeenth century, to amend the poor law as constituted by the statute of Elizabeth, and that of Charles II. The legislation of the reign of William III. contains, in its recitals and enactments, first, a recognition of the great liability to abuse of the provisions for the poor, under the statute of Elizabeth; secondly, an equally distinct recognition of the injurious influence of the statute of Charles II. on the distribution of labour; and lastly, some most insufficient provisions for redressing the grievances which were so clearly recognised.

When the remedy applied was so inadequate, we shall not be surprised to find that the symptoms of the disease were soon aggravated. Bishop Burnet, writing under Queen Anne, expresses a wish for the law of settlement and removal being "well reviewed, *if not entirely taken away*." *

* Burnet, *History of his Own Times*, vol. vi. Conclusion, p. 213. ed. Oxford, 1823.

CHAP. X.

THE PAUPERISM AND POOR LAWS OF ENGLAND DURING THE EIGHTEENTH CENTURY.

Il faut à mesure que la nation s'enrichit, que tous soient mieux nourris, mieux vêtus, mieux logés ; que tous aient plus de sécurité dans leur existence, plus d'ésperances dans leur avenir ; il faut que tous enfin trouvent, dans leur participation à la richesse croissante, un motif nouveau de bienveillance mutuelle.—SISMONDI.

THE increase of pauperism which followed the passing of the statute of Charles II., seems to have continued till some time after the accession of George I. Abuses in the administration of the law, arising in part from the power given to justices of the peace to order relief, and to make certain allowances, were beginning to be felt at the very commencement of the eighteenth century, and were noticed by parliament in the year 1722. It seems that the annual outlay in relief of the poor before the accession of George I., had reached the large sum of one million sterling.

That a great part of this outlay was expended in the relief of *able-bodied* poor, cannot be doubted. In the year 1704, Sir Humphrey Mackworth introduced into Parliament a bill which must have originated in a desire to render productive the labour of able-bodied paupers, then maintained in idleness by the contributions of ratepayers. The object of this proposed legislation, was a complete organisation of labour, by establishing great parochial manufactories, and raising capital by poor-rates, in order to carry on, in each such manufactory, a trade, in which paupers might be employed as labourers. The wild scheme met with the complete approbation of the House of Commons, and was passed there with great applause, but was rejected by the other House. While this bill was before the Commons, the celebrated De Foe published an address to Parliament, entitled, "Giving Alms no

Charity," in which is contained much that, if attended to, might have saved the House of Commons the discredit of having passed such a bill.

Among the topics which De Foe urges, is one which has seldom, if ever, been attended to: that prevention of pauperism should rather be sought after, than its cure; and that "the erection of parochial manufactures, in order to parcel out work to every door, would be ruinous to the manufacturers themselves; would turn thousands of families out of their employments; and would take the bread out of the mouths of diligent and industrious families, to feed vagrants, thieves, and beggars, who ought much rather to be compelled, by legal methods, to *seek* that work which it is plain is to be had." The improvidence and drunkenness peculiar to the uneducated and neglected poor, form a prominent topic of his address. He says, "I can give an incredible number of examples in my own knowledge, among our labouring poor. I once paid six or seven men together on a Saturday night, the least 10*s*., and some 30*s*. for work, and have seen them go with it directly to the ale-house, lie there till Monday, spend it every penny, and run in debt to boot, and not give a farthing of it to their families, though all of them had wives and children. From hence comes poverty, parish charges, and beggary. If ever one of these wretches falls sick, all they would ask, is a pass to the parish they lived at, and the wife and children to the door a-begging."

About this time it would seem, that the idea of doing something towards educating the poor, obtained a share of public attention. In 1714, the author of the "Fable of the Bees," gave some reasons why the labouring classes should not be educated: and it must be owned that the country has, at least, escaped all evils, if there could have been any, likely to have resulted from providing, generally, for education; for no such provision has been made. Mandeville says, "Going to school, in comparison to working, is idleness; and the longer boys continue in this easy sort of life, the more unfit they will be, when grown up, for downright labour, both as to strength and inclination. Men who are to remain and end their days in a laborious, tiresome, and painful station of life, the sooner they are put upon it at first, the more patiently they will submit to it for ever after.—The poor have nothing to stir them up to labour, but their wants, which it is wisdom to relieve, but folly to cure. The maxim is not less calculated for the real advantage of the poor, than it appears to be for the benefit of the rich. For, among the labouring people, those will ever be the least wretched as to themselves, as well as most useful to the public, that, being meanly born and bred, submit to the station they are in with cheerfulness; and, contented that their children should succeed them in the same low condition, inure them from their infancy to labour and submission." What has been already said is a sufficient comment on doctrines such as these.*

In 1722, we are informed, by the preamble of the statute of 9 Geo. I. c. 7., "An Act for amending the Laws relating to the Settlement, Employment, and Relief of the Poor," that, under colour of the proviso contained in the statute of 3 & 4 W. & M. c. 11. s. 11. †, many persons had applied to justices of the peace, without the knowledge of any officers of the parish, "and thereby, upon untrue suggestions, and sometimes upon false or frivolous pretences, have obtained relief, which hath greatly contributed *to the increase of the parish rates;*" for remedy whereof it enacts, that no justice of the peace shall order relief to any poor person, until oath be made before such justice of some matter, which he shall judge to be a reasonable cause for such relief, and that the same person had applied for relief to the parish, and been refused.

The evils of the jurisdiction now more distinctly conferred on justices of ordering relief, undoubtedly tended greatly to aggravate all the other evils of the poor laws, and continued in active and general operation until the year 1834. The exercise of this power only served, during its entire continuance, to increase the amount of poor-rates, and to add to the demoralisation of the labouring classes; and although a

* Above, p. 88. and following.

† Above, p. 238.

sort of privilege of a powerful body in the state of England, it could no longer be maintained, after its effects were exposed by the Poor Law Inquiry of 1833.

Another clause of the statute of 1722, authorised parishes to purchase or hire, or unite in purchasing or hiring, a workhouse, and to contract for the maintenance there of their poor; and enacted, that any persons who should refuse to be lodged in such houses, should not be entitled to collection or relief. This clause seems to have had a beneficial effect in reducing the amount of yearly expenditure for relief of the poor. The purchase of workhouses enabled the parochial administration of the day to apply a reasonable test of destitution, and to limit their relief to worthier objects than in the early part of the century had begun to obtain it. Parochial accounts, preserved by Sir Frederick Eden, show how great a diminution, in the amount of poor-rate, in many parishes, followed the passing of this statute.

But workhouses alone cannot extinguish pauperism, or remove many of its causes; and it may be observed, in connexion with the diminution in the amount of relief paid to the poor, between 1720 and 1750, that the average price of wheat, during the whole of that period, was greatly below 40*s.* a quarter. During the ten years from 1731 to 1740, it was 1*l.* 17*s.* $3\frac{1}{5}$*d.* per quarter, and during the next ten years, it was only 1*l.* 13*s.* $9\frac{4}{5}$*d.* per quarter.* The relief of the poor, in 1750, cost 689,971*l.*, or 2*s.* per head on the then population of the country: the same relief, in the reign of Queen Anne, at the very commencement of the century, seems to have amounted to a million a year.†

Gilbert's Act, passed in 1783 (22 Geo. III. c. 83.), and the allowance system, introduced in 1795, should both be enumerated, as probably, in some degree, having contributed to the increased pauperism of the latter half of the eighteenth century, both having had the same direct and necessary tendency, though in a different degree, to degrade the working man, and destroy in him any such principles of virtuous inde-

* Smith's *Wealth of Nations*, vol. i. p. 420. ed. M'Culloch.

† Eden, *State of the Poor*, vol. i. p. 264.

pendence and honest industry as nature or accident might have instilled into his uneducated mind. Even Gilbert's Act, on its first passing, had a considerable effect in compensating for previous carelessness and neglect to carry out the provisions of the statute of Elizabeth, and effected some diminution in the poor-rates of the places where it was adopted.

The relief of the poor, which, in 1750, had cost only 689,971*l.*, amounted, in 1776, to 1,530,800*l.*: on the average of 1783-4-5, it attained to 2,004,239*l.*; and in 1801, it was 4,017,871*l.* A review of the latter half of the eighteenth century, makes it clear, that increase of the pauperism of England, even exceeded, in its proportion, the increase of national wealth which took place in the same period.

At the commencement of this half century, began a change in the condition of the country, which, in its nature, is deserving of a very attentive consideration, but which it is not necessary, at this moment, to dwell on, further than to point out that it was accompanied, during the greater part of its continuance, by an uniform increase of pauperism. The American war, the wars with France, an extensive increase of the British dominion in the East, and a vast accumulation of wealth during the whole period from 1750 to 1800, was accompanied by an increase, till then unprecedented, in the destitution and misery of the great body of the labouring classes.

Of all the evils which the labourer suffers, whether produced by the law of settlement, or by any other law, few can be compared, in magnitude, with those arising from his want of decent and convenient house-room. His present condition, in the middle of the nineteenth century, in this respect, will be considered in a future chapter. It is now proposed to indicate briefly, by a few contemporary witnesses, both what that condition must have been, during the latter half of the last century, and how it arose.

Before calling forward these witnesses, it may be observed, that the law of settlement and removal of 1662, would necessarily make all landowners desire, that the birth or residence, which might confer a settlement, and thereby create a perpetual burden on their land, should occur in any neighbouring parish, rather than in their own. Hence arose a tendency to clear estates of the cottages in which agricultural labourers, employed on such estates, would naturally reside, and to drive such labourers to seek for places of residence elsewhere, travelling, daily, as far as might be needful, to their work. It is undoubted that the law of settlement created this tendency to pull down cottages, and grievously restricted the cottage accommodation of the poor. It is even considered by many writers, that the difficulty and want of decent cottage accommodation, thus created, in agricultural districts, was such as to have been a material check on marriage, among the labouring classes, during the greater part of the eighteenth century. The more miserable and degraded the class of labourers were rendered by the want of a decent residence, the less powerful would such a check be; and its effect, as a check on marriage (the only good tendency, perhaps, that it ever had), must have been completely neutralised by the allowance system, which was adopted in 1795, even if such a check had any substantial influence down to that period.

It seems hardly possible to deny or question that the law of settlement and removal has had a most injurious effect on the health, morality, and comfort of the whole labouring population, by holding out to the owners of parishes an inducement to diminish the amount of cottage accommodation within their parochial boundaries, and to draw from neighbouring districts even the daily supply of labour needed to cultivate their lands. We shall see hereafter*, how great the sufferings of the poor have been, and still are, in consequence of this abuse, by the proprietors of parishes, of the legal rights of property, and of this neglect of moral duties co-extensive with those rights. The effect must have begun to be felt soon after the passing of the statute of Charles II., and was generally prevalent in the middle of the last century. Dr. Burn's testimony, in his "History of the Poor Laws," published in

* *Post*, Chapter XIV.

1764, is conclusive as to this palpable consequence of the law of settlement. "In practice, the office of an overseer of the poor seems to be understood to be this: to keep an extraordinary look-out to prevent persons coming to inhabit, without certificates, and to fly to justices to remove them; and if a man brings a certificate, then to caution all the inhabitants not to let him a farm of 10*l.* a year, and to take care to keep him out of all parish offices.—*To pull down cottages; to drive out as many inhabitants, and admit as few, as possibly they can; that is, to depopulate the parish, in order to lessen the poor-rate.*" *

Mr. Young, in "The Farmer's Letters to the People of England," mentions the destruction of cottages, and complains of the effect of the law of settlement in bringing it about. "It is too much the interest of a parish, both landlords and tenants, to decrease the cottages in it, and, above all, to prevent their increase, that, in a process of time, habitations are extremely difficult to be procured,—and this conduct is found so conducive to easing the rates, that it universally gives rise to *an open war against cottages.*—Nay, how often do gentlemen who have possessions in a parish, where such cottages come to sale, purchase them, and immediately erase them from the ground, that they may never become the *nests*, as they are called, *of beggars' brats;* by which means their tenants are not so burthened in their rates, and, of course, their farms *let* the better: for the *rates* are considered as much by tenants as the *rent* of a new farm. In this manner cottages are the perpetual objects of parish jealousy."† Increase in the size of estates and farms, and a corresponding diminution in the number of landowners and occupiers, seems to have been a leading characteristic of the agricultural economy of England, during the latter half of the eighteenth century.

In a pamphlet, entitled "Thoughts on the Cause of the

* Burn, *The History of the Poor Laws*, p. 211. It is only as this sheet is passing through the press (in January, 1852), that I first obtain a sight of this book.

† *The Farmer's Letters to the People of England*, pp. 288, 289. 2nd ed. 8vo. London, 1768.

Increase of the Poor," published in 1787*, it is said that the burden of the poor-rate arises "from the absorption of smaller farms in greater, and by depriving a poor labourer of a portion of land round his cottage." Goldsmith, in his "Deserted Village," gives earlier and immortal testimony, to what his own eyes had probably witnessed, as well in England as in his native country:

The man of wealth and pride
Takes up a space that many poor supplied;
Space for his lakes, his park's extended bounds,
Space for his horses, equipage, and hounds. — †
His seat, where solitary sports are seen,
Indignant spurns the cottage from the green — ‡:
Where then, ah! where, shall poverty reside,
To scape the pressure of contiguous pride? §

Small proprietors who cultivated their own fields, and formed so striking a characteristic of the English nation in the age of Fortescue ||, had been greatly reduced during the two following centuries, but still there were numbered in England, in the seventeenth century, not less than "160,000 proprietors, who, with their families, made up more than a

* Ruggles, *History of the Poor*, Letter XXV. p. 32.

† So in Imperial Rome: in Quintilian, Declam. xiii., a small landowner says, "Nec ab initio vicinus divitis fui: pares circa me habitavere domini, et *frequentibus villis* concors vicinia parvos limites coluit." Ib. "Quod cives pascebat, nunc divitis unius *hortus* est."

‡ Ib. "Postquam proximos quosque revellendo terminos ager locupletis latius inundavit: æquatæ solo *villæ*, et excisa patria sacra."

§ Ib. "Quid agimus inquam? Undique *vallo divitiarum* clausi sumus. Hinc hortuli locupletis, hinc arva, inde vineta, hinc saltus, nullus terræ datur exitus." Such exile as clearances have since produced on so grand a scale, both in the Scottish Highlands and in Ireland, is also described by Goldsmith, and is mentioned, with a remarkable similarity of expression, in the prose of the Latin writer:

"Good heaven! what sorrows gloomed that parting day
That call'd them from their native walks away;
When the poor exiles, every pleasure past,
Hung round the bowers, *and fondly looked their last.*"

"Æquatæ solo villæ, et excisa patria sacra, et cum conjugibus parvisque liberis, *respectantes patrium larem*, migraverunt veteres coloni: et lætæ solitudinis indiscreta unitas facta est."

|| Above, p. 168.

seventh part of the whole population, and derived their subsistence from their little freehold farms."* It has been computed, that the number of persons who then occupied their own land was greater than the number of those who farmed the land of others.† This class of proprietors has long been diminishing; their most rapid progress towards extinction, probably occurred towards the latter half of the eighteenth century. The wealth of the country continued greatly to increase, while the number of those among whom it was distributed seems to have thus constantly diminished. The analogy of all this to what occurred in ancient Rome is obvious.

Sir Frederick Eden, towards the end of the eighteenth century‡, speaks of the "impossibility of procuring habitations," as the greatest difficulty under which the poor laboured: and, mentioning the repeal, by 15 Geo. III. c. 32., of the statute of Elizabeth, which prohibited the building of cottages unless four acres of land were laid to each cottage, he adds, truly enough, "there does not seem to be much danger, at present, of cottages becoming too numerous."

The want of cottage accommodation for labourers, forced itself on the notice of the magistrates of Hampshire, in 1795, in consequence of an inquiry under an order made at their Epiphany sessions of that year. The justices who inquired reported§, among other things, that "it would much improve the condition of labourers, if cottages were multiplied and dispersed about the estates where they labour, with small pieces of ground annexed for their own proper cultivation and advantage; by which the loss of time, and the actual labour of going to and from work at a distance, would be saved from such fruitless waste, to be employed in the fruitful cultivation of such pieces of ground."‖ A contemporary

* Macaulay, *History of England*, vol. i. p. 334. † Ibid.

‡ Eden, *State of the Poor*, vol. i. p. 361.

§ Report on the Inquiry into the General State of the Poor, instituted by order of the last Epiphany Quarter Sessions for Hampshire. Published by Young, *Annals of Agriculture*, vol. xxv. pp. 349—398.

‖ Report, p. 258.

testimony tells us, at the same time, that "the condition of the poor was every day made more wretched than ever, although the rates, from the late and present scarcity, were most rapidly increasing."*

In a tract published in the year 1800, it is stated, that a very great quantity of land had been taken from under the plough and thrown into pasture, and that "the reduction in the number of farms in England would scarce be credited, was not the fact, unfortunately, too well proved. Not one county in the kingdom has more than half the number it formerly had; most counties are reduced to one-third; and one county in particular has not the fourth part of the number it had a few years ago."†

Such are some of the more prominent characteristics of the pauperism of England during the eighteenth century.

But the manifest injury to all classes of the community from the poor man's liability to removal, under the act of Charles II., whenever an overseer thought him even *likely* to become chargeable, continued, in all its severity, to disgrace the statute book. The overseer's power, arbitrarily to refuse a certificate‡, was never qualified. The overseer's authority, in this respect, has been of slight moment to the poor since the year 1795, for a statute was then passed, under which actual chargeability to the removing parish was justly made a necessary condition, on which alone any order of removal could be granted§; and thereupon certificates became practically useless. The statute effecting this tardy improvement and mitigation of the law, very distinctly characterises the principle of the previous legislation, and its effect on the rights and happiness of the poor.

Its language is, "Whereas many industrious poor persons, chargeable to the parish, township, or place where they live,

* Rev. J. Howlett, on the 30th November, 1795, in Young's *Annals of Agriculture*, vol. xxv. p. 602.

† Brooke, *The True Cause of our Present Distress for Provisions*, p. 6. London, 1800.

‡ Above, p. 239.

§ 35 Geo. III. c. 101. The provision for badging the poor was also repealed in the same year, 1795.

merely from want of work there, would, in any other place, where sufficient employment is to be had, maintain themselves and families without being burthensome to any parish, township, or place; and such poor persons *are, for the most part, compelled to live in their own parishes, townships, or places,* and *are not permitted to inhabit elsewhere,* under pretence that they are likely to become chargeable to the parish, township, or place, into which they go for the purpose of getting employment, although the labour of such poor persons might, in many instances, be very beneficial to such parish, township, or place."

The description given by the legislature*, nearly a century before this act passed, of the injurious consequences of the statute of Charles II., was much the same as that which is here exhibited.†

What a contrast is there between this recital of the act of 1795, and that of the statute of Charles II. Then it was declared to be a great defect in the law, that poor people were *not restrained from going out of* one parish into another. Now the defect is, that the poor are *compelled* to *live in* their own parishes, and are *not permitted* to inhabit elsewhere.

A reference to the political history, as well as to the social condition, of England in 1795, will probably give a reasonable explanation of the passing, at that moment, of the statute 35 Geo. III. c. 101., in so far as it mitigates the cruelty and

* In the preamble to the stat. 8 & 9 Will. III. c. 30., passed in 1697, and set out above, p. 238.

† The same statute, 35 Geo. III. c. 101., mitigated another practical grievance of the poor, under the statute of Charles II. A common cause of destitution being bodily sickness, it frequently happened that orders of removal were obtained, and (as the statute 35 Geo. III. c. 101. s. 2. informs us) "poor persons were often removed, or passed to the place of their settlement, during the time of their sickness, *to the great danger of their lives*:" the act therefore gave the power of suspending the execution of orders of removal, in the case of poor persons, whose sickness rendered it dangerous for them to be removed. The same act also defined new conditions of litigation between parishes respecting these suspended orders, and the amount of costs of relief which might be incurred under them. It is impossible to modify any abuse of this settlement and removal law, without affecting pecuniary interests of the hostile and belligerent districts, into which it divides the whole country.

oppression of the law of settlement and removal. That statute limits, for the first time, the power of removal to the case of those who were in actual need of parish relief. The time was, at least, one of general distress. Wheat, during several years, had become dearer and dearer; and the horizon of agricultural districts was lurid with the rick-burnings of discontented incendiaries. The price of wheat had risen as follows:

Year.	Wheat per Quarter. £	s.	d.
1792	2	2	11
1793	2	8	11
1794	2	11	8
1795	3	14	2
1796	3	17	1

As economical science advanced in the last century, and before the statute 35 Geo. III. c. 101. had passed, thoughtful men began to discover that the interests of the employer and the employed, in truth, equally required the entire repeal of our law of settlement and removal; and the few then knew, what has since been added to the stock of knowledge of the many, that the labour of the free man is cheaper to its employer than the labour of a slave, or serf, or pauper bound to his parish by the practical serfdom of his settlement. It was declared, by the voice of a great teacher of mankind, that, by the abolition of the law of settlement, there would be opened to the labourer an unrestricted selection of the best market for his industry, so that his employer would necessarily obtain the best supply of labour, while the labourer's condition would clearly be bettered, and the relation between employer and labourer in every respect improved.

Adam Smith loudly and earnestly denounced the impolicy and injustice of the law, which, however, easily withstood his attack. It still survives, with all its miserable associations of sorrow and suffering, to show how hard a matter it can sometimes be, to abate an almost universally admitted nuisance. "To remove a man who has committed no misdemeanour," said the author of the Wealth of Nations, "from the parish where he chooses to reside, is an evident violation of natural liberty and justice. The common people of England, however, so jealous of their liberty, but, like the common people of most other countries, never rightly understanding wherein it consists, have now, for more than a century together, suffered themselves to be exposed to this oppression without a remedy. Though men of reflection, too, have sometimes complained of the law of settlements, as a public grievance; yet it has never been the object of any general popular clamour, such as that against general warrants, an abusive practice undoubtedly, but such a one as was not likely to occasion any general oppression. There is scarce a poor man in England, of forty years of age, I will venture to say, who has not, in some part of life, felt himself most cruelly oppressed by this ill-contrived law of settlements."* "Break down the exclusive privileges of corporations, and repeal the Statute of Apprenticeship, both which are really encroachments upon natural liberty, and add to those the repeal of the law of settlements, so that a poor workman, when thrown out of employment, either in one trade or in one place, may seek for it in another trade or in another place, without the fear, either of a prosecution, or of a removal." †

The doctrine of the great and excellent Turgot, agrees with that of Adam Smith. The celebrated edict, by which corporate privileges were abolished in France, under Louis XVI., is prefaced by a solemn declaration, that labour is the poor man's property, that no property is more sacred, and that neither time nor authority can sanction the violation of his right, freely to dispose of this, his only resource. ‡

* Smith, *Wealth of Nations*, vol. i. p. 194.; ed. Edinb. 1817.

† *Wealth of Nations*, vol. ii. p. 264.; ed. Edinb. 1817.

‡ Turgot, *Sur la Suppression des Jurandes*. "Dieu en donnant à l'homme des besoins, en lui rendant nécessaire la ressource du travail, a fait du droit de travailler la propriété de tout homme, et cette propriété est la première, la plus sacreé, la plus imprescriptible des toutes." The decree (Edit du Roi, portant suppression des jurandes, donné au mois de Février 1776), is given in Turgot, *Œuvres*, tom. viii. p. 330., and commences as follows: "Louis, par grace de Dieu, etc. Nous devons à tous nos sujets de leur assurer la jouissance pleine et

Two centuries sufficed to emancipate the middle classes, and especially inhabitants of towns, from the unjust restrictions, in the employment of their industry, to which corporate privileges subjected them. The Statute of Apprenticeship, passed in the reign of Queen Elizabeth, was repealed early in the nineteenth century *, and no longer impedes the skilled workman from exercising his art or mystery, when and as he may see fit; but the poor labourer, in ruder forms of industry, still suffers under the legislation of a by-gone age.

entière de leurs droits; nous devons surtout cette protection à cette classe d'hommes, qui n'ayant de propriété que leur travail et leur industrie, ont autant plus le besoin et le droit d'employer dans toute leur étendue les seules ressources qu'ils aient pour subsister. Nous avons vu avec peine les atteintes multipliées qu'ont donné à ce droit naturel et commun, des institutions, anciennes à la vérité, mais que ni le tems ni l'autorité qui semblent les avoir consacrées n'ont pu légitimer."

* It was repealed by 54 Geo. III. c. 96.

CHAP. XI.

PAUPERISM AND POOR LAWS OF ENGLAND, FROM 1800 TO 1834.

Omne in præcipiti vitium stetit: utere velis,
Totos pande sinus. — JUVENAL.

THE whole interval between the commencement of the present century, and the passing of the Poor Law Amendment Act in 1834, is marked, in the history of our poor, by a continuous increase of pauperism. This increase was in part produced by the systematic abuse and disregard of the provisions of the statute of Elizabeth, and in part, by the operation of the law of settlement and removal. The labourer, looking on his parish as the place to which, under the latter statute, he was bound, was led, by abuses in the administration of relief, to regard that same parish as bound to him, by a bond still more indissoluble than that of his own serfdom. True it was, that he could not prudently leave his parish and seek for work elsewhere, but that parish did much, as if to prevent all desire to leave it, by opening as wide as possible the portals of public support for all settled parishioners; and even undertaking to pay each of them a yearly income, accurately adjusted to the extent of his necessities: increasing from year to year, with the increase of his family, and increasing from week to week, with any increase in the price of corn. The slave on a West India plantation, was not more completely deprived of every incentive to prudence; and although, on the one hand, the English agricultural labourer could not hope ever to mend his condition, yet, on the other, he was released from all fear of materially injuring himself by any prodigality or misconduct of which he might be guilty.

This allowance system, as it was called, and which has been already alluded to as introduced in 1795, was first formally sanctioned by resolutions of the justices of peace, in Berkshire, and soon became general throughout the country. The resolutions of the Berkshire magistrates were adopted "at a general meeting of the justices of this county, together with several discreet persons assembled by public advertisement, on Wednesday, the 6th day of May, 1795, at the Pelican Inn, in Speenhamland (in pursuance of an order of the last Court of General Quarter Sessions), for the purpose of rating husbandry wages by the day or week, if then approved of."

These resolutions were as follows: "1. That the present state of the poor does require further assistance than has been generally given them. 2. That it is not expedient for the magistrates to grant that assistance by regulating the wages of day labourers, according to the directions of the statutes of the 5th Elizabeth, and 1st James; but the magistrates very earnestly recommend to the farmers and others throughout the county, to increase the pay of their labourers in proportion to the present price of provisions; and agreeable thereto, the magistrates now present have unanimously resolved, that they will, in their several divisions, make the following calculations and allowances, for the relief of all poor and industrious men, and their families, who, to the satisfaction of the justices of their parish, shall endeavour (as far as they can) for their own support and maintenance; that is to say, when the gallon loaf of seconds flour, weighing 8lbs. 11oz., shall cost 1*s.*, then every poor and industrious man shall have for his own support 3*s.* weekly, either procured by his own, or his family's labour, or an allowance from the poor-rates; and for the support of his wife, and every other of his family, 1*s.* 6*d.* When the gallon loaf shall cost 1*s.* 6*d.*, then every poor and industrious man shall have 4*s.* weekly for his own support, and 1*s.* 10*d.* for the support of every other of his family. And so in proportion, as the price of bread rises or falls, (that is to say,) 3*d.* to the man, and 1*d.* to every other of his family, on every 1*d.* which the loaf rises above 1*s.*"

On the 20th of February, 1834, the Commissioners for Inquiry into the administration and practical operation of the Poor Laws, made the Report to which frequent reference has been made in the previous pages, and which sufficiently shows what had been the condition of England, in respect of its pauperism, during the previous part of the present century. It appears from that Report, and the other folio volumes of evidence * on which it was founded, that in the greater part of the districts throughout which a most extensive and elaborate examination was then made, the fund provided under the statute of Elizabeth (and thereby directed to be employed in setting to work children and persons capable of labour, but using no daily trade, and in the necessary relief of the impotent), "was applied to purposes opposed to the letter, and still more opposed to the spirit, of that Law, and destructive to the morals of the most numerous class, and to the welfare of all." †

Throughout the whole mass of evidence collected by the Commissioners, it is easy to discern ample proof, that, independently of all the glaring abuses in the administration of relief, under the statute of Elizabeth (which abuses might easily be prevented, by amending the mere machinery of administration), the law of settlement and removal had largely contributed towards bringing about the evils then so justly complained of, and felt to be unendurable. Several of the more intelligent witnesses examined, expressed opinions wholly adverse to the law of settlement and removal.

When we shall come to consider, in a future chapter, the necessity of a complete abolition of that law, some of the principal evils, to which it gives rise, as they pervade the agricultural counties of England, must be stated. Such evils, as they have revived, and now exist, in 1851, are, to a great extent, identical with those described by witnesses under the inquiry of 1833; and it is clear that a great part of the very abuses which led to the passing of the Poor Law Amendment Act, and which, at the same time, led so many persons to think that the law of settlement and removal ought to be

* Consisting of, 1st, one volume of Reports of Assistant Commissioners; 2nd, two volumes of Answers to Town Queries; 3rd, four volumes of Answers to Rural Queries.

† Report, p. 8.

repealed, or greatly reformed, still exist to show the present necessity of such repeal or reform.

So far respecting the pauperism of the period from 1800 to 1834. The progress of poor law legislation, during the same interval, is very trifling. One most injudicious provision was made in 1815, extending the mischievous power already adverted to *, and so long exercised by justices of peace. By the statute 55 George III. c. 137., it was provided, that any justice or justices of the peace, may order relief to be given to poor persons, at their own homes, for any period not exceeding three months; and that two or more justices may make a further order for relief, for any period not exceeding six months, and so on from time to time, as occasion should require: and such justices might order the discontinuance of such relief. This provision, like many others in poor law legislation, had a very different effect from that which its framers must have anticipated. The evidence taken before the various committees who subsequently investigated the subject, showed plainly enough the extremely injurious result which arose from this power, and perhaps a little consideration might have enabled the collective wisdom of the nation to foresee the inevitable result of such an act of legislation.

All the mitigation which the law of settlement and removal underwent between the years 1800 and 1834, so far as its substantial evils are concerned, is hardly worthy of notice, although those evils were constantly felt, and almost as constantly evidenced, by a never-failing series of statutory regulations, and modifications of existing rights and liabilities of parishes. The wisdom of Parliament was sometimes employed in devising and amending mere forms of procedure; more frequently in defining anew the conditions on which this annexation of the poor man, by the bond of an arbitrary settlement, to a particular parish, should be effected. The changes thus introduced, invariably imposed further restrictions on the acquisition of settlements, and usually gave rise to a good deal of litigation. Settlement by renting a tene-

* Above, pp. 238. 245.

ment, may be mentioned as one of the greater heads of this small legislation. The statute of Charles II., required a residence of forty days only. In 1819, this arbitrary term of forty days was changed into an equally arbitrary term of one year, and in order to acquire such a settlement, subsequent to 2nd July, 1819, various additional conditions were to be fulfilled.* But, as if in a pious horror of uniformity of law, the old settlement by forty days' residence, prior to the 2nd July, 1819, was to be preserved, as to all settlements then acquired. Subsequent statutes, passed on 22nd June, 1825†, on 31st March, 1831 ‡, and on 14th August, 1834 §, imposed still further restrictions on the acquisition of a settlement by renting a tenement, each statute defining the settlement for the future only, and leaving all the previous heads of settlement, by renting a tenement, uninterfered with. Hence it has followed, that since the passing of the Poor Law Amendment Act, there are no less than five distinct heads of settlement, by renting a tenement alone.

In a former chapter, the indefensible injustice of removing a man, by warrant, from his place of residence, to some distant part of the kingdom, and then trying the question, whether he ought to have been removed or not, has been adverted to.|| Three different attempts appear to have been made between 1662 and 1850, to obviate this scandal: but, like most other poor law grievances and abuses, it long bore "a charmed life," and each of the two first attempts to destroy it entirely failed. The first of them was made in 1819, by bill brought into the House of Commons, and rejected.¶ The second was made in the Report of February, 1834 **, by the Commis-

* 59 Geo. III. c. 50.

† 6 Geo. IV. c. 57.

‡ 1 Will. IV. c. 18.

§ 4 & 5 Will. IV. c. 76.

|| Above, pp. 241, 242.

¶ See the next note.

** Report of 1834, p. 194. "We further recommend, that instead of the present mode of first removing the pauper, and then inquiring whether the removal was lawful, the inquiry should precede the removal. We find this measure in a bill brought into the House of Commons in 1819, and printed in the Parliamentary Papers of that year, No. 211. That bill empowers the justice, who shall order a

sioners, whose advice the legislature did not adopt; for, in the Poor Law Amendment Act of the same year, it was merely provided (4 & 5 Will. IV. c. 76. s. 79.), that no poor "person should be removed under any order, until twenty-one days after a notice in writing of his being chargeable, should have been sent to the overseers of the parish, to whom such order should be directed;" and, in effect, a power was thereby given to every parish, of exercising an option, and appealing against an order, either before its execution, by the removal of the paupers, or after such removal.

Paupers, therefore, continued to be dragged across the country under orders of removal, before the legal right to remove them was contested on appeal; and it was not till the year 1849 *, that a third attempt to put an end to the disgrace and scandal of so preposterous a procedure, was made and succeeded.

Another great cause of wholly unnecessary litigation respecting settlements arose, and still continues to arise, under the statute of Charles II., as follows. On an appeal, appellants answer the settlement acquired in their own parish, by proving a subsequent settlement to have been gained elsewhere. Now the law, in such a case, might easily have

removal, to suspend its execution, and to forward (which might be effected through the post-office) a copy of the examination of the pauper, and of the order of removal, to the overseers of the parish in which the pauper has been adjudged to be settled. It then enables parties, who think themselves aggrieved by the order, to appeal to the quarter sessions within twenty-eight days, and the sessions to decide on the question, as if the removal had actually taken place. In the absence of appeal, the order is to be conclusive. The expediency of this measure is so obvious, that it is difficult to account for its rejection in 1819, unless we are to believe a tradition, that it was defeated by a combination of persons interested in creating litigation and expense."

* By 11 & 12 Vict. c. 31. s. 9., which provides that "no appeal shall be allowed against any order of removal, if notice of such appeal be not given, as required by law, within the space of twenty-one days after the notice of chargeability shall have been sent;" and gives a further time of fourteen days only, in the event of the appellant parish applying within the twenty-one days for a copy of the depositions on which the order was made. This and other provisions of the act effected a useful small reform of the law, in the matter of parish appeals; and relieved the Court of Queen's Bench from having to decide many trifling points.

required the appellants to give notice of their intended answer, not only to the respondents, but to the third parish, by which, if the answer were true, the pauper ought to be maintained. Thus the real place of settlement would have been ascertained on such appeal. The law, however, has made no such provision. The appellant answers the *primâ facie* case against him by proving a subsequent settlement, in a third parish, and the order is therefore quashed. The second deal of the cards of litigation next takes place, on a removal, by the defeated respondents, to this third place, in which the last settlement appears to have been acquired, and which now first hears of the claim on its funds. The third parish thinks fit to appeal, and a second appeal is therefore tried, in which the same question of settlement, in this third parish, now a litigant party, is to be again decided. The quarter sessions, consisting, perhaps, of different justices from those who heard the former appeal, taking a different view of the effect of the evidence adduced, decide that the subsequent settlement is *not* proved.* The

* It must have happened to every counsel of much experience at sessions to have known innumerable instances of such second removals; and when appealed against, they are by no means exempt from the ordinary uncertainty of litigation. I have known a different view taken in two such appeals as are above described, even by the same chairman. *Idle*, in the West Riding, some years ago, removed a large family of paupers to *Calverley*. *Calverley* showed, by way of answer, on appeal at the sessions, that a subsequent settlement, by renting a tenement worth 10*l.* a year, *had* been gained in *Thirsk* in the North Riding. Hereupon the order was quashed, and *Idle* now removed to *Thirsk*. The case of *Calverley* against *Idle* had been decided in January, and at the following July sessions, *Thirsk* against *Idle* came on to be heard. The result of a full consideration of the whole case, at the July sessions, led the Court then to decide that the settlement in *Thirsk* had *not* been gained. The same chairman of sessions presided both in January and July, a man of excellent sense and judgment, sufficient legal knowledge, and, in every respect, most competent to the efficient discharge of all his judicial duties. I believe that each decision was right. A court must always judge "*secundum allegata et probata*" on the case actually before it. Had Thirsk been compelled to defend itself on the first trial, the supposed settlement there would not have been successfully made out; and Calverley, the real place of settlement, would have been fixed with the paupers. The costs incurred in this litigation, by the two successful parishes, Calverley and Thirsk, were very heavy. How much was the outlay of Idle, which failed twice, I know not. I was myself counsel for the appellants on each occasion.

legal result of the two appeals, therefore, is, that of these three parishes, the *innocent* parish, as it is called, the only one parish in which admittedly the pauper is *not* settled, is to maintain him, and can never remove him again to either of the two parishes, in one or the other of which, admittedly, the pauper *is* settled.

But it would exhaust my reader's patience, and waste his time, further to dwell on such minute details. There now exist throughout England great grievances, equally suffered by those who pay relief to the poor, and by those who receive it. Such grievances will be discussed in subsequent pages; will probably be found to spread over a wide field for comprehensive legislation; and will at least require a total repeal of the law of settlement and removal.

CHAP. XII.

THE PAUPER LEGISLATION OF THE YEAR 1834.

Regemque dedit, qui fœdere certo
Et premere, et laxas sciret dare jussus habenas. VIRGIL.

THE Poor Law Amendment Act of 1834, is, and will ever remain, a most important step in the history of the pauperism and poor laws of England. Nevertheless, it was little more than an improvement in administrative machinery, and merely provided means of ensuring a due performance of that duty of relieving the poor, the neglect of which had been attended by great injury to all classes of the community. Parliament did little to cut away the root of those evils, which were glaring and admitted, and which no merely administrative change could remove. The most valuable part of the Report of the Commissioners is, perhaps, that which was least attended to by Parliament, and which shows the evils produced by the law of settlement and removal.

It is greatly to be regretted that the Poor Law Amendment Act did not adopt the judicious recommendation of the Commissioners in respect of an extensive reform of that law. The Report had stated the opinion of the Commissioners, that (subject to the obvious exception of persons born in prisons, hospitals, and workhouses,) the settlement of every legitimate child, born after the passing of the intended act, should follow that of the parents or surviving parent of such child, until such child should attain the age of sixteen years, or the death of its surviving parent, and that, at the age of sixteen, or on the death of its surviving parent, such child should be considered as settled in the place in which it was born.* This advice, if adopted, would have been a great simplifying of the

* Report, folio edition, p. 193.

law, and would have conferred a great benefit on the community. By the variety of successive statutory restrictions introduced into the law of settlement and removal, that law, by 1834, had greatly increased in complexity and uncertainty. Speaking of settlements, in a comparatively simple state of the statute law, Dr. Burn had said, in 1764, "It has been the work of an age to ascertain the law respecting them!"

That good work, if accomplished in 1764, was certainly rendered of little use in the nineteenth century, when every session of parliament added something to the previous patchwork of arbitrary legislation. Our mixed state of social luxury and pauperism, perhaps, not unnaturally, led to many legislative provisions. "Corruptissima civitáte, plurimæ leges." But, notwithstanding the multifariousness of these laws, and of the evils produced by them, and many of which were pointed out by the Commissioners of 1833, the legislature, in 1834, did but little, either to simplify the law, or to remove the evils. This will probably be the inference of every one who compares the Report of the Commissioners of 1833, with the Poor Law Amendment Act of 1834. The legislature certainly did a great deal less than the Commissioners thought absolutely necessary, to mitigate the evils of the law of settlement. Attention was mainly given by the legislature, in the statute 4 & 5 Will. IV. c. 76., to improvement in the mere administration of relief, to the organisation of the union boards, and to the control conferred on a central authority. One head of settlement alone was repealed, and trifling restrictions were imposed in respect of some others; but the main and essential evils of the law of settlement and removal, were not substantially interfered with.

Among many prominent evils of the law, to which the attention of the legislature was in vain invited by the Commissioners, were those flowing from settlement by apprenticeship. Mere chance, in the first instance, often ascertained only by an expensive litigation, occurring forty or fifty years after the event in dispute, decides whether one parish or another is to keep a family, in which there is such an inheritance as a settlement by apprenticeship. The state of the law, as it still exists in 1852, is correctly set forth in the Report of the Commission of 1833.* "An apprentice is settled finally in the parish where he sleeps the last night in his condition of apprentice, provided he has slept there, either continuously or at different times, though with intervals, even of years, for forty days in the whole. In the meantime he carries with him, wherever he goes, a contingent right of settlement, and may, in fact, gain as many settlements as there are periods of forty days in the period of his apprenticeship; each fresh settlement, suspending all the previous ones, subject to their revival, if his last night is spent in any parish, in which he has slept, as an apprentice, for thirty-nine days. Bitter complaints are made of this grievance, by the ratepayers of towns having ports, or situated on the banks of navigable rivers. — And it is on absurdities like these that the question depends, whether parish A, or parish B, neither of which has any real connection with the pauper, neither of which could, by any vigilance, have prevented his acquiring a settlement, is to support him and his family for ever. — To these evils must be added the perjury and falsehood which seem peculiarly incidental to these inquiries. — Settlements are claimed by hiring and service under masters who have long been dead, under apprenticeship when the indentures are lost or destroyed, by renting a tenement when houses have been pulled down. And they are rebutted or supported by narratives of conversations which occurred, perhaps, twenty years before, and which were not of a nature to dwell on the memories of those who proffer to report them."

Some of the reasons for abolishing settlement by apprenticeship, were again distinctly stated by the Poor Law Commissioners many years ago in their annual Report. "Pauper boys and girls have often been apprenticed merely to get them a settlement in another parish, and without any reference to the ability of the master to maintain or instruct them. A species of slavery of the worst kind is thus created. Needy persons take the apprentices for the sake of the premiums,

* Report, pp. 88, 89. 91.

nominally to teach them a trade, really to employ them as mere drudges in household work."*

The changes introduced into the law of settlement, by the Poor Law Amendment Act, were, practically speaking, quite trifling, excepting that it prospectively repealed, but retrospectively preserved, settlement by hiring and service for a year.† The various objections to this head of settlement were so universally admitted, that it could not be wholly retained; but the miserable half-measure of its merely prospective repeal, may be judged of by the fact that a large proportion of orders, even now, are made on alleged settlements by hiring and service prior to 1834. In 1841 no less than 2341 orders out of the 8412 of the year, were made on this single ground.‡

The wisdom of Parliament, therefore, provides for the removal of a grievance from some future race, but leaves the present and the next generation to endure all the evils which arise from the litigation of such questions.

We now discuss the hiring and service of a father or mother; and in another quarter of a century, should the law of settlement and removal remain unaltered, the father will have become a grandfather, the mother a grandmother, and the hiring and service of grandfather or grandmother will be the turning point of an appeal at sessions.

It may be supposed that the settlement by hiring and service, completed before the passing of the act, was preserved on account of an imagined, but most mistaken analogy between a settlement and a right of property; and there was once a time, as appears by the Law Reports, when judges used to speak of a settlement as a thing to be favoured in the law, and when they seemed to consider it not in its real light of a great restriction on natural liberty, but as a pecu-

* Ninth Annual Report of the Poor Law Commissioners, 1843, p. 50. On subsequent occasions, the same Commissioners have again expressed their unfavourable opinion of that state of servitude, which is created by the apprenticeship of parish children. Eleventh Annual Report, 1845, p. 16.

† 4 & 5 Will. IV. c. 76. s. 64.

‡ Ninth Annual Report of the Poor Law Commissioners, p. 45.

liar privilege of the poor. The abolition of settlement by hiring and service, and the various restrictions introduced in respect of the acquisition of other settlements, have, upon the whole, had a great effect in rendering it in all cases difficult, and in the vast majority of cases impossible, for any adult labourer ever now to acquire a settlement at all.

If no further change should take place in the law, more and more will the question of settlement resolve itself, as it has already begun to resolve itself, into one of pedigree, and into determining the locality of a father's or a grandfather's birth.

The existing law of birth settlement is most absurd, and involves parishes in great uncertainty and expense. The absurdity consists in this: that any derivative settlement, from either parent, is held to prevent that of the proper place of birth from arising; and, as the law now stands, any order for a pauper's removal to any birth settlement, whether his own or that of his father or mother, grandfather or grandmother, may be quashed, on appeal, by showing the birth settlement of a more remote ancestor. The more remote the derivation of the settlement, the greater is the uncertainty and cost of proof. In the course of my experience, I have, on two occasions, known the settlement of a great-grandfather satisfactorily made out, on the trial of appeals against orders of removal; but so made out with great difficulty, and at much expense.

It would seem that the whole title of "derivative settlement," or "settlement by parentage," which now occupies a large space in treatises on the poor laws, is founded on an unnecessary and erroneous construction of the statute of Charles II.; but the error is one that was adopted more than a century ago, and cannot now be rectified by anything less than an act of Parliament.*

* It has always appeared to me that the intention of the statute of Charles II. would have been far better carried out, if the Court of King's Bench had not engrafted on it this monstrous excrescence of derivative settlements. There is nothing in the statute to indicate an intention of the legislature to make a man removable to the place in which his father or grandfather was born: the re-

Obviously the place of a man's settlement is no longer the place of his industrial residence; and is likely enough to be a place in which he is an entire stranger. An agricultural labourer working, since 1834, under a yearly contract of hiring and service, from youth till old age, in the parish of his birth, will still be settled, at seventy years of age, in any extremity of the kingdom in which his father may have happened to be born; while, on the other hand, a mere child, if apprenticed by parish officers, and, as is very generally done, so apprenticed by them into a parish different from their own, would even now, in 1851, by forty days residence in such parish, acquire a settlement there*, and, in all likelihood,

moval is to be, to the place, either of the man's own nativity, or the place in which he may have resided for forty days in some character specified in the statute. The words of the statute authorised removal "to such parish where he or they were last legally settled, either as a native, householder, sojourner, apprentice, or servant, for the space of forty days at the least." The error of construction seems to have been committed in consequence of an attempt made, by order of removal, to separate the unemancipated child from its parent. The Court thereupon held, that the parent's birth, or other settlement, was transmitted, as an inheritance, to his unemancipated child; instead of merely holding, as it would seem they ought to have done, that although irremovable from the parent while unemancipated (or up to seven, fourteen, sixteen, or twenty-one years of age, as might have been thought most consistent with the principles of the common law respecting the relation of parent and child), yet that such child, as soon as separable from the parent, should be removed to the place of his own birth, not to that of his parent. That the vast arena of suffering of the poor (opened by the doctrine of derivative settlements, and the consequent transportation of the poor, under removal orders, to foreign and distant counties), arose as above suggested, will be apparent to any one who takes the trouble of reading the case of *St. Katherine and St. George*, in Fortescue's Reports, p. 218. Lord Chief Justice Parker there says, "It is as *unnatural* to force a child from the mother as from the father; so that *if she gains a settlement, the children must too.*" The only principle needed in these cases, is found in Ulpian, lib. 20., ad Sabinum, in D. XXXIII. 7. De instruct. vel instrum. legato, 12. 7. "Uxores quoque et infantes eorum, qui supra enumerati sunt, in eadem villa agentes, credendum est voluisse testatorem legato contineri, neque enim *duram separationem* injunxisse credendus est:" And "agnatio vel affinitas" was equally respected, in the case of serfs or colons adscriptitiæ conditionis (the settled agricultural labourers of the Roman empire), by a Constitution of Constantine, C. iii. 38. (Commun. utr. jud.) 11. "Quis enim ferat, liberos à parentibus, à fratribus sorores, à viris conjuges segregari?"

* On a recent occasion, I was counsel in a case of appeal, in which the parish of St. J. C. (not in any union) had apprenticed a parish pauper into St. L. M.,

no subsequent act of his life would ever free him from that settlement.

The statute 9 & 10 Vict. c. 66., preventing removal of the poor, in certain cases of long-continued residence, will be considered in the next chapter. In the meantime we may say of this law of settlement, that it is substantially as bad now as it was fifty years ago; and that, so far as its operations on the poor is concerned, it still deserves all the reprobation which was justly bestowed on it by those who, in the eighteenth century, pointed out its impolicy and injustice.

the master having been induced to take the child by a fee of 5*l.*, provided by some charity funds in the hands of the churchwardens. The child served and resided with his master more than forty days in St. L. M.; fell into society like that to which little Oliver Twist was exposed; was charged with felony, convicted, and imprisoned. His indenture was hereupon cancelled; and, on his discharge from prison, he wandered back to the parish of St. J. C. within six months of the day of his original binding: whereupon an order of *removal* was obtained for conveying him to the parish of St. L. M., in which, by virtue of the operation of the parish officers of St. J. C., a settlement had been created. The appeal was against this order of removal, which, however, on the trial, was properly confirmed, the present law undoubtedly sanctioning such a binding.

CHAP. XIII.

THE PAUPERISM AND POOR LAWS OF ENGLAND, SINCE THE PASSING OF THE POOR LAW AMENDMENT ACT, IN 1834.

Hocc' est, advorso nixantem trudere monte
Saxum, quod tamen a summo jam vertice rursum
Volvitur, et plani raptim petit æquora campi. LUCRETIUS.

SLIGHTLY as the Poor Law Amendment Act of 1834 interfered with the principle of previous legislation, nevertheless, the creation of a central board able to repress administrative abuses, effected a great and immediate reduction in the sum annually expended in relieving the poor. The outlay of 6,790,799*l.* in 1833, was reduced, for the year 1837, to 4,171,692*l.*, the price of wheat being nearly the same sum, 52*s.* 9*d.* the quarter, in each of those years. But even Gilbert's Act, 22 George III. c. 83., and its administrative reforms, seems to have been followed, at first, by a considerable diminution in the expense of maintaining the poor, although the provisions of that statute involved a wide and dangerous departure from the principle of the statute of Elizabeth.

The Poor Law Commissioners, created by the statute of 1834, at first caused the workhouse test to be applied with great severity; and perhaps the sudden and great diminution in the cost of pauperism, which ensued, was, in part, owing to the severe application of that test. The merely "official pauperism" of relief lists, must vary with the nature of the conditions on which such relief is given. In the Third Annual Report of the Poor Law Commissioners, it is stated, in reference to the reduced expenditure of the previous year, that the new system of administration had passed through the ordeal of an extremely severe winter, and of a general rise in the cost of provisions; and latterly, moreover, through a severe commercial embarrassment.* The Commissioners contrast the expenditure of 1,002,810*l.* in parishes then in union, with an average expenditure, before 1834, amounting to 2,189,810*l.* in the same parishes. A clear diminution of 46 per cent. in this parochial expenditure was exhibited. The Commissioners could hardly restrain their exultation, even while preparing a formal Official Report to the Secretary of State. They seem to have believed that the severe application of the workhouse test had already proved a panacea for the social evils of centuries †; and would, in a little while, emancipate England from the fatal embrace of her pauperism!

In later years, the administration of the Poor Law Commissioners and the Poor Law Board, by greatly restricting the application of the workhouse test ‡ (so often injurious in its necessary incidents and tendency), has, perhaps, effected as much good, and as little accompanying evil, as can be effected in carrying out the existing law. No one doubts the ability and earnestness with which, for many years, the duties of the onerous and important office of President of the Poor Law Board, have been discharged. Notwithstanding this able and just administration, the expenditure, for the relief of the poor, which, for the year ending on 25th March, 1837, was 4,171,692*l.*, with wheat at 52*s.* 3*d.* per quarter, had become, for the year ending on 25th March, 1850, no less than 5,395,022*l.*, wheat being, on the average, only 42*s.* 7*d.* per quarter.

In the year 1848, the expenditure had attained the enormous sum of 6,180,764*l.*, but the average price of wheat in that year was 64*s.* 6*d.* the quarter, so that the number of quarters

* Third Annual Report of the Poor Law Commissioners, 1837, p. 52.

† For instance, in the Third Annual Report, p. 51., the Commissioners say: "The amount of annual payments by the parishes, for illegitimate children, was fully 300*l.* There is not now a single instance of payment for illegitimate children." The burden of the almost lyrical strain of the Commissioners, resembles that which, in ancient Greece, the mysteries of Eleusis used to call forth from religious enthusiasts, who contrasted the evils from which they had escaped, with the bliss which their regenerate nature enjoyed.

‡ Above, pp. 12, 13.

for which the money could have been exchanged, was not so great then as it has been in each subsequent year.*

It is unquestionable, that the Poor Law Amendment Act only removed mere abuses in the administration of the law, and that those abuses vanished, and could not but vanish at once, as soon as the new system of a central control, and an efficient audit of accounts, was established. All the essential evils of our poor laws are still unmitigated, or, at the most, have been very slightly mitigated, by the Act of 1834; and we now find that, during the long years between 1834 and 1852, Poor Law Commissioners, and Presidents of the Poor Law Board, have been successively employed in the mere labour of Sisyphus; and that the stone which they have been condemned to turn, has become heavier and heavier, with the efforts of each successive year.

The main change in the law, effected since 1834, was introduced by the statute 9 & 10 Vict. c. 66. The year 1846, in which this statute passed, was signalised, and will be ever memorable, in the annals of Great Britain, by the triumph of the principle of Free Trade, in the total repeal of the Corn Laws. That repeal was likely to make it necessary for the legislature soon to apply some effectual remedy to the evils of the law of settlement and removal; and Sir Robert Peel, when, on 27th January, 1846, he first moved, to the consternation of the country gentlemen, that the House of Commons should go into committee on the Customs and Corn Importation Act, studiously explained, to the great party which he had once before divided, but of which he had again become the chosen defender and leader, how he had taken care to relieve them from the pressure of "the Law of Settlement,—a law grievously complained of, and justly, by the agricultural interest." The great convert to Free Trade, depicted the hardship of sending back, to a rural district, in a time of manufacturing distress, those labourers whose industry had been invited, years before, to a manufacturing town, and there exercised in the interval. Such poor men were removed

* Above, p. 6.

back, "greatly to their own annoyance and suffering; and not only is a great injustice inflicted on the rural districts, but a shock is given to the feelings of every just and humane man."*

Thus originated the proposal to make a residence of five years confer the privilege of irremovability. "The alteration we propose," said Sir Robert Peel, "will be a moral improvement in the law, just in itself, and a *great advantage to the agricultural districts;* while at the same time it will be the remedy of a *gross injustice, under which the labouring man now exists.*"

Temporary sickness or accident, if the only cause of chargeability, was, by the proposed statute, no longer to be a sufficient ground of removal. "Here again," exclaimed the Prime Minister†, "we shall be gaining a great social advantage, and also relieving the agricultural districts of a burden which is certainly very great."

Fortunate was it for the labouring man, that at length the interest of the landowners of England was understood to be identified with a partial mitigation of the law of settlement and removal. From 1662 till 1846, the necessary evils and hardships of that law had been endured by the poor with patience, and witnessed by the legislature with fortitude or indifference; and although the operation of the law may daily have shocked "the feelings of every just and humane man," who witnessed its cruelty and oppression, yet no serious attempt was made in the legislature, by any English statesman, to prevent the recurrence of such shocks.‡ It was the good fortune of the poor man, that his partial emancipation from the bondage of his settlement was supposed, in 1846, to be essential to transferring the burden of his poverty, present and future, from the agricultural to the manufacturing interest. §

* Hansard, Third Series, vol. lxxxiii. pp. 266, 267.

† Hansard, ibid. p. 268.

‡ The benevolent but vain endeavour of a member of the House of Commons, Mr. Hay, has been already mentioned, above, p. 240.

§ In the following year, 1847, a committee of the House of Commons sat, for many weeks, on the subject. See below, pp. 307, 308.

Sir Robert Peel manifestly thought that the repeal of the corn laws, would greatly change the conditions under which agricultural industry must be exercised in England; and probably he was well aware, even in 1846, that freedom of trade in corn, ought to be speedily followed by freedom for the circulation of agricultural and other labour. But the experience of the session of 1845, had taught both Sir Robert Peel and his distinguished colleague, Sir James Graham, the great difficulty of persuading the then House of Commons to make any substantial change in the law of *settlement*: the Cabinet measure of 1846, was therefore so prepared, as to leave all question of *settlement* untouched, and merely to prevent removal of the poor, under given circumstances, from their places of residence.

Much inconvenience and some injustice was foreseen as likely to result from passing such a measure on this narrow and isolated question of non-removal; and Mr. J. E. Denison moved and carried an instruction to the committee, on the committal of the bill, to adopt a union settlement. But as soon as the corn laws were repealed, Sir Robert Peel and Sir James Graham ceased to hold office; and the Whigs, by whom they were succeeded, took up the original bill of Sir Robert Peel and Sir James Graham, adjourning any change in the law of settlement, for future consideration. That adjournment has been repeated, from time to time, by both Government and Poor Law Board, down to the commencement of the session of 1852.

The promise held out, early in the session of 1846, by Sir Robert Peel, was realised under the Whigs, on the 26th August in the same year. The statute then passed, 9 & 10 Vict. c. 66., provides, that "no person shall be removed, nor shall any warrant be granted for the removal of any person, from any parish in which such person shall have resided for five years next before the application for the warrant." A subsequent section of the statute prohibits removal of persons becoming chargeable in respect of relief, made necessary by sickness or accident, except such as will produce permanent disability.

By passing this act, the Legislature seems to sanction the principle that it is for Parliament, at any time that it may see fit, by a fresh repartition of the burden of local taxation, to relieve any one class of ratepayers directly at the expense of any other. The change effected was not made by removing an existing burden from landowners in agricultural districts, and placing it on the public generally, but by removing it from one *class* of local ratepayers, residing in one part of the country, and placing it on another *class* residing elsewhere: and it must be owned that it was a strong case of legislative interference with existing relative rights and duties of different *classes* in the State. In 1843, the Poor Law Commissioners had prepared an elaborate scheme of small changes in the law of settlement and removal: they thought that all which could be done, was "so to modify the existing laws as to meet *some* of the evils arising from them, without at the same time giving an exclusive advantage either to the rural or the town parishes."*

This statute was certainly a mitigation for the poor, to some extent, of the hardship of the previous law of removal, and it was most unquestionably a great change, for the ratepayers of England, in the distribution of their burden. A very large immigration of labourers had been long taking place, from the agricultural into the manufacturing districts. Hence, when the statute passed, an immense number of paupers, whose places of settlement in country parishes were unaffected by the statute, had been resident in towns for five years, and so had become irremovable. The consequence of this statutory protection was, that the protected parishes now refused that contribution towards the maintenance of their settled, but no longer removable, poor, which they had previously given.

Thus the boon promised to the country gentlemen by Sir Robert Peel, when he moved the repeal of the corn laws, was, so far as concerned many places, fully realised by the result. The vast multitude of paupers settled in country parishes, and

* Ninth Annual Report of the Poor Law Commissioners, 1843, p. 49.

now suddenly thrown for support on the ratepayers of the towns of their residence, proved so grievous a burden to the oppressed towns, that Parliament was obliged to interfere. The relief to agriculture, sanctioned by 9 & 10 Vict. c. 66., was maintained, but it was found necessary for the Legislature to transfer the burden of maintaining all classes of poor persons, who were rendered irremovable, under the provisions of the statute 9 & 10 Vict. c. 66., from the parish of residence to the whole union in which it was comprised. This was effected, in 1847, by Mr. Bodkin's Act of 10 & 11 Vict. c. 110.

Great relief was thus afforded, in some parts of the country, to the pressure created by the statute. The burden which had been taken from the shoulders of the country gentlemen, and placed at first on the town parishes, was now diffused over the wider space of the town unions; and in many large towns and cities, the weight was hard and grievous to bear. Norwich was thus fixed with an absolute increase of about 5000*l.* per annum, in the cost of maintaining its resident and now irremovable poor. Exeter and Canterbury, in each of which places the poor of the whole city are governed under local acts, much in the same way as in Norwich, suffered similarly.* In Leeds the increase of annual burden was about 3000*l.*†; and so, very generally throughout all towns, the statute found ample materials to work on, and the agricultural and country interest was everywhere benefited, at the expense of what may be called the manufacturing and town interest. A few additional examples may be adduced to show the extent of the change.

In three parishes of the Radford Union, which surrounds the town of Nottingham, and is in turn surrounded by close parishes‡, the expense of maintaining the poor, for the two years next after the statute of 1846 came into operation, was above three times as great as it had been during previous years.§

* Vain attempts were made by Norwich and Exeter to get rid of this new burden by a legal discussion of clauses in their local acts. *Regina* v. *Forncett St. Mary*, Queen's Bench Reports, vol. xii. p. 16.; and *Regina* v. *Ide*, New Sessions Cases, vol. iv. p. 438.

† On the increase of burden in these towns, see the evidence given before Mr. Charles Buller's Select Committee on Settlement and Poor Removal, in 1847.

‡ Reports to the Poor Law Board, 1850, p. 127. § Ibid. p. 126.

This increase of poor-rate is stated to have caused a decrease in the value of property in the parish of Radford, to the extent, in some instances, of 50 per cent.*

The town of Kendal† seems to have suffered, immediately, to the extent of more than 1000*l.* a year, and Doncaster to half that amount.‡ It would probably be difficult to find an instance in which property, in a town surrounded by an agricultural district, was not suddenly injured by the change in the law; and the sum total of the annual burden thus removed from one class of property, and placed on another, throughout England and Wales, would be difficult to estimate, and almost impossible to ascertain.

The effect of the statute was most strikingly exhibited in the close agricultural parishes, those happy regions, each of which belongs to one or two proprietors, and not unfrequently constitutes a sort of oasis, in a surrounding desert of pauperism.§ Rightly to understand this effect of the statute,

* Reports to the Poor Law Board, 1850, p. 126.

† Appendix, No. 4. p. 331., in the Sixth Report of the Commons' Committee of 1847.

‡ Sixth Report of the Commons' Committee, 1847, J. Falconar, 6238, and Appendix, p. 333. "Comparative Statement of Chargeability caused by 9 & 10 Vict. c. 66."

§ The evils of the close parishes, which have been known for a century, were distinctly pointed out in 1833, in the Report of the Commission of Inquiry, p. 87. folio ed. "When a parish is in the hands of only one proprietor, or of proprietors so few in number as to be able to act, and to compel their tenants to act, in unison, and adjoins to parishes in which property is much divided, they may pull down every cottage as it becomes vacant, and prevent the building of new ones. — They may thus depopulate their own estates, and cultivate them by means of the surplus population of the surrounding district. Against such conduct as this, a parish in which the property is much divided, and that is the case in all towns, has no defence. Small master bricklayers and carpenters, and retired tradesmen, with trifling accumulations, find cottages and houses inhabited by the poor, a most lucrative investment. They must exercise, indeed, great vigilance and occasional harshness; they must be ready to wring their rents from their tenants, or to extort them from the overseer, by constantly threatening, and sometimes effecting, distresses and executions; and as no educated person could bear to seize the small property of the poor, or to turn whole families into the streets, those who seek a profit by providing accommodation for the labouring classes, are generally persons whose habits have rendered them not merely indifferent to the general prosperity of the parish, but anxious to promote the pauperism that creates the demand for their crowded and unhealthy habitations."

in relieving the *close* parishes of a portion of that small amount of poor-rate which they had been wont to pay, and in throwing a new burden on their already oppressed neighbours, it is only necessary to refer to the voluminous reports of evidence received before the late Mr. Charles Buller, and the other members of the Select Committee on the Law of Settlement and Removal, in 1847, and to the more precise and specific information collected in reports made in 1848, to the Poor Law Board, by several of its inspectors. It will be necessary again to advert to such close parishes in the next chapter, which will treat of the cottage accommodation of the poor. In the mean time, it may safely be stated, that the inconvenience and loss, amounting to 3*d.* or 4*d.* of the wages of each day's labour, and the injury, both to the health and morals * of those who reside in open parishes (at a great distance from their places of work, in neighbouring close parishes), as well as the hardship on payers of poor-rate in such open parishes, are now fully demonstrated. In the close parishes, population has remained stationary, or has diminished, while it has increased all round them. In many instances, the population of close parishes is reduced, in 1851, to one-half of its amount in 1801, although more labour is now requisite for the proper cultivation of the land, and the general population of England has more than doubled in the interval. All the evils previously existing and felt in the neighbourhood of such privileged close parishes, were vastly aggravated by the statute of 9 & 10 Vict. c. 66. Not only was the proprietor of the close parish substantially freed from bearing the burden of great part of the pauperism which properly belonged to him, but a further premium was held out to *clearing* such parishes, and driving all their labourers into *residence* elsewhere; for the new statute would now give a

* "Mr. Vines, one of the surgeons of the Reading Union, informed me that he had observed the bad effect produced on the morals of the families of the agricultural labourers, by the distance the parents have to go away from home to their daily work. He had found the children of this class of persons always the most dirty, the most dissipated, and the most depraved."—*Reports to the Poor Law Board*, 1850, p. 51.

permanent protection to the *close* parish of settlement, against any removal of its settled poor from any neighbouring place in which they might have resided for five years.

Wholly independent of the statute 9 & 10 Vict. c. 66., and of the general excess of pauperism in agricultural districts, local causes have occurred, both in towns and in the country, to throw most unequal burdens on neighbouring places, where one is mainly inhabited by the poor, the other mainly inhabited by the rich. Some change in the law, with a view to a more just repartition of these unequal burdens, is very generally felt to have become absolutely necessary.

In large towns, composed of more than one parish, where the wealthy and the working classes are generally found inhabiting separate localities, the increased pressure of the poor-rate on the poorer districts "is apparent, and its injustice is generally felt and inveighed against."*

The different causes which have produced this inequality in the incidence of the poor-rate, seem to have operated, with almost equal effect, to diminish the burden of the rate, where that burden was light, and to increase it where it was heavy. Instances of this might easily be multiplied.

The statute of Elizabeth provided some relief for such cases, by means of a *rate in aid*, to be levied on the parishes of greater ability; but a convenient mode of laying the rate in aid was not provided, and the remedy has certainly not been

* See, in the Reports to the Poor Law Board, 1850, the Report on the County of Northumberland, W. H. Hawley, p. 190.; also G. A. à Beckett's Report, p. 38. and p. 39. The attention of the public and of the legislature has recently been called to the hardship and injustice of "the present law of settlement, and rating to the relief of the poor," by the Court of Common Council of the City of London. That Court, on 8th May, 1850, resolved, "That it is the opinion of this Court, that the present law of settlement, and rating for the relief of the poor, is unjust, partial, and oppressive in its operation throughout the City of London, inasmuch as it annually relieves those parishes, where the property is of the greatest rateable value, and trade most extensive, from their share of providing for the relief and maintenance of the poor, and at the same time throws a most unfair and oppressive burden on those parishes in which the houses are small, and where the poor *can find a residence*." The resolution of the same Court, "that petitions be presented to both Houses of Parliament, praying for an alteration of the law of settlement, and rating for the relief of the poor," has been already referred to, above, p. 41.

found available in practice, although there have been some instances in which it has been resorted to with success.

This inequality of burden is strikingly exemplified by instances found in London and Middlesex, which have been already mentioned.* The Colchester Union, in Essex, furnishes another instance of the same inequality. This union consists chiefly of town parishes; and, in the best and most valuable parts of the town of Colchester, there are no dwellings for the working classes, who are therefore driven for residence into impoverished parishes, in which alone their resident destitution can demand relief. Hence, the parish of St. Leonard, the poorest of the whole town, has to pay yearly poor-rate to the amount of 9*s.* 10*d.* in the pound; and the ratepayers there, "who are paying, or trying to pay, 9*s.* 10*d.* in the pound, are naturally dissatisfied when they see that in the opulent parish of All Saints, inhabited chiefly by persons retired from business, and generally in affluent circumstances, the demand for poor-rate is only 2*s.* 4*d.* in the pound, or less that one-fourth the amount asked for from the poverty-stricken parish of St. Leonard's."†

Inequality of burden between close and open, or rich and poor, parishes, is further aggravated by the provision for distributing what are called the establishment charges of every union, among the several parishes of the union, not in proportion to their ability, but to their parochial burdens. The recent additions to these charges aggravate this grievance.‡ Ability of parishes, which is the true basis, or, at least, a condition of the imposition of the tax, as contemplated by the statute of Elizabeth, would be measured by the proportion between the net rateable value of the parish, and the amount of its poor-rate, but certainly is not in any way indicated by the mere amount of that poor-rate. In short, the union charges, if really what they are called, ought to be imposed

* Above, pp. 38—40.

† G. A. à Beckett's Report on the Counties of Suffolk, Norfolk, and Essex, p. 38.

‡ See Mr. Rowsell's evidence, Report from the Select Committee of the House of Lords, on the Laws relating to Parochial Assessments, 1850, No. 663 to 812.

on the property, and not on the poverty, of the several parishes in the union.

Let us revert to the direct consequences of the law of settlement, when followed and accompanied by the law of 9 & 10 Vict. c. 66. So long as we have this double law in force, and the narrow circle of either parish or union is the place of settlement, locally and wholly maintaining its settled poor, cases like the following will be found to occur. In Cambridgeshire, a landowner having a quantity of land in one parish, and a slip in the adjoining parish, recently pulled down his cottages in the first parish, and built others on the slip in the second, for the residence of his labourers. In the Newark union, is a parish of *Harby*, of which we read, in the Report of a poor law inspector (Mr. Howell), that a landed proprietor "bought a piece of land in this parish close to his own parish of *Swinethorpe*, and on it built some cottages for his own parish labourers;" and that some of the men have been a burden to Harby *, the place which has the ill-fortune to have this rich neighbour. Similarly, in the neighbourhood of Reading is the close parish of Newlands, belonging to two proprietors, and, in this parish (which has only one pauper), cottages have been pulled down, and the son of one of the two proprietors avows "the facility with which the poor can be kept out of Newlands, by running up a few houses in Wokingham, a town close by, and very conveniently situated for the purposes of the neighbouring parish." †

Thus, the labourer employed in one parish, in case of destitution, can only come on the poor-rate in the other.

According to medieval principles, and medieval jurisprudence, the serfs or villeins, like cattle, were said to be "levant and couchant" on the lands of their lords; and it was reserved for a period of higher civilisation to discover and exemplify this new principle, whereby the landowner creates a levancy and couchancy of his own bondmen on the land of his neighbour.

Such instances are not confined to agricultural districts.

* Reports to the Poor Law Board, p. 138.

† Ibid. p. 53.

Manufacturers have placed themselves on the same "bad eminence" since 1846, in thus pulling down labourers' cottages in the close parish, and even replacing them by building others in an adjoining open parish, merely that the man who ought to pay the poor-rates, may not pay them, and that his innocent and helpless neighbours may be made to pay them for him.*

A wealthy proprietor of an extensive manufactory, in the district of the Potteries, is the owner of nearly the whole parish in which his works are situate. In that parish he has pulled down cottages in which his labourers lived, and in the adjoining parish he has purchased a slip of land, and run up cottages along it, just opposite to his works, but on the further side of a brook, which forms the parish boundary. And thus his labourers, when thrown out of work by temporary sickness, and chargeable (though *settled* in their master's parish, in which they still work), are, under 9 & 10 Vict. c. 66., irremovable, and entitled to relief at the expense of the *neighbours* of the manufacturer.

I am informed that, in some cases the sickness, and in others the death, of workmen, have already made their families and widows chargeable to the unfortunate adjoining parish to which I refer. The chargeability having occurred under circumstances which bring the case within 9 & 10 Vict. c. 66., and prevent removal to the parish of settlement, the manufacturer, by this abuse of his rights of property, is already greatly benefited under the recent statute; and yet, at the present time, the main and substantial protection of the five years' residence has not been gained, the cottages having

* Events like these were predicted by the Commission of Inquiry of 1833, Report, p. 88., folio ed., where, after recounting the practices which had arisen in the close agricultural parishes, the Commissioners proceed: "The instances of similar practices on the part of the manufacturers are comparatively few; but we cannot hope that so obvious a source of profit will long be overlooked. If the present system continues, we may expect to see manufactories erected on one side of a parochial boundary, and cottages for workpeople on the other; so that all the allowances to the labourers, all the casualties to which they are subject, and the great casualty of the failure of the manufactory, may fall exclusively on that parish in which the master manufacturer owns, perhaps, nothing but the three or four acres which he has covered with his cottages."

been built *since* the passing of the statute, and the five years of residence not being yet completed.

Although, upon the whole, the statute has probably been beneficial to the poor, yet in many parishes it has occasionally aggravated the evils of their condition.

Mr. Revans's observations on the effect of the Act, seem to be well founded, when he says that, until it was passed, "a man out of work would be allowed to remain in the parish in which he had long resided and exercised his industry, provided the parish of his settlement would reimburse the relief meted out to him: but since the Act, the labourer is no sooner the applicant for relief, than the opportunity is seized of hurrying him back to his settlement. Every hour that he remains in the parish, in which he may have worked with skill and with diligence, in which he may have conducted himself with propriety and with honesty, is looked upon with jealousy as an hour nearer to the acquirement of a five years' residence, and the right to a maintenance, during sickness and during infirmity, for himself and his family.*

Just the same result arises, in this respect, in towns, as in country places. The approach towards a completion of a five years' residence, everywhere puts the parish officers on the alert, and a single application for a shilling, or a loaf of bread, in the way of parish relief, if made by a man who has resided in a parish for nearly five years, is sure to be followed by the immediate taking out of an order for his removal.†

The statute made it greatly the interest of parishes, first, to prevent the completion of the five years' residence; and, secondly, to coerce or induce poor persons, legally protected

* Report of John Revans, Esq., to the Poor Law Board, on the operation of the Law of Settlement in Dorsetshire, Hampshire, and Somersetshire, published in Reports to the Poor Law Board, 1850.

† Removal under an order of justices (although the pauper may instantly return to the parish of his residence), effects a constructive break in the residence, and disentitles the pauper to include in his five years, any residence previous to such constructive break. *Regina* v. *Halifax*, Queen's Bench Reports, vol. xii. p. 111.; *Regina* v. *Seend*, ibid. p. 133.; and *Regina* v. *Caldecote* (decided by the same court, on 10th May, 1851), Jurist, vol xv. p. 537.; S. C. 4 New Sessions Cases, 687.

from removal by such residence, to go to reside, for however short a term, elsewhere, so as to lose their privilege. A section of the statute, meant to protect the poor from undue influence of parish officers, has not always been effectual.* The violation of that section has been the subject of investigation, not merely in board-rooms of guardians, or in petty sessions, but in courts of quarter session; and has even been the subject of judicial decision in the Court of Queen's Bench.†

Many of the evils which have, in fact, resulted from the passing of this statute, were distinctly foreseen by some of those who took part in the debates on the measure, between the time of its introduction, by Sir James Graham, as Home Secretary in Sir Robert Peel's Cabinet, and its final passing under the care of the Whig ministry, which succeeded Sir Robert Peel.‡

Some of the same evils had been pointed out in the Report of the Commissioners of 1833, as likely to result from any such measure. Every argument that was advanced, in 1833, against settlement by residence, is applicable to the new irremovability by residence, which this statute introduced. The well-founded expectation of the Commissioners was expressed as follows: "The demolition of cottages, and the *forcing of the agricultural population into the towns and the parishes in which property is much divided,* though we fear that they must, to a certain degree, arise under any law of settlement what-

* 9 & 10 Vict. c. 66. s. 6. enacts that if any parish officer, with the intent to cause any poor person to become chargeable to any parish, to which such poor person was not then chargeable, procure any poor person to be conveyed out of the parish, or give, directly or indirectly, money or assistance for such conveyance, or make any promise, or use any threat, to induce any poor person to depart from such parish, " and if, in consequence of such conveyance or departure, any poor person become chargeable to any parish to which he was not then chargeable," such officer is to be liable to a fine of from 40*s.* to 5*l.*, on conviction before two justices.

† As in *Regina* v. *St. Marylebone,* decided on 22nd January, 1851, Jurist, vol. xv. p. 289. ; S. C. New Sessions Cases, vol. iv. p. 444.

‡ See Mr. J. E. Denison's speech, as reported in Hansard, Third Series, vol. lxxxvii. pp. 44—50. ; and Sir James Graham's speech in the same debate, and afterwards on 13th July, 1846, *ib.* 1069., and on 23rd July, 1846, *ib.* 1393, 1394.

ever, *would be much promoted* by a law which would fix on a parish every labourer who should have been allowed to reside there for any given period, unless the period were so long, as to render the law almost inoperative."*

Upon the whole, it may fairly be said that the statute 9 & 10 Vict. c. 66., although a beneficial mitigation of the previous law, so far as it tended to strike off from the poor man the fetters of his settlement, has inconveniently increased some of the evils which were previously endured by both paupers and ratepayers, and now furnishes an additional ground for repealing the law of settlement altogether, and for modifying the gross injustice found in the present distribution of the burden of relieving the poor.

* Report of the Commissioners for Inquiring, &c. p. 194. folio ed.

CHAP. XIV.

EFFECT OF THE LAW OF SETTLEMENT ON THE DWELLINGS OF LABOURERS IN AGRICULTURE.

Health, brightest visitant from Heaven,
  Grant me with thee to rest!
And through the term by Nature given
  Be thou my constant guest:
Each charm of life that solaces the heart
Attends on thee, blest Health, and must with thee depart.

ARIPHRO OF SICYON *

BENEVOLENCE has been very active of late years, both in making known, and alleviating, some of the evils which characterise the habitations of the poorer classes in our large towns. The condition of the agricultural labourer in respect of the cottage in which he is compelled to reside, has attracted less attention. It will probably be found that the amount of suffering and demoralisation, the injury to health, and the shortening of life, to which the agricultural labourer and his family are exposed, *from preventible causes*, is even greater than that which has excited so much sympathy on behalf of the town population. In examining into this question, we must not too hastily or harshly condemn the owners of property, for the degraded and wretched condition, in which we shall find a large part of the labouring population. It must be borne in mind, throughout this chapter, that the law of settlement and removal has long tended to stimulate into action the baser and more sordid feelings of human nature, by threatening with a permanent future charge, the landowner who allowed any settlement to be acquired in his parish.

* *Ὑγίεια πρεσβίστα μακάρων, | μετὰ σεῦ ναίοιμι | τὸ λειπόμενον βιοτᾶς· | Σὺ δέ μοι πρόφρων σύνοικος εἴης· | Μετὰ σεῖο, μάκαρ Ὑγίεια, | τέθηλε πάντα καὶ λάμπει Χαρίτων ἔαρ· | σέθεν δὲ χωρὶς οὔ τις εὐδαίμων.*

Many intelligent and enlightened landowners are well aware of the paramount necessity of a great change in the condition of the agricultural labourer, with respect to his dwelling; and do all they can to amend that condition. Some of them, greatly to their own honour, have endeavoured to impress on the understanding of the legislature the necessity of providing the labourer with a dwelling near his work, and above all, giving him better cottage accommodation.*

The law of settlement and removal has tended, during the whole period of its existence, to deter the owners of close parishes from building cottages, and has thus deprived the poor, in numberless agricultural parishes, of the possibility of residing near the place in which their labour is employed. Landowners are found who forget, or have not learned, that the ownership of land imposes moral duties, co-extensive with the legal rights which it sanctions. Throughout extensive districts not a union can be found in which the agricultural labourer is not put to great straits, for want of a residence near his work. A journey of two, three, four, or five miles, has to be performed early and late, morning and night, at every season of the year, and in all weathers, that the unhappy biped may aid in tilling the land, to which he performs his daily pilgrimage, while it is only his more fortunate quadruped companions that are housed there.

The interference of the law of settlement, with the proper supply of cottage accommodation for agricultural labourers, is so manifest, and the resulting evils are so great, that some boards of guardians have been led to rest their condemnation of the existing law of settlement mainly on the ground of that interference, and those evils.

In the Ongar Union, the guardians recently came to a unanimous resolution, "that the abolition of the law of settlement and removal would be very beneficial to the deserving labourers, by encouraging the owners of property to build

* Such was the language of Mr. J. E. Denison, himself an owner of close parishes, in the excellent speech which he made on 5th June, 1846, in moving an instruction to a committee of the House of Commons, to provide for the establishment of union settlements. This speech is referred above, p. 286, note †.

cottages on their estates for the accommodation of their labourers; and that the present law of settlement and removal operates to the injury of the labourers, by limiting the market of their labour, and discouraging the building of cottages, so that the poor are crowded into miserable dwellings, at the sacrifice of health, comfort, and morality." *

It is undoubted and indisputable, that wherever the deficiency of cottage accommodation exists, as it does so generally, it entails a fearful catalogue of calamities on the unhappy labourer and his family. They usually become a subject of traffic to small building speculators, who extort a high rental for a wretched hut; and who profit by the misery and degradation of those among whom all sense of decency is destroyed, while health is injured, and life itself greatly shortened, by their being crowded together, often without any regard to distinction of age or sex.

The last few years have brought forward an imposing array of witnesses, whose voices have been lifted up against the abomination of the wretched places, unfit for human habitation, in which, to the utter destruction of the poor, and the great injury of all other classes of society, pauperism and disease are permitted, and even constrained, to lurk and propagate themselves.

Among the varied objects exposed, at the World's Great Fair of 1851, to the admiration of visitors, none more deserved examination than the model cottages for labourers, placed at the very threshold of the Exhibition by his Royal Highness Prince Albert. Any one who has forced himself to contemplate the mass of social evil which springs from this single source of defective cottage accommodation in England, must look on the Prince's cottages as furnishing, not only conclusive testimony to the qualities, both of head and heart, of the exhibitor, but as a declaration, from the highest quarter, to the wealthy, that they should make some better provision, than they have hitherto done, for the observance of the ordinary decencies of human life, by that great and helpless

* Reports to the Poor Law Board, 1850, p. 45.

class of Her Majesty's subjects, the poor. Nor have examples been wanting among the landowners themselves, of men who are fully alive to, and willing to discharge, all their moral duties to the race of labourers. Such men have addressed their fellow landowners in direct and urgent terms of advice and entreaty on this important subject. Bedfordshire, owing, perhaps, to the excellent example set by the Duke of Bedford, is, as a whole, a little better off, in respect of cottage accommodation for labourers, than many other counties. "From landlords," said the Duke, in an address published nearly three years ago, "it is surely not too much to expect that, while they are building and improving farm-houses, homesteads, and cattle-sheds, they will also build and improve dwellings for their labourers, in sufficient numbers to meet the improved and improving condition of the land."* How much remains to be done, even in Bedfordshire, before this excellent advice will have been properly acted on, we shall see in the course of this chapter.

Unexceptionable witnesses have proved, conclusively, how widely spread, and fearful, are the evils engendered among the whole labouring population, in agricultural districts, by this want of decent and convenient cottages. Perhaps the most striking testimony on the subject is that given by the Special Assistant Poor Law Commissioners, who had to report, in 1843, on the employment of women and children in agriculture. The Commissioners were told to direct their main attention to the employment of children; and the question of the want of cottage accommodation for the labouring classes seems, in the course of their inquiry, to have forced itself, unasked after, on their attention. The following are passages from their Reports. "The want of sufficient accommodation," says Mr. Austin, "seems universal. Cottages generally have only two bedrooms (with very rare exceptions); a great many have only one. The consequence is, that it is very often extremely difficult, if not impossible, to divide a family so that grown-up persons of different sexes, brothers

* Duke of Bedford, *Letter, dated 9th March*, 1849, published in the "Journal of the Royal Society of Agriculture," vol. x. pp. 185—187.

and sisters, fathers and daughters, do not sleep in the same room. Three or four persons not unfrequently sleep in the same bed."

"This, I was told, was not an extraordinary case, but that, more or less, every bedroom in the village was crowded with inmates of both sexes, of various ages, and that such a state of things was caused *by the want of cottages.*

"It is impossible not to be struck, in visiting the dwellings of the agricultural labourers, with the general want of new cottages, notwithstanding the universal increase of population."

Mr. Austin was informed, by an agent of my Lord Lansdowne, that "in Studley (in Wilts) it is not at all uncommon for a whole family to sleep in the same room. The number of bastards in that place is very great; the number of unmarried women is greater than in the neighbouring places. I do not think this state of things is attributable to the women working in the fields, but more *to the want of proper accommodation in the cottages.*"

The benevolent rector of Bryanston, in Dorset, says, "Within this last year I saw, in a room about thirteen feet square, three beds; on the first lay the mother, a widow, dying of consumption; on the second, two unmarried daughters, one eighteen years of age, the other twelve; on the third, a young married couple, whom I myself had married two days before. A married woman of thorough good character told me, a few weeks ago, that on her confinement, so crowded with children is her one room, they are obliged to put her on the floor in the middle of the room, that they may pay her the requisite attention: she spoke of this as, to her, the most painful part of that, her hour of trial. I do not choose to put on paper the disgusting scenes that I have known to occur from this promiscuous crowding of the sexes together. Seeing, however, to what the mind of the young female is exposed, from her very childhood, I have long ceased to wonder at the otherwise seeming precocious licentiousness of conversation which may be heard in every field, where many of the young are at work together."

We learn, from a surgeon at Blandford, that "generally

the cottages are too small for the families living in them, and tend to produce and aggravate disease, from the inmates living so closely together. Two years ago, typhus fever occurred in a neighbouring parish; — there were more than forty cases of typhus, and the spread of the disease must be attributed to the people living so densely packed together."

Let any one, who either cares about the sufferings of his fellow men, or would reduce poor-rates, refer to the clear account which Dr. Southwood Smith gives* of the parochial burden inevitably produced by typhus fever among the poor. It is heads of families who are most commonly attacked by typhus. Suppose that, out of these forty cases, there were only two deaths of heads of families. Two widows, and several fatherless children, are, at once, thrown on the parish; and in addition to the expense of several pauper families, chargeable during the illness of the forty persons attacked, and to the expense of the funerals, there remains, after the fever is over, a charge which may last for an uncertain period of months or years, in maintaining widows and their children. And all this disbursement of the money of ratepayers in some country towns, — all this sacrifice of human happiness, and waste of human life, among the labouring population, simply because a neighbouring landowner includes, within his ring fence, a whole parish, and refuses to allow cottages to be built for the use of those whom he compels daily, and in all weathers, to perform a wearisome journey, to and from their labour on his estate!

Mr. Vaughan, another commissioner, says: "The undivided state of the larger families, acting upon the scantiness of house-room, and general poverty, or high rent, often crowds them together in their sleeping apartments, so as seriously to infringe on the decencies which guard female morals. — It is very common for tradesmen and builders to erect tenements in the villages, for which they are enabled, owing to the demand for house-room, to obtain a higher rent than that which is taken by the larger proprietor of the soil"

* Above, p. 50.

Near Reigate, we are told, that "many cottages have but one room, and the whole family sleep in one bed." And the curate of Farnham in Surrey, "mentioned a case within his own knowledge, where two sisters and a brother, all above fourteen, habitually slept together."

"In Northumberland," says Sir Francis Doyle, also a commissioner on the same inquiry, "the ordinary cottages contain but one room, perhaps 17 by 15 feet; in point of construction and ventilation there is nothing to be said for them; but as the Northumbrians are, in spite of every thing, a healthy and vigorous race of men, such inconveniences do not amount to a crying evil: but when we find that a whole family, father and mother and children, of both sexes, and of all ages, live together, and have to sleep together in one and the same room, any degree of unchastity ceases to surprise, and the only wonder is, that the women should behave as well as they do."

Mr. S. C. Denison, another commissioner engaged on the same inquiry, gives the following account of the "Ganging system" found in Norfolk, and which has arisen from the neglect of landlords to provide cottage accommodation for the poor. "Castle Acre is what is called an *open* parish; that is, in the hands of a considerable number of proprietors, while the neighbouring parishes are each owned by one or two (or very few) proprietors. These last, partly in order to prevent an increase of birth settlements, and to keep down the rates, partly from an unwillingness to invest money in cottage property, not only allow no new cottages to be built, but let the old ones fall into ruin. The resident population of these parishes is thereby gradually reduced, as the labourers are forced to quit them, and come to reside in Castle Acre. Thus, while, in the adjoining parishes, there are not hands enough left to cultivate the soil, Castle Acre is overstocked with inhabitants that do not properly belong to it, and who are, generally speaking, the worst characters in the parishes from whence they come. The competition caused by these new comers, raises the house-rent throughout the parish; and as they are at the mercy of those who have land at Castle

Acre, they are forced to pay exorbitant rents for very wretched dwellings.—From these two causes, viz., the excess of labourers in Castle Acre, and the defect of them in neighbouring parishes, sprung the *gang system* of employment. The neighbouring occupiers wanted hands, and applied to a person in Castle Acre to supply them. This was easily done, owing to the great numbers living there, all together, anxious for employment.—As the only object of the gangmaster is to fulfil his contract, he regards the labourer solely as a living instrument, valuable only in proportion to its available power: hence all sorts of characters, from all the neighbouring parishes, are mixed up in the gang, male and female." It is said that, "owing to ganging," nearly three-fourths of the girls become prostitutes.

Mr. Denison's conclusion is as follows:—"If, in the present state of the parish, 'ganging' were suddenly put an end to, I fear that a vast number of persons would be thrown out of work, and the immorality and crime of the place would be increased by idleness and distress. I believe those who first (unintentionally and unknowingly) caused the mischief, can alone cure it: I mean *the neighbouring landowners*. If those 103 stranger families, who now swell the amount of crime and misery at Castle Acre, were living in their own parishes,—Castle Acre would not be reproached as 'the coop of all the scrapings in the country;' its own native population would be uncontaminated by the refuse of other parishes; the gang-system would necessarily cease; and Castle Acre would no longer be, what it now is, the most miserable rural parish I ever saw anywhere."*

In a previous chapter†, reference was made to certain landowners, who rigorously enforce their legal rights, but neglect to perform their corresponding duties. The clergyman of the parish there alluded to, states, that "the most serious detriment to the success of the school, arises unhappily

* S. C. Denison, Report to the Poor Law Commissioners on the Counties of Suffolk, Norfolk, and Lincoln, pp. 221, 222. 225, 226.

† Above, pp. 90, 91.

from the pernicious system of agricultural labour pursued in this district, known as the gang-system."*

The condition of labourers in respect of their cottage accommodation, is largely noticed in the Reports made by Poor Law Inspectors to the Poor Law Board in 1848 and 1849. Mr. Weale, one of those inspectors, reports of the county of Bedford, that, in many instances, although the mere *number* of existing cottages is said to be sufficient, yet "complaints are made of their being sadly deficient in the necessary accommodation for a family; and that it is a very common thing for whole families, with grown-up sons and daughters, to occupy the only bedroom the cottages afford." †

Clergymen of various parishes in Bedfordshire give testimony, which will serve as a sufficient indication of the condition of that part of the country in respect of the cottage accommodation of agricultural labourers. I select a few of these cases, naming each parish before giving the answer of its clergyman to Mr. Weale's question—"Are there many cases in which different families are crowded in the same cottage?" It may safely be assumed that each clergyman has nothing extenuated, nor aught set down in malice; but has given us a truthful statement of what his parochial ministration had taught him.

Ampthill.—"Many of the cottages are inconveniently crowded with more than one family." Houghton Conquest.—"The great mischief is that of huddling up a large family of children, growing up to man and woman's estate, in the same small bedroom, frequently shared also by the father and mother." Cople.—"Yes, many; several instances of cottages being too small for one family, to the utter violation of decency, and to the detriment of health and morals."

* Minutes of the Committee of Council on Education, 1850-51; the Rev. M. Michell's Report, p. 252.

† Reports to the Poor Law Board, 1848, p. 148. Mr. Weale states, that the Duke of Bedford, the largest proprietor in Bedfordshire, has been erecting for the last two or three years, and is about to erect on his estate generally, very superior cottages, which he lets at moderate rents, and on terms calculated to improve the moral condition of his cottage tenants. Some other proprietors are mentioned as doing, or about to do, the same thing.

Harrold.—"No; but many instances in which the same families are crowded in their cottages, to a great extent. There are cottages with only one small room, in which six, seven, or eight persons sleep." Thurleigh.—"Not many; but there are many instances in which cottages have only one sleeping apartment, in which the whole family herd together." Yielden.—"The accommodation in some of the cottages in this village is wretched in the extreme, and the poor themselves feel sensibly this wretched state, not to mention the impropriety of so living." Biggleswade.—"A very great many, where the sons and daughters have married, and live with their parents. The cottages are in a most deplorable state as to necessary accommodation and convenience." Meppershall.—"Only one case of two families; a few cases of single persons living with families, and many cases of members of families most improperly crowded together in bedrooms." Eaton Bray.—"No; many of the cottages are inconveniently small; and, in some cases, crowded without regard to common decency." Barton.—"The cottages are shamefully deficient as to bedrooms." Poddington.—"The want of proper accommodation produces great immorality, and is severely felt by the poor."

Another poor law inspector, in a Report to the Poor Law Board, made in 1848, respecting the counties of Surrey and Sussex, gives the following as his compendious view of the cause and character of this grievous condition of the agricultural labourer.

"The law of settlement is, no doubt, one of the causes which contribute to the scarcity of residences for the poor observable in the rural parishes of these counties. If, by any combination amongst the landowners, or by the determination of one person owning the whole parish, residences for the poor can be got rid of, and cottages permanently kept off the land, the payment of rates is, in a great measure, avoided, and the charge of the poor shifted from their own to some neighbouring parish. The sad evils resulting from a scarcity of cottages have been already detailed; the injury done to the labourer re-acts, also, on his employer; the strength the labourer loses in his long walk is so much deducted from the day's work he would otherwise perform." *

"The small number, and untenantable state, of many of the cottages," says the writer of a prize report, on the farming of Devonshire, "compel a large proportion of the workmen to reside in the *nearest town or village*,—a circumstance unfavourable to his comfort and morals, as well as those of his family, and a loss of time and labour to his employer. Here, discomfort at home drives the father to the ale-house; the sons, from a similar cause, forsake their homes, and, meeting with others similarly circumstanced, they too often congregate together, and lead each other on to the committal of crime." †

Mr. Acland, the author of an article, recently published, on the farming of Somerset ‡, says, "There is a strong and just feeling among many tenants, that landlords ought to do more to provide the labourers with *decent cottages near their work, instead of driving them into towns and villages*, where they must pay as much as 4*l.* for a miserable house without a garden. A very distinguished tenant farmer has sent me a calculation, showing that the time lost by the labourer walking four miles daily is equal to several years of his life; and yet, he says, *at this time* (1850), *landlords are taking down cottages on their estates*."

Although landlords are thus acting, yet the farmers cannot but feel, and do feel, that they would derive a great benefit from having, near at hand, places of residence for their labourers. Sometimes farmers, even under the present law, have induced their landlords to render assistance towards remedying this crying evil and injustice. Instances of the erection of such cottages in close parishes, at the expense of the farmers, have occurred; and, in other cases, a tenant has given up his farm, "because his landlord would not let him

* Captain Robinson, R. N., Report to the Poor Law Board, 1850, p. 83.

† Mr. Henry Tanner's Prize Report, *The Farming of Devonshire*, "Journal of the Royal Society of Agriculture," vol. ix. pp. 454. 491.

‡ T. D. Acland, jun., *On the Farming of Somersetshire*, "Journal of the Royal Agricultural Society," vol. xi. pp. 666—764.

have cottages on the land for the accommodation of the labourers." * Elsewhere, covenants have been introduced into leases, restricting the farmer, under a penalty, from doing any act to give a man a parish settlement.†

The more this question is considered, the greater will appear to be the advantages likely to result to the whole community from providing everywhere adequate cottage accommodation for all those who are needed to till the ground.‡

In North Nottinghamshire are the two unions of East Retford and Worksop, each deserving of a moment's notice, as showing that even on the verge of the great manufacturing district of the West Riding, and in an agricultural region where the pauperism is light, the evils of the law of settlement are most grievous, in the vicinity of close parishes, with respect to its effect on the cottage accommodation of the poor. In the East Retford Union, of fifty parishes, comprising a considerable agricultural district (100,010 acres), there are many close parishes, the property of great proprietors. Instances occur of the labouring man having daily to walk as much as three miles and a half, in one instance even seven miles is mentioned, from his place of residence to the close parish which requires his labour for its cultivation, but in which no cottage is allowed to shelter him. Cases are here frequent, "of labourers having to walk two and three miles to and from their work;" and it is stated to be a "clearly defined object in the minds of landed proprietors, so

* Reports to the Poor Law Board, 1850, p. 53. † Ibid. p. 53.

‡ Reports to the Poor Law Board, 1850, p. 50. "Mr. May, a farmer in this neighbourhood, showed me the cottages he had built at his own cost, that is to say, he had found the labour, and his landlord had, most reluctantly, found the materials; for the latter was greatly averse to anything being done which might lead to the making of a settlement, while the former felt so strongly interested in having cottages for his workmen, that he had erected two habitations at an expense of 75*l*. They are comfortable dwellings with good gardens, and had been let at 2*s*. a week each, so that Mr. May had just about got back, in the seven years during which they had been standing, the original outlay he had incurred. His landlord, who had been disinclined to the building of these cottages, is not a very large owner in Caversham, but holds a considerable quantity of property in Maple Durham, and is the same gentleman who had been plaintiff in an action against a tenant, to recover a penalty for breach of covenant, by the making of two settlements."

to manage their estates as to keep down poor-rates." In the Worksop Union, containing a great part of the well-known district called "the Dukery," and being about 77,791 acres in extent, are many close parishes, and some extra-parochial places, the seats of landowners. "There are many labourers living at Worksop, who work for Lord Manvers at Thoresby *, for the Duke of Newcastle at Clumber, for the Duke of Portland at Welbeck, and for Mr. Foljambe at Osberton; some of these men go regularly backwards and forwards, and have done so for ten or fifteen years, three, four, five, and as much as six miles †, to their work; they generally walk, some few keep donkeys." ‡

These poor labourers are crowded into unhealthy dwellings, in the worse parts of Worksop. What they suffer, and what the ratepayers of the parish of Worksop suffer, by these agricultural labourers being thus refused a cottage near the domains on which they are employed, is sufficiently shown by a recent Report to the Board of Health; and may be taken as an example of what is now occurring over some millions of acres of highly cultivated land, and in scores, if not hundreds, of country towns, in the midst of such land, in different parts of England. §

A table in the Appendix will show how unequally the burden of pauperism is distributed throughout even lightly-burdened unions, like those of Worksop and East Retford, when they contain close parishes. Out of the twenty-six parishes of the Worksop Union, there are two, in which the

* See above, p. 90, *note*.

† Such distances remind us of Columella, who (De Re Rustica, i. 2. 10.) describes some of the *præpotentes* of his own day, "qui possident fines gentium, quos ne circumire equis quidem valent; sed proculcandos pecudibus, et vastandos feris derelinquunt; aut occupatos nexu civium, et ergastulis tenent."

‡ Reports to the Poor Law Board, p. 142. It is said that a laugh or titter was produced in the House of Commons, when the late Sir Robert Peel mentioned this evil of the agricultural labourer's present condition.

"Sed risu inepto res ineptior nulla est."

§ See, in the Appendix, the evidence of Mr. Henry Hase, as published in the Report to the General Board of Health, on a preliminary inquiry into the sanitary condition of the town of Worksop, by William Lee, Superintending Inspector.

year's poor-rate amounts to only 2*d.* in the pound on the rental; eight in which it varies from 2½*d.* to 7*d.*; while, in eight other parishes of the union, where the burden of poor-rate is greatest, it varies from 1*s.* to 2*s.* 3*d.* in the pound.

In cases where the owners of land have had the courage to disregard the tendencies of an unjust law, and adequately to discharge their duty to the poor labourer, by providing him with a decent cottage, the happiest effect has been produced. "To give an instance," says the late steward to the Earl of Scarborough, "of the effect upon the poor of a little kindness and attention, we rebuilt, in Wellow *, eight cottages, that were in a most miserable state: we made them clean and comfortable, and it seemed quite to change the nature of the inhabitants; from being the most dirty and wretched people they became neat and orderly, and took a great pride in showing you a clean house. They told me, that before they had nothing to cling to, they had not even a floor to clean." †

The dreadful condition of the cottages of agricultural labourers in respect of bedroom accommodation, leads not unfrequently, in courts of criminal justice, to investigations of cases unfit for all publication. More than once it has occurred to me to hear Mr. Justice Coleridge state, when performing his judicial functions, that a large proportion of crime, in his opinion, is produced by this want of proper cottage accommodation for the labouring classes. The same learned judge has said, more recently, in addressing a Labourers' Friends Association, "From my own experience as a judge, the painful conviction has been forced upon my mind, that very much of the crime which disgraces our country, is mainly attributable to the mixture of sexes and of ages in the dwellings of the poor; a practice that debases and demoralises the human mind, and which, unless counteracted, must effectually neutralise every effort made towards the elevation or improvement of the people." ‡

* Wellow is in or on the verge of Sherwood Forest, and in or on the verge of the region of "the Dukery" mentioned above.

† Reports to the Poor Law Board, 1850, p. 133.

‡ I quote from the Dean of Hereford's *Suggestive Hints*, p. 169.

The present Dean of Hereford *, after justly observing that this opinion, sanctioned by such authority and experience, is entitled to the highest attention, himself avows, that the opinion "is one to which every inquiring mind must come, that has witnessed the low and degrading habits to which such practices lead."

Such are some of the physical and moral evils afflicting the daily life of the agricultural labourer, throughout England, and which are mainly owing to the law of settlement and removal of the poor.

* Ibid. p. 169.

CHAP. XV.

ON THE NECESSITY OF A TOTAL REPEAL OF THE LAW OF SETTLEMENT AND REMOVAL OF THE POOR.

Cuncta prius tentata: sed immedicabile vulnus
Ense recidendum, ne pars sincera trahatur. OVID.

MANY of the evils under which the whole country has long suffered, and which arise mainly from the law of settlement and removal of the poor, have presented themselves for consideration in the course of the previous pages. But the most striking, and most extensively injurious, of all the evil influences of that law remain to be pointed out; and will be found in the necessary effect of such a law on the distribution and wages of labour throughout the country.

If a farmer, acquainted only with the neighbourhood of manufacturing regions of the North, occupying a farm in Nottinghamshire, or North Lincolnshire, or the West Riding of Yorkshire, were suddenly made acquainted with the condition of an agricultural labourer in Devon, or Somerset, or Hants, or any of our ten selected counties of pure agriculture and unmitigated operation of the law of settlement, he would hardly be able to credit, still less to understand, what he would find. The week's wage of the labourer which, in the one part of the country, is 11*s.*, or 12*s.*, or 13*s.*, becomes, in the other, only 7*s.*, or 8*s.*, or 9*s.* The work done is the same in both districts; and if the necessities of existence had anything to do with the matter, the necessities of the man who receives the lower sum are the greater.*

The effect of the law of settlement and removal affords the only explanation of this remarkable state of things. The natural and necessary tendency of such a law to produce

* For instance, the price of fuel is much higher in the Eastern, Southern, and Western districts, than in the Northern.

such results, has been sufficiently pointed out, and explained, by most impartial and competent witnesses, and to their reports reference will shortly be made. *

But grievous as is the hardship thus produced throughout these purely agricultural counties, on the whole mass of the labouring population, still greater social evils than even this extreme of poverty, are due to the law of settlement. The practice of hiring labourers by the year, once enforced by law as a binding obligation on all employers of labour in husbandry, has generally ceased; and the labourer is employed from day to day, or at the most from week to week, as he is wanted by the farmer. Hence it follows that, in the winter season, many men are thrown out of work, and at once become a charge on the parish.

The selection of labourers for employment during the winter, is very generally made in parishes, at all events in the pauperised agricultural district, with a mere view of keeping down the poor-rate, and in total disregard of the character and skill of the candidates for work. A single man of unblemished reputation, an excellent workman, is certainly the first to be thrown out of employment (especially if he should have saved as much as will maintain him for two or three months): and the ill-conducted drunken spendthrift, who has a wife and family, as certainly will have employment given him, in order to save the parish from a heavy weekly charge for so many mouths in the union-house.

On the inquiry of 1833, it appeared, that a large part of the social evil of the pauperism of England was caused by the law of settlement and removal alone; and was not necessarily incident to the administration of relief under the humane provisions of the statute of Elizabeth. It need not, therefore, excite any surprise that the very same evils as were then brought to light, should be found in existence at the present day. Such evils are essentially inherent in the law of settle-

* Adam Smith observed (*Wealth of Nations*, vol. i. p. 193.), "The very unequal price of labour which we frequently find in England, in places at no great distance from one another, is probably owing to the obstruction which the law of settlements gives to a poor man who would carry his industry from one parish to another without a certificate"

ment and removal, and must necessarily arise under the administration of that law.

The Rev. H. H. Bailey, a witness examined on the inquiry of 1833, then stated: "I consider the present law of settlement renders the peasant, to all intents and purposes, a bondsman: he is chained to the soil by the operation of the system, and it forbids his acquiring property, or enjoying it openly or honestly.—I have no doubt, that if the labourers were freed from their present trammels, there would be such a circulation of labour, as would relieve the agricultural districts.—I am certain that the poor labourers of those parishes, with which I have been connected in the country, are fully aware that it is not to their interest to advance their condition by the acquisition of property. I once congratulated my bailiff on the prospect of his inheriting, by his wife, a little real property; he replied, 'It would be of no use to me, Sir; for I should be less able to get employment, and could obtain no relief until it was all spent.' When the gentlemen and clergy of Henley contemplated the establishment of a savings bank in their neighbourhood, I thought it my duty to address the young men on the subject, after morning service, and urge upon them the propriety of saving for their protection against the contingencies of sickness and old age. They listened to me very attentively. One or two persons asked me, whether I honestly thought it would not be for the benefit of the parish, more than themselves, if they saved? I was startled by the inquiry; but, on consideration, I found that I really could not state that it would be for their benefit to save. The decided conviction of the whole body of the labourers was, that any saving would be for the benefit of the parish and the farmers, and not for the benefit of the individuals saving."*

The Dean of Hereford, whose testimony I am always glad to invoke, observed, while residing in his rural parish of King's Somborne, the way in which the law of settlement in-

* Extracts from information received by Her Majesty's Commissioners, as to the administration and operation of the Poor Laws, pp. 271, 272. London, 1833, 8vo.

terferes with the fair remuneration of labour, and saw clearly how great is the evil effect of the same law, in obstructing all educational advancement of the labourer. He adopts the opinion that "a modification, or even the total repeal of our present law of settlement, would do more than anything else to secure the immediate success of any attempt which may be made to educate the poorer classes. At present the labourer possesses no inducement to improve himself, to establish a good character, or to acquire knowledge or skill. He has no hope of benefiting himself in any way, do what he may—nor can he ever look forward to receiving higher wages than those which are given to good and bad workmen alike, or to securing for himself a better position than that of his fellow-labourers. He has no motive for improving himself, because, by doing so, he would not improve his condition; nor has he any motive for recommending himself to the employers of labour, because, whether they like him or dislike him, they must employ him, and at the same wages as the rest of their men. If there were no law of settlement, every farmer would seek for the most industrious and intelligent labourers, just as a tradesman or manufacturer does, and he would pay them in proportion to their value, because they would be sought after. This would be a direct premium upon good conduct, intelligence, and skill. Education amongst the agricultural poor is deprived of its marketable value, as an investment of time and attention, and it is therefore deprived of almost all motive, by our present law of settlement. Those, therefore, who are desirous of seeing the poor well educated, ought to be desirous of seeing this great obstacle to their education removed as speedily as possible."*

A conviction that such are the necessary consequences of this law, has become widely diffused; and the words of Adam Smith, denouncing its impolicy and injustice, recognised as true, only by the few who appreciated his great work, during the eighteenth century, are now adopted by the many, and may be said to express the views of the great

* Dawes, *Remarks occasioned by the present Crusade against the Educational Plans of the Committee of Council on Education*, pp. 48, 49. London, 1850.

majority of those who are brought into daily contact with the administration of relief to the poor.

The late President of the Poor Law Board, Mr. Charles Buller, was desirous, as it would seem, "to make assurance doubly sure," in respect of pronouncing a just condemnation on the law of settlement, if it was to be condemned. He, therefore, after presiding over the labours of the Committee of 1847, instituted further inquiry into the operation of that law on the welfare of all classes of the community. Much time was bestowed, in the year 1848, by many able and diligent Poor Law Inspectors, in again investigating the practical working of the law. At the same time, the opinion of local boards of guardians, which, if adverse to the existing system, would be entitled to great weight, was inquired into and ascertained.

The results of this inquiry were fully known to the Poor Law Board in 1848 and 1849; they were communicated to the public in 1850, nearly two years ago.* The inspectors employed to report, certainly obtained plenty of evidence, and that evidence showed conclusively that a great part of the existing evils of the pauperism of England and Wales, is owing to the law of settlment and removal.

In 1847, a Select Committee of the House of Commons, appointed to inquire into the operation of the law of settlement and removal, and of the statute of 9 & 10 Vict. c. 66., passed in the previous session of parliament, reported to the House, from time to time, a vast body of evidence which they heard; and ultimately agreed in opinions embodied in the following resolutions, which, however, were not reported to the House.

1. *Resolved*, "That the law of settlement and removal is generally productive of hardship to the poor, and injurious to the working classes, by impeding the free circulation of labour."

* Reports to the Poor Law Board on the Laws of Settlement and Removal of the Poor, presented to both Houses of Parliament, by command of Her Majesty, 1850.

2. *Resolved,* "That it is injurious to the employers of labour, and impedes the improvement of agriculture."

3. *Resolved,* "That it is injurious to the ratepayers, by occasioning expense in litigation and removal of paupers."

4. *Resolved,* "That the power of removing destitute poor persons, from one parish to another, in England and Wales, be abolished."

These resolutions are of great weight, for, in the first three of them, the committee were unanimous; and in the majority by which the fourth was carried, are found the concurrent opinions, not only of friends of political progress, and free-traders, but of Tories or Conservatives, and Protectionists.

Much evidence respecting the evils of the law of settlement had been adduced before this committee, and the opinion of many competent witnesses was then given in favour of the unqualified repeal of that law, as the only adequate remedy. The subsequent investigation amply confirmed that opinion, if it needed confirmation; and also showed, that those whose attention had been especially called to the subject, including in their number magistrates and clergymen, landowners and farmers, guardians and clerks to guardians, overseers and relieving officers, were very generally satisfied that the law ought to be abolished. *Delenda est Carthago,* is the almost universal feeling.

The Poor Law Board appears to have taken care that this important investigation should be extended through a sufficient number of counties to make it certain that its results might safely be adopted as true for the length and breadth of England. Why the Poor Law Board should ever since, for so many years, have pursued a Fabian policy of continuous delay, when the grievances complained of call so loudly for redress, it is neither easy to see, nor very material now to ask. The evidence reported to the Board, was obtained throughout a wide breadth of country. The East was amply represented by the counties of Suffolk, Norfolk, and Essex; the West, by Dorset and Somerset; the South, by Hampshire, Surrey, and Sussex; the Midland district, by Berkshire, Buckinghamshire, Oxfordshire, Bedfordshire, and Nottinghamshire; and the extreme North, by Northumberland. Premising that the inspectors have drawn the only possible conclusion which could be drawn from the facts before them*, I will set forth what those conclusions are, in the very words of the Official Reports. It will probably suffice to select language used by two of the inspectors, embodying as it does, the substance of the views of all. The first extract is from the Report on Surrey and Sussex.

"The difficulty the labourer finds in shaking off these shackles to his free agency, depreciates his labour. The skilled and unskilled, the industrious and the idle, are paid alike. The payment of labour is regulated, not by its reproductive value, but with reference to the minimum on which a labourer can live. He has no direct interest that his work should be of the best quality; there is no inducement to him to be thrifty, even if he had the power; an early marriage is rather to his advantage than otherwise. If there is a scanty demand for employment, a preference will be given to the married over the single man, and he will often receive higher wages. He knows that he must be kept by the rates if he is out of work, and that it is more expensive to maintain him and his in the Union, than to pay him the current rate of wages. The tendency of the law is to reduce his condition to that of a serf, and to render his labour, therefore, of the least possible value."

After stating the great deficiency, caused by the law of settlement, in the cottage accommodation of labourers throughout the two counties in question, the Inspector adds, that the feelings of most persons conversant with the effects of the law may be summed up in an expression which he often heard: "The masses of labour are wrongly distributed, and cannot right themselves till set free from the law of parochial settlement." The conclusion arrived at by the Inspector is, that every one connected with the management of the poor is impressed with "a strong desire that this law should be abolished

* The facts are set out in the Reports to the Poor Law Board, which were printed and made public in 1850.

altogether, and a conviction that such a course would be for the benefit of the ratepayers."

The following extract is from the Report on Dorset, Hampshire, and Somerset, by another poor law inspector, Mr. Revans, who was officially familiar with the evidence obtained on the condition of the poor at the time of the Commission of Inquiry in 1833 and 1834, and who accurately appreciates, and very lucidly states, the practical working of the law. Mr. Revans, after premising what is undeniable, that it is now almost impossible for a working man to acquire a fresh settlement, proceeds as follows: *

"Excepting during short and very busy periods in agriculture, as at harvest, a working man will be refused employment, save in his own parish; for, at all other times, the ratepayers postpone the execution of work till those periods when employment is likely to be scarce, and when the labourers, who have settlements, would constantly fall upon the rates. It is nearly useless, therefore, for a working man, with the existing laws of settlement, to attempt to obtain work beyond the bounds of his parish. He will be answered with, 'We have enough to do to find employment for our own people.' Should one, however, by the force of accident, obtain employment away from his settlement, the first occasion on which there shall be the slightest deficiency of employment for the labourers who belong to the parish, will cause him to be removed to his settlement; though he may have passed half his life in the parish from which he is removed, have there gained fresh acquaintance and friendship, and his children shall have been born and educated there.

"And now comes his reward for having gone forth in search of employment. When arrived at his settlement he will find that the cottage, which had been occupied by himself and his family, has been given to another, or perhaps pulled down, and that the only residence open to him is the Union-house. Possibly he will find a lodging in the market town of the district, or in some other open parish belonging

* Reports, pp. 90. 92. 94.

to several proprietors, and, therefore, better provided with labourers' dwellings. But then he must be content to walk three or perhaps five miles morning and evening, winter and summer, during good weather and during bad weather, to and from the parish of his settlement, the only one in the district which will provide him with employment, and where nominal work will be given him on the roads, and at wages just sufficient to keep body and soul together; an employment rendered yet more painful by the avowal that it is only found for the purpose of keeping the unwelcome applicant and his family from becoming a more severe burden to the rate-payers, by entering the Union-house. Returned to his settlement, he has bitterly to lament the energy and the industry which urged him to go forth from his parish, in order to earn, by skill and assiduity, a better and more independent provision for his family; and as he trudges to and from his distant, and oft degrading work, he moves a daily warning to every labourer in the surrounding district, of the folly of endeavouring to improve his condition, by leaving the parish to which the law has awarded him."

Mr. Revans, after justly observing that the existing law is most powerful in driving the working man back to the parish of his settlement, and in deterring those who are in their's from leaving it, proceeds: "Under such a system of settlement, the economical distribution of labour is entirely disregarded. Labourers are no longer found in each district in proportion to the quantity of employment which offers, but according to the accident of their birth. A surplus population may frequently be found in one place, whilst a scarcity of labourers will exist in some other, and neither place need be more than ten or a dozen miles distant from the other. The farmers even who frequent the same market table will be found to pay wages differing to the extent of fifty per cent. The wages on the extreme north of the market district will be 8*s.* and 9*s.* a-week, whilst the wages on the extreme south, and for equally good workmen, will not exceed 6*s.* and 7*s.*; and whilst the employer in one district is heavily burdened with poor-rate, the employer in the other has only to support a few aged and infirm persons."

The following passages in the Report of the same inspector are especially deserving of attention.

"Those who are familiar with the history of poor-law management previously to 1834, will recognise in the above the worst evils which were then attributed primarily to maladministration. Amongst the effects of the present system of settlement, I detect the existence of every one of those evils which were attributed by the English Poor Law Inquiry in 1834, to the then mode of administration under the old parochial management. As the secretary to that inquiry, the whole of the details were so deeply stamped on my memory, that their presence and similitude instantly attracted my attention. I am certain that all those evils, and in more than their pristine vigour, will in a few years burst forth, unless the laws of settlement are placed upon a sound principle; for there is ample evidence to show that the maladministration of relief which was corrected in 1834, was only the most glaring effect of the disease, but not the disease itself. The disease lay in the settlement laws; and, so far from having been subdued by the Poor Law Amendment Act, it has been considerably strengthened thereby.

"It is not wonderful, perhaps, that in 1834, the mischiefs connected with the poor laws should have been attributed to the administration of the relief, which was in fact only the most prominent symptom. Large masses of the most graphic facts exhibiting the maladministration of relief in its most pernicious form, dazzled the mind and drew it from the less obtrusive appearance of the settlement laws, themselves the cause of the maladministration and of its long train of secondary evils."

Mr. Pigott, another poor law inspector, concludes his Report on the counties of Berks, Buckinghamshire, and Oxfordshire, by saying of the laws of settlement and removal (p. 174.), "that the evils everywhere inseparable from poverty have been greatly increased in this country by these laws, and that without their total repeal, no measures, however well intended, can avail much for the improvement of the condition of the labouring classes."

All who take the pains of perusing the *evidence* obtained by the different poor law inspectors on this investigation, will probably agree in the conviction produced on the mind of each inspector, by what he saw and learnt. But in that evidence, as printed in the published Reports, are found opinions of guardians of the poor, the very men who are constantly employed in administering this law; and these opinions are deserving of special notice and attention. Such guardians, by formal resolutions at Board meetings, very generally declare that the law of settlement and removal ought to be abolished. They seem to have formed their judgment, not on the mere ground of the pecuniary relief to be expected by ratepayers from such abolition, but from a wider consideration of the various evils incident to the law. A few extracts from such resolutions of guardians, taken exclusively from a single county, Suffolk, will be sufficient as a specimen of them all.

The Stowmarket Union resolved, "That in the opinion of this Board, it is expedient the law of settlement should be abolished, and any person requiring relief should be provided for wherever he may require assistance."

The Bosmere and Claydon Union resolved, "That the law of settlement and removal operates injuriously for the poor, and that its abolition would be desirable; but that such an alteration would render necessary a more extensive and equitable distribution of the burden of maintaining the poor."

The Ipswich Union resolved, "That it is the opinion of this Board, that it is expedient to repeal the laws relating to the removal and settlement of the poor; and that the poor be relieved by a general rate made upon the entire property of the kingdom."

The Woodbridge Union resolved, "That it is desirable the law of settlement should be entirely abolished, and that every poor person born in England or Wales be relieved in the parish where he may reside, from the general funds of the Union in which such parish is situated."

The Mildenhall Union resolved, "That the law of settlement as at present existing is extremely oppressive to the poorer classes, by frequently compelling their removal in old age to a distance from their families and connections, to spend their few remaining years among strangers.

"That the said law has always been found prejudicial to the interest of the ratepayers, from the great amount of litigation it has involved, and the heavy expenses necessarily incurred thereby.

"That for the above and other reasons the Board of Guardians are of opinion that the law of settlement *should be totally and absolutely abolished.*

"That in lieu thereof *some means should be devised for equalising the tax for the relief of the poor,* by an improved and uniform system of rating through every Union, combined with an Act rendering compulsory the relief of destitution *wherever it may exist,* without reference to any local circumstances of previous residence or otherwise of the applicant for relief."

An immense progress of public opinion on this subject, of the law of settlement and removal, is certainly manifested by such resolutions of Boards of Guardians. Still that dread of change which "perplexes monarchs," which has always been a powerful obstacle to just improvement in the laws of this country, and which has generally made the legislature follow slowly, and at a great distance, the progress of opinion out of doors, will doubtless have some influence in Parliament, whenever it shall be proposed totally to repeal the unjust and injurious law. The late Lord Eldon would probably have wept over any proposal to abolish it, and have spoken of its preservation as equally essential with penal laws in matters of religion, and with the punishment of death in cases of stealing to the value of 5*l.* in a dwelling-house, to the security of the rights of property, and the stability of all the most valued institutions of our Church and State of England.

It may, however, be affirmed with confidence, that the law of settlement and removal is finally doomed, that its days are numbered, and that it must soon be abolished for ever. Its evils were denounced by Adam Smith nearly a century ago; they were apparent and appalling in 1833, but were then in part mistaken, by superficial observers, for evils supposed to be necessarily incident to every poor law; they have been greatly aggravated, so far as inequality and injustice of incidence on the ratepayer is concerned, by the legislation of 1846; and they were sufficiently exposed before the Select Committee of the Commons in 1847.

Again were they exposed and denounced, by the Official Reports addressed to the Poor Law Board, in 1848 and 1849; and at last a legislative remedy was promised, although the promise is as yet wholly unfulfilled. It may safely be averred, that the supineness of the Government will cease the very moment that the people of England once understand this question, and express an opinion "out of doors" upon it. Such an opinion will prove a sure warrant for the removal of "pauper settlements" from the region of Legislation into that of History, there to serve with "Wager of Battel," and "Benefit of Clergy," and other now abrogated absurdities of "Father Antic the Law," as memorable examples of the slow progress of reason and justice among the rulers of a just and reasonable people.

CHAP. XVI.

REMEDY BY ABOLISHING REMOVALS, AND SUBSTITUTING MONEY ORDERS.

Sedes ubi fata quietas
Ostendunt. VIRGIL.

SOME benevolent reformers have been sufficiently struck with the more palpable evils of the present law of removal, and especially with its cruel operation on the poor in the day of their distress, to propose that all *removals* should cease. They would not, however, in any respect, change the law of settlement, but would merely substitute, for the present order of removal, under the statute of Charles II., an order of justices, granted at the instance of the parish of the pauper's residence, and requiring payment, by the parish of settlement, of all necessary relief to be given to the pauper. No doubt such a change in the law may easily be made. The question of parochial charge, in the event of an appeal against such an order, would thus be determined between the contending parishes, as is now done in the case of lunatic paupers, without, in any case, inflicting on the pauper the hardship, or on the parish the expense, of an actual removal.

Certainly it would be a good thing to prevent parish officers from daily traversing the country, with paupers in their custody, under warrants of removal. The unfortunate paupers are often dragged, on the occasion of merely temporary want of their usual work, from the only home they have ever known; from the scene of their youth, and the residence of all their relations and friends; and, what is still more important to ratepayers, often from a manufacturing to an agricultural, or from an agricultural to a manufacturing, district; from the place where their industry is usually able to maintain them, to a place where they will prove a permanent parochial burden.

Such removals must continue to take place, under the existing law of hereditary settlement, often to some distant parish, with which the only connexion of the pauper is the accident of a father or a grandfather, or some other ancestor, paternal or maternal, having been born in it, or having, fifty or sixty years ago, resided in it for forty days, on a tenement worth 10*l.* a year, or having, perhaps, slept in it, as long ago, on the last night of a year's service, or of an apprenticeship, or having, in any other way, acquired a settlement there.

Many of those employed in Parliament in making laws, and in courts of justice in administering them, have had their attention but little called to the sufferings which, during the last two centuries, the ill-contrived and unjust law of settlement and removal has constantly inflicted on the indigent poor.* Could the numerous body of assistant overseers and relieving officers of the present day, be jurors for deciding on the truth of the grave charges brought against the present law, I believe it would be impossible, out of the whole of that body, to pack a single jury, that would give a verdict in favour of the power of removal. The Law would be unanimously condemned by the very men who are employed in its administration; who well understand the whole practical working of its injustice and cruelty; and who can best appreciate how slight a mitigation it effects, of any temporary pressure on ratepayers, and how grievous the hardship which it frequently and necessarily inflicts on the poor.

Any change which should free the English name and nation from the reproach of treating its indigent poor as they

* Since the whole of the present chapter, and most of those which follow it, were written, I have seen the cover and title-page of a "Report to the Poor Law Board on the Law of Settlement and Removal of the Poor, being a further Report, in addition to those printed in 1850," by George Coode, Esq. The pressure of professional and other engagements, has made it impossible for me, as yet, to peruse this Report; which I much regret, knowing well, as I do, from the contents of the Report on Local Taxation, published in 1843, Mr. Coode's great ability and learning. It may, however, be assumed, that Mr. Coode comes to much the same conclusion (namely, that the law of settlement ought to be wholly repealed) as was arrived at by Mr. Revans and the other poor law inspectors, whose Reports were published in 1850.

have been treated, for nearly two centuries, by this power of removal, under the statute of Charles II., would justly be considered as a national gain.

It may, no doubt, be objected, by some, that the abolition of the power of removing the poor to some place or other of "settlement," would increase the amount of parochial rates; and that the guardians of any union, in bestowing relief, would do so more liberally if acting as mere agents for the ratepayers of a distant parish of settlement, than if they were paying away their own funds. But some grounds exist for thinking that the boards of guardians, who would pay for their own paupers residing in other unions just as they received for other paupers residing with them, may be trusted in such a matter as this, and would do neither more nor less than their duty.

Every board of guardians already acts in this character of agent to other boards, in numerous cases of giving relief. The yearly amount of money paid to resident non-settled poor, by the guardians of every union, as mere agents for the guardians of some other union in which such poor are settled, is many times greater than the amount of relief actually distributed yearly, by the same union, to those whom it provides for, under the coercion of orders of removal. In such cases, therefore, the sense of justice and convenience, pervading the breasts of those who have to administer relief to the poor, silently repeals the law of removal; and serves to suggest that a similar mode of proceeding ought to be established in all cases, if any law of parochial or union settlement be retained.

It must, however, be conceded, that the due performance of the duty to the distant parish of settlement would be far better secured, if the relieving parish had some direct and substantial interest in the payments made to relieve its resident destitution. Such an interest may easily be created. The law may so apportion the burden of relief, in all cases of its bestowal by one parish on "non-settled" poor, when another parish is looked to for reimbursement, as to ensure fidelity in the discharge of the duty of relieving. For instance, the liability to pay one-third of the money due under the order, may be thrown on the parish of residence, and two-thirds on the parish of settlement. It is manifest that, by such a change as this, which I now suggest, a good deal of the utterly useless expense and hardship of the present law of settlement and removal would be avoided.

It may also be objected that the proposed change in the law, by substituting an order for reimbursement of relief in the place of an order of removal, would tend to make the indigent poor apply for relief in some cases in which the terrors of the present power of removal prevent them from doing so. It is probable that such would be the result of the change; but, on the other hand, there would be a corresponding economy in respect of all the money now expended in travelling, and other charges incident to the actual removal.

Neither would it be desirable to preserve any such terrors as those of the despotic power of removal. The existence of such a power over the poor does not furnish a convenient or just test of destitution in any case; and there is no doubt that, in many instances, it produces only mendicancy, vagrancy, and other offences, by the commission of which, society loses much more than it can ever gain by the exchange of paupers between parishes.*

Another reason why the expense and hardship of these

* Sixth Report of the Commons' Committee, 1847, H. Coppock, 5206. "If it is a case of destitution; if a man has no means of labour to obtain a livelihood, and is in want of food (and I presume those are the only cases in which the poor laws ought to relieve); if you refuse that relief which is requisite, by making it so oppressive to that poor man's feelings that he would rather beg, steal, or use any unfair means of getting a living, you do a great injury to society, by allowing that test to be applied."—5209. "I have known men frequently say, especially the Irish at the present moment, and I have heard it said by Englishmen, 'I would rather die here than be removed there!'"—5219. "What you mean is, that the horror of removal is so great, that people will submit to the most dreadful privations, and very often privations ending in death itself? No doubt about it."—5226. "When you say that a man is driven to shift for himself, and that men who are destitute are often driven to shift for themselves from the knowledge that they are liable to be removed, you do not mean that they prefer the alternative of starvation, but that in many cases they may resort to mendicancy and vagrancy, or something short of starvation, under pressure of their necessities? No doubt of it."

actual removals of paupers from one parish to another ought to be done away with, even if the law of settlement be retained, is found in the undoubted fact, that such removals frequently fail to effect the transfer of the burden of destitution to the place of settlement. An order for repayment of relief given by the parish of the pauper's residence, would much more certainly effect the transfer to the parish of settlement of that burden which, according to the present law, the place of settlement ought to bear.

When a man is removed with his family from a place where, perhaps, he is likelier to maintain himself and them, than he will be in the place to which he is removed, it often turns out, after all the trouble and expense incurred, that a merely momentary change of burden is effected; for the paupers frequently return, sometimes on the same day*, to the home from which the law has removed them,—and they so return in total disregard of the vain threat of punishment for vagrancy held out to all who return and again become chargeable to the place which had removed them.

Men of great experience in the administration of relief to the poor, are of opinion, that the forced removal of the poor, is the occasion, in the majority of instances, of just as much money as such removal costs being entirely thrown away; "for," say they, "more than half of the paupers removed will come back again." "They generally return, because they have their connections in the place from which they have been sent, and, being known there, are likely to obtain

* R. Long, in Reports to the Poor Law Board, 1850, p. 60., speaking of the Ipswich Union, says: "Many, after a heavy expense incurred by removal, return with a weekly allowance from their settlement parish. Many of this class (able-bodied men, with wives and families, removed in consequence of temporary sickness, or want of work) have returned *the same day* they were removed, and the *generality of them, after a short time,* if they have had a few years' residence in the parishes from which they were removed." In the same volume, W. G. Dennis, speaking of unions in Essex, says: "With reference to removal of the poor, I can say, from my experience as a guardian of two unions, that in many cases when paupers have been removed, perhaps at a considerable expense and trouble, they will return within a very short period, and I have known them to occupy the same residence."

some employment, the suspension of which has rendered them for a time chargeable." *

During the period of severe distress in Stockport, in the years 1841 and 1842, an unprecedented number of removals was effected by the parochial authorities there. The following table exhibits their amount during the three years between March, 1840, and March, 1843.

REMOVALS FROM PLACES WITHIN THE STOCKPORT UNION.

	Families.	Persons.
During 9 months between March and 31st Dec. 1840 -	73	263
During the year ended 31st December, 1841 - -	195	627
During the year ended 31st December, 1842 - -	272	920
During the 3 months ended 25th March, 1843 - -	50	187
Total - - - -	590	1997

Mr. H. Coppock, of Stockport, the clerk to this Union, was asked by the House of Lords' Committee on the Burdens affecting Real Property, in 1846 (6471.)—"Have you any means of knowing whether many of them (the persons so removed) came back again in times of manufacturing prosperity?" His answer was—"Many of them came back again, *even in the time of distress. We found this occurred with a great number of paupers. Very frequently the paupers would get back again faster than the removal officer who was sent with them.*"

The exact average proportion of those who return after removal under orders, it would be difficult to ascertain; but in the case of removal from populous towns, it is undoubtedly very large. Whenever the poor, who have been so removed, return, and again become chargeable, a second order of removal is, practically speaking, the only available remedy

* Reports to the Poor Law Board, 1850; Mr. G. A. à Beckett's Report, p. 39. Mr. Howard, the clerk to the Board of Guardians of the Lexden and Winstree Union, *ib.* p. 40., states his belief, founded on a long experience, that in the case of the able-bodied man, removal is almost wholly ineffectual. "It frequently happens that paupers removed, after much litigation and considerable cost, will completely defeat the law by returning whence they came, or at all events quitting the place that has been declared chargeable with their maintenance."

by which the place of residence can seek to obtain temporary relief from the burden of maintaining such non-settled paupers. When such a second order of removal is obtained, the expense of that proceeding, and of removing the paupers under it, is again thrown on the parish which obtains it, even if there should be no appeal against such order, and the burden of the future maintenance of the paupers should ultimately be transferred to the parish to which the removal is directed.*

A proceeding for vagrancy against the husband or father, in such a case of return from removal under an order, would only have the effect, so far as parish funds are concerned, of making the wife and children chargeable, during the whole period of the husband's imprisonment for his contravention of the law. On his release from prison, more degraded and less capable of earning his living than he was before, there would be less chance than ever of his supporting his family; and all that the parish could now do, if disposed to stir further in the matter, would be again to obtain an order of removal, the only available means, after all, of relieving itself from the burden of such non-settled paupers.

In some parishes the mere *threat* of a prosecution for vagrancy may, for a while after the return of the pauper, prevent any application by him for parish relief; but actually to put in force the vagrant law, in any such case, would inevitably add to, instead of diminishing, the amount of the parish burdens.

An intelligent officer of a populous manufacturing town in Yorkshire, recently informed me, that on one occasion in particular, the return of paupers from their removals, had been

* The second order of removal is sometimes founded solely on the fact of a former order and removal, made and acquiesced in. Such a second order occasionally becomes the subject of an appeal at sessions, not on the real facts of the settlement, but on the correctness of the different steps in the formal proceedings. The former order, if duly signed and sealed, good on its face, well executed, and either unappealed against, or confirmed on appeal at sessions, operates as what the law calls an *estoppel* on the parties; and so renders any inquiry into the facts on which the first order was founded immaterial. I have known such *second* orders quashed on appeal on some legal point, although the first was acquiesced in, and not appealed against.

extremely numerous. "We found out," he said, "that *a majority* of the paupers returned, and it was of precious little use having removals at all." The threat to put in force the Vagrant Act against any poor man, who, after so returning, should apply for relief, was hereupon used, and greatly diminished the cases of application for relief from persons so circumstanced. But the undoubted fact, that a very large proportion of those who are thus removed, do shortly return to the places where they have long been accustomed to reside, and return in a state of destitution as great as that in which they were removed from it, is a strong argument against the use of so harsh, and expensive, and ineffectual a proceeding as an order of removal; and certainly shows that an order, for the repayment of the relief bestowed in the place of the pauper's residence, would be open to much less just objection, than attaches to the actual removal of all who require such relief.

After all, the power of removal is of extremely little use to the ratepayers of populous places, even during periods of distress. That this is so, will be made perfectly clear, by our dwelling for a moment on what has occurred in the towns of Nottingham, Stockport, and Sheffield respectively, during such periods.

From July 1837 to July 1838, was a time of severe, and almost unprecedented suffering, among the dense manufacturing population of the town of Nottingham. From this suffering population of 50,000 people, "an enormous proportion of whom were, at that time, receiving relief from the poor-rates," the whole number of persons placed under orders of removal was only 178; they were included in 80 orders. Whether the whole number of them was actually removed, is not known. We may well agree with those who have thought and said, that the removal of 178 persons from such a population, "can hardly be looked upon as any substantial relief to the ratepayers of Nottingham, at that period."*

The distress and suffering by which Stockport was visited, in the latter part of 1841, and in 1842, were quite appalling. A

* Sixth Report of the Commons' Committee of 1847, 6671.

government commission of inquiry was issued on the subject; the guardians of the poor availed themselves largely of the right to apply for orders of removal: but the whole number of *orders* actually executed by the removal of the paupers during the year of distress, was only 272, and this was a much larger number than that of either the previous or following year.

The case of Stockport may, therefore, fairly be considered, like that of Nottingham, as showing that the power of removal does not confer any great amount of relief on a distressed locality. Inconvenience and loss to the very ratepayers of such districts, is, however, sure to follow such removals: a sort of retributive justice for useless suffering, to which the poor have been exposed by the removal, overtakes the removants; and the manufacturer's capital lies idle for some time, after a revival of trade, before a sufficiency of hands is found to take the places of those who have been scattered over the country, to burden the poor-rates of agricultural parishes. The poor man, whose life has been spent in spinning or weaving, is not likely to find employment in a place where his knowledge of spinning or weaving is useless, and where, perhaps, there is already a surplus amount of settled labour.

The evidence given before the Commons' Committee of 1847, by Mr. H. Coppock, of Stockport, town-clerk of that borough, as well as Clerk to the Board of Guardians of the Stockport Union, respecting the pecuniary benefit or protection afforded to ratepayers by the power of removing the poor, even under the pressure of distress like that of 1842, is very striking.*

* Sixth Report of the Commons' Committee of 1847, 5258. "There is not the sort of population to be obtained at a short notice that would work the mills if a good trade exists, and therefore if you remove or disperse the working population, you very much injure the manufacturers, because, when trade revives, they must either obtain that population back again, or their mills must be inefficiently worked. Therefore the wise course would be, to deal with the case of pauperism where it arose, and let it survive the badness of trade in the place in which it arises; let it remain there till trade revives. To disperse the population would injure the population. A person brought up to the cotton trade must be some time before he can be an efficient workman in any other trade or calling; therefore, it is no advantage to send him to an agricultural township, and another

Mr. Coppock was examined on this same subject, before the Lords' Committee on Burdens on Land, in the year 1846; and his evidence on that occasion, already adverted to, enables us to estimate, for Stockport, the value of the power of removal, as an alleviation of the local burden of poor-rate, during a period of distress. This comparison we obtain from a former table*, and the following, also laid, by Mr. Coppock, before the Lords' Committee.†

Year ended 25th March,	Number of Persons relieved.			Money Expended.
	In-door.	Out-door.	Total.	
				£
1841	1,668	12,918	14,586	8,132
1842	2,122	21,391	23,513	11,990
1843	1,469	14,504	15,973	9,224
Totals	5,259	48,813	54,072	29,346

The average number of persons receiving relief, therefore, in the Stockport Union, during each of these three years, was 18,024, and the average number of persons who, as appears by the table already given*, were removed yearly under orders during the same period, was 665, or 3·7 per cent of those who constituted the mass of paupers during each year. Allowing for the immediate returns of many of the persons removed, it is therefore apparent, that the power of

township which is manufacturing is no better off as regards trade. It would be better to keep him where his friends reside; let him remain there till he is again wanted by his employer." — 5263. After the removals from Stockport in 1842, "the masters were some time before they obtained hands; when trade revived they had not a sufficiency of hands." — 5265. "I think there was a period of six months before the full number of hands could be obtained again." — 5268. "The experience of 1842 confirms my opinion that it would be wise to do away with the law of settlement and removal altogether." — 5271. "My opinion is that there was no advantage" (in the removals of 1842) "corresponding with the misery caused." Mr. Coppock states (5281) that, out of the persons removed in 1842 (above, p. 321.), 250 returned at once to Stockport, so that less than 700 in fact were got rid of by removal; 700 hands would, however, work a large factory.

* Above, p. 321. † Report of the Lords' Committee, 1846, p. 583.

removal is of trifling use, as an alleviation of local burdens in populous districts, during severe temporary distress.

Mr. Coppock informs me that the numbers of the preceding table, are those of the *cases;* and therefore include instances of persons who become chargeable more than once in each year. A correction is therefore required, to enable us to compare exactly the number of persons removed, with those relieved.

Such a comparison will be accurately given by the following table for the Sheffield Union, the rateable value of which is 165,788*l.*, and which, in 1851, contained 103,602 inhabitants. The year preceding the 25th March, 1849, was one of great depression in the trade of Sheffield, and of severe distress among its inhabitants.

Year ending Lady-day.	Amount of Poor Rate in the Pound.	Number of Paupers.		Per Centage of Paupers removed on the Number relieved.
		Relieved (excluding Vagrants).	Removed under Orders of Removal.	
	s.			
1847	3	12,853	13	·001
1848	3	13,123	33	·002
1849	6	23,808	52	·002
1850	4	16,728	74	·004
1851	2	13,770	35	·002

Out of 10,685 additional claimants on parochial relief, in the year ended at Lady-day, 1849, only 19 were removed, under this law of settlement and removal; yet in the year 1848, the distress in Sheffield was very great; and, as we see, the amount of poor-rate was twice as great in that year, as it was in the previous year.

These data show that the supposed benefit of any power of removal is wholly illusory, and that no substantial relief from the burden of pauperism, as borne by populous places, in times of great commercial distress, has ever been obtained, or ever will be obtained, from any such law.

Indeed it seems that of late years, in many unions, a sense of the injury which forced removals cause, both to ratepayers and to the poor, has largely spread, and has effected a great diminution in the number of actual removals. Parish officers, by avoiding the costs of removal, not unfrequently save more than they expend in relieving those whom they might remove, but do not. "A great deal of expense, much bad feeling between parish and parish, and a great deal of hardship to the poor themselves, have been saved by this course."*

The numerous evils attendant on actual removal of the poor, when they thus prevent the carrying out the law, in effect compel the parishes of resident destitution to forego the only remedy given for enforcing relief by the parishes of settlement. If, therefore, there be anything of reason or justice in the principle of a law of settlement, it must be the duty of the legislature, at least to provide means by which the burden of providing for settled poor, wherever resident, may more effectually be thrown on those who, according to the law, ought to bear it. Such means would certainly be found in substituting an order for repayment of relief, in the place of the order of removal.

When the conveyance of the poor man to a distant place of settlement, under an order of removal, is effected, and is not followed by his speedy return, it sometimes happens, as we have seen, that a revival of trade makes his labour wanted in the very place in which, shortly before, during a depression of trade, he could not find employment. The power of removal, if exercised freely during temporary stagnation of trade, so disperses the hands employed, as to make it extremely difficult, if not impracticable, to regain them, when again wanted. Hence, some manufacturers, employing many hands, "find it imperative upon them to endeavour to find work for their people, even when trade is bad, and the sale of their manufactures is but slow."† When manufacturers make such

* Mr. Marriott, clerk to the Southwell Union, Reports to the Poor Law Board 1850, p. 130.

† Reports to the Poor Law Board, 1850, p. 116. Mr. Hardisty, the head of a firm of extensive silk and crape manufacturers, employing more than 800 hands in the town of Shepton Mallet in Somersetshire, complains, that whilst himself and his partners are compelled to maintain their own people, during a slack time, the settlement laws throw the most unfair burden upon them as ratepayers; for, during the season when agricultural labourers have not em-

sacrifices, to prevent the law of removal from being put in force, we may feel well assured of the extreme inconvenience, which is apt to result to all parties interested, from the compulsory removal of poor workmen to places of settlement.

Upon the whole, therefore, it may safely be concluded, that a change which should substitute the delivery of a mere order directing the payment of money, in the stead of an actual removal of the indigent poor from one parish to another, would, as far as it went, be a very decided improvement in the law; but its realisation would still leave unchecked the greater part of the social evil which the poor-law legislation of the last two centuries has created and fostered, and would leave, in undiminished energy, most of the demoralising influences to which that law still subjects the labouring population.

ployment, they fall upon the parish, and the landowners of neighbouring parishes, by pulling down cottages, compel Shepton Mallet to provide a large part of the relief needed by poor people, whose residence alone is in Shepton Mallet, but whose labour is employed in close parishes four or five miles distant.

CHAP. XVII.

PROPOSED REMEDY BY UNION SETTLEMENT AND UNION RATING.

Æstuat infelix angusto limite. — JUVENAL.

THAT the substitution of the *union*, in the place of the *parish*, as the district of a pauper's settlement, would remove some existing inequalities in the incidence of the poor-rate, and would slightly palliate other evils of pauperism, may perhaps be conceded. But the review of former legislation shows, that the principle of district or union settlement, has been once tried in this country, during a long period, and rejected. The simple provision of the statute of Elizabeth, which, on that rejection, was substituted for the union or district settlement, was found capable of convenient administration, and, during a period of about sixty years, the evils of pauperism in England appear mainly to have arisen from neglect to carry out that simple provision. It must be admitted that, in our own day, the project of union settlement is likely to find favour with reluctant bit-by-bit reformers, men who never act on any principle except that of temporary expediency, and whose greatest triumph it would be to patch up or palliate for the moment, any evil, however great, and to leave to other hands the application of a real remedy, whenever inevitable necessity for such remedy might arise. It seems, also, that an idea has of late prevailed, that union settlement will prove a panacea for every evil of the poor law, and especially that it will remove the inequality in incidence of the poor-rate, which has long been complained of as existing in different districts, even of the same union. It is undoubtedly such inequality which has mainly caused the cry for union settlement, and union rating. This inequality "is so apparent," says a poor law inspector, "and its injustice is so generally felt and inveighed against," that "the propriety of uniting such parishes for the joint support of the poor, can no longer be doubted."* It can certainly no longer be doubted, that a great change in the law is needed, and it may be conceded that a union of such parishes, for both settlement and rating, would be a sufficient remedy, in many cases, for the single evil of this inequality of burden. But, to make such union an effectual remedy, of even this single evil, it must include union rating, which shall deal with the union as if it were one parish, and shall levy the funds needed for relieving the poor, upon real property throughout the union, in proportion to the value of such property, without regard to the parish in which it is situate.†

Inequality of burden, as now complained of, would, by the adoption of this proposal, be completely removed, so far as the relative contribution of different parts of each separate union is concerned; but it may well be doubted, whether such a remedy would not be, in many respects, worse than the existing disease. Its adoption seems, in the first place, necessarily to involve greater interference with existing rights than is requisite for the reasonable adjustment of existing burdens. In some unions the effect would be to *increase* the rate, on some of the parishes, to an amount many times greater than that which such parishes had previously paid; it would, in many unions, raise the rate on parishes which have heretofore maintained their poor at an expense of less than half the average of the burden throughout England, to double the amount of that average.‡ It seems to me that a sufficient ground for rejecting such a proposal is found in the fact that, in many of the districts which it would subject to an entirely new burden, the rates would be thus increased,

* Report on the County of Northumberland, by W. H. T. Hawley, p. 190.

† A modification of this principle has been proposed; and will be adverted to, in the next chapter.

‡ This would occur wherever a few parishes lightly burdened are in union with many parishes, the burdens in which are heavy, as in the Newcastle-upon-Tyne Union, which pays an average rate of 2*s.* 5*d.* in the pound, and contains in the whole eleven parishes, of which Fenham now pays 4½*d.*, Heaton 7¼*d.*, Elswick 8¾*d.*, and Jesmond 11*d.*, making an average of 7¾*d.* for the four.

from an amount much below, to an amount greatly exceeding, the average rate of the whole country. This test may justly be considered as decisive against the adoption of the union area of taxation.*

That there would not be wanting great inequalities between different unions, even at the very moment of adopting the new area of taxation, is apparent; for the now *average* poor-rate of each union, if ascertained, will be found to be widely different even in different unions of the same county. In the Tewkesbury Union in Gloucestershire, the average of the year's rate is 10¾*d.* only in the pound, while that of the Dursley Union, in the same county, is 3*s.* 5½*d.* In the North Riding of Yorkshire, the Darlington Union pays, on the average, 8*d.*, and the Reeth Union 2*s.* 6¼*d.* In Northumberland, the Haltwhistle Union 7*d.*, and the Newcastle Union 2*s.* 5*d.* Not only would inequalities like these be created, but, in short, all pauperised *districts*, containing unions such as are mentioned in a subjoined table†, would obtain no relief whatever from such a change as that proposed.

The extent of inequality in amount of burden, which would at once be found in different unions, under the paltry reform of this "union settlement and union rating," will receive further illustration, by a reference to a former chapter, in which the existing inequality of the burden of poor-rate, as borne by different unions and districts of the metropolis, is pointed out.‡ Every such instance of present inequality in distribution of that burden, would, by any scheme of mere union settlement and union rating, be left wholly unredressed.

A list of unions, six in each of the six different counties

* Sir John M'Neill adopts the same criterion: see Evidence before the Lords Committee on Parochial Assessments, 1850, p. 376., answer to question 2730. "Though I might largely increase the rate (of the parish that was to suffer by a change of rating), I would not be deterred by that, *unless I was increasing it much above the average rate of the country.*"

† Appendix, p. 389.

‡ See Chapter II., especially pp. 35. 38, 39, 40.

of Gloucester, Lincoln, Salop, Middlesex, North Riding of York, and Carnarvon, laid before a Select Committee of the Lords, on the 6th June, 1850, gives the following result as to the inequalities in the thirty-six unions there tabulated.*

Average Rate in the Pound.	Under 1*s*.	At 1*s*., above 1*s*., and under 2*s*.	Above 2*s*., and under 3*s*.	Above 3*s*., and under 4*s*.	At 4*s*.
Number of Unions -	14	11	6	4	1

Now the inequality here shown to exist, in the incidence of the average poor-rate, as it falls on different unions, is just as great as the inequality ordinarily found to exist between the different parishes of a union.

In some instances, the present difference in amount of poor-rate, levied for different parishes in the same union, is much less than is found in comparing the average poor-rates of different unions. In the Alnwick Union, of sixty-two parishes, there are only ten parishes in which the annual rate exceeds 1*s*. in the pound, and of the ten, only one, Alnwick itself, in which it reaches 2*s*. In the Bedford Union, of forty-four parishes, the amount of poor-rate in each parish, in 1847, was as follows:

Average Rate in the Pound.	Under 1*s*.	Above 1*s*., and under 2*s*.	Above 2*s*., and under 3*s*.	Above 3*s*., and under 4*s*.	Above 4*s*.
Number of Parishes -	5	23	13	3	0

The adoption of union settlement and rating would, no doubt, to some extent, diminish the number and extent of the instances of inequality in the incidence of the poor-rate; and, if it should appear that any very great improvement would be effected, in the condition of the indigent poor, by such a change in the law, its advantages, in that respect, might, in

* See Mr. G. L. Hutchinson's evidence before the Select Committee of the Lords on the Laws relating to Parochial Assessments, 1850, p. 171.

some measure, compensate for its utter inefficiency, as a reform in the incidence of the rate.

But no substantial improvement in the labourer's condition could justly be looked forward to from any such trifling change in the law. By the substitution of union for parochial settlement, the narrow circle, within which labour has been so long restricted, would, undoubtedly, be somewhat enlarged, and a slight palliative of the injurious effects upon industry of the law of settlement would, therefore, be obtained; but the expectation of any great amount of benefit, from so slight a modification of the law, would certainly prove wholly illusory. It would seem that an opinion, in favour of union settlement, prevailed much more generally a few years ago, than it does now; that recent discussion has done much to change that opinion; and that a conviction of the utter insufficiency of such a change in the law to remove the ills justly complained of, as resulting from the present law of settlement, and in any way materially to improve the condition of the labourer, has gradually spread, and is now very generally adopted.

It is true there is a notion, so prevalent that it may be termed popular, according to which this change in the law would almost put an end to removals. The removals would be comparatively few, say the advocates of the plan, for the only interchange of paupers would be between unions instead of between parishes. So removals would diminish to one twenty-third of their present number, there being, on the average, twenty-three parishes in each union.

Unfortunately, the internecine warfare of parishes, and its necessary and continual sacrifice of paupers and ratepayers, would not thus cease: the mere diminution in the number of citadels of the belligerents could not materially diminish either the number of the forces engaged, or the frequency of their conflicts.

There is a palpable fallacy in thus contrasting the small number of 620 unions with 15,000 parishes, as if, in future, there would only be 620 orders of removal, for every 15,000 which are now obtained. This fallacy was exposed, in evidence given before the Commons' Committee of 1847. "Unions contain, on the average, twenty-three parishes," says Mr. Richard Hall, then an assistant Poor Law Commissioner, "and I think it is evident, that every cluster of twenty-three parishes would be able to remove into every other parish in the kingdom, whether it were a union or not. In point of fact there would be, so to speak, one party removing from these 23 parishes, all the persons not settled in any of these parishes, instead of 23 parties, and there would be 580 parties * to be defendants in the removal, so to speak, instead of 14,980, as the number is now. All the non-settled paupers in a union would be removable out of that union, after the alteration, just as they are now; only they would not be removable from one parish to another in the union. If a non-settled pauper were dwelling in a union of twenty-three parishes, and the law were altered in the manner proposed, there would be only twenty-two parishes out of all the parishes in the country into which he could not be removed.—In asking for opinions on union settlement, and in discussing it at boards of guardians, I find that is the view they take of it at once. They *always* say, 'It would do nothing for us; we do not remove as between parishes in our own union.'"†

Removals between parishes in the same union have certainly been very rare, throughout the whole country. In many cases, any question of disputed settlement, between two parishes in the same union, is referred to the decision of the Board of Guardians ‡; if the facts are admitted, and a point of law is the only matter in dispute, parishes in the same union frequently state a case for the opinion of counsel

* Mr. Hall refers to the number of unions existing in 1847.

† Mr. Hall's answers, 6991 and 6999, to questions put by the Select Committee of the Commons, in 1847; see the Sixth Report, pp. 236, 237.

‡ Sixth Report of the Commons' Committee, 1847, J. Livesey (Guardian of the Preston Union, in Lancashire), 6172. "The decision in our union, of the Board of Guardians, has always been considered final: we have *never had a single case* of removal within the union since it was formed."

of some standing at the bar, agreeing to be bound by his decision. Thus, in some parts of the country, "cases of disputed settlement, belonging to two places in the same union, are never taken into court." *

An elaborate statistical inquiry would probably show that the utmost mitigation of the grievance experienced by ratepayers and paupers, in removals and consequent litigation, would be measured by a diminution of orders of removal in the proportion of one in ten, and of appeals against them in about the same proportion.† The change of legal adviser, respecting settlements and appeals, from the attorney of each parish to the clerk of the guardians of each union, might make a difference in the costs of litigation; it would probably increase them in some unions, and diminish them in others.

It is moreover to be feared, that although the fixing a pauper by settlement, in a union, instead of a parish, will not substantially diminish the evils of the present law, as they affect either the poor man or the ratepayer, yet the change may have some injurious consequences, beyond those pointed out; and, upon the whole, do more harm than good. It will, in the first place, necessitate a considerable change in the staff of union officers: but I shall assume such change to be effected in the best possible way; and that any increase in the expense of administration, which might be incurred, is not worth notice. A much graver objection to the plan is, that it would, on the average, reduce the interest of each guardian, in examining into any case of alleged destitution in his own parish, to the twenty-third part of its present amount; for there are, on the average, twenty-three parishes

* Mr, Bryant, Clerk to the Wimborne and Cranborne Union, Reports to the Poor Law Board, 1850, p. 123.

† The same witness (Sixth Report of Commons' Committee, 1847, 6697, 6698.) gives exact statistical details on the subject, for a population of 1,177,365 (in 46 unions containing 554 parishes). and shows that in a whole year 668 orders were made directing removal from within a union to some place without it, of which 77 were litigated, and in the whole 600 executed; the whole number of orders between parishes, both of which were situate in the same union, was only 66, of which 5 only were litigated, and 53 only executed.

in every union. After such a change, the guardian would not attend to the union interests, as he now does to those of his own parish. It is well known that the establishment or union charges at present existing, are not the object of the same vigilant and jealous care with which every parochial burden is regarded.

The probable result of abrogating the parochial and adopting this union settlement would be, the necessary transfer of duties, now well performed by the unpaid guardians, to paid officers; and such result would be a great, and, I think, a most injudicious change. It would not only cause additional expense in the administration of the altered law; but would amount to an unnecessary step towards the centralisation of powers, which are still vested in independent local authorities, and the due administration of which powers is now guaranteed, both by the existing local interest of those in whom they are vested, and by the amply sufficient control of the Poor Law Board.

Moreover, the proposed union settlement would be wholly inoperative, to redress many existing grievances which have arisen since the passing of 9 & 10 Vict. c. 66., and equally so to prevent future hardship, in the extremely unequal incidence of the poor-rate, in the various instances pointed out, and also in other cases, such as that of Norwich, and some large towns. Yet, powerless for good, as the substituted system would be, in various important classes of cases of existing inequality and hardship, it would nevertheless, in another class of cases (equally entitled to consideration in any alteration of the law), be irresistible for evil, in producing sudden, violent, and wholly unnecessary disturbance of actual burdens. The change would, in truth, overturn and confound all existing rights and duties, attached to the possession of property in respect of parochial rates, and would do this, too, with a rudeness and injustice so gross and unendurable, that, as is admitted by an apologist of the project, it would be requisite for some of the existing unions to be entirely reconstructed, "remodelled," before they could endure the shock of so sudden and violent an attack and devastation. "I do not think," says an assistant Poor Law Commissioner, in advocating the change, "that there would be a large number of unions that would require remodelling; but if no power of remodelling was given, I think a considerable amount of inconvenience would result in individual instances, but I think they are few compared to the whole."* Perhaps so; if they amount to only ten per cent. of the whole, there will be more than sixty unions so circumstanced. Whatever the number, great care and consideration of the cases of expected injury, and of the new union arrangements, as preliminaries to any legislative establishment of union settlement and rating, would be required; and the necessity of any such preliminary investigations and decisions, constitutes another objection to the change. Lastly, the authority of parishioners in vestry, which still exists to some extent, and ought, perhaps, rather to be increased than diminished, would, the moment "union settlement and rating" became the law of the land, be practically abrogated for all purposes relating to the poor.

Such a change could only be justified on the clearest proof that the great national benefit which it seeks for, and a very small part alone of which it could secure, is unattainable by less violent means. It will be shown plainly enough, hereafter, that a modification of the present mode of levying the poor-rate may be adopted, which, setting the labourer free from any bondage of a settlement, will nevertheless, preserve a sufficient local interest in the administration of relief, to make it practicable, substantially to continue all existing local authorities in the performance of their present functions. At the same time, this better proposal will protect the owners of property from such sudden and extreme alteration, in the amount of their burdens, as union rating would, in many instances, effect, and will produce a reasonable approach to equalisation of present inequalities, in numerous and important classes of cases, which would be left comparatively without redress, by the adoption of union rating.

* Second and Third Reports of the Commons' Committee, Mr. Gulson, p. 52. question 1313.

Upon the whole, therefore, the probable benefits of the change, which has been considered in this chapter, do not countervail its inherent inconveniences and dangers; and since, at the very most, it would, from omitting totally to repeal the law of settlement, only palliate to a small extent, the main evils of our pauper code, it deserves no further serious consideration.

CHAP. XVIII.

PROPOSED REMEDIES. — UNION RATING. — CHARGE ON THE CONSOLIDATED FUND. — NATIONAL RATE ON REAL PROPERTY. — NATIONAL PROPERTY TAX. — SPECIAL INCOME TAX. — ASSESSMENT OF TITHE COMMUTATION RENT CHARGE. — TRANSFER TO THE STATE OF ALL ESTABLISHMENT OR UNION CHARGES. — TRANSFER TO THE STATE OF PART OF THE CHARGE OF LUNATIC PAUPERS.

> Others apart sat on a hill retir'd,
> In thought more elevate, and reason'd high: —
> Vain wisdom all, and false philosophy!
> Yet with a pleasing sorcery could charm
> Pain for a while, or anguish, and excite
> Fallacious hope. MILTON.

VARIOUS plans have been put forward for raising the funds needed to relieve the poor. The raising of these funds has always been a burden on land; and, in making any attempt equitably to adjust, between the several classes of the community, the pressure of general taxation, the legislature will always bear in mind, on the one hand, that the real estate of England is exclusively burdened with poor-rate and other local taxes; and, on the other hand, that the land tax is inconsiderable. It is quite true, that some of these local taxes are as old as the Conquest; that even the poor-rate has existed during more than two hundred and fifty years, under the very words of the statute of Queen Elizabeth, and was, in its origin, a substitution for a burden which had been mainly borne by the land, from the time when Christianity was first established in the island. And it is equally true, that the owners of real estate in England enjoy, as a class, some peculiar and not insignificant advantages over owners of other property. But all these burdens and privileges, of land and landowner, are sure to meet with ample consideration in parliament, whenever a serious attempt shall be made towards effecting a just and satisfactory repartition of the general taxation of the country.

All the various plans which will be considered in this chapter, have been suggested, as more equitable than the present mode of raising the funds required for the relief of pauperism, and equally assume the repeal of the law of settlement, and provide for the distribution of relief where it may be needed. There is, however, a great difference between these plans in their modes of raising the many millions which they yearly distribute; and, according as one or the other of them shall be adopted, an equally great difference in social consequences, to all classes of the community, may probably ensue. I propose briefly to state these plans, and to point out some of the objections which may justly be urged against each of them. Having done so, I shall venture to suggest a mode of raising the funds for the relief of the poor, which possibly may be found preferable to any hitherto put forward.

It may safely be assumed that, on the repeal of the law of settlement, it would be wise and necessary to provide a better mode than the present of raising the funds for relieving pauperism. The first suggestion made is, that a union rating should be established. In what respect does such a proposal recommend itself as a provision for the state of things to be produced by repealing the law of settlement? Every topic which was urged in the last chapter against such a mode of raising the funds required for the relief of the poor will equally apply now. The objections urged against a union rating, as coupled with a union settlement, seem to lose none of their weight by supposing the law of settlement to be wholly repealed. Perhaps they are rather strengthened than weakened by that supposition. If such repeal of the law of settlement would be likely to expose particular localities, especially the great manufacturing towns, to an occasional aggravation of their local burdens, greater than any already experienced, so much more grave are the reasons against inflicting on the owners of land, heretofore comparatively free from the burden of pauperism, an equal share of the sorrows and sins of its neighbours, "three, or four, or five miles" off.*

Terrible local distress arises whenever a great focus of manufacturing industry is obliged to come to a sudden temporary stoppage in the career of its material prosperity; and so to exhibit, in all their concentration and horror, those sufferings of the many which seem to be everywhere the fatal and inseparable accompaniment of the aggregation of capital in the hands of the few. It may be, that in order to alleviate the sufferings produced by such a temporary crisis, a rate in aid over a wide district, or even a contribution of some kind of assistance from the State itself, might not unjustly be called for. And at all events it is clear, that, on the repeal of the law of settlement and removal, a union rating will not effect a reasonable adjustment of the burden now so unequally pressing on those by whom pauperism is supported, and that some other remedy, for the inequalities present and future of which ratepayers may justly complain, ought to be devised and adopted.

A modification of this plan of union rating, and an approach towards a more centralised system, is found in a proposal of an Assistant Poor Law Commissioner, Mr. G. Pigott, "That every poor person, for every purpose of relief, shall be deemed settled wherever he becomes destitute; that the poor of the whole kingdom shall be relieved from one general fund, under the control of government commissioners; that this fund shall be supplied by payments from the ratepayers of each union throughout the kingdom, in the proportion of their last calculated average payments, for the relief of their poor; that, after each lapse of three years, new averages be taken of the amount of relief legally administered within the union during each of the three preceding years, which new averages shall regulate the payments of each union to the general fund

* Second and Third Reports of the Commons' Committee of 1847, Question 1359. Evidence of Mr. Gulson (an Assistant Poor Law Commissioner)—"What area would you add to such a town as Nottingham?—I would add an area of perhaps three, or four, or five miles."

during the three years ensuing; that each union be constituted as one parish, for the purposes of rating; and that the *payments of each parish*, to the union rate, *be fixed in perpetuity*, at the proportion which the expenditure of each parish, for the relief of the poor, bore to the expenditure of the union on the 26th August, 1847.*

This plan would cause future payments towards the relief of pauperism to be made by parishes quite irrespectively of the amount of actual destitution calling for relief in each parish: the burden would be apportioned among the parishes of each union in proportion to their relative payments, at the time when the new principle was first adopted. Enormous inequalities of burden would soon grow up under such a scheme: and in less than half a century, parishes of the greatest pauperism would, in many places, be those of the least payment towards the relief of that pauperism.

Any plan of union rating, tending thus to stereotype inequalities of burden, existing at the moment of adopting the new proposal, and to make future proportions of charge between different parishes depend on averages of the amount of their past or present burdens, seems to be wholly inadmissible. Twenty years, under such an arrangement, would suffice, in districts where changes of population are rapid, to produce a result of great inequality and oppression. A whole parish, with a poor-rate commuted at one-fifteenth part of the amount now paid by the rest of the union, might, by change of circumstances, contain property, equal in rateable value to half that of the whole union, and might contain much more than half the pauperism of the whole union, yet it would still contribute, according to the plan proposed, only one-fifteenth part towards the maintenance of the pauperism which it had itself mainly created.

Of all the various projects which have been put forward for a new distribution of the burden of pauperism, the most violent and revolutionary is that which would ignore or repudiate the traditions and obligations of centuries, and would

* Fifth Report from the Select Committee on Settlement and Poor Removal, 1847, p. 56. Question 3433.

provide for the poor out of the consolidated fund alone. Such spoliation of the industrial classes, who mainly pay the general taxation of the country, accompanied by such a withdrawal from the poor of their right and guarantee of subsistence, now secured on the whole rental of the landowner, is not likely ever to be adopted, or generally approved, in England. It has been well said of Religion and Charity, that, in this country, they have the guarantee of landed property, and are its safeguards in return. "All those who value genuine piety, the pure offspring of our Established Church, and who, unprejudiced by the abuse of the poor laws, still venerate their humane origin, and appreciate their utility when cautiously administered, all these (and they form the best part of our community) will strenuously resist any change of security, or transfer of the charge from land to funds. The clergy and the landowners, the poor and the proprietors, are coparceners in the soil; they must stand or fall together on their existing tenure."*

It seems unnecessary to add anything further to the observation already made on this iniquitous and insensate scheme. Its gigantic injustice is only equalled by its stupendous folly.†

Another plan is that of a national rate on real property, which would, in the main, keep the burden on the same shoulders as have heretofore borne it; but, by centralising the whole administration, would strike a fatal blow at the principle and practice of local government, would necessarily remove local safeguards, would destroy local interest in the administration of the funds raised for relieving the poor, and would tend greatly and rapidly to increase the general burden of pauperism.

Two of the answers of Sir John M'Neill, the judicious chairman of the Board of Supervision for Relief of the

* Sir James Graham, *Corn and Currency*, p. 16.

† See above, p. 135., note * Some of the immediate consequences which would necessarily follow from the adoption of such a plan, are well pointed out by Mr. Cornewall Lewis, in his evidence before the Select Committee of the Lords on Parochial Assessments, 1850, Answer to Question 2357.

Poor in Scotland, given before the Lords' Committee on Parochial Assessments, in 1850, suggest the chief objections to any such national rate. "It must be borne in mind that a poor-rate is, in its nature, unlimited; it is limited only by the necessities and rights of the parties who are to be relieved; you, therefore, would propose to raise from one portion of the community an unlimited amount of money, to be paid to another portion of the community by parties who have no sufficient immediate interest in keeping down the expenditure. As an instance of the laxity which is produced by a national fund of that description, I think it is sufficient to look to the readiness with which people, for local purposes, seek for funds from the revenue of the country. We all contribute to the revenue of the country; but we contribute in so small a proportion to the whole fund, that wherever a fund is wanted for local purposes, every body is ready to increase the general taxation of the country, if he can get a considerable sum for his local purposes.—It is certainly consistent with my experience, that if the public money can be got for local purposes, no one is deterred from seeking it, because it may increase the general taxation of the country. In the same way, in respect to the poor fund, if it is to be a general fund for the whole country, each parish, at the risk of increasing the general taxation for the poor, will endeavour to get as much for itself as it can, and you will, therefore, have a competition in extravagance, as I believe, instead of a competition in economy." * Again; the same witness, in answering the question, whether his conclusion was, that "the only practical safety in the administration of the poor law is in establishing a narrow and close connexion between the taxation necessary to raise the pecuniary means, and the application of those pecuniary means, in each case?" justly said, "I think that a very close connexion must be established, in order to be safe; but I would guard myself against pretending to define what the best limit is; because, while on the one hand you require to

* Report of the Select Committee of the House of Lords, appointed to consider the Laws relating to Parochial Assessments, Session 1850; answer to Question 2693.

preserve that close connexion with the man's own personal interest who administers the poor funds, on the other hand, you must so extend your area of taxation, as not to throw an undue burden upon parts of the community which are incapable of bearing it."

The present mode of collection of poor-rate in England, the application of the fund on the spot where it is raised, and by those who have contributed to raise it, has unquestionably prevented the occurrence of far greater evils than any which have, as yet, been felt under the poor laws. Great as are the evils of the existing law, it would nevertheless, be better to bear them, than to fly to others, the extent of which cannot be measured, or even estimated. Had a national fund been provided for relieving the poor in 1795, when the allowance system was first introduced, it is pretty plain that the institution of National Workhouses, or *Ateliers Nationaux*, as our neighbours recently called analogous establishments, would, in a few years, have swallowed up much of the accumulated capital of the country. The wealth of England would have been unequal to feed such a ravenous *communism*, increasing daily by what it fed on.

It will appear, in the next chapter, that a rational remedy for many of the existing evils of our pauperism may be found, without abandoning the principle of local government, and without plunging into any such unfathomed abyss as that of a national charge.

The next project is a general property tax, specially appropriated to the relief of the poor. The liability, in strict law, of inhabitants of a parish, to be included in the poor-rate, under the statute of Elizabeth, in respect of visible and personal property locally found in the parish*, has been the pretext on

* The Court of King's Bench decided, in the latter part of the 18th century, when Lord Kenyon was chief justice, that "stock in trade, if it be the property of the person in possession, and productive, is rateable to the poor." (Rex *v.* Darlington, *Term Reports*, vol vi. p. 468.) In cases which occurred previously, Lord Mansfield had strongly leant against holding personal property to be within the statute of Elizabeth. (Rex *v.* Ringwood, *Cowper's Reports*, p. 326.) But the ordinary practice continued unaltered; and, as a general rule, personal property has not been rated, even in the cases in which it was declared to be

which this most unwise and unjust proposal for so violent a change in the distribution of the burden of maintaining the poor has been rested. Such a proposal would transfer the burden of pauperism to the State, but would raise the requisite funds by a general tax on income, derived from personal as well as real property. This plan is wholly inadmissible, on the same grounds as render inadmissible any other general state provision. Such a change would also be open to objection on the score of injustice, in suddenly removing, or reducing by half, one of the direct taxes to which real property is liable, and which, in substance, real property alone has paid in this country. It would also be open to some of the objections which are found to exist in Scotland, against any assessment on "means and substance." Such assessment, when resorted to, usually produces either gross injustice or gross fraud.*

The Earl of Malmesbury has proposed a plan for substituting, instead of all parochial rates for relief of the poor, a special tax, to be assessed and levied as an income tax. This proposal has been expounded by its author, before a Committee of the House of Lords. Its adoption would undoubtedly

rateable. The whole extent of this rateability is, that "personal property, if *visible* and *profitable*, is rateable." (Regina *v.* Lumsdaine, *Adolphus & Ellis's Reports*, vol. x. p. 157.) Ever since the year 1840, the strict right to tax visible personal property has been suspended by temporary statutes, which have been highly beneficial, by relieving overseers from a duty which, in the existing condition of society, it is absolutely impossible for them to perform.

* Sir John M'Neill (Minutes of Evidence before the Lords Committee on Parochial Assessments, 1850, p. 367.; Answer to Question 2660.) says, "From the year 1845-6, when the Board of Supervision made its first report, till the 29th of June, 1850, there has been an increase in the number of parishes assessed of 198; of those 198, 193 have resolved to assess upon rental, and five upon means and substance." The few new instances of adopting the assessment on means and substance seem to have arisen from a desire of ratepayers "to catch some one wealthy individual in the parish." In one case, "a person who considered himself as improperly assailed in this way, successfully resisted it by an arrangement of his property with his family, which put it out of the power of the parish to touch it." In the city of Glasgow it has recently been thought fit to abandon all attempts to rate on means and substance, and to recur to the better principle of rating on rental of real estate. In the attempt to rate on means and substance it was found, that the amount to be paid by each individual became a matter of mere arrangement between him and the parochial board. (Sir John M'Neill, ibid., Answer to Question 2664.)

have the effect of relieving the landowner from about three-fourths of his present burden; and a great part of the burden so removed from accumulated capital, would be placed on productive labour. The noble lord frankly avows, that he means his proposed income tax, under the name of poor tax, to affect all incomes, "down to the smallest."* Any skilled labourer earning from three to four pounds a week (and there are many such in manufacturing and commercial districts), would therefore be liable to pay, like any landowner with ten thousand a-year, both under Sir Robert Peel's general income tax, and under Lord Malmesbury's special income tax. But, under the measure now proposed for adoption, the labourer who earned only 10*s.* or 12*s.* weekly, although exempt from the general income tax, would, even the day before, or the day after his own chargeability to his parish, be liable to pay this additional impost on the wages of his labour, in order to exempt landowners from a part of the burden of poor-rate, which, in an "ignorant impatience of taxation," some of them are anxious to place on any shoulders other than their own.

His Lordship adds,—what he calls "the most important of all,"—that he fixes a maximum! "Therefore there is not the danger which a national tax would have connected with it, of people having an uncertain sum to pay: if you look the thing in the face, you know the worst at once; you know that for ten or twenty years, or whatever term you please to fix, this national tax, called the poor tax, cannot be levied beyond the amount of 5,300,000*l.*, but that it may be less than that, if the country increases in prosperity, and the parishes are well managed."†

As the only argument or commentary called for by this project, which is open to at least every objection urged against the adoption of a general property or income tax, I refer to the ancient story of King Canute, and his command to the waves of the sea, not to advance beyond the line which he had drawn.

* Report of the Lords' Committee on the Laws relating to Parochial Assessments; Minutes of Evidence, Questions 2419 and 2420, and Answers.

† Ibid. p. 332.; answer to Question 2417.

Among the different classes of society which are interested in the just repartition of the burden of local taxes, the beneficed clergy stand in a very prominent rank. Any inequality in the incidence of that burden on tithe commutation rent charge, as compared with other real estate, must press with great force on the owners of so large an amount of that valuable kind of property. Greatly indeed, is it to be regretted, that excess of zeal, and lack of discretion, should have been displayed by some of the most respectable witnesses, but most injudicious advocates, who have given testimony and argued, in behalf of the inferior clergy in this matter. The justice of the complaint made by the clergy respecting the mode of assessment to parochial rates, now very generally prevalent in parishes, seems however, notwithstanding what has been said by their advocates, to be unquestionable.

So long as it shall be the interest of those who make rates to have the total valuation for poor-rate in each parish lower than its true amount, so long will the clergy suffer as they now do, and pay more than their fair share of such rates. The annual value of real property, as assessed for different purposes, in 1847, in thirteen parishes of the county of Bedford, appears to have been as follows*:—

Annual Value of Property in Thirteen Parishes of Bedfordshire, assessed in 1847 to			Expended in the same Thirteen Parishes, in Relief of the Poor.
Property Tax.	County Rate.	Poor Rate.	
£ 92,522	£ 77,530	£ 69,933	£ 6,547

The total amount of tithe commutation rent charge included in these several assessments was 4979*l.* 0*s.* 4¾*d.* Now, this rent charge will appear at its full amount in the lowest of the three assessments; its value is always known: and, looking at the difference in the above assessments in these thirteen parishes, it may safely be assumed that the occupiers are generally rated to poor-rate at a sum about 25 per cent below

* For the details, see Appendix.

the real rateable value of their holdings; in other words, the clergyman pays on the full value of his rent charge, and the landowner, by his tenants, pays on only three-fourths of the value of his farm.

The obvious remedy for this manifest inequality and injustice is a better mode of rating. The insufficiency of the Parochial Assessments Act to effect its object has long been notorious. One single valuation ought to be used for all local and other rates. It is preposterous and absurd to incur the expense and trouble of having *separate valuations* for poor-rate, highway-rate, property tax assessment, and so many other rates and assessments, all imposed mainly on the same property, and all easy to levy on the basis of one single valuation, and to collect by the hand of one single collector.

Instead of advocating so simple a reform, giving complete redress to the clergy, for a real grievance of which they most justly complain, their right reverend and reverend representatives have contended for an impracticable rating of personal property, or an unfounded exemption of the clergy in respect of the value of their spiritual ministrations.

A venerable archdeacon has even expressed the opinion, that, "if you go back to the original endowment, you should likewise go back, if it were possible, to the mind of the person who so endowed the benefice. Had he at all conceived that, in five or six centuries, all these new burdens would have been laid upon his endowment, the endowment would, in all probability, have been increased by him in consideration of them."* It may, perhaps, be owned, that the obligation of the statute of Elizabeth is a "new burden" as to property in lay hands; but a little consideration of the history of tithes, and of the ancient duty of the clergy to maintain and relieve the poor, shows that those who gave tithes to the church would not have been likely to increase their donations, had they known that an average payment of about 1*s.* 7*d.* in the 1*l.* yearly would be the whole contribution legally ex-

* Report of the Select Committee of the House of Lords on the Laws relating to Parochial Assessments, 1850, p. 277.; answer to Question 2075.

pected, in 1852, from the inferior clergy, towards the relief of their poor parishioners.

The title of the clergyman to his rent charge is now precisely the same as that of any layman to the same kind of property*, or of any landowner to his ordinary rent; and it is to be regretted that a claim to exemption, destitute of all legal foundation, should be thus put forward, tending, as it does, to obstruct a practicable reform, and to perpetuate injustice, under which the clergy themselves suffer.

Reference has already been made to the establishment or union charges, which, in terms first created by the Poor Law Amendment Act of 1834, have since been largely extended. They now include, among other things, the whole expenditure in respect of many of the poor, such, for instance, as are irremoveable from any parish by reason of the statute 9 & 10 Vict. c. 66.†

Two years ago a proposal was made by Mr. D'Israeli, "that from the 25th March, 1850, the establishment charges for the relief of the poor should be defrayed out of the general revenue of the State:" and it was added, "No one can attempt to contend, that the burden of the establishment charges have been inherited or acquired with the estates which the owners of land now hold. The time at which those charges were

* Lay lords appear to have obtained possession of tithes and other ecclesiastical property at an early period. Such holdings were very common in the 11th and 12th centuries, and restrictions were placed on the transfer of such property from laymen to the church. The exchequer of Normandy, in the year 1210, decided, that the tithes of a knight's fee, when so in the hands of a layman, might be given in alms, that is, bestowed on the church, (for the terms were in those days synonymous,) provided they did not exceed the third part of the whole inheritance. Brussel (*Usage général des Fiefs*, tom. ii. p. 839.), "Decimæ de fœdo loricæ possunt *eleemosynari*, si non excedant tertiam partem illius hereditatis." See also Marnier, *Établissements et Coutumes, Assises et Arrêts de l'Échiquier de Normandie au treizième siècle.* A constitution of Saint Louis (A. D. 1269) gave complete authority to the lay holders of tithes to convey them to the church, without any consent of the king. (Brussel, l. c. p. 841.)

† Above, p. 278. An obscurely worded clause of the statute 11 & 12 Vict. c. 103. s. 5. (interpreted by Regina *v.* Wigton, *New Sessions Cases*, vol. iv. p. 476.), has added the cost of maintenance of a considerable class of lunatic paupers to the previous items of establishment charges.

created is not so much within the memory of the oldest inhabitant of this house, as rather of the youngest."*

It may properly be observed, that many of the charges alluded to are, in reality, as old as the poor law, and have always been a parochial burden. Their name of establishment or union charges merely indicates that they are apportioned among the different parishes of each union, according to the rule prescribed by statute, and already adverted to.† The proposer of this scheme stated, in moving its adoption, "it is perfectly well known that these charges are not necessarily connected with local administration, and virtually are almost entirely independent of it. Such a change would have no bearing whatever upon our admirable system of self-government;—that system would remain intact, its machinery unaltered, its chain of checks and control as before."‡

* Mr. D'Israeli, on his motion in the House of Commons for a Committee to take into its consideration such revision of the poor laws as might mitigate the distress of the agricultural classes, made on 19th February, 1850. (Hansard, Third Series, vol. cviii. p. 1041.) The honourable member thought fit, on this motion, to speak as follows of Lord John Russell and the house of Bedford. "Neither is it true with respect to very considerable portions of the land of England (that it was inherited or enjoyed subject to poor-rates). I cannot forget," proceeded Mr. D'Israeli, with curious infelicity, "that I am standing opposite the noble Lord, the son of one of our greatest houses, a house which I am willing to admit has exercised its vast possessions for the honour and dignity of England—which certainly did not inherit or otherwise acquire those vast possessions, subject to the provisions of the 43rd of Elizabeth. As a matter of fact, therefore, the assertion is not true." No doubt the house of Bedford possesses extensive domains, which, until the dissolution of the monasteries by Henry VIII., were the property of the Church, but were, on that very account, as has been seen above, especially subjected to the burden of maintaining the poor. They were not, it is true, acquired subject to the provisions of the statute of 43rd of Elizabeth; but it is equally true that the old Church lands are the only lands in England, of which it can be said, that they have always been liable to the burden of maintaining the poor, latterly under the statutory provisions which the Reformation introduced, formerly under the not less binding obligation which the Church acknowledged. But on a serious parliamentary discussion, in the middle of the nineteenth century, as to the desirableness of a change in the incidence of poor-rate, it can hardly be worth while to consider the burdens of land, in respect of maintaining the poor, prior to the statute of Elizabeth. If a usage of 250 years cannot give a title or create an obligation, it would be difficult to say what can.

† 4 & 5 Will. 4. c. 76. s. 28., and above, p. 278.

‡ Hansard, Third Series, vol. cviii. p. 1040.

That these ideas are utterly unfounded, is apparent to every one who knows what is the meaning of the words "establishment charges." One of such charges being the relief bestowed on all persons exempt from removal, under the statute 9 & 10 Vict. c. 66., it follows that a necessary and immediate consequence of throwing the establishment charges on the State would be to separate, from the general pauperism of every parish, a class of poor to be provided for by the State alone.

A condition of things would thus be produced unlike anything known in any other country of Europe, but closely resembling what has long prevailed in one of the states of the North American Union. In Massachusetts, the whole of such relief as is given by overseers of parishes to casual and non-settled poor, has long been a national burden.

Destitution, even in a young country, seems to "grow by what it feeds on," when fed by the State; and Massachusetts, which has been so unwise as to make this state provision for part of its poor, suffers more from pauperism than any other state in the Union.* In the year 1820, the amount so expended in Massachusetts was five times as great as it had been in 1793, only twenty-seven years before. Legislation has been had recourse to on various occasions (in 1798, 1821, 1823, and 1830), to ensure a very strict administration of this relief. Nevertheless, the expense of relieving the state poor in Massachusetts attained to nearly an equal amount with the whole expense of relieving the settled poor of the country; and at length commissioners were appointed to report to the House of Representatives on the pauper system of the state. Their Report is printed in the Appen-

* Foreign Communications, APPENDIX F. to the Report of the Commissioners for Inquiring into the Poor Laws, 1834; Paper No. 6. p. 57. F. By a Report of the Secretary of State of New York, Feb. 9. 1824, it appeared that in several States of the Union, the number of paupers, in proportion to the population, was as follows:—

New York	1 in 220
Massachusetts	1 in 68
Connecticut	1 in 150
New Hampshire	1 in 100
Delaware	1 in 227

dix of Foreign Communications, subjoined to the "Report of the Commissioners for Inquiry into the Administration of the Poor Laws," published in 1834.

The commissioners advert to the proportion which the State's poor had borne to the parish, or town's poor, as in itself "a fact of startling interest." A passage in the Report of these commissioners shows some of the results of such a State provision in Massachusetts. "It is not to be doubted that a large proportion of this excess of the State's poor more or less assisted during the year, consists of those who are called in the statements herewith presented, 'wandering or travelling poor.' The single fact of the existence among us of this class of fellow-beings, especially considered in connexion with the facts that *nearly all of them are State's poor, and that, to a great extent, they have been made what they are by the State's provision for them,* brings the subject before us in a bearing in which we scarcely know whether the call is loudest to the pity we should feel for them, or the *self-reproach with which we should recur to the measures we have sanctioned,* and which have alike enlarged their numbers and their misery."

It may fairly be inferred, that, if the establishment charges of unions, as now existing, were transferred to the State, a great temptation would be held out to all local authorities to increase those charges: they probably would soon exceed, in amount, all other expenditure for relief of the poor: would become an intolerable burden to the tax-payer: and, at the same time, a source of demoralisation and degradation to the whole class of receivers of such relief.

Descending from plan to plan, for altering the incidence or the whole or part of the burden of pauperism, we now come to the smallest, and the last, which has been put forward.

Sir Charles Wood, Chancellor of the Exchequer, when, in his great struggle of 1851, "magnas inter opes inops," he had to deal with a surplus revenue, which nearly overwhelmed him, at first proposed to disturb the local taxation of the country, by applying towards the maintenance of lunatic paupers the modest sum of 150,000*l.* raised by the general taxation of the country.* The project was received with disapproval, and even derision, and withdrawn. Anything more illusory, as relief to agricultural distress, could not have been imagined; yet, illusory as it was for all practical good, it involved, in principle, the whole of that disregard of prescriptive obligation, and of local government, which has been discussed and denounced in the earlier pages of this chapter.

The only ground on which it appears to have been suggested that the State ought to relieve parishes of part of the burden of maintaining their insane poor, was that no act of the parochial authorities could prevent persons so afflicted from becoming chargeable.† The same argument might be put forward in favour of the State's undertaking to pay most other heads of parochial outlay. It is not easy to see how the prudence of overseers can prevent any of the direct causes of pauperism; and it is impossible to draw any such distinction between one sort of disease and another as would justify the providing for the one by the State, and leaving the other a burden on the parish.‡

The working classes generally are especially liable to bodily injuries, and men are frequently disabled from maintaining themselves and their families by such causes. Whether the disability be produced by accident, by insanity, or by any other form of disease, the burden of providing for it should manifestly fall on the same shoulders. A difference in the nature of disease cannot possibly be a ground for difference in the incidence of the burden of providing relief.§

* Hansard, Third Series, vol. cxiv. p. 734.

† Sir Charles Wood, ib. p. 734. "It is a reason for taking some portion of this charge, that no foresight, no sacrifice, no care, on the part of the ratepayers, can prevent the charge from being thrown on the parish."

‡ Sir John M'Neill, on 2nd July, 1850, before the Lords' Committee on Parochial Assessments, says (Answer to Questions 2747, 2749.), "I do not know that the disability produced by that form of disease (lunacy) is not as reasonable a ground of charge as the disability produced by any other." "A person disabled, by whatever cause, whether by fever, lunacy, accident, age, or infirmity of any kind, becomes entitled to relief. I do not know on what ground of justice I can exclude a man disabled by lunacy from the right to parochial relief, any more than a man disabled from any other cause."

§ While predial slavery existed, and while, on many farms, all the labourers

The insanity prevalent among the labouring population of the agricultural districts, as we have already seen, is one of the many remarkable features of our present social condition. The land ought surely to maintain, under every form of disease and disability to work, the labourer whose industry has been devoted to making such land productive.

were serfs or slaves, the landlords did not repudiate, or seek to place elsewhere than on the land, the obligation of providing not only ordinary sustenance, but necessary medical care, in cases of sickness and accident, for the labourers whom they employed, and who have always constituted, in every form of agricultural industry hitherto prevalent, a necessary and most important part of the farming stock, the *instrumentum fundi.* M. Varro (*De Re rusticâ*, i. 17. 1.) states that, by some, farming stock was divided into three parts: "Alii in tres partes, instrumenti genus vocale, et semivocale, et mutum. *Vocale* in quo sunt *servi: semivocale* in quo sunt *boves: mutum* in quo sunt *plaustra.*" Columella (*De Re rusticâ*, xi. 1. 18.): "Agat cujusque maximam curam (villicus): sive quis, quod accidit plerumque, *sauciatus in opere* noxam ceperit, adhibeat fomenta: sive aliter languidior est, in valitudinarium confestim deducat, et convenientem ei cæteram curationem adhiberi jubeat. Eorum vero, qui recte valebunt, non minor habenda erit ratio, ut cibus et potio sine fraude a cellariis præbeatur."

CHAP. XIX.

THE AUTHOR'S PROPOSAL.

L'homme propose, et Dieu dispose.
FRENCH PROVERB.

MY proposal is, that the law of settlement be wholly repealed; that the various provisions for raising and administering relief to the poor be consolidated into one statute; that the yearly sum needed for such relief continue to be raised by parochial rates on real property; that two-thirds of this sum be raised by a pound-rate, equal throughout the whole country; and the remainder by a further pound-rate, raising in every parish a sum equal to one-third of the actual expenditure of such parish.

If the whole net rental of real property in England, when correctly estimated, should amount to 120,000,000*l.* yearly (and it certainly does amount to some such sum), it follows that a year's relief of the poor, taken at the extravagantly high amount of 6,000,000*l.*, will be raised by a pound-rate of 1*s.* on such rental. Of this 1*s.*, every parish, by the proposed plan, would equally contribute 8*d.* in the 1*l.* on its net rental. Thus, by an equal charge of a moderate amount, two-thirds of the whole sum needed, or 4,000,000*l.*, would be raised. The remaining 2,000,000*l.* would be contributed by property in different parishes, in exact proportion to the pauperism found in each parish.

If further detail of the machinery required to carry out the proposal, be needed, I add that the Poor Law Board, on or before the 1st March in each year, should define the general pound-rate for the ensuing year, commencing on 26th March; and the estimate, by each parish, of its own expenditure during such ensuing year, should be made at Easter, by the parishioners in vestry, when nominating their parish officers. The general estimate of the Poor Law Board, and the local estimate of each parish, should be embodied in one rate for the whole year, and such rate should be payable by quarterly instalments. A power should be reserved to the inhabitants to meet in vestry, and lay a supplemental rate, if the local estimate should be exceeded, and further parochial funds required.

The parishes of every union might pay to the union treasurer, or receive from him, the excess or deficiency of the sum thus raised, in each parish, above or below its own actual expenditure; and the balance, due to or from each union treasurer, might be paid through the medium of a clearing house, for the adjustment of accounts between different unions.*

It will be convenient to point out a few instances of the practical working of the proposed plan, and of the effect likely to be produced, by its adoption, on the amount and distribution of parochial burdens.

Kensington now raises, for relief of the poor, a rate of $8\frac{1}{4}d.$ in the pound on the parish rental.† Under the suggested change, it would have to raise, first, the amount of general rate, say 8*d.*, and next, the third of its own disbursement, or $2\frac{3}{4}d.$, making a total of $10\frac{3}{4}d.$ in the pound on its rental. The adjoining parish of Chelsea now raises 2*s.* 7*d.* in the pound on its rental ‡; it would have to raise its average proportion of 8*d.*, and the third of its own actual expenditure, or $10\frac{1}{3}d.$, making a total of 1*s.* $6\frac{1}{3}d.$ St. Christopher le Stock now pays nothing §; it would have to pay 8*d.* St. Mildred, Bread Street, now pays 8*s.* ‖; it would have to pay 8*d.* + 2*s.* 8*d.* = 3*s.* 4*d.*

Every parish which now pays above the average of all England, must still pay more than that average, although its burden would be lightened; and every parish which now

* Such clearing house might well be established in the office of the Poor Law Board, and probably this might be done without making any addition to the staff of secretaries and clerks now employed.

† Above, p. 39. ‡ Above, p. 39.

§ Above, p. 40. ‖ Above, p. 40

pays less than the average of what is paid throughout the country, must continue to pay less than such average, although a small new burden would be laid on broad and powerful shoulders, well able to bear it.

By the proposed plan, we should recur to, and carry out, the very principle which was sanctioned at the time of the Reformation. According to one of the earliest statutes then passed, any surplus funds, in rich parishes, were to be distributed in relieving poor parishes of their burden*; and under the statute of Elizabeth, the provision for laying a rate in aid, little as that provision has been practically used, shows strongly, that although it was intended to ensure the strictly parochial administration of relief to the poor, it was not intended equally to limit the mode of raising the funds to be distributed in such relief.†

The precedent afforded by the legislation of 1846, and by a resolution of the Select Committee of the House of Lords, appointed, in 1850, to consider the laws relating to parochial assessments, appears to go much further than is required to sanction all that I propose. The principle of the statute referred to, has already been pointed out‡, and the Select Committee of the House of Lords resolved, wisely and justly, as it seems to me, that places which have heretofore enjoyed absolute immunity from relieving indigence, ought to be suddenly subjected to the full weight of that local burden.§

* Above, p. 204.

† 43 Eliz. c. 2. s. 3. enacted, "That if the said justices of peace do perceive that the inhabitants of any parish are not able to levy among themselves sufficient sums of money for the purposes aforesaid, that then the said two justices shall and may tax, rate, and assess as aforesaid, any other of other parishes, or out of any parish within the hundred where the said parish is, to pay such sum and sums of money to the churchwardens and overseers of the said poor parish, for the said purposes as the said justices shall think fit;" and in case of inability of the hundred, the justices "shall rate and assess as aforesaid any other of other parishes, or out of any parish within the said county for the purposes aforesaid, as in their discretion shall seem fit."

‡ Above, p. 277.

§ The Committee agreed to the resolution, "That it is expedient in every extra-parochial place, to require the appointment of an overseer of the poor, and to facilitate the annexation of such places to an adjoining parish, by the Poor Law Commissioners, on petition of the owners of property of three-fourths in value in each parish."

They resolved, further, with like wisdom and justice, that whole masses of real estate, not included in the statute of Elizabeth, and enjoying till now absolute exemption from liability to be rated, ought to contribute towards the relief of the poor.* They propose to rate all mines below the surface of the earth; they no longer exempt from a common burden, any sacred Precinct, or College, or Temple, in which, till now, overseers and poor-rates have been equally unknown; and thus, in effect, a Committee of Lords Spiritual and Temporal, solemnly resolve that it is necessary now to correct, by legislation, the inequalities and injustice which omission of the legislature, two hundred and fifty years ago, whether accidental or wilful, has produced, and which has received the confirmation of a uniform observance during the whole of that period.

The proposal which I have ventured to put forward, will involve a smaller disturbance of existing rights than these resolutions of the Lords' Committee would alone, in many cases, produce, and infinitely less than has been produced in numberless instances by the statute of 1846.

A little consideration of the existing distribution of the burden of poor rate, will show that no great or oppressive change in its incidence would accompany or follow the adoption of the plan proposed.

It is now found that there are, on the one hand, 1650

* The Committee agreed to the resolution, "That it is expedient that all mines should be assessed as coal mines are now assessed, inasmuch as the exemption from rates of mineral mines is founded on no sound principle, and depends on the form of agreement made between landlord and tenant." The Court of Exchequer Chamber had held, in the case of Crease *v.* Sawle (*Queen's Bench Reports*, vol. ii. pp. 862. 886.), that as, according to previous decisions, the occupier of every mine, except coal mines, is exempt from poor-rate under the statute 43 Eliz. c. 2., so "he who receives a portion of the ore, in an unmanufactured state, is liable to be rated." The Court, resting their judgment entirely on the previous decisions, intimate that the statute of Elizabeth was in truth framed "with a view to render rateable all occupiers of every description of real estate; and it might be very questionable whether occupiers of mines of any description were exempt." They, however, "abstain from the discussion of such questions, and abide by the construction which numerous decisions have given to the words of the statute, and which has been for a long time acted on."

parishes which pay less than sixpence in the pound for relief of the poor, and 440 which pay more than four shillings.*

As a specimen of existing anomalies, which my proposal would satisfactorily remove, I subjoin a table containing forty parishes, in rural districts of Dorset, Norfolk, Sussex, and Wilts, twenty of which parishes expend yearly in relieving their poor, the sum of 79*l.* only, or $1\frac{1}{4}$*d.* in the pound on their rental; and the other twenty expend yearly, for the like purpose, 12,408*l.*, or 6*s.* $2\frac{1}{2}$*d.* in the pound on their rental. The burden of pauperism, in the latter parishes, is, therefore, about sixty times as heavy as in the former!

It is to be noticed, that parishes in which poor-rates are either extremely high, or extremely low, are, for the most part, small parishes. Those in which the rate is less than 6*d.* in the pound, will probably not average 1500*l.* rental, in each parish throughout all England.† It follows, therefore, that the great relief which my proposal will give to the most heavily burdened parishes, will scarcely be appreciable as an increase of the general burden of poor-rate throughout the country. Looking at the whole number of parishes in England and Wales, the substance of the burden to be re-distributed, will be found in parishes now assessed at from 6*d.* to 2*s.* 6*d.* in the pound. Upwards of 3000 such parishes, now assessed at less than 1*s.* in the pound, would have to bear a small increase of burden; and upwards of 3000 now assessed at more than 1*s.* 6*d.* in the pound, would experience a corresponding alleviation.

Such is the outline of the principal change in the distribution of burden among ratepayers.

That the simple repeal of the law of settlement would ensure a large and permanent benefit to the agricultural interest, is unquestionable. This interest would probably

* Parliamentary Paper, No. 735, Commons, Session of 1848, and Mr. Hutchinson's Table, Minutes of Evidence before the Lords' Committee on Parochial Assessments, 1850, pp. 168, 169.

† This will appear by a table in the Appendix, p. 401., of all the parishes in one county, Wilts, in each of which the year's expenditure for relief of the poor in 1847, was less than 6*d.* in the pound on the rental.

acquiesce in such repeal unaccompanied by any provision for re-distributing the burden of relief, and would be willing to leave that burden solely on the parish, where the necessity of giving relief might arise.

But, if the law of settlement should be wholly repealed, without any modification being introduced into the mode of raising funds for the relief of destitution, it can hardly be doubted that the labouring population would be exposed, especially in and near all close parishes, to hardships and oppression, exceeding even what they have already experienced; and would be driven, still more than they have already been, to reside out of the parishes in which their labour is required. A higher premium than ever would be given to indiscriminate and remorseless clearances; and we should have the pain of witnessing, in England, scenes of misery and suffering similar to those which have disgraced the modern history of other parts of the empire.*

It seems, moreover, to be almost universally admitted, both in agricultural districts and elsewhere, that if the law of settlement itself be repealed, the incidence of the burden of

* Dr. Sutherland, at p. 74. of his Report on Cholera in Glasgow (Appendix A. to the Report to the General Board of Health on the Epidemic Cholera of 1848 and 1849), describes the effects on our town population of such clearances: "Every cabin that is razed to the ground sends one or more families to find house room in the cities of England and Scotland, and of this element of disease Glasgow obtains its full share. A great proportion of these poor people are young men and women in the prime of life. They come from the fresh country air, and a diet just sufficient to support health in it, to inhabit for a time those wretched dens of misery, disease, and death, the low lodging-houses. It is only, however, for a time; for a diet still further reduced, and a pestilential atmosphere do the rest. The young and healthy soon become the prey of epidemic disease, and their deaths go to swell the catalogue of those who have been prematurely cut off by typhus. Others again, driven by sheer necessity and the vile examples they meet with, find their way to the prison and the convict ship; and not a few young women, virtuously brought up in their native parishes in the Highlands, or in Ireland, are seduced, ruined, abandoned to prostitution and an early grave. Such are the notorious results of the social system at present in operation in Glasgow and other large cities. The overcrowding and wretchedness of late years has brought typhus with it, a disease that not long ago was as rare in the large cities of Scotland as the ague is now; and wherever typhus has prevailed, there cholera now prevails, or has done so recently."

poor-rate must be altered. Resolutions of Boards of Guardians, unanimously entered into in favour of that repeal, have usually been accompanied by suggestions as to the future mode of raising the funds needed for the relief of the poor.* The different boards all agree as to the necessity of repealing the existing law, but differ widely as to what system should be adopted in its stead. Everybody, desirous to escape from a present incubus, exclaims, like Macbeth, —

> Take any shape but that, and my firm nerves
> Shall never tremble !

The proposed plan, it is submitted, will sufficiently remove the great inequality in the parochial burden of pauperism which now exists, and will effectuate as close an approach towards an equal repartition of the whole of that burden, as can with justice and safety be sanctioned.

It will be seen by every one, that the adoption of this plan will leave unimpaired the existing duties and offices of all local functionaries, such as guardians, overseers, assistant overseers, and relieving officers. The duties of assistant overseer, in hunting out evidence for obtaining orders of removal, or for supporting them when appealed against, and in removing paupers under such orders, are the only duties of parish officers which it is proposed to abrogate.

Some persons, and especially inhabitants of great cities, suppose that on the repeal of the law of settlement, a vast number of poor will commence a course of peregrination up and down the country, lodging at the public expense in union poor-houses, and staying a longer or shorter time in any such house, according as they like their quarters. Doubtless when the barriers of parochial settlement are once removed, the free circulation of labour throughout the country will be greatly increased; and some addition may possibly be made to the number of persons entitled to relief as "casual poor," who will be strangers in the places where they apply to the relieving officers: but there is no rational ground for supposing that mere vagrancy will be increased by such a change in the law.

* Above, pp. 313, 314.

Of the whole number of honest wayfarers who would be called into existence by the repeal of the law of settlement, the great majority would be chargeable to the parish of their fixed residence, if they remained at home. If, at the very time when, in endeavouring to better their condition by seeking for work elsewhere than in the place of their proper domicile, they should occasionally, when on their journey, have to ask for shelter in a union house, it is not easy to see any great harm in their doing so. Such freedom as a repeal of the law of settlement will confer, is eminently desirable for the interests of the labouring population, and of the whole community. The accidental necessities by which the exercise of this new freedom may now and then be attended, are only an instance of what we see every day, that few, if any, of the arrangements of society are quite perfect; and the probability that such necessities will occur, does not form a rational objection to the proposed change. Even if a great increase of real vagrancy should be the immediate result of such change, the experience of 1848, already adverted to, shows that the present vagrant law is sufficiently stringent to protect society from any such evils. Each union workhouse has only to establish a "vagrant ward," with an appropriate dietary, and to administer a bath to each suspected vagrant, enforcing at the same time a complete change of clothing on the part of their guest, and in other respects following the directions of Mr. Buller's minute of 4th August, 1848*, and there will be no fear of vagrancy overwhelming or injuring them. In 1848, a large proportion of the vagrants who infested England, were natives of Ireland.† The power of removing Scotch and Irish paupers, is felt to be of considerable importance to the interests of English parishes; and such a power might properly be retained after the abolition of removals from one English parish to another.‡

* Above, p. 227.

† The "Irish vagrancy" of 1848, in England, is particularly dwelt on by Captain Robinson, Reports to the Poor Law Board, 1850, p. 86.

‡ Although, in these days, no English parishes will ask for such protection against the ravages of Irish pauperism as was afforded in the year 1572, by the

Union workhouses would, therefore, need no enlargement in their vagrant wards, in consequence of the proposed change. At the same time great alteration is called for in the administration of workhouses; and the moment of so great a change in the law would be most convenient for improving their existing organisation. A moment's consideration of a subject so important to the welfare of a large class of the most helpless members of our community, will not be out of place in this concluding chapter.

During the last ten years, I have visited many prisons and lunatic asylums, not only in England, but in France and Germany. A single English workhouse contains more that justly calls for condemnation in the principle on which it is established, than is found in the very worst prisons or public lunatic asylums that I have seen. The workhouse as now organized, is a reproach and disgrace peculiar to England: nothing corresponding to it is found throughout the whole continent of Europe. In France, the medical patients of our workhouses would be found in "hôpitaux;" the infirm aged poor would be in "hospices;" and the blind, the idiot, the lunatic, the bastard child, and the vagrant, would similarly be placed, each in an appropriate, but separate establishment. With us a common *malebolge* is provided for them all; and, in some parts of the country, the confusion is worse confounded, by the effect of prohibitory orders, which, enforcing the application of the notable workhouse-test, drive into the same common sink of so many kinds of vice and misfortune, the poor man whose only crime is his poverty, and whose want of work alone makes him chargeable.

Each of the buildings which we so absurdly call a workhouse, is, in truth, 1. A general hospital; 2. An almshouse; 3. A foundling house; 4. A lying-in hospital; 5. A school house; 6. A lunatic asylum; 7. An idiot house; 8. A blind

statute of 14 Eliz. c. 5., already referred to, imposing a penalty on the bringing into England of any such "as shall be *likely to live by begging*, being born in Ireland or the Isle of Man" (above, p. 197.), yet, probably, neither Lancashire nor London would feel themselves safe in giving up the power of removing non-settled Irish poor to their native land.

asylum; 9. A deaf and dumb asylum; 10. A workhouse: but this part of the establishment is generally a *lucus a non lucendo,* omitting to find work, even for able-bodied paupers. Such and so various are the destinations of these common receptacles of sin and misfortune, of sorrow and suffering of the most different kinds, each tending to aggravate the others with which it is unnecessarily and injuriously brought into close contact.

It is at once equally shocking to every principle of reason, and every feeling of humanity, that all these varied forms of wretchedness should be thus crowded together into one common abode: that no attempt should be made by law to classify them, and to provide appropriate places for the relief of each. The attempt at classification, in the existing workhouses, can easily be made on parchment or paper, in the form of orders from a Central Board; but practical and efficient classification, can only be effected by the complete separation of the buildings in which relief is to be bestowed on each different class of paupers.

It would be out of place here to describe the abominations which result from the present organisation of our workhouses. They mainly arise from this want of classification. In every union workhouse may be seen great numbers of those, whose age and infirmities render such a house their necessary place of residence till death. Hard by this class of inmates, are lodged pregnant and recently delivered women, in the "lying-in ward," or "lying-in hospital." Another room, "the nursery," contains infants and little children, some of them foundlings, and most of them born in the workhouse. Children under sixteen form another numerous class in the establishment.* A step or two from the lying-in hospital,

* Any one who doubts or is ignorant of the paramount necessity of establishing district schools, already pointed out (above, pp. 22–31.), should make himself personally acquainted with the condition of the existing schools in some large workhouses; where he will find, under one schoolmaster or schoolmistress, from 100 to 200 children, of all ages, from 2 to 16. These children are inmates o the "house" for long and short terms, some staying for years, and others only for a few days, and they are mixed together, without possible classification, in a way highly injurious to the morals and progress of those who remain long in the school.

will bring us to the "fever ward," and a little further on is found the quarter of idiots and lunatics.* But why say more than that the plain and true description by Crabbe, of these "regions of sorrow," is as appropriate in the middle of the nineteenth century, as it was towards the end of the eighteenth?

There children dwell who know no parents' care;
Parents, who know no children's love, dwell there!
Heart-broken matrons on their joyless bed,
Forsaken wives, and mothers never wed;
Dejected widows with unheeded tears,
And crippled age with more than childhood fears;
The lame, the blind, and, far the happiest they!
The moping idiot, and the madman gay.
Here too the sick their final doom receive,
Here brought, amid the scenes of grief, to grieve.†

As to lunatics, nothing can be more objectionable than what I have myself witnessed, in cases of their detention in workhouses; and the present system is as injurious to the interest of the ratepayer, as it is to the welfare of the poor lunatic. The timely application of proper treatment would frequently restore the lunatic to society, and prevent a permanent charge on the poor-rate.‡

* The "lunatic, insane person, or idiot," is not, if "dangerous," to be detained in any workhouse "for any longer period than fourteen days" (4 & 5 Will. IV. c. 76. s. 45.); but if not dangerous, may be detained in a workhouse till released from it by death. The lunatic or idiot is also liable to *removal* to the place of his settlement, and is sometimes so removed by parish officers, instead of being sent to an asylum: Regina *v.* Barnsley (*Queen's Bench Reports*, vol. xii. p. 193.).

† Crabbe, *The Village*, book i.

‡ In a Report of the present Commissioners in Lunacy, made in 1847, after expressing a conviction, in which every one, except the keepers of private asylums, will agree, "that the lunatic poor of England will never be altogether properly provided for, until public asylums for the benefit of every county shall have been erected:" (Further Report of the Commissioners in Lunacy to the Lord Chancellor, 1847, p. 63.) they mention numerous instances of the improper detention in *workhouses* of persons of unsound mind, "whose case is of recent origin, or otherwise presents hope of cure through the timely application of judicious treatment, or who is noisy, violent, and unmanageable, or filthy and disgusting in his habits, and must, therefore, be a nuisance to other inmates." Ib Appendix A. p. 269. The Commissioners state, that in upwards of a hundred instances they procured the removal of such persons to lunatic asylums; and that if they had been able to interfere in all such cases, the instances would have been greatly more numerous. Ib. p. 270.

The great importance of improving our incoherent, ill-digested, and obscure law respecting lunatics, and especially of making such provision as shall prevent the detention of any lunatic in either a prison or workhouse, is unquestionable.*

As an example of one of the obvious reforms of the poor law which may advantageously be effected, I will point out what I think should be done respecting idiots. Their number now confined in lunatic asylums and workhouses, may be taken at not less than 2500.† They should be removed from their present abodes, and lodged in public idiot asylums, four of which would probably be sufficient for the requirements of the whole country. The expense of maintaining each idiot in such establishments need not be more than from 3*s.* 3*d.* to 3*s.* 9*d.* per week; less than half of what, on the average, idiots now cost their parishes, when maintained in county asylums, and scarcely exceeding one-third of the present charge made to parishes by keepers of private licensed houses. A subjoined table shows that a single metropolitan union now maintains, in lunatic asylums, more than one-third of all its idiot paupers; and that the average cost of their maintenance in such asylums, is 9*s.* 3¼*d.* per head, per week.‡

* At least one public asylum ought to be provided for all criminal lunatics, many of whom are highly dangerous, and some of whom are now lodged in county asylums, to the great inconvenience and discomfort of those establishments; while others, "according to the form of the statute, in such case made and provided," are severally detained, "during Her Majesty's pleasure," in common gaols.

† Further Report of the Commissioners in Lunacy to the Lord Chancellor, 1847, Summary at pp. 384, 385. The Reports of the Poor Law Board give only the total of chargeable "lunatics, insane persons, and idiots," distinguishing the males, females, and children, under sixteen; and do not give the number of idiots separately. The Returns of the Poor Law Board on this, as on other heads, are limited to parishes *in union* in England and Wales; hence a difference in the numbers of the limited returns published by the Poor Law Board, and of the more complete returns of the Commissioners in Lunacy, which difference seems recently to have puzzled the learned writer of a paper on the Vital Statistics of Scotland, Dr. Stark: *Journal of the Statistical Society of London*, vol. xiv. pp. 48. 53.

‡ See Appendix, p. 402.

In each of such large establishments for idiots, there must be a great majority of inmates whose health and comfort would be promoted by constant employment, and whose useful labour would make nearly all their own shoes and clothes, and would cultivate, by spade husbandry, extensive grounds, so as to produce a supply of fruit and vegetables abundantly sufficient for the use of the whole establishment. Such an employment, even of lunatics, is now largely effected in the asylum for the North and East Ridings of Yorkshire, at Clifton near York. Productive labour is there found to be equally advantageous in the medical and the pecuniary point of view; and certainly the results obtained, redound greatly to the credit of the medical superintendent, Dr. Hill, under whose vigilant and able care, this most unobjectionable "organisation of labour" is carried out.* In this asylum, the average weekly cost per inmate was reduced, in 1849, to 7*s.* 1¼*d.*, on an average number of only 157 inmates.

The establishment of such idiot asylums as I propose, would immediately produce immense relief to workhouses and lunatic asylums, by the removal of all idiots from them; the idiots removed from workhouses would be greatly benefited by the change; and the daily comfort of all other classes of the poor inmates of workhouses would be much increased by the removal of the idiots.†

Before concluding, a word should be said as to the probable general effect which my proposal for a repeal of the law of

* Report of the Committee of Visitors of the Lunatic Asylum for the North and East Ridings of Yorkshire, presented at the Epiphany Quarter Sessions for the respective Ridings, 1850, p. 11. This asylum is one of the best conducted public establishments that I have ever visited in any country.

† Since the whole of this chapter was written, and while the present sheet is passing through the press, I have had an opportunity of visiting the branch establishment at Highgate, belonging to that excellent institution the Asylum for Idiots, which has houses at Highgate and Colchester, and of seeing Dr. Maxwell, the resident physician at such establishment. It is highly satisfactory to me to find that his special experience and mature judgment entirely confirm the soundness of the views which I had formed on this subject. He is strongly of opinion, that the probable expense per patient, in each of such large public establishments as are suggested, confined to the reception and care of idiots, would be even less than the sum which I have mentioned.

settlement, and a new distribution of the burden of pauperism if adopted, will produce in the metropolitan, the agricultural, and the manufacturing districts respectively. As to the metropolis, it has been seen that the principal poor law grievance there complained of, is the unequal distribution of the burden of ratepayers in different parishes and districts.* For this grievance, the proposal made, although it accepts traditions of the past, and realities of the present, as the basis of the future, must be allowed to be an effectual remedy.

Throughout agricultural districts the effect of the change would, in the first instance, be chiefly felt in the great and general diminution of the burden on ratepayers; but must also be experienced by farmers† in the improved cottage accommodation of the agricultural labourer, who would very soon and generally be enabled to reside near his work.‡

But by far the most important of all the results of the change would be found in the immense improvement which may confidently be anticipated in the condition, physical and moral, of the agricultural labourer. Skill and character would become of value to him, which now they are not.§ Early education and training, to which an unjust and debasing law has rendered the whole labouring population utterly indifferent, would be eagerly sought after. Under the circumstances of a greatly improved physical condition, moral, intellectual, and religious advancement would be rendered possible, and even easy, to the peasantry of England; and they would cease to be the shame and reproach of their country. Lastly, the landowner, who would at least share with the farmer the benefit of a great reduction in the direct money cost of pauperism, would find no slight addition to the pleasures of a country life in this inevitable improvement in the character of the whole labouring population.

In manufacturing districts, the great and permanent, though less immediate benefit of the proposal, would be most strikingly exemplified during moments of great temporary stagnation of trade, and consequent suffering among all the in-

* Above, pp. 40, 41.

† Above, pp. 298, 299.

‡ Above, p. 289.

§ Above, p. 96., and p. 306.

habitants of such districts. It must be owned, looking at the immense accumulation of a population living mainly from hand to mouth in our great towns, that, on occasions of sudden depression, succeeding a long period of commercial and manufacturing prosperity, the ratepayers are now subjected to the pressure of a great and injurious local burden. By the adoption of the proposed plan, direct alleviation of all such pressure, whenever it may occur, will be amply secured. A crisis of greater suffering than was experienced in 1842, can hardly be anticipated. In Stockport, the average weekly income of 15,823 persons, was 1*s.* 4¾*d.* each; in Manchester there were said to be 9000 families, earning on an average only 1*s.* a week; and in Leeds, 4025 families, one-fifth of the whole population, were dependent on the poor-rate.* Disturbance of the public peace, accompanied or followed this distress, as it accompanied the sufferings of the agricultural labourers in 1830. "No one can have forgotten the formidable riots that took place in the midland counties in the summer of 1842, and which sufficiently attested the desperate condition to which the operatives were reduced. Almost everywhere, and in every manufacture, the complaint of the workman was the same, of the difficulty of obtaining employment, and the utter impossibility of earning a competent livelihood." †

It seems to me to be no slight advantage, both economical and political, of the plan proposed, that it would provide so great an alleviation for distress of this kind. The grievous injury which such a crisis, and poor-rates suddenly raised to twice or thrice their ordinary amount, inflict on owners of property, is, in some cases, only less than is endured by the poor themselves.‡ Commercial and manufacturing towns would, therefore, by the adoption of the proposed plan, be protected against any such severe temporary pressure of the burden of

* Thornton, *Over-Population*, vol. i. pp. 37, 38. † Ibid.

‡ The effect on owners of property, produced by the increase of chargeable poor suddenly thrown on places in the Radford Union, near Nottingham, by the mere passing of the statute 9 & 10 Vict. c. 66., has been mentioned above, p. 279.

pauperism, as took place at Stockport and Nottingham, at Leeds and Manchester, in 1841 and 1842, at Sheffield and Birmingham in 1848, and at Liverpool during the recent famine in Ireland. Two-thirds of the whole charge of such sudden and violent aggravations of that burden would always be substantially removed, by being shared by the country at large, with the place in which they occur. At the same time, the contribution, by the parish in which such pauperism receives its relief, of one-third of the actual outlay, will preserve a sufficient local interest in the due administration of the relief fund, to secure to the country the indispensable services of the ratepayers themselves, in attending, by their own locally elected officers and guardians, to the administration of their own affairs.

Much inquiry and consideration induce me to think, that a less interest than the payment, by each parish, of one-third of its own actual expenditure, would be insufficient to keep up, in proper activity, the attention of parish guardians at union boards, and of other parish officers and ratepayers, to the administration of the poor-law. And it is a matter, not only of economical, but political importance, in no respect to impair that great principle of local government, which serves to distinguish England from some countries of the European continent, heretofore possessing a share of freedom, but in which the smallest matters of local interest are now subjected to the direct control of a central absolutism.

The proposals which I have made are consistent with the truest principles of English constitutional freedom, and, by their adoption, the personal liberty of the body of the people would receive a larger extension than has been secured by any legislative measure passed since the Revolution of 1688. With the more general diffusion of the means of education the labourer would find opportunity and motive for intellectual and moral advancement; and it may reasonably be hoped that he would soon be raised from his present miserable and debased condition. The small, but powerful, section of the community, who alone have suffered by the repeal of the Corn Laws, would be justly relieved from a disproportionate burden of local taxation. The centres of commercial and manufacturing industry, by the distribution of the poor-rate over so much wider and less variable a basis, would receive a benefit, not so immediate or manifest, but still of a large and permanent character. And the ratepayers of England would all contribute, in more just proportions, towards the maintenance of the poor.

These benefits would be secured even if the present amount of pauperism were not diminished. But a greater benefit than all these would be found in the diminution of pauperism, obtained by removing the restrictions to which the circulation of labour is subjected by the law of settlement, and in the advantages which would result, to all classes of the community, from the accompanying improvement in the physical and moral condition of the labouring population.

APPENDIX.

APPENDIX.

Chap. I.

Table showing the Population, according to the Census of 1851, the Average Number of Out-door Paupers receiving Relief, on each Day of the Year ended 25th March, 1851, and the Number of Out-door Paupers relieved during the whole or any part of the Half-year ended 25th September, 1850. —(*Referred to at page* 11.)

Name of Union, Parish, or Township.	Population (Census of 1851).	Average Number of Out-door Paupers receiving Relief on each Day of the Year ended 25th March, 1851.	Number of Out-door Paupers relieved during the whole or any part of the Half-Year ended 25th September, 1850.
Birmingham - -	173,878	4,349	9,206
Bradford (Wilts) - -	11,604	850	1,400
Bradford and North Bierley (York)	181,977	2,149	4,418
		1,940	2,726
Chelsea, St. Luke - -	56,543	1,809	3,796
Doncaster - - -	34,669	1,106	1,910
Halifax - - -	120,943	4,044	5,806
Holbeach - - -	19,151	736	1,328
Holborn - - -	46,571	1,574	5,126
Leeds (township) -	101,331	4,088	6,644
London, East - -	44,407	2,771	6,956
London, West - -	28,829	1,406	3,715
Manchester - - -	228,437	8,939	17,724
St. George in the East -	47,362	1,480	3,130
St. Martin in the Fields	24,557	581	990
St. Olave, Southwark -	19,367	673	1,931
Scarborough - -	24,611	853	1,212
Sheffield - - -	103,602	3,330	6,258
Skipton - - -	28,764	1,981	2,593
South Stoneham - -	16,002	556	1,214
Stepney - - -	110,669	3,937	9,937
Stockbridge - - -	7,479	501	1,174
Stockport - - -	90,205	1,412	2,685
Stoke-upon-Trent -	57,946	1,296	2,808
Strand - - -	44,446	1,442	3,293
Thirsk - - -	12,760	439	645
Uxbridge - - -	19,500	774	1,799
Watford - - -	18,800	941	1,748
Whitechapel - -	79,756	2,109	8,033
Worksop - - -	19,210	665	1,357
Totals - - -	1,773,376	58,731	121,562

The following are two specimens of the thirty returns on which the above table is founded. After repeatedly failing to obtain, from clerks of guardians, the information which my questions, addressed to them, were intended to elicit, I spent some hours in an examination of the accounts of a union; and so learned how to draw out, in blank, in a form which it should be almost impossible to misunderstand, the returns which I wanted. For the following tables I am indebted to the care and attention of Mr. Rider, of Thirsk, and Mr. Smith, of Leman Street, the respective clerks of the unions named. Such figures as are here printed in broader type, fill up the only blanks left by me in the forms sent to the several clerks to whom I applied.

Thirsk Union. Population (1851) 12,760.

In-door Relief (Vagrants excluded) for the Four Quarters of the Year ending at Lady-Day, 1851.

Half-year.	Quarter.	No. of In-door Paupers at the Commencement of the Quarter.	No. of Births in the Quarter.	No. admitted during the Quarter.	No. discharged during the Quarter.	No. of Deaths during the Quarter.	No. of In-door Paupers at the End of the Quarter.	No. of In-door Paupers on July 1. 1850.	No. of In-door Paupers on Jan. 1. 1851.
Half-year from Lady-day to Michalemas, 1850	1st Quarter	**103**	**5**	**74**	**119**	**7**	**56**		
	2nd Quarter	**56**	**2**	**42**	**49**	**0**	**51**	**54**	
Half-year from Michaelmas, 1850, to Lady-day, 1851	1st Quarter	**51**	**0**	**58**	**47**	**2**	**60**		**60**
	2nd Quarter	**60**	**4**	**24**	**34**	**3**	**51**		

The number of those included as "admitted," who had been previously "discharged," and were re-admitted during the year, and are thus numbered twice in the Table, is about **20**.

[N.B. The Workhouse Master is likeliest to judge correctly of this number.]

Out-door Relief (including Lunatics and Non-settled Poor, and excluding Vagrants) for the Year ending at Lady-day, 1851.

Total Number relieved															
On March 25. 1850.		From Lady-day to Michaelmas, 1850.		On Sept. 25. 1850.		From Michaelmas, 1850, to Lady-day, 1851.		In the Second Half-year who had been on the Relief List of the previous Half-year, and had ceased to be chargeable before 25th Sept., and so are entered twice.		On March 25. 1851.		On July 1. 1850.		On Jan. 1. 1851.	
491		**645**		**428**		**573**		**20**		**470**		**436**		**422**	
Able-bodied Adults, Male (M.) Female (F.), included in the above Totals.															
M.	F.	M.	F.	M.	F.	M.	F.	M.	F.	M.	F.	M.	F.	M.	F.
,,	,,	**36**	**68**	,,	,,	**25**	**57**	,,	,,	,,	,,	**7**	**34**	**9**	**31**

To "deduct," as persons relieved both in-door and out-door, and included twice in the official "Statistical Statement:"

First half-year, **11**: Second half-year, **12**: Total, **23**.

WHITECHAPEL UNION. Population (1851) 77,654.

In-door Relief (Vagrants excluded) for the Four Quarters of the Year ending at Lady-day, 1851.

Half-year.	Quarter.	No. of In-door Paupers at the Commencement of the Quarter.	No. of Births in the Quarter.	No. admitted during the Quarter.	No. discharged during the Quarter.	No. of Deaths during the Quarter.	No. of In-door Paupers at the End of the Quarter.	No. of In-door Paupers on July 1. 1850.	No. of In-door Paupers on Jan. 1. 1851.
Half-year from Lady-day to Michaelmas, 1850	1st Quarter	976	25	529	654	52	824		
	2nd Quarter	824	23	620	566	54	847	833	
Half-year from Michaelmas, 1850, to Lady-day, 1851	1st Quarter	847	36	816	625	83	991		
	2nd Quarter	991	33	929	829	127	997		1013

The number of those included as "admitted," who had been previously "discharged," and were re-admitted during the year, and are thus numbered twice in the Table, is about **94**.

[N.B. The Workhouse Master is likeliest to judge correctly of this number.]

Out-door Relief (including Lunatics and Non-settled Poor, and excluding Vagrants) for the Year ending at Lady-day, 1851.

Total Number relieved															
On March 25. 1850.		From Lady-day to Michaelmas, 1850.		On Sept. 25. 1850.		From Michaelmas, 1850, to Lady-day, 1851.		In the Second Half-year who had been on the Relief List of the previous Half-year, and had ceased to be chargeable before 25th Sept., and so are entered twice.		On March 25. 1851.		On July 1. 1850.		On Jan. 1. 1851.	
2413		8033		1860		9109		2320		2413		1885		2281	
Able-bodied Adults, Male (M.) and Female (F.), included in the above Totals.															
M.	F.	M.	F.	M.	F.	M.	F.	M.	F.	M.	F.	M.	F.	M.	F.
,,	,,	880	1542	,,	,,	1189	1891	,,	,,	,,	,,	76	360	167	451

To "deduct," as persons relieved both in-door and out-door, and included twice in the official "Statistical Statement."

First half-year, **394**: Second half-year, **325**: Total, **719**.

Table, showing the Average Number of Persons receiving Relief, In-door and Out-door, in several Manufacturing Towns, during the Year ended the 25th March, 1851.—(*Referred to at page* 12.)

Name of Union.	Average Number of Persons receiving Relief.	
	In-door.	Out-door.
Birmingham - - -	683	4,369
Bradford (York) - - -	125	1,145
Halifax - - - -	236	4,044
Leeds - - - -	397	4,223
North Bierley - - -	52	1,940
Norwich - - - -	257	7,085
Sheffield - - - -	374	3,325
Total - - -	2,124	26,131

Table showing the Number of able-bodied adult Paupers, and the corresponding Number of Paupers of all Classes, receiving Out-door Relief, on the 1st July, 1850, and the 1st January, 1851, and during an entire Half-year, in Thirteen Unions, containing a Population of 850,892.—(*Referred to at page* 18.)

Name of Union.	Pop. Census of 1851.	Number of able-bodied adult Paupers receiving Out-door Relief						Total Number of Paupers receiving Out-door Relief		
		On July 1. 1850.		On Jan. 1. 1851.		From Mar. 25. to Sep. 25. 1850.		On July 1. 1850.	On Jan. 1. 1851.	From March 25. to Sep. 25. 1850.
		Male.	Female.	Male.	Female.	Male.	Female.			
Bradford (Wilts) -	11,604	12	50	16	47	61	107	850	861	1,400
Doncaster -	34,669	27	121	12	65	132	243	1,134	1,073	1,910
Leeds - -	101,331	187	772	257	781	666	1,477	3,992	4,118	4,003
London, West -	28,829	117	273	83	190	506	834	1,592	1,220	3,715
Manchester	228,437	621	1,454	842	1,721	2,485	4,206	7,913	8,940	17,724
St. George in the East -	47,362	46	327	27	150	265	656	1,864	1,094	3,130
Sheffield -	103,602	99	509	111	535	465	1,102	3,450	3,200	6,258
Stepney -	110,669	139	799	164	764	820	1,719	3,798	3,960	9,937
Stockbridge	7,479	110	224	134	235	272	404	466	536	1,174
Stockport -	90,205	67	190	71	182	216	454	1,418	1,406	2,685
Stoke-upon-Trent -	57,946	2	154	1	157	16	346	1,295	1,245	2,801
South Stoneham -	16,002	27	60	29	64	180	199	532	559	1,214
Thirsk -	12,760	7	34	9	31	36	68	436	422	645
Totals -	850,895	1,461	4,977	1,756	4,922	6,120	11,751	28,740	28,634	60,596

TABLE showing the Population and the Number of Soldiers of several Provinces of the Austrian Empire, containing a Population equal to that of England and Wales, extracted from the "Tafeln zur Statistik der Oesterreichischen Monarchie, für die Jahre 1845 und 1846." Wien, 1850. — (*Referred to at page* 19.)

Countries.	Population.	Of whom Soldiers.
Lower Austria - - -	1,531,034	36,635
Upper Austria - - -	870,676	13,982
Styria - - - -	1,023,153	20,079
Carinthia and Carniola - -	796,143	11,357
Kuestenland - - -	507,903	7,802
Tirol - - - -	866,078	6,828
Bohemia - - - -	4,409,792	61,830
Moravia and Silesia - -	2,290,449	39,855
Gallicia - - - -	5,189,004	83,446
Dalmatia - - - -	418,063	7,075
Total - - -	17,902,295	288,889

THE following is the Table of Persons relieved in the different Arrondissements of the City of Paris, given by M. Buret, *De la Misère des Classes laborieuses en Angleterre et en France*, tom. i. p. 267. — (*Referred to at page* 20.)

Arrondissements.	Persons relieved, 1835.			
	Adults.		Children.	
	Males.	Females.	Males.	Females.
1st	814	1,488	632	665
2nd	593	1,160	444	449
3rd	545	1,012	371	478
4th	735	1,350	512	532
5th	1,061	1,873	862	903
6th	1,633	2,842	1,175	1,286
7th	896	1,594	694	752
8th	2,290	3,586	2,077	1,985
9th	1,210	2,033	795	886
10th	1,061	2,376	791	845
11th	902	1,791	577	626
12th	2,759	4,643	1,932	2,028
Totals - -	14,499	25,748	10,862	11,435

TABLE showing the Number of Widows receiving Out-door Relief, and the corresponding Number of Paupers of all Classes receiving Out-door Relief, on Five given Days, in the Years 1849, 1850, 1851.—(*Referred to at page* 20.)

Days.	Widows relieved out of the Workhouse.	All Persons relieved out of the Workhouse (Vagrants excluded).
1st January, 1849 -	52,441	815,044
1st July, 1849 - -	50,088	736,828
1st January, 1850 -	53,151	769,687
1st July, 1850 - -	50,669	708,571
1st January, 1851 -	50,628	723,851
Total - -	256,977	3,753,981
Average - -	51,395	750,756

CHAP. II.

TABLE of Charities in the Metropolis, with the Income derived from Voluntary Contributions, and from Property, extracted from Low's "Charities of London," p. 452.—(N.B. I omit from this Table one class of charities, included in the text at p. 34., and which seems not to be appropriated to the poor.)—(*Referred to at page* 34.)

Charities.	Number.	Income from Voluntary Contributions.	Income from Property.	Total.
		£	£	£
General Medical Hospitals -	12	31,265	111,641	142,906
Medical Charities for special purposes - - -	50	27,974	68,690	96,664
General Dispensaries - -	35	11,470	2,054	13,524
Relief of General Destitution and Distress - - -	14	20,646	3,234	23,880
Aiding the Resources of the Industrious - - -	14	4,677	2,569	7,246
For the Blind, Deaf, and Dumb - - - -	11	11,965	22,797	34,762
Colleges, Hospitals, and other asylums for the aged -	103	5,857	77,190	83,047
Charitable Pension Societies	16	15,790	3,199	18,989
Asylums for Orphans and other necessitous Children	31	55,466	25,549	81,015
	286	185,110	316,923	502,033

TABLE showing, in each Union or Parish in the Metropolis, the Population in 1851, the Net Rental of Property as assessed to the Poor Rate in 1847, and the Amount expended in Relief of the Poor, in the Years ended at Lady-day, 1847, and at Lady-day, 1850. — (*Referred to at page 34.*)

Districts and Unions, &c.	Population in 1851.	Net Rental of Property as assessed to the Relief of the Poor in 1847.	Amount expended for the Relief of the Poor in the Year ended Lady-day, 1847.	Lady-day, 1850.
Western District.		£	£	£
Kensington - - -	119,990	518,191	23,920	38,143
Chelsea - - -	56,543	147,932	13,854	19,193
St. George, Hanover Sq.	73,207	661,582	21,363	18,205
Westminster - -	65,609	212,396	13,914	16,875
St. Martin in the Fields -	24,557	249,555	12,839	16,850
St. James, Westminster -	36,426	296,949	14,816	14,182
Totals - - -	376,332	2,086,605	100,706	123,448
Northern District.				
Marylebone - - -	157,679	840,216	51,686	63,352
St. Pancras - - -	167,198	} 625,491	32,782 {	42,322
Hampstead - - -	11,986			6,135
Islington - - -	95,054	287,518	13,131	17,646
Hackney - - -	58,424	198,007	12,160	15,608
Totals - - -	490,441	1,951,232	109,759	145,061
Central District.				
St. Giles in the Fields -	54,062	232,005	16,465	14,658
Strand - - -	44,446	219,914	14,100	15,728
Holborn - - -	46,571	144,668	13,004	14,063
Clerkenwell - - -	64,705	183,529	14,283	14,268
St. Luke - - -	54,058	135,688	15,181	15,538
London, City - -	55,908	667,943	50,440	62,888
London, East - -	44,407	139,038	17,569	16,781
London, West - -	28,829	154,929	15,693	18,501
Totals - - -	392,986	1,877,714	156,735	172,425
Eastern District.				
Shoreditch - - -	109,209	211,251	21,421	37,188
Bethnal Green - -	90,170	96,816	11,066	12,270
Whitechapel - -	79,756	201,068	18,444	18,895
St. George in the East -	47,362	143,383	16,474	16,537
Stepney - - -	110,669	241,774	23,559	27,123
Poplar - - -	47,157	173,980	13,201	11,805
Totals - - -	485,336	1,068,272	104,165	123,818
Southern District.				
St. Saviour, Southwark -	35,729	123,119	12,542	10,575
St. Olave - - -	19,367	83,431	7,204	8,587
Bermondsey - - -	48,128	112,646	13,823	13,283
St. George, Southwark -	51,825	109,161	14,737	15,698
Newington - - -	64,805	148,164	18,328	18,781
Lambeth - - -	139,240	438,220	35,367	39,719
Camberwell - - -	54,668	184,742	8,817	12,876
Rotherhithe - - -	17,778	54,704	7,193	7,810
Greenwich - - -	99,404	242,884	23,455	26,166
Wandsworth - -	50,770	218,729	16,257	17,327
Lewisham - - -	34,831	130,985	5,881	6,333
Totals - - -	618,049	1,845,695	163,604	177,155
Total of the Metropolis -	2,363,144	8,829,518	634,369	741,907

TABLE showing the Population of the Metropolis in 1851, and the Average Number of Paupers receiving Relief, whether In-door or Out-door, on each Day of the Year ended 25th March, 1851.—(*Referred to at page* 36.)

Name of Union or Parish.	Population in 1851.	Average Number of Paupers relieved on each Day of the Year ended 25th March, 1851 (Lunatics included, and Vagrants excluded).	
		In-door.	Out-door.
Bermondsey - -	48,128	569	1,225
Camberwell - - -	54,668	374	1,065
Chelsea - - -	56,543	376	1,718
Clerkenwell - - -	64,705	390	1,238
Fulham - - -	29,669	365	955
Hackney - - -	58,424	403	1,462
Holborn - - -	46,571	642	1,437
Islington - - -	95,054	488	1,404
Kensington - - -	44,048	257	950
Lambeth - - -	139,240	1,519*	4,800
London, East - -	44,407	731	2,741
London, West - -	28,829	473	1,406
Marylebone - - -	159,679	1,661	4,527
Newington - - -	64,805	601	1,763
Rotherhithe - - -	17,778	230	1,058
Shoreditch - - -	109,209	828	3,942
Stepney - - -	110,669	1,118	2,992
Strand - - -	44,446	583	1,488
St. George, Hanover Sq.	73,207	656	770†
St. George in the East -	47,362	871	1,479
St. George, Southwark -	51,825	574	1,309
St. James, Westminster	36,426	674	673
St. Luke - - -	54,058	487	1,803
St. Martin in the Fields	24,557	797	581
St. Olave, Southwark -	19,367	354	673
St. Pancras - - -	167,198	1,230	4,501
St. Saviour, Southwark -	35,729	428	873
Wandsworth - -	50,770	484	1,532
Whitechapel - -	79,756	923	2,083
Total of the above Districts - - -	1,857,127	18,886	52,448
Residue of the Metropolitan Districts - -	505,109	4,921‡	14,265‡
Total of the Metropolis -	2,362,236	23,807	66,713

* In-door, and in lunatic asylums.

† Of this number eighty-two are lunatics, or idiots, confined in lunatic asylums.

‡ Estimated from the ascertained number of paupers of "the above districts."

TABLE showing the Net Rental, and the Amount expended in Relief of the Poor, for the Year ended on 25th March, 1847, in the Holborn, and the East and West London Unions, and in the Parishes of St. Matthew, Bethnal Green and St. George, Southwark.—(*Referred to at page* 38.)

Name of Union or Parish.	Net Rental.	Amount expended in the Relief of the Poor for the Year ended 25th March, 1847.
	£	£
Holborn - - - -	144,668	14,063
St. Matthew, Bethnal Green -	96,816	12,270
East London - - -	139,038	16,781
West London - - -	154,929	18,501
St. George, Southwark - -	109,161	15,698
Totals - -	644,612	77,333

TABLE showing the Population in the City of London Union, and the East and West London Unions, in the Years 1841 and 1851, the Net Annual Value of Real Property assessed to the Poor-rate in 1847, and the Rate per Head of the Net Annual Value of Property assessed to the Poor-rate, on the Population of 1851.—(*Referred to at page* 40.)

Name of Union.	Population in		Net Annual Value of Real Property assessed to the Poor-rate in 1847.	Rate per Head of the Net Annual Value of Property assessed to the Poor-rate in 1847, on the Population in 1851.
	1841.	1851.		
			£	£ s. d.
City of London -	56,009	55,908	667,943	11 19 11¼
East London and West London	89,626	98,465	293,967	2 19 8¼
Totals - -	145,635	154,373	961,910	6 4 7¼

TABLE showing the Population of the City of London Union (including the City within the Walls), and the Number of Inhabited Houses, in the Years 1841 and 1851 —(*Referred to at page* 40.)

Year.	Inhabited Houses.	Inhabitants.
1841	7,921	56,009
1851	7,329	55,908

With nearly the same number of inhabitants in 1851, as in 1841; the City, therefore, now contains 592 fewer houses, for their accommodation, than it did ten years ago.

TABLE exhibiting the contrast between the Parishes of St. George, Hanover Square, St. James, Westminster, and St. Martin in the Fields, with the Parishes of Lambeth, Shoreditch, Rotherhithe, and the East London Union, in respect of the Proportion between In-door and Out-door Poor.—(*Referred to at page* 42.)

Name of Parish or Union.	Average Number receiving Relief.	
	In-door.	Out-door.
St. George, Hanover Square - -	656	770
St. James, Westminster - - -	674	673
St. Martin in the Fields - - -	797	581
Totals - - -	1,927	2,024
Lambeth - - - -	1,519	4,800
Rotherhithe - - - -	230	1,058
Shoreditch - - - -	828	3,942
East London Union - - -	731	2,741
Totals - - -	3,308	12,541

TABLE exhibiting the Deaths from Cholera, in Three different Classes of Society, mainly residing in different Localities, during the Sixty Weeks ending on 24th November, 1849.—(*Referred to at page* 46.)

District.	Proportion of the different Classes.			Total.
	Gentry.	Tradesmen.	Mechanics.	
Western District -	3·7	12·9	83·5	100·
Eastern District -	1·0	11·6	87·4	100·
Whole Metropolis -	2·6	15·7	81·7	100·

TABLE showing the Number of inhabited Houses, and the Number of Inhabitants, in the Holborn and East London Unions, and the Parishes of St. James, Clerkenwell, St. Margaret and St. John, Westminster, and St. Mary, Whitechapel, in the Years 1841 and 1851, and the Increase or Decrease in the Number of Houses, and the Increase in the Number of Inhabitants in that Interval. —(*Referred to at page* 51.)

Name of Parish or Union.	Number of inhabited Houses.		Number of Inhabitants.		Difference between 1841 and 1851 in respect of	
	1841.	1851.	1841.	1851.	Inhabited Houses.	Inhabitants.
Clerkenwell - -	6,946	7,259	56,799	64,705	+313	+7,906
East London -	4,796	4,785	39,718	44,407	− 11	+4,689
Holborn - -	4,603	4,517	44,532	46,571	− 86	+2,039
Westminster (St. Margaret's and St. John's) - -	6,439	6,647	56,802	65,609	+208	+8,807
Whitechapel -	8,834	8,832	71,879	79,756	− 2	+7,877
Total - -	31,618	32,040	269,730	301,048	+422	+31,318

Chap. III.

Table showing the Population, Number of Acres, the Number of Poor on the Register, in 1850, and the Proportion of the Registered to the whole Number of Inhabitants, throughout Scotland. —(*Referred to at page* 60.)

(The instances of "proportion of paupers to population," in Scotland, mentioned in the text, at p. 60, was obtained by comparing the paupers of 1850 with the population of 1841. Now that the population of each county in 1851 is published, it is better to compare the paupers of 1850, with the population of 1851.)

Counties.	Population, 1841.	Population, 1851.	Acres.	Number of the Poor on the Roll, or registered, in 1850.	Proportion of the Number of the registered Poor *in* 1850, to the whole Number of *Inhabitants in* 1851.
1. Aberdeen - -	192,893	214,658	1,260,800	6,663	1 in 32·21
2. Argyll - - -	96,824	88,567	2,054,400	3,552	1 in 24·93
3. Ayr - - -	164,477	189,286	668,800	4,506	1 in 42·00
4. Banff - - -	48,463	53,935	414,080	1,852	1 in 29·12
5. Berwick - -	34,345	36,287	282,880	1,306	1 in 27·78
6. Bute - - -	15,740	16,576	105,600	488	1 in 32·80
7. Caithness - -	37,410	38,542	446,080	1,761	1 in 27·56
8. Clackmannan -	20,041	22,985	30,720	642	1 in 35·81
9. Dumbarton - -	46,005	44,923	165,760	1,132	1 in 39·65
10. Dumfries - -	72,855	78,057	808,320	2,470	1 in 31·60
11. Edinburgh - -	225,276	258,824	226,560	11,496	1 in 22·51
12. Elgin or Moray -	35,879	38,671	307,200	1,495	1 in 25·86
13. Fife - - -	139,729	153,011	300,800	4,169	1 in 36·70
14. Forfar - - -	170,395	174,731	570,880	4,792	1 in 36·46
15. Haddington - -	35,835	36,396	174,080	1,328	1 in 27·40
16. Inverness - -	98,417	96,328	2,716,810	3,845	1 in 25·05
17. Kincardine - -	33,550	34,743	244,480	1,222	1 in 28·43
18. Kinross - -	7,834	8,913	50,560	145	1 in 61·47
19. Kirkcudbright -	41,119	43,310	533,760	1,707	1 in 25·37
20. Lanark - -	427,738	532,114	604,800	24,373	1 in 21·83
21. Linlithgow - -	27,466	30,044	76,800	906	1 in 33·16
22. Nairn - - -	7,186	9,966	126,720	301	1 in 33·30
23. Orkney and Shetland:					
Orkney -	30,507	62,313	281,600	780	1 in 40·12
Shetland -	30,558		563,200	773	
24. Peebles - -	10,558	10,582	204,160	303	1 in 34·72
25. Perth - - -	137,854	139,216	,688,320	3,906	1 in 35·64
26. Renfrew - -	154,160	159,064	145,280	5,013	1 in 40·72
27. Ross and Cromarty	79,941	82,625	,904,000	3,756	1 in 21·99
28. Roxburgh - -	46,271	51,570	457,920	1,791	1 in 28·79
29. Selkirk - -	7,413	9,797	169,280	212	1 in 46·21
30. Stirling - -	80,535	85,726	321,280	1,940	1 in 44·18
31. Sutherland - -	23,715	25,771	1,152,640	1,039	1 in 24·80
32. Wigton - -	39,195	43,253	293,760	1,790	1 in 24·16
Total - -	2,620,184	2,870,784	19,352,330	101,454	1 in 28·29

The county of Sutherland, contains a surface of 1,152,640 acres (of which 30,080 are water), and the population of the county, which was 25,538 in

1831, is only 25,711 in 1851. The following table shows that the density of population, even of the Shetland and Orkney Islands, is more than thrice as great as that of the county of Sutherland.

Counties.	Number of Acres corresponding to each Person.		
	1831.	1841.	1851.
Orkney - - - - -	9·429	13·653	13·592
Shetland - - - - -	18·617		
Sutherland - - - -	43·990	45·469	44·726
Average of Scotland - -	8·009	7·205	6·753

The county of Sutherland, therefore, as found in the preceding table of the pauperism of the counties of Scotland, if contrasted with the Orkney and Shetland Islands, furnishes a striking exception to the general distribution of pauperism mentioned in the text, at p. 60. Although it cannot be said that the wilds of Sutherland equal the wynds of Glasgow in the destitution and suffering of their pauperised population, yet the whole county of Sutherland, belonging mainly to one great proprietor, is afflicted by a pauperism far exceeding the average of that which prevails throughout Scotland. Its pauperism is sixty per cent above that of the Orkney and Shetland Islands, in which there is found a numerous class of small and even poor proprietors.

The only explanation which I can suggest of the difference in the pauperism of Sutherland and the Orkney and Shetland Islands, is that furnished by Lord Bacon (above, p. 213.), that "subversion of houses breeds decay of charity, and *charges to the poor.*"

The subversion of houses in Sutherlandshire, the expulsion of the indigenous clansman population of tillers of the soil, the introduction in their place of "a shepherd and his dog," the "latæ solitudinis indiscreta unitas," are matters not only of British, but of European history. In the Statistical Account of Scotland, it is said of the single parish of Farr, in Sutherland, that "the census of 1831, compared with the return of 1790, shows a decrease of 400 in the population. This was owing to the introduction of the sheep-farming system: by its adoption, the farmers and tenants who occupied the straths and glens in the interior, were, in 1818 and 1819, all removed from their possessions." (p. 73.) In the same work, at p. 79., it is stated of the same parish of Farr, that the straths in which hundreds of families had lived comfortably, were then tenanted by about twenty-four families of shepherds. In justice to the great proprietor of the county of Sutherland, it must be owned that other landowners, in the Highlands and in Ireland, have done just the same thing as was done by the house of Sutherland in its proper county.

As an additional note on this subject, it may be observed, that the great proprietors to whom the Campagna of Rome belonged, appear, in the fifteenth and sixteenth centuries, to have adopted exactly the same course, doing their utmost to clear off all human incumbrances from their broad acres, and to people them with herds and flocks. The profits of pasturage seemed to the Roman, as well as to the British grandees, to be greater than could be got from tillage. See Nicolai, *Dell' Agro Romano*, tom. ii. pp. 30, 31. (cited by Sismondi, *Études*, tom. ii.

p. 28.), quoting a constitution of Pope Sixtus IV. (1471-1484), re-enacted by Clement VII. in 1523.

At the best, the substitution of pasture in the place of tillage, is rather going backwards in the scale of civilisation; and undoubtedly the fiat of a great land-owner, "Veteres migrate coloni!" when he sweeps away a whole population of tenants, produces great and deplorable human suffering. Such a deed is, "the snapping of a chain linked by centuries; the destruction of the dearest local attachments, the dissolution of the earliest friendships;" and, as has been said, with reference to the more recent exhibition of this selfishness and oppression, persons invested with the legal power to produce such scenes of woe, should remember "the ties which must be broken, the villages which must be deserted, the gardens to be laid desolate, the second nature of habits which must be altered, the hearts which must sink, the hands which may rebel under trials such as these"*

TABLE showing the estimated Population of England and Wales in 1850; the Total Amount expended for the Relief of the Poor, in the Year ended Lady-day, 1850; the estimated Number of Paupers relieved during the whole or some Part of the Year; the Average Amount expended on each Pauper, and the Rate of the whole Sum expended, per Head, on the Population.—(*Referred to at page* 61.)

Estimated Population in 1850.	Total Amount expended in Relief of the Poor in the Year ended Lady-day, 1850.	Estimated Number of Paupers relieved during the whole or some part of the Year.	Average Amount expended on each Pauper, Man, Woman, or Child.	Rate per Head on the Population.
	£ *s.* *d.*		£ *s.* *d.*	*s.* *d.*
17,725,934	5,395,021 12 0	3,000,000†	1 15 11½	6 1

CORRESPONDING Tables for Belgium, and for the most densely peopled and most pauperised Department of France, are as follows:

Country.	Population, in 1846.	Sum distributed by Bureaux de Bienfaisance.	Number of poor Persons relieved.	Average Sum per Head for each poor Person.	Rate per Head on the Population.
		francs. cts.		fr. cts.	fr. cts.
Belgium -	4,377,206	5,726,912 61	455,658	12 56	1 30
Departement du Nord, France	1,132,980	1,791,567 0	188,711	9 49	1 58

The data on which this Table is constructed are found in the "Annuaire du Bureau des Longitudes," 1851, in an essay by M. Wolowski, published in his "Études d'Économie Politique et de Statistique" (première partie), Paris, 1848, in Ducpetiaux, "Mémoire sur le Paupérisme dans les Flandres," Bruxelles, 1850.

* Sir J. Graham, *Corn and Currency*, p. 83. † See Chap. I. pp. 10, 11, 12.

TABLE showing the Average Mortality of the Population of the Ten selected Agricultural Counties, as compared with the Three Manufacturing Counties, the Metropolitan Registration District, and with the Average of England and Wales.—(*Referred to at page* 69.)

Counties.	Number of Persons living for each Death in a given Year on the Average of the Seven Years 1838-1844.	
	Males.	Females.
Agricultural Counties :		
Bedford - - -	46·4	47·8
Berks - - -	50·1	50·7
Bucks - - -	46·5	47·3
Dorset - - -	51·0	53·2
Essex - - -	48·4	50·7
Norfolk - - -	46·7	50·2
Oxford - - -	48·1	47·5
Suffolk - - -	50·6	51·0
Sussex - - -	53·1	55·7
Wilts - - -	49·1	48·9
Manufacturing Counties :		
Lancaster - -	35·8	39·0
Stafford - - -	43·7	45·2
West Riding, York -	43·6	46·2
Metropolitan District -	36·5	43·3
England and Wales - -	44·1	47·5

TABLE showing the Number of Acres of Land corresponding to each Individual of the Population of the Ten selected Agricultural Counties, compared with the Three Manufacturing Counties, and with the general Average of all England.—(*Referred to at page* 70.)

Counties.	No. of Acres corresponding to each Person.		
	1831.	1841.	1851.
Bedford - - - - -	3·103	2·745	2·293
Berks - - - - -	3·310	3·003	2·379
Bucks - - - - -	3·223	3·027	3·228
Dorset - - - - -	4·042	3·684	3·531
Essex - - - - -	3·090	2·840	2·846
Norfolk - - - - -	3·320	3·139	2·979
Oxford - - - - -	3·042	2·862	2·744
Suffolk - - - - -	3·272	3·073	2·734
Sussex - - - - -	3·445	3·129	2·680
Wilts - - - - -	3·866	3·575	3·601
Average of the above Ten Counties -	3·341	3·094	2·901
Lancaster - - - - -	·845	·677	·542
Stafford - - - - -	1·845	1·485	1·167
West Riding, York - - -	1·688	1·427	1·211
Average of the above Three Counties	1·253	1·023	·861
Average of England and Wales -	2·628	2·294	2·037

TABLE showing the Acreage, the Population in 1841 and 1851, the Net Rateable Value in 1847, and the Expenditure in Relief of the Poor in 1840 and 1850, of a Region of Selected Agricultural Unions, and of the Eastern District of the Metropolis, comprising Shoreditch, Bethnal Green, Whitechapel, St. George in the East, Stepney, and Poplar.—(*Referred to at pages* 75, *and* 331.)

Counties.	Names of Unions.	No. of Parishes in Union.	Statute Acres.	Population in 1841.	Population in 1851.	Annual Value of Property rated to the Poor in 1847.	Amount expended in Relief of the Poor in the Year ended Lady-day			
							1840.		1850.	
						£	£	s.	£	s.
Bedford	Biggleswade	26	56,560	20,694	23,438	83,319	7,778	8	8,395	17
Berks	Farringdon	31	65,880	15,582	15,733	95,303	6,932	16	8,280	4
	Hungerford	21	96.436	19,892	20,409	97,063	8,892	19	9,444	2
	Wantage	34	80,850	16,826	17,431	97,894	8,717	17	9,674	2
Bucks	Aylesbury	40	73,630	22,134	23,094	110,201	12,412	11	12,941	2
	Newport Paguell	45	69,340	22,999	23,108	108,531	9,083	14	9,673	14
	Winslow	17	33,851	8,376	9,376	47,700	4,771	17	5,336	8
Dorset	Blandford	33	66,590	13,856	14,798	54,270	6,777	19	6,559	6
	Cerne	20	45,990	7,259	*8,239	51,413	3,558	14	3,787	9
	Wareham & Purbeck	27	92,930	16,542	17,413	62,529	8,519	16	8,464	17
Essex	Chelmsford	31	82,260	13,476	*15,313	103,076	16,467	2	16,468	11
	Lexden & Winstree	35	70,490	20,881	21,665	99,338	8,726	14	8,218	10
	Ongar -	26	44.019	11,804	11,857	62,729	5,162	10	6,153	2
Norfolk	St. Faith -	30	47,851	11,556	11,981	55,994	6,868	9	6.364	9
	Swaffham -	33	76,222	13,084	14,311	76,576	7,937	3	7,218	5
	Walsingham	50	74,214	20,960	22,023	117,911	11,384	18	11,565	10
Oxford	Chipping Norton	33	75,071	16,151	17,423	78,573	7,881	18	7,003	5
	Henley -	24	46,327	17,544	17,905	71,465	8,178	6	10,328	16
	Thame -	35	53,463	15,605	15,616	77,133	11,513	11	11,067	15
Suffolk	Bosmere & Claydon	39	58,270	16,521	17,219	80,167	7,388	10	8,389	19
	Mildenhall	13	61,339	9,184	10,351	37,968	4,026	19	3,742	12
	Thingoe -	46	85,130	18,031	19,024	86,579	9,657	4	8,823	6
Sussex	E. Grinstead	7	56,623	12,619	13,223	43,027	6,596	11	7,184	19
	Midhurst -	26	60,865	13,320	13,581	44.538	6,912	5	7,005	18
	Petworth -	5	36,916	9,681	9,628	27,350	5,205	2	5,552	2
Wilts	Alderbury -	22	52,337	14,171	14,950	64,045	7,400	12	8,154	14
	Marlborough	14	39,220	9,234	10,283	53,144	5,668	19	4,867	15
	Mere -	12	30,333	8,498	8,431	43,418	4,585	2	5,052	1
Total of the above Agricultural Unions		773	1,733,007	416,480	437,823	2,031,257	219,008	6	225,518	10
The Eastern District of the Metropolis		20	5,632	392,444	485,336	1,068,272	104,165†		123,821	14

* Estimated population, the "Census of Great Britain 1851," published in July 1851, not giving it separately.

† This is the amount expended in 1847. There are no published returns from which the corresponding amount for 1840, can be stated.

TABLE showing the Amount expended in Relief of the Poor in the Parish of Birmingham, the Number of In-door and Out-door Paupers relieved respectively on the 25th March, and during the Whole, or any Part of the Half-years ended on that Day, in the Years 1850 and 1851.—(*Referred to at page* 72.)

Year.	Amount expended in Relief of the Poor for the Year ended on 25th March.	Number of In-door Paupers relieved on 25th March.	Number of Out-door Paupers relieved on 25th March.	Total Number of In-door and Out-door Paupers, relieved during the Half-year ended on 25th March.
	£ *s.* *d.*			
1850	37,548 15 0	768	5,453	19,031
1851	33,613 4 0	628	4,309	12,125

TABLE contrasting the Pauperism of the Three Commercial and Manufacturing Towns, Birmingham, Liverpool, and Stockport, with the Two Agricultural Counties, Cambridge and Huntingdon.—(*Referred to at page* 79.)

	Estimated Population in 1847.*	Amount expended for Relief of the Poor, in the Year ended Lady-day, 1847.	Rate per Head on the whole Population of the Sum expended for Relief of the Poor.
Counties :		£	*s.* *d.*
Cambridge -	180,893	81,334	8 11¾
Huntingdon -	59,611	29,608	9 11
Totals -	240,504	110,942	9 2½
Towns :			
Birmingham -	159,611	37,863	4 8¾
Liverpool - -	242,854	67,184	5 6¼
Stockport - -	29,721	4,678	3 1¾
Totals -	431,586	109,725	5 1

* Obtained by adding to the population of 1841 six-tenths of the increase from 1841 to 1851, as shown in the census of 1851.

TABLE showing the Population of the Ten selected Agricultural Counties, and the Number of Persons committed for trial, or bailed, with the Number of Committals to every 1000 of the Population, during the Five Years 1844—1848, compared with the Four Counties, Northumberland, Cumberland, Westmoreland, and Lincoln, and with the whole of England and Wales. — (*Referred to at page* 86.)

Counties.	Population in 1851.	Number of Persons committed for Trial, or bailed, during the Five Years 1844—1848.	Number of Persons committed in every 1000 of the Population.
Bedford - - -	129,789	910	7
Berks - - -	199,154	1,492	7½
Bucks - - -	143,670	1,472	10¼
Dorset - - -	177,597	1,240	7
Essex - - -	343,916	3.044	9
Norfolk - - -	433,803	3,590	8¼
Oxford - - -	170,286	1,428	8⅖
Suffolk - - -	335,991	2,508	7½
Sussex - - -	339,428	2,354	7
Wilts - - -	241,003	3,002	12¼
Totals - - -	2,514,637	21,040	8⅓
Northumberland - -	303,535	1,042	3⅖
Cumberland - - -	195,487	653	3⅓
Westmoreland - -	58,380	224	3⅘
Lincoln - - -	400,266	2,360	5⅞
Totals - - -	957,668	4,279	4½
Total of England and Wales	17,922,768	135,134	7½

TABLE showing the Degree of Ignorance above and below the Average throughout England and Wales, as evidenced by the Number of Men signing the Marriage Register with Marks, in the Year 1844. — (*Referred to at page* 89.)

Counties.	Proportion per Cent above and below the Average throughout England and Wales, of Men signing the Marriage Register with a Mark, in the Year 1844.
Agricultural:	
Bedford - - - - - -	+ 53·0
Berks - - - - - -	+ 28·6
Bucks - - - - - -	+ 30·2
Dorset - - - - - -	+ 10·1
Essex - - - - - -	+ 42·4
Norfolk - - - - - -	+ 38·1
Oxford - - - - - -	+ 5·0
Suffolk - - - - - -	+ 42·0
Sussex - - - - - -	— 7.5
Wilts - - - - - -	+ 26·5
Manufacturing:	
Lancaster - - - - - -	+ 22·1
Stafford - - - - - -	+ 31·3
West Riding of Yorkshire - - - -	+ 17·9

COMPARATIVE Statement showing the Number of Children of Age to attend School, and the Number actually attending School, in Provinces of the Austrian Empire (extracted from the "Tafeln zur Statistik der Oesterreichischen Monarchie, für die Jahr 1845 und 1846"). — (*Referred to at page* 115.)

Provinces.	Number of Children.					
	Of Age to attend School.			Attending School.		
	Boys.	Girls.	Total.	Boys.	Girls.	Total.
Lower Austria	80,008	79,349	159,357	78,958	77,236	156,194
Upper Austria	45,061	44,908	89,969	44,551	43,287	87,838
Styria - -	46,452	51,104	107,556	44,925	36,566	81,491
Tirol - -	52,814	49,917	102,731	55,005	49,758	104,763
Bohemia -	275,441	266,702	542,143	261,906	249,538	511,444
Moravia and Silesia	146,410	143,623	290,033	141,424	136,057	277,481
Totals -	646,186	635,603	1,291,789	626,769	592,442	1,219,211

TABLE showing the Proportion per Cent of Illegitimate Births in the Selected Counties, Agricultural and Manufacturing, above and below the Average of England and Wales. — (*Referred to at page* 121.)

Counties.	Proportion per Cent above and below the Average of England and Wales.	
	1842.	1845.
Agricultural:		
Bedford - - -	+15·1	+17·5
Berks - - -	+ 9·1	+14·3
Bucks - - -	+ 8·8	+ 2·6
Dorset - - -	− 0·2	− 0·7
Essex - - -	+21·2	+19·1
Norfolk - - -	+47·2	+53·1
Oxford - - -	+11·4	− 0·1
Suffolk - - -	+20·1	+20·7
Sussex - - -	− 0·6	− 0·4
Wilts - - -	+ 8·5	+ 4·8
Manufacturing:		
Lancaster - - -	+28·8	+16·6
Stafford - - -	+10·2	+ 9·7
West Riding of Yorkshire -	+ 5·3	+ 3·9

The Tables giving the Average of the three years 1849, 1850, and 1851, mentioned at page 120, are mislaid as this sheet is passing through the press. I substitute the following Table, which gives nearly the same results:—

TABLE showing the Total Number of Paupers, and the Number of Illegitimate Children, relieved in *Union* Workhouses on the 1st January, 1850, in the Ten Selected Agricultural Counties, in the Three Manufacturing Counties, and in the Whole of England and Wales.

Counties.	Total Number of Paupers relieved in Union Workhouses on 1st January, 1850.	Number of Illegitimate Children relieved in Union Workhouses on 1st Jan., 1850.
Agricultural Counties:		
Bedford - - - -	1,055	69
Berks - - - -	2,754	219
Bucks - - - -	1,541	177
Dorset - - - -	1,772	196
Essex - - - -	4,716	314
Norfolk - - - -	3,513	425
Oxford - - - -	1,541	119
Suffolk - - - -	4,080	430
Sussex - - - -	3,648	288
Wilts - - - -	3,003	385
Total of the above Ten Counties -	27,623	2,622
Manufacturing Counties:		
Lancaster - - - -	8,269	329
Stafford - - - -	2,376	192
West Riding of Yorkshire - -	3,042	137
Total of the above Three Counties -	13,687	658
England and Wales - - -	110,328	7877

The proportion of illegitimate children to the whole number of paupers relieved is, therefore, in

The Ten Agricultural Counties - - - - 1 in 10·53

The Three Manufacturing Counties - - - 1 in 20·80

The Whole of England and Wales - - - 1 in 14·00

TABLE showing the Population, and the Number of Pauper Lunatics and Idiots chargeable to Parishes in Unions, &c. in the Ten Selected Agricultural Counties, the Three Manufacturing Counties, the Counties of Middlesex and Surrey, and the whole of England and Wales, on the 1st of January, 1847. (Obtained from the "Summary of Returns of Pauper Lunatics and Idiots chargeable to Parishes and Townships in the several Unions in England and Wales, and also to Parishes and Townships not in Union, on the 1st January, 1847," found in Appendix (I.) to "Further Report of the Commissioners in Lunacy to the Lord Chancellor," presented to Parliament, and printed, in 1847.)—(*Referred to at page* 126.)

Names of Counties.	Population of Unions, &c. in 1847.	Lunatics.			Idiots.			Grand Total: Lunatics and Idiots.
		Male.	Female.	Total.	Male.	Female.	Total.	
Agricultural:								
Bedford -	112,379	38	41	79	33	33	66	145
Berks - -	190,367	63	84	147	75	84	159	306
Bucks - -	138,255	41	50	91	37	40	77	168
Dorset - -	167,874	68	86	154	35	40	75	229
Essex - -	320,818	66	114	180	80	77	157	337
Norfolk -	405,123	139	153	392	119	140	259	551
Oxford - -	159,476	54	73	127	67	60	127	254
Suffolk - -	314,722	98	163	261	77	75	152	403
Sussex - -	278,608	65	94	159	88	103	191	350
Wilts - -	243,322	94	108	202	68	94	162	364
Total - -	2,330,944	726	966	1,792	549	746	1,425	3,107
Manufacturing:								
Lancaster -	1,709,959	439	478	917	249	269	518	1,435
Stafford -	442,348	109	116	225	117	135	252	477
West Riding of York -	879,492	221	247	468	175	162	337	805
Total - -	3,031,699	769	841	1,610	541	566	1,107	2,717
Middlesex -	1,574,465	616	940	1,556	180	202	382	1,938
Surrey - -	577,775	224	316	540	105	122	227	767
Total - -	2,152,240	840	1,256	2,096	285	324	609	2,705
Totals of England and Wales	15,906,741	4,499	5,930	10,429	3,637	3,999	7,636	18,065

COMPARATIVE Statement, showing the Population, the Number of Insane Poor Persons, and their Proportion to the Population, in Six Commercial and Manufacturing Departments of France; in the remaining Seventy-six Departments; and in the whole of France.—(*Referred to at page* 127.)

Name of Departments, &c	Population in 1846.	Number of Insane Paupers, "Aliénés Indigents," supported by the Department.	Proportion of Insane Paupers to the Population.
Seine - - - - - -	1,364,933	2,536*	1 in 538
Seine Inférieure - - - - -	758,852	410	1 in 1,850
Bouches du Rhône - - - - -	413,918	358	1 in 1,156
Rhône - - - - - - -	545,635	320	1 in 1,705
Nord - - - - - - -	1,132,980	270	1 in 4,196
Calvados - - - - - -	498,385	230	1 in 2,166
Total of the above 6 Departments -	4,714,703	4,124	1 in 1,143
Remaining 76 Departments - -	30,687,058	8,162	1 in 3,759
The whole of France - - -	35,401,761	12,286	1 in 2,881

* The number given by M. De Watteville, *Essai Statistique sur les Établissemens de Bienfaisance*, is 2356, and not 2536: the results drawn in the text (at p. 127.), are not materially affected by the difference.

TABLE showing the Amount expended in the Relief of the Poor in the Ten Selected Agricultural Counties, during the Years 1844 and 1845, and the Increase per Cent in 1845, as compared with 1844.—(*Referred to at page* 132.)

Counties.	Amount expended in the Relief of the Poor in the Year		Increase per Cent in 1845, compared with 1844.
	1844.	1845.	
	£	£	
Bedford - - -	42,469	44,341	4
Berks - - -	88,913	92,615	4
Bucks - - -	67,900	70,545	4
Dorset - - -	76,329	79,398	4
Essex - - -	147,046	154,158	5
Norfolk - - -	160,586	169,769	6
Oxford - - -	72,735	77,395	6
Suffolk - - -	136,658	144,964	6
Sussex - - -	112,263	114,975	2
Wilts - - -	125,493	126,410	1

CHAP. XIV.

EVIDENCE of Mr. Henry Hase, as published in the Report to the General Board of Health, on a Preliminary Inquiry into the Sanitary Condition of the Town of Worksop. — (*Referred to at page* 300 §.)

"I have been practising as a surgeon fifteen years in Worksop. I have been medical officer of the Worksop district of the union thirteen years. I have the whole town of Worksop and the workhouse under my care. There is a considerable number of persons receiving medical union relief. In the workhouse and the parish I average twenty-five patients per day. *I have had very extensive opportunities of becoming acquainted with the condition of the poor people.*—In the Low Town and Mere Croft there are several families in one house. *In the crowded parts, where the poor live, the rooms are eight to ten feet square, and from six to eight feet high, but some are much less than that, and are low, confined places, and in bad repair.* The average would be five inmates per house, as near as I can tell, but perhaps more in the Mere Croft. *I have seen, in cases of fever, four in a bed, and in some instances five; and I have seen grown-up sons and daughters of the same family sleeping together. The cottages have seldom more than two bedrooms. There are many with only one bedroom. Many of the windows cannot be opened. The lodging-houses are in an abominable state. I have seen*, in harvest, *ninety persons in a house in Norfolk Street, with only seven bedrooms, and a garret in the tiles. There are seven of these houses in Norfolk Street. They will average twelve to fifteen persons per night.* There are no water-works in the town. *I am not aware of one cottage-house with a supply of water in it. They are not drained. There is not such a thing as a house-drain in the town.* Filth, manure, and excrementitious matters, are generally thrown close to the doors. The usual prevailing epidemics found in this town are influenza, dysentery, and diarrhœa, frequently running into fever of a low typhoid character. We usually have such attacks twice a year, in spring and in autumn. They arise from causes that might in a great measure be removed. Typhus and typhoid fevers are the most serious epidemics of a preventible character, and we have them in cycles of five or seven years, with an awful increase of mortality. In the milder cases the fever is obstinate, and the patients are long before they are restored to health; the return to convalescence is retarded by the bad condition of the places where they live. It generally occupies from two to four, or six weeks, before a person of thirty years of age, or ordinary constitution, with every advantage of medical attendance, is fit for work; but if it goes on to typhus it may be three months. *It is within my experience that many persons have been thus brought upon the parish who would not otherwise have become paupers.* I think that influenza and typhus have destroyed more persons than cholera. Typhus is a more expensive disease than cholera. I imagine the effects of influenza and typhus would far exceed that of cholera upon sick societies, &c., because, in the former, there may be three months continuance, but the latter only a few hours or days. We have typhus fever every year, but we have only had cholera twice in this country, and therefore, *there may be an indigenous epidemic disease more disastrous to the general health and prosperity of a town than a disease of the nature of cholera,* AND SUCH I BELIEVE TYPHUS TO BE. It varies in intensity in different neighbourhoods, and I find it worst where the houses and their inmates are dirtiest, and the ventilation most defective."

TABLE showing the Population (Census, 1841) and the Net Rental of the several Parishes within the Worksop Union, the Sums expended in the Relief of the Poor in such Parishes, and the Amount of such Relief as a Pound Rate on the Net Rental in the Year 1850. (Compiled from Returns with which I have been furnished by Mr. Whall, the Clerk to the Guardians of the Worksop Union.)—(*Referred to at page* 300.)

Name of Parish or Township.	Population Census, 1841.	Amount of Parish Valuation for Poor-rate, 1850.	Total of Year's Expenditure *for Relief of the Poor* ended Lady-day, 1850.	Proportion in the Pound of Expenditure to Rateable Value.
		£	£	*s. d.*
Worksop - -	6,129	24,042	1,667	1 4½
Carburton -	193	838	35	0 10
Cuckney - -	625	1,273	111	1 8¾
Norton - -	362	1,121	58	1 0¼
Holbeck - -	266	1,243	54	0 10¼
Langwith -	443	1,507	28	0 4¼
Carlton - -	1,049	4,983	286	1 1¾
Blyth - -	758	3,425	183	1 0¾
Hodsock - -	225	4,118	76	0 4¼
Styrrup - -	634	3,720	154	0 9¾
Harworth -	546	4,176	115	0 6½
Whitwell -	1,125	4,026	173	0 10¼
Clown - -	660	2,415	172	1 5
Barlbro' - -	800	6,300	320	1 0
Elmton - -	433	2,038	88	0 10¼
Thorpe Salvin -	390	2,409	55	0 5¼
Harthill - -	709	4,803	200	0 10
Anston - -	863	2,313	261	2 3
Woodsetts -	181	836	22	0 6¼
Gildingwells -	91	567	6	0 2½
Dinnington -	279	1,160	36	0 7¼
Letwell - -	129	1,153	10	0 2
Firbeck - -	191	1,492	40	0 6¼
St. John's -	69	837	7	0 2
Todwick -	214	1,922	42	0 5¼
Wales - -	310	834	25	0 7
Totals -	17,674	83,551	4,224	1 0

The details of the census of 1851 not being as yet published, it is necessary to use those of the census of 1841 in this Table. The population of the whole of this Union, in 1851, was 19,210.

Chap. XVIII.

Table showing the Tithe Commutation Rent Charge payable to Parochial Incumbents, the Annual Value of Property in 1847, as assessed to the Property Tax, County Rate, and Poor Rate respectively, and the Amount expended in the Relief of the Poor in the Year ended Lady-day, 1847. (Compiled from the Parliamentary Papers 298. and 735.— Session 1848.)—(*Referred to above, at page* 348.)

Names of Parishes.	Tithe Commutation Rent Charge payable to the Parochial Incumbent.			Annual Value of Property as assessed in 1847 to			Expended for the Relief of the Poor in the Year ended Lady-day, 1847.
				Property Tax.	County Rate.	Poor Rate.	
	£	s.	d.	£	£	£	£
Bletsoe - -	343	18	9	3,273	2,695	2,188	216
Bolnhurst - -	104	16	6	1,923	1,610	1,120	178
Goldington -	233	8	0	5,163	4,320	2,733	270
Hawnes - -	524	18	0	4,103	4,120	2,967	375
Higham Gobion -	307	0	0	1,894	1,700	1,471	92
Leighton Buzzard*	492	7	9	16,274	11,370	10,985	1,109
Luton - -	1,350	15	0	39,134	33,000	32,910	2,546
Melchbourne -	74	3	10¾	3,144	2,900	2,424	89
Meppershall -	535	0	0	2,701	2,400	2,042	254
Stagsden - -	350	8	6	3,147	3,450	2,917	337
Stotfold - -	180	0	0	4,624	2,350	2,432	315
Turvey* - -	253	4	0	5,075	5,495	4,178	563
Willington -	230	0	0	2,067	2,120	1,566	203
Totals -	4,970	0	4¾	92,522	77,530	69,933	6,547

* Clerical appropriators and their lessees.

CHAP. XIX.

TABLE showing the Annual Value of Property as assessed to the Relief of the Poor, in 1847, the Sum expended in relieving the Poor, and the Amount of such Expenditure as a Pound Rate on such Annual Value of the Property assessed, in Twenty Parishes of the Counties of Dorset, Norfolk, Sussex, and Wilts, followed by a like Table, respecting Twenty other Parishes, in the same Counties. (Obtained from the Parliamentary Paper, No. 735, Commons, 1848.)—(*Referred to at page* 360.)

Counties and Parishes.	Annual Value of Property rated to the Poor-rate in 1847.	Expended for the Relief of the Poor, for the Year ended Lady-day, 1847.	Amount of Rate in the Parish.
	£	£	*s.* *d.*
Dorset:			
Turnworth - - - - -	1,054	6	0 1¼
Winterbourne Tomson - -	424	2	0 1¼
Upper Cerne - - - -	1,058	9	0 2
Winterbourne Herrington -	732	5	0 1¾
Farnham - - - -	435	2	0 1
Norfolk:			
Bexwell - - - - -	1,537	9	0 1½
Ryston - - - - - -	1,007	8	0 2
Bawsey - - - - - -	345	1	0 0¾
Thuxton - - - - -	1,640	3	0 0½
Roudham - - - - -	864	7	0 2
Sussex:			
St. Mary Bulverhithe - -	577	1	0 0½
Hangleton - - - - -	995	5	0 1¼
West Blatchington - - -	550	1	0 0½
Parham - - - - - -	645	3	0 1
Middleton - - - - -	480	4	0 2
Wilts:			
Avon - - - - - -	438	2	0 1
Biddleston St. Peter - -	268	2	0 1¾
Foxley - - - - - -	799	2	0 0½
Pertwood - - - - -	400	2	0 1¼
Fifield Bavant - - -	809	5	0 1½
Total - - - - -	15,057	79	0 1¼

A Like Table respecting Twenty other Parishes in the last above-mentioned Counties. (Obtained from the Parliamentary Paper, No. 735, Commons, 1848.)—(*Referred to at page* 360.)

Counties and Parishes.	Annual Value of Property rated to the Poor-rate in 1847.	Expended for the Relief of the Poor, for the Year ended Lady-day, 1847.	Amount of Rate in the Pound.
	£	£	*s.* *d.*
Dorset:			
Charlton Marshall - -	1,329	365	5 6
Stourpaine - - -	1,468	425	5 9¼
Holy Trinity - - -	1,811	654	7 2¾
Lady St. Mary - -	2,497	649	5 2½
Arne - - - -	358	118	6 7
Norfolk:			
St. Faith's - - -	3,782	1,142	6 0½
Horsford - - -	2,541	806	6 4¼
Winterton - - -	517	319	12 4
New Buckenham - -	1,124	331	5 10¾
South Lopham - -	1,766	661	7 5¾
Sussex:			
Holy Trinity - - -	293	111	7 7
Fernhurst - - -	1,592	585	7 4¼
Lodsworth - - -	1,474	491	6 8
Alciston - - -	1,391	369	5 3½
Chalvington - - -	844	227	5 4½
Wilts:			
Fisherton Anger - -	3,086	816	5 3½
Hindon - - -	1,052	486	9 3
Horningsham - - -	3,191	925	5 9½
Corsley - - -	3,837	922	4 9¾
Wilton - - -	5,996	2,006	6 8¼
Total - - -	39,949	12,408	6 2½

TABLE showing the Net Rental, and the Amount expended in Relief of the Poor in all the Parishes in the County of Wilts, being Twenty-one in number, in each of which the Poor-rate is under Sixpence in the Pound. — (*Referred to at page* 360.)

Parishes.	Annual Value of Property rated to the Poor-rates in 1847.			Expended for the Relief of the Poor for the Year ended Lady-day, 1847.			Rate in the Pound of Expenditure for the Relief to the Poor, for the Year ended Lady-day, 1847, on the Annual Value of rateable Property in 1847.	
	£	*s.*	*d.*	£	*s.*	*d.*	*s.*	*d.*
Alderbury Union:								
Odstock - - -	805	0	0	13	0	0	0	3¾
Standlinch - - -	540	0	0	6	0	0	0	2¾
Amesbury Union:								
Allington - - -	862	0	0	18	0	0	0	5
Boscombe - - -	1,226	0	0	28	0	0	0	5½
Orcheston, St. George -	1,724	0	0	17	0	0	0	2½
Rollstone - - -	642	0	0	10	0	0	0	3¾
Bradford Union:								
Great Chalfield - -	1,079	0	0	8	0	0	0	1¾
Calne Union:								
Bowood - - -	1,072	0	0	12	0	0	0	2¾
Chippenham Union:								
Avon - - - -	438	0	0	2	0	0	0	1
Biddlestone, St. Peter -	268	0	0	2	0	0	0	1¾
Ditteridge - - -	552	0	0	8	0	0	0	3½
Tytherton Kelways -	470	0	0	9	0	0	0	4½
Devizes Union:								
Allington - - -	1,464	0	0	28	0	0	0	4½
Malmesbury Union:								
Easton Grey - -	1,781	0	0	31	0	0	0	4¼
Foxley - - -	799	0	0	2	0	0	0	0½
Mere Union:								
Pertwood - - -	400	0	0	2	0	0	0	1¼
Tisbury Union:								
Berwick, St. Leonard -	940	0	0	15	0	0	0	3¾
Wilton Union:								
Little Langford - -	845	0	0	8	0	0	0	2¼
Fifield Bavant - -	809	0	0	5	0	0	0	1½
Tetbury Union:								
Ashley - - -	932	0	0	13	0	0	0	3¼
Long Neuriton - -	2,638	0	0	58	0	0	0	5¼
Total - - -	20,286	0	0	292	0	0		
Average - - -	1,014	6	0	14	12	0	0	3½

Tables showing the Number of Lunatics and Idiots chargeable to the Whitechapel Union, or some Parish therein, on the 1st January, 1852. — (*Referred to at page* 367.)

	Number of Lunatics and Idiots relieved.				
	In the Workhouse.	In County Asylums.	In Private Licensed Houses.	At their own Residences.	Total.
Lunatics -	4	81	2	1	88
Idiots - -	18	12	- -	2	32

	Average Cost per Head, per Week, for their Maintenance.			
	In the Workhouse.	In County Asylums.	In Private Licensed Houses.	At their own Residences.
	s. d.	*s. d.*	*s.*	*s.*
Lunatics -	2 7	9 3¼	11	2
Idiots - -	2 7	9 3¼	11	2

INDEX.

INDEX.

THE END.

LONDON:
SPOTTISWOODES and SHAW,
New-street-Square.

For EU product safety concerns, contact us at Calle de José Abascal, 56–1°, 28003 Madrid, Spain or eugpsr@cambridge.org.

www.ingramcontent.com/pod-product-compliance
Ingram Content Group UK Ltd.
Pitfield, Milton Keynes, MK11 3LW, UK
UKHW041140300926
15471UKWH00011B/16
* 9 7 8 1 1 0 8 0 3 7 0 0 6 *